THE IDEALIST TRADITION

THE LIBRARY OF PHILOSOPHICAL MOVEMENTS

GENERAL EDITOR: *Paul Edwards*

The
Idealist Tradition

FROM BERKELEY TO BLANSHARD

EDITED WITH AN INTRODUCTION AND COMMENTARY

by A. C. EWING

THE FREE PRESS
GLENCOE, ILLINOIS
&
 THE FALCON'S WING PRESS

Preface

The Idealist Tradition is the first in a series of books which will
make available to the general public some of the most interesting
work of philosophers of very diverse viewpoints. Each volume will
deal with one or, in some cases, with two, philosophical "schools"
or "movements." It is fortunate that philosophers are rarely united
by the kind of common purpose which inspires political or religious
"movements." Nevertheless, it is frequently helpful to consider the
work of different writers according to the similarities in their aim
and content; and this is the policy which has been adopted in design-
ing the *Library of Philosophical Movements*.

Each book in the series will contain selections from important
representatives of the school and, wherever space allows, from critics
as well. There will also be an introduction by the editor, setting out
the main doctrines and some of the criticisms to which they have
been subjected. At the end of each book there will be a fairly detailed
bibliography.

An attempt will be made to include in the new books selections
from important works which have long been out of print and pieces
which are not easily accessible to the general reader and often not
even to the specialist. In the present volume there are no new translations since most of the foreign classics of idealism have had English
editions. However, other volumes now in preparation will feature a
large number of items never before published in English.

It is inevitable that, because of space restrictions, there will be
regrettable omissions in all the books in this series. Dr. Ewing originally sent me many more selections than those actually used. He
has asked me to enumerate the writers whose work we decided to
delete. They are Brightman, Calkins, Gentile, Inge, Lotze, Perry,
Rhadakrishnan, Sorley, Stace, Stout, and Urban. Extracts from Kant
and McTaggart also had to be sacrificed, but in the case of these
two writers very substantial selections remain. The grounds for deciding what was to be included or deleted were in most cases quite
complex, and it should not be inferred that the philosophers now
omitted are necessarily less significant than the others.

[v]

I am very much indebted to my friend, Professor Ernest Nagel, for most valuable advice in the planning of the entire series and for constant encouragement while putting the plans into effect. I wish to thank my friend and former student, James Bayley, without whose tireless aid publication would have been delayed for a long time. I also wish to thank my friends, Professor Arthur Pap, Toni Hoeltzli, Sheila Meyer, and my students Bernard Berofsky, Marilyn Charney, Charles Evans, Ruth Hoffman, Vera Scharman, and John Viscide, who helped me in many ways in the preparation of this book. Finally, I should like to express my gratitude to the Free Press, whose unusual generosity and devotion to scholarship have made possible the publication of the *Library of Philosophical Movements*.

PAUL EDWARDS

New York City
October 1956

CONTENTS

THE IDEALIST TRADITION

Editor's Introduction

THE TERM *idealism* has a wider and a narrower meaning. It has been defined as covering "all those philosophies which agree in maintaining that spiritual values have a determining voice in the ordering of the universe."[1] If the term were seriously taken in as wide a sense as this, all theists would have to be included in the school of idealists. This would be neither in accord with common philosophical usage nor suitable for my purpose. It would be most unusual in a philosophical treatise to call Thomas Aquinas, Descartes, Locke and all believers in God idealists. Such a wide use would also burden us with a load of selections which one particular volume in this series could not bear. Further, while most idealists do hold the belief mentioned, this is not true of all. It could hardly be affirmed of the pessimist, Schopenhauer, for example. In philosophical terminology, the contradictory of idealism is not materialism or naturalism, but "realism."

What then is it that distinguishes idealists from other philosophers who believe that "spiritual values have a determining voice in the ordering of the universe" but who would not be called idealists? I do not think there is a clear-cut answer to this question. There seems to be general agreement on the *extension* of the term—in spite of the most striking differences between some of the philosophers from whose works I have made selections, they would almost all be unanimously considered idealists—but it does not seem possible to give a precise, water-tight definition.

No definition, I think, could cover all philosophers who are by general admission idealists without including some who are by general admission not idealists. This is not altogether surprising; it is notorious that there is a certain looseness about the meaning of all -isms, just as there is about the distinctive principles of parties in politics. I shall in fact not commit myself to a definition, but instead just give some brief general account of the main features of the movement which has played such an important part in philosophy in the last 150 years or more. Many will feel that it is

---

1. Kemp Smith, *Prolegomena to an Idealist Theory of Knowledge*, p. 1.

rather a phenomenon of past history than a living school today. This is certainly the case in Great Britain and, I suppose, in most universities in the United States, though not on the whole on the European continent. But in any case we may be certain that we still have a great deal to learn from it and that its indirect effects on prevailing philosophies cannot be eradicated lightly. As regards nomenclature one must treat it mainly as a phenomenon of past history. Few philosophers in English-speaking countries, though I think a good number in certain other parts of the world, would call themselves idealists to-day, and only two or three of the idealist philosophers from whom I have made selections are still alive. The ways of looking at the universe which were characteristic of idealists are not ways which are popular now, but this does not necessarily mean that even their most neglected doctrines do not contain important truths which the philosophers of the present urgently need to learn.

BERKELEIAN IDEALISM

Idealism starts with Berkeley. I do not think it is desirable in a book of selections characteristic of the idealist movement to go back further, although Plato and Platonists are often called idealists in a rather different sense of the word. Berkeley based his attack on matter on three main types of argument, and these arguments can, I think, all be found in some form in most philosophers who have been called idealists, while almost all use at least one. Thus they can serve to give the school a distinctive unity without tying one down to a rigid definition. Firstly, there are arguments which purport to show that the mere fact that we know something implies that it is relative to mind. Secondly, there are arguments to the effect that the specific qualities we ascribe to physical objects are such that their *esse* is *percipi* and that consequently they could not exist apart from an experiencing being. Thirdly, there are negative arguments to the effect that we could not possibly justify the belief in matter. It should be noted that, while Berkeley denies the existence of matter, he insists that he does not deny the existence of particular material things like chairs, trees or human beings. We see and touch them, and therefore they exist. What he says is that, although they exist, they are only ideas in human minds or in the mind of God. This is similar to the line generally adopted by idealists (whether they introduce God in Berkeley's way or not) and finds its logical culmination in the present-day phenomenalists who say that physical object-propositions are true but have to be analyzed in terms of sense-data or human experience.

Most later idealists have felt that there was a certain crudity about Berkeley's treatment of physical objects as ideas in the mind of God, and have also taken a more rationalist view of our sense-experience, insisting that sense-experience does not result merely from the passive reception of given sense-data, but from the organization of sense-data by thought. Berkeley indeed admitted this in his last work, *Siris*. But these three lines of argument have, nevertheless, all played a fundamental part in the idealist controversy. It has been denied that they were used by Hegel and the most important philosophers influenced by him, but this does not seem true to me. If anything can be plain about Hegel, it is plain that he used at least the first kind of argument, and Bradley certainly used both the first and the second.

There are two other arguments used by Berkeley which could not be employed to refute all, but only some, forms of realism. One is the argument against Locke's substance conceived as distinct from its qualities, which Berkeley rejects as completely vacuous and therefore meaningless. The other is the argument that, if there were a world of material things existing unperceived, we should have to suppose that God had created a vast number of completely useless beings, since he could quite well have given us all the experiences we have without creating these beings. Both arguments seem to me to have considerable force, but obviously the former could be used only to refute a particular kind of realist view and not all realism—many realists would hold a different view of substance than Locke or even say that material things were better regarded as events or connected series of events than as substances —and the latter argument would only at most be valid against a realist who also accepted theism.

To return to the first three arguments. Nowadays, I suppose, the most usual view would be that, while the third of them presented serious difficulties, the first and second were purely fallacious. The fallacies, though subtle, are quite easy to point out. The principle one involves confusing the *object* with the *act* of sensing, perceiving, conceiving or knowing—a confusion which is facilitated by the fact that the same words may be used for both object and act. It is obvious that "sensation," taken as meaning the *act* of sensing, must be mental, but it does not follow that "sensation," taken as the *object* sensed, will be so. The confusion of *object* with *act* remains even if the argument is put in dispositional terms. To say that something which I sense or cognize is the object of certain dispositions on my part is not the same as to say that it is identical with those dispositions in me or in any other person.

But the exposure of such fallacies does not by any means always make an idealist abandon his epistemological views.[2] The issue certainly cuts deeper than this. It is not a case just of a single specious argument, but of deciding which of two rival theories of knowledge does more justice to the facts (or indeed whether there be a third alternative which combines the advantages of both). The difficulty for a realist theory is to explain how we can cross the gulf between the knowing mind and what is known: the difficulty for an idealist theory is how we are to reconcile idealism with the specific character of what we cannot help admitting we know. If we are to have an epistemological idealism which can reconcile our knowledge of other minds or of general laws or even of our own past with the dependence of what is known on the knowing or the thinking of it or the inseparability of it from that, we must distinguish between knowing Mind as such and *our* knowing or *our* minds. We must do this whether we think of the knowing Mind as transcendent relatively to all finite minds or immanent in them or both. Truth will then consist in conformity not with something independent of thought but with the nature of mind or thought as such. And since the nature of thought is shown in the making of a coherent system it follows that the test and the nature of truth lie in coherence and not either in correspondence with given fact or in verification by sense-experience. Insofar as I fail in the making of a coherent system I am acting irrationally and not *qua* thinking mind.

I do not myself accept—I have not been able adequately to think my way into—an idealist theory of knowledge, but in fairness it must be admitted that there are difficulties on both sides. Certainly modern controversy has revealed great, if not insur-

2. Berkeley already sees the need of defending himself against the charge of having committed the fallacy in question (*Dialogues between Hylas and Philonous*, Everyman ed., pp. 226-29; Fraser Selections, pp. 146-49).

mountable, difficulties in the notion of correspondence between our thought and the real. This problem cannot in my opinion be evaded by a "semantic theory of truth" which just declares that to say "p is true" is merely to say more emphatically "p." After all, when we assert "p" we are still talking about something distinct from any judgment of ours, and all the problems still remain about the relation between our judgment and the things of which we are talking when we judge. Further, realists have jumped too rapidly from the true proposition that knowing is not a process of altering things (though it may incidentally alter them), or of producing what is known, to the conclusion that we are entitled to assert what the objects of knowledge are like in themselves apart from their relation to any mind which knows them. Perhaps we can, but epistemological arguments like those of Royce and Blanshard are still impressive, and they have not been adequately considered by contemporary philosophers.

The contention that the *esse* of physical things is *percipi*, backed as it is by a consideration of their alleged properties severally, is, I am afraid, one of those of which it must be said that a man either does or does not see it. There is no way of settling, through argument, the dispute between those who do and those who do not. The contention takes various forms. Berkeley maintains that, if we consider carefully any of the qualities we ordinarily ascribe to physical objects, these turn out to be really only sensations or ideas; Bradley contends that every piece of existence of which we can think must consist of sentient experience or it would be nothing;[3] Green argues that relations imply mind because the terms related are both together and separate in a way which we can only think intelligibly if we think them as held together by a mind.[4] But all the arguments seem at some point to depend on an insight or alleged insight which can only be described as intuitive. The insight is intuitive not in the sense that men have it before philosophical reflection on the subject, but in the sense that it is not vindicated by any formal logical argument from generally accepted premises. That the being of physical objects is inseparable from their being experienced has certainly seemed obvious to a great variety of philosophers. Among them are not only metaphysical idealists, but also those positivistically inclined moderns who cannot envisage the possibility of understand-

3. *Appearance and Reality*, p. 145.
4. v. below pp. 119ff.

ing physical object-propositions except as propositions about human experience. The theory can therefore hardly be treated with contempt. The only thing for each person to do is, after carefully reading the idealist arguments, to decide for himself whether he can or cannot conceive significantly the existence of, for example, shape, without a mind experiencing or thinking shape. I cannot believe that the difficulty many thinkers have felt in conceiving this is due wholly to the fact that in order to give an affirmative answer at least one mind would have to conceive it; namely, one's own. To this the reply is all too obvious that what depends on our conceiving it is not its existence but only the possibility of our knowing it to exist. We must indeed admit that we can only conceive what a physical object is like by conceiving how it affects experience, and what it would be like to experience it under various conditions. At the same time it seems to me personally quite clear that we may intelligibly suppose a quality to exist unexperienced, in a categorical and not merely a hypothetical sense. It is a mere tautology that we can only experience a quality which is experienced. It would be most unreasonable to argue from this inductively that there are no cases of the quality existing unperceived. Such an argument would be even more unreasonable than it would have been (to take an example of Lord Russell's) for Kant, who had never been out of East Prussia, to argue that all the cows he had seen were in East Prussia and therefore all cows probably were in East Prussia. But clearly the idealist argument is not inductive but *a priori*. It cannot be consistently admitted by anybody who will not admit informative *a priori* propositions.

Idealists would of course commonly say not only is it logically absurd to suppose there might be qualities existing unperceived by anyone, but that it follows from their specific nature that none of the qualities we commonly ascribe to physical objects could be conceived as so existing. This again, however, is something which we either see intuitively or can see no point whatever in asserting. I think the formal arguments which have been used to support it can be dismissed as fallacious. Once this has been pointed out I do not see any way of showing by argument that the theory cannot be true. Some philosophers are, after careful reflection, convinced that it is as clear as daylight that colour or even shape and size could not exist unperceived except in the hypothetical sense that under certain conditions they would be experienced; others, equally intelligent, do not feel the slightest temptation to suppose this true. So, leaving the reader to make up his own mind, let us turn to questions in regard to which it is rather a matter of evaluating the logical force of arguments than of claiming or repudiating an intuition.

I shall mention just one more point which is urged in support of the contention that the *esse* of physical objects is inseparable from *percipi* and which seems to me to involve a definite fallacy. It is easier to persuade a person in the case of the "secondary" qualities—taste, sound, color, felt hardness or felt heat, and others —that they are inseparable from experience than in the case of the "primary" qualities,[5]—shape, size, and motion. Against a person who accepts the former, but denies the latter proposition, it is contended that primary qualities are inseparable from secondary, so that their existence also must be inseparable from experience. We cannot conceive a shape without either colour or tactual properties. Primary qualities are relational, and relations imply terms. To have extension we must have qualities spread out in space; there must be something extended for there to be shape, size or motion, and the something extended cannot be a bare substance without qualities. Now it does seem to me logically impossible that there could be things which had the primary qualities without having *any* other qualities. But it does not in the least follow from this that objects could not have the primary qualities without having other qualities like those we perceive. The argument does show that their qualities cannot be limited to those called primary. We have no right, however, to assert what their other qualities are like. These may be totally different from anything we can experience or conceive, but this does not mean that the possession of such qualities is inconceivable in the sense of being logically absurd. It is therefore quite possible to maintain both that the secondary qualities we know are all inseparable from experience, and yet that there are things with primary qualities existing independently of being experienced. I say it is possible, although it is not a view that I should myself hold. For while it is difficult to see how we could justify the proposition that, e.g., the actual colors I perceive sometimes qualify things existing unperceived in a sense in which this could not be reduced

---

5. I have used the term "quality" here, as this is the ordinary usage, but I think the "primary qualities" really should be called relational properties with the exception of size, which is a quantity rather than a quality.

to a proposition about possible experiences, it does not seem to me that its falsity is either self-evident or capable of establishment by an argument of any sort.

A great deal of controversy has been directed to the question whether we can know the existence of independent physical objects in perception or have any good argument by which we can infer it from our perceptual experience. The difficulties in giving an affirmative answer to either question have in recent times led a great many philosophers who had no sympathy with idealist metaphysics to maintain that we are entitled to assert physical object-propositions only if we analyze these as propositions about human sense-data or human experiences. Such a view urgently calls out for explanation as to why our experiences go on persistently as if they were of independent physical objects. Our predictions based on beliefs about these objects are continually fulfilled just as if the objects existed and just as if they had the properties attributed to them. This in itself seems to me a strong argument for realism as against phenomenalism, but not necessarily against an idealism which provided a metaphysical explanation of some kind for this circumstance. Whatever we may think of Berkeley's view in general, it could not be used as an argument against him. If Berkeley's God wished to arrange that our predictions of future experiences should be fulfilled in the same way as if physical objects existed independently without their really so existing, he could no doubt do this. And the idealists who dismiss as crude Berkeley's view of physical objects have metaphysical explanations of their own which would account for our having the experiences we do. To account for the fulfilment of our predictions an idealist philosophy must maintain that a non-human mind deliberately wills our experience to take the course it does. In the case of less personal forms of idealism it would have to be maintained that in the single absolute experience or in the realm of spiritual entities there is somehow a *structure* similar to that which we ordinarily ascribe to the physical world. Scientific predictions are not logically required to be derived from the assumption that the causes of our perceptions have qualities just like those we experience in the perceptions that we regard as veridical. They depend only on assumptions as to the structure of these causes. Provided the causes have or contain something which has a structure like that we ordinarily attribute to physical objects, we are not bound by the argument to suppose that they are really extended spatially.

This being so, it is very hard to see how idealism can be refuted. It is customary among English philosophers nowadays to fall back on common sense and say that of course we know that physical things exist; and that this is more certain than any philosophical argument on the subject could possibly be. But if so, it is at least incumbent on the philosopher to give some satisfactory analysis of what exactly we know when we know physical object-propositions to be true, and how we know it, which is surely no easy thing to do. Many philosophers who have maintained the common sense view in question have gone on to insist that physical object-propositions have to be analyzed as propositions as human sense-data. They have thus taken away with one hand what they gave with the other.

If we accept my suggestion that some metaphysical explanation is necessary of the continual fulfillment of our predictions based on the belief in physical objects, and if it is thought that there are fatal objections to realism, the way is paved for a transcendent idealist metaphysics of some kind. But an idealist who adopts this line must be very careful indeed not to include in his criticism of realism any arguments which, if valid, would show that we cannot justify the assertion of anything beyond the experience of human beings. This has to be emphasized since some arguments used by idealists have aimed at precisely this conclusion.

THE UNREALITY OF SPACE AND TIME

Other idealist arguments have been based on the alleged self-contradictoriness of the spatial and temporal world, especially the so-called antinomies about infinity. Space, time, and the world in space and time must, it would seem, be either finite or infinite. Yet either alternative, it has been alleged, gives rise to contradictions. Reality has therefore been declared by some idealists to be non-temporal as well as non-spatial. This, if taken literally, is a very bold statement indeed. For we apprehend not only physical objects but ourselves as in time, and consequently not only all our judgments about physical objects but all our introspective judgments will be mistaken if we are not really in time. They will be mistaken, moreover, not merely in a superficial detail, but in a feature so fundamental that not one element of our experience would be recognizable in its absence.

Kant, the most famous philosopher to employ this line of argument, thinks indeed he can avoid the conclusion that these judgments are false and says instead that they are true, but true only of appearances. It may be objected that this is an inconsistent compromise. If our judgments about space and time are true even of appearances, they must be true of something real, since to say something is an appearance is to say that we really experience it; and if they are true of anything, they cannot offend against the law of contradiction. Whether this is a valid criticism or not depends on whether, as Kant thought, it is the case both that the contradictions are insoluble if time is conceived as belonging to an independent world, and that they disappear if time is made relative to human experience.

Other philosophers have adopted what seems to me the more consistent but incredible view that all our judgments involving time are false. This would seem to be the necessary logical consequence if time is really self-contradictory. Yet even if the antinomies *seemed* insoluble, it appears far more likely that there was some undetected philosophical mistake in the reasoning than that all empirical judgments ever made by us should be wrong to an enormous and incalculable extent in fundamental points. For every concept we can form of anything in our psychological and physical life is inseparably bound up with change and so with time.

Recent achievements in mathematics and the philosophy of mathematics are relevant to those arguments against the reality of space and time which depend on the problem of infinity.[6] We must not be too confident that, because thinkers like Russell have removed any logical difficulty in maintaining that infinite and infinitesimal numbers can exist in whatever sense numbers do exist, therefore there is necessarily no difficulty in supposing that there exist infinitesimal things or an infinite number of things. We have after all long known that there is no absurdity in admitting negative numbers, but this does not prove that there could be a negative number of things in the universe. It must be admitted however, that Kant has not given an adequate proof that there really are insoluble

---

6. McTaggart's argument (p. 228) does not. It is criticized by C. D. Broad in *Examination of McTaggart's Philosophy,* Vol. II, Part I, Chapter 35.

antinomies. While it would take a bold man to say there was no difficulty, it would today take a still bolder one to assert on the strength of the difficulties about infinity that time is unreal.

There are other philosophers who say that time is unreal or mere appearance, but who mean something rather different by this assertion. I am here referring to the Hegelians and to Bradley and Bosanquet. For them, reality is a matter of degree and to call something unreal is to say that it does not occupy an important place in the structure of the universe. To be understood in its place it would have to be viewed very differently from the fashion in which we inevitably view it. The philosophers I am considering do often say that all our judgments are partly false. I think it is plain that they are here not using "false" in its ordinary sense but rather to mean "conveying an inadequate impression in some respects." (I may come to view events in my childhood very differently from the way in which I viewed them when they occurred, but this does not necessarily make false in the ordinary sense my childish judgment as to how I felt at the time.) These thinkers call everything that is in time appearance, but do not regard appearance as something outside the ultimately real. They regard experiences as imperfectly understood parts of the latter. Moreover, they claim that since any element of the whole taken by itself becomes unintelligible there is nothing in reality but appearances—a claim that would be self-contradictory and absurd in Kant's use of the term "appearance." By this they mean that reality is such a closely-knit system that, if we regard any element in it apart from the rest, as human limitations make it inevitable that we should, we distort it and our concept of it turns out to be self-contradictory. Similarly nothing that I have said is intended as an objection to the highly probable supposition that, whether we accept a philosophy like Bradley's or like Kant's or neither, the really right philosophical view of time would give a quite different impression of its nature and real place in the universe from any we now have.

KANTIAN IDEALISM

Kant's general argument for idealism is of a rather different type from any I have yet mentioned. In fact Kant may be specially recommended today as a philosopher who had absorbed much, I should say the most important part, of the considerations which support positivism. No great philosopher of the past, with the possible exception of Hume, should have anything like the appeal of Kant for the modern positivist. The chief difference is the absence of those constant references to language that characterize contemporary positivism, but they are absent also in Hume. Kant, like the positivist, finds a great difficulty in synthetic *a priori* judgments. Only he does not therefore reject them. The problem is solved for him by thinking of them as ways of organizing our experience by a *synthesis* so as to give us knowledge. Experience is for him the *tertium quid* which links together subject and predicate so as to make a synthetic judgment possible. For this reason he denies the possibility of synthetic *a priori* judgments beyond the realm of actual and possible experience. Unlike any of the other thinkers from whom I have made selections, Kant regarded his idealism as consisting not in the building up of a metaphysics but in the *denial* of the possibility of any metaphysics. In the sense in which he was an idealist, Kant may be said to have been one just because he was too much of an empiricist to be anything else. He was a ("transcendental") idealist because he did not see how the transition from experience to judgments about independent things in themselves could be justified; but he called himself also an ("empirical") realist because he wanted to insist that physical object-judgments are still true, though true only in the realm of actual and possible experience. He meant by this approximately what a modern phenomenalist means when he says that physical object-propositions are true but analyzable in terms of sense-data.

Kant makes, however, an important addition: he argues in effect that the analysis must be in terms not just of sense-data but of causal laws connecting our sense-data (the proofs of the second and third Analogies). His reason for this is that, even if we interpret physical object-propositions in terms of human experience, we must still make a distinction within experience between the subjective and the objective, otherwise the merest illusion will be on the same level as the best warranted conclusions of natural science. Yet they cannot be distinguished by means of their empirical content. With any empirical content it is conceivable that it might be illusory and also conceivable that it might be objective. Therefore the distinction, Kant concludes, can only be made in terms of causal laws governing our experience. The objective is for Kant what is determined by laws valid for human percipients as such. An objective sequence is one which it is not in our power to reverse by attending first to one object and then to the other as we can reverse our perceptions of the coexistent. To the criticism that we cannot prevent ourselves having illusions and that there are causal laws which make all human beings have them in certain contexts, Kant would reply that at any rate we in some way use conformity with causal laws as the criterion for distinguishing between those perceptions which are veridical and those which are illusory. This can hardly be doubted. Those perceptions which, if regarded as giving properties of physical objects, fit into a causal system are taken as veridical; those which, if so regarded, do not fit in, are condemned as illusory and explained causally in a different fashion by refracted light-rays, defects of our sense-organs, or even by repressed desires. And it is certainly plausible to say that, if we are to analyze physical object-propositions in terms of experience, we must regard physical things as systems of actual and possible experiences connected by causal laws. So objectivity for Kant involves causal necessity, and this is his argument for the view that every event in the world of appearances is causally determined by previous events. This must not indeed be taken in too strong a sense: probably Kant, like Berkeley, held what we should nowadays call the regularity or uniformity theory of causation as regards the physical world. He believed, like Berkeley, that there was a more ultimate explanation, but it lay for him in the unknowable realm of things-in-themselves. What he insisted, however, was that the general principle that every event is caused is not derivable empirically but is necessary, i.e., *a priori* in character. The reason why it can be known *a priori* is not for him that we, by pure thought, have an insight into the nature of reality, but simply that it is a necessary condition of our making the ordinary factual judgments which we cannot help making. The principle cannot therefore be proved of reality but only of appearances, and the same applies to all synthetic *a priori* principles on Kant's view. Metaphysics in the sense in which Kant rejects it involves the attempt to prove propositions about reality by the use of principles which can only be justified in application to appearances. Those synthetic *a priori* principles which, like causality, are necessary if we are to make our ordinary empirical judgments about succession in time or position in space are called "categories" or "concepts of understanding," and are regarded as proved. Those principles which are useful for the advance of science and provide valuable rules of method for the scientist but are not necessary for the very possibility of organizing our experience sufficiently to give knowledge, are called "regulative principles" or "ideas of reason." Kant claims to know only the synthetic *a priori* to be true. He makes no such claims about the truth of the regulative principles, leaving open the possibility that these might only be methodological fictions. One difference between Kantian and Hegelian epistemology seems to me to be that Hegelians take principles of this second type as known also, thus leading them to affirm dogmatically a degree of system in the world much greater than would have been admitted by Kant. Kant's view was the beginning of a far-reaching theory of knowledge, later known as the coherence theory,[7] according to which knowledge is organization into a system and conformity with the system becomes the sole criterion of truth. Kant did not explicitly develop it this far, but he was the first philosopher of importance to put forward the conception of science as the organization of our experience rather than as the discovery of independent reality, a view which, whether true or false, certainly has had a great vogue recently among philosophers and even among scientists.

Kant is also responsible for another conception which has played a very important role in subsequent idealist philosophy. According to Kant, not only does an object imply a subject, but a subject equally implies an object. Kant holds both that physical objects can be thought only as existing for a mind and that a mind can have existence only in relation to objects which it thinks. For otherwise the mind would be without content, and so a mere empty nothing. Self-identity itself (the "transcendental unity of apperception"), Kant insists in the "Transcendental Deduction," is realised only in the organization of the given manifold into physical things. Further, Kant argues, at least in the second edition of the *Critique of Pure Reason,* that the self can know itself only in time against a permanent background of physical things. This has been held irreconcilable with his idealism, but it need not be if we add the proviso that propositions about the permanent things would have to be "analyzed phenomenalistically," as a modern thinker would say.

So far Kant's philosophy is not incompatible with some form of positivism, but there are certain reservations in his condemna-

---

7. v. below p. 21.

tion of metaphysics which no positivist would approve. He believed
in synthetic *a priori* propositions in ethics, though not in metaphysics. He also thought it legitimate to argue from the truths of
ethics to the truths of some metaphysical propositions. The argument would not amount to a strict proof, but would nontheless
justify our belief in the latter. An example of this is our belief in
the existence of God. The particular form in which Kant cast his
argument for the existence of God is open to and has received a
great deal of criticism. However, it may be stated in general terms,
less open to criticism, as an argument to the effect that the good
man recognises his obligation to act as if there were a God and that
therefore we are entitled to believe there is a God. The premise, it
will be noted, does not entail the belief in God, but, Kant holds, it
does justify it. Kant argues similarly for immortality, and with still
greater confidence for freedom as a presupposition of morality.
The propositions in question are not known, Kant insists, with
objective theoretical certainty. Nor do we have any clear conception of what they involve, as we have in the case of scientific propositions. Yet we are justified, he says, in holding them with objective
certainty. There is no doubt that he means that they are true and
not merely that we ought to treat them as if they were true. Hence
Kant's philosophy does leave a place for religion, not merely as an
attitude of mind, but as including a very limited set of metaphysical
beliefs. But it is a religion based almost wholly on ethics. He is not
prepared to allow any validity either to metaphysical, as opposed
to ethical, arguments for the existence of God or to the claim often
made to awareness of God in religious experience. It has been questioned whether what he does claim is at all consistent with his
sceptical attitude toward theoretical knowledge of reality. The
question arises chiefly because his religious position involves the
application of the categories beyond the realm of appearances when,
for example, God is thought of as creating (causing) the world.
Kant meets this by a distinction between determinate knowledge
and indeterminate thinking. We do not know God according to the
categories but we can think of God by means of them, at least in a
certain fashion. Kant's philosophy of religion, more than most, did
full justice to the element of agnosticism that should be present in
religion and to the inevitable limitations of human thought which
must, at best, make the conception of the deity an obscure one.

Similar attacks on Kant's concept of the thing-in-itself are perhaps harder to meet. If we posit things-in-themselves of which the natural world is the appearance, we must think of them as in some sense causing or helping to cause appearances; and we may defend this use of a category in the same way as in the case of God. But had Kant a right to say that things-in-themselves existed at all? Is not that itself a metaphysical dogma like the others which Kant wished to refute? There is no argument from ethics to support the belief in things-in-themselves as there was to support the belief in God. However that may be, the concept of the thing-in-itself has certainly an important and valuable part to play in Kant's philosophy, if only as a concept of something the possibility of which he could not deny, even though he was not entitled to assert that it was realized in fact. It has value at least as a "problematical concept," setting limits to our knowledge, as in one passage Kant himself suggests. For if he had denied even the possibility of things in themselves, there would have been nothing left but minds and objects existing only relative to minds, i.e. he would have become what he called a dogmatic idealist and so contradicted his critical philosophy altogether. In using the term "things-in-themselves" of the metaphysical grounds of our perceptions, Kant did not indeed mean to exclude the possibility that they might be minds—he meant to leave open the question what they were or rather to dismiss it as insoluble. But he was concerned to insist that we were not in the least entitled to deny the dependence of our perceptions on something quite outside human life and furthermore that the very conception of appearances implies a reality, unknowable in itself, which appears. However the thing-in-itself was the first element in Kant's philosophy to be dropped by the members of the idealist school he founded. When the thing-in-itself had been eliminated, the theory became idealism, which in some form was the dominant philosophy in many countries for a long period.

One feature of Kant's philosophy and of very much idealism is the diametrical contrast between two aspects of the self. The first aspect is the self as known to introspection and ordinary psychological study, in which capacity it is one object in time among others. The second is the self as knower in which capacity it transcends time and space. The antithesis is at its sharpest in Kant; he accepts a phenomenalistic account like Hume's of the self as object of introspection, but the self as subject he conceives in a totally different way. This distinction is made the basis of what he thinks to be the sole possible solution of the problem of reconciling human freedom with the causal determination of all phenomena. As is well known, the solution was effected by maintaining that the real self is timeless and therefore exempt from determination by phenomena, being itself that for which all appearances exist. Kant is not indeed an indeterminist: he thinks of the real self as determined but not determined by previous events. It is not determination as such, but determination by the past which is irreconcilable with freedom. If I am determined by the past, even my own past, he says I am determined by something which it is not now in my power to change. This difficulty is avoided if our free causation is in reality timeless, and Kant was not deterred by the impossibility of conceiving what timeless determination could be like. After all it follows necessarily from his philosophy that human beings cannot know their own real nature any more than the nature of things-in-themselves. I do not want to commit myself to accepting Kant's view of freedom, but we must realise that he could reply to most of the objections to it by saying simply that they arose from insisting on asking questions which must from the nature of the case be unanswerable for human beings.

Kant's complete dualism between the real and the apparent self was retained by few of his successors. However, some radical distinction between two aspects of the self—the self as member of the natural world on the one hand and the self as knower, agent and maker of appearances on the other—is essential to most forms of idealism. Such a distinction is apparently a consequence of any idealism which does not treat knowing as merely one event among others or confines the creative side of knowing to a transcendent God.

HEGELIAN AND ABSOLUTE IDEALISM

The philosophy of Hegel deserves perhaps as much study as that of Kant, but this study has been gravely hampered by his obscurity. Hegel is regarded, at any rate by most of his more modern interpreters, as an idealist in a different sense from Berkeley or from Kant. He certainly does not seem interested in using the ordinary idealist arguments to show that the physical world is dependent for its existence on a mind or minds conceived personally, whether human or non-human. Yet he does insist on "spirit" or "the absolute idea" as the ultimate categories in terms of which to interpret reality. He has been, however, understood in different ways. He has been thought to teach that reality consisted of a single "Absolute Spirit" like the Christian God, only viewed in a rather more pantheistic way than has usually been considered orthodox. At the other extreme he has been considered a realist who merely teaches that reality bears the characteristics of Mind in the sense of forming a rational system and in the sense that the nature of reality is most fully expressed in the consciousness of developed minds and spirits. Even so, however, his philosophy emphasizes the importance of mind and insists on the element of rational structure in the world in a way which is sharply antithetical to ordinary naturalism. It is also difficult to accept the second interpretation (i.e., of Hegel as a realist) as giving the whole truth in view of his arguments from the relativity of an object to a subject and in view of the very elaborate and emphatic way in which he works out the relativity of the lower categories to those of spirit. The true interpretation presumably lies somewhere between the two extremes, but the difficulty of arriving at it seems to me almost insuperable.

The most important feature of Hegel's philosophy is his *dialectic,* an argument in triads which starts by taking a particular concept as starting-point (the "thesis"), finds this self-contradictory, replaces it by its opposite (the "antithesis"), finds this likewise self-contradictory or even, when logically developed, identical with the discarded thesis. and replaces the antithesis in turn by a "synthesis" (in a very different sense from that in which Kant used the word). The synthesis solves the problem not by asserting one of the conflicting principles and denying the other, but by combining both in such a way as to remove the immediate contradiction. But when this is done the synthesis itself develops new contradictions, which result in a repetition of the triadic development of thought (thesis, antithesis, synthesis) again and again till the nature of reality is disclosed in higher and higher categories as the expression of spirit. The dialectic seems to be viewed by Hegel as a logical argument to refute and correct in succession a series of inadequate ways of conceiving the world, as a history of philosophical thought showing the laws of its development apart from unessential oscillations, and as an account of the logical structure of reality as such. It culminates in a series of categories which imply mind or spirit. It is by no means clear, however, that the method itself necessarily involves idealism and very much of it could be accepted by a realist. Today, ironically enough, it lives chiefly in the philosophy of the communists, who regard the idealists as their worst philosophical opponents. Whatever we may think of their applications of it, we must admit that the mode of thought, expressed by the three terms, thesis, antithesis, synthesis, is a very common, important and often highly illuminating one. The right way of thinking commonly proceeds by the reconciliation of opposites and the correction of one-sided extremes.

The school of idealists which was most prominent in the nineteenth and at the beginning of the twentieth century, often called the Absolute Idealists, was very much influenced by Hegel. They usually thought of Reality as a single "Absolute Mind" or a single "Experience," which they were more or less inclined to personify, according to their sympathy or lack of sympathy with Christian theology. They regarded reality as a whole as in some sense perfect. This is a position with which people find it particularly hard to sympathize today, but it was actually combined with a wholehearted condemnation of many things in the world. These are condemned when viewed by themselves or in the context of a limited number of conditions and effects. The very perfection of a closely-knit whole, it is said, implies that its parts when taken separately, as we have to take them since we do not know everything, must be imperfect and in some measure evil just because they are incomplete. The main reason such thinkers have (apart from intuitive religious convictions) for holding reality to be perfect was perhaps the following. If we are to have any criterion of truth at all, it must depend on the principle that what satisfies the intellect is true. Reality must therefore satisfy our intellect. But we are after all a unity. So nothing can ultimately satisfy the intellect which would not also satisfy all the other sides of our nature at their best. Such an argument is given in the third selection from Bradley.[8]

These thinkers strongly emphasize rational system as the central feature of thought and a fundamental characteristic of reality. This emphasis is shown in two theories which led to much controversy at the beginning of the century; namely, the internal theory of relations and the coherence theory of truth. The senses in which relations have been said to be internal are very varied. I have myself elsewhere distinguished ten and was rightly criticized for having

8. v. below, pp. 140-44.

omitted an eleventh. In its most important and usual sense, however, the theory roughly asserts that all relation involves a logical connection so that the existence of any relation follows necessarily from the nature of its terms. The implications of this are very far reaching. For we must admit that everything in the world is in some way related to everything else. Consequently the theory implies that Reality is a logically connected system in which nothing can be different from what it actually is. Many who revolted against the theory were influenced by their repugnance to the determinism it implied. Apart from this the view is of course diametrically opposed to generally current views of logic today, which make necessary connection a matter of symbolism and not anything present in reality. Another conclusion drawn concerns the relation between knowing and what is known: since knowing must be related and so internally related to its object, we could never know what an object was like apart from the knowing of it and so must dismiss the notion of objects existing otherwise than in relation to a knowing mind as unthinkable or even logically absurd.

The reasons why the internal theory of relations was held were not always made very clear. The following seem to have been the chief: (a) It was thought somehow to follow from the nature of relations as such. Arguments were used such as that a relation could not hold together its terms unless it were rooted in their nature. (b) It was assumed that everything was completely determined causally by something, and causally connected directly or indirectly with everything other than itself, while causality was viewed not as mere regular sequence, but as a logically necessary connection. Our estimate of the validity of this argument will therefore depend largely on our view of causation. It has been contended that the view of causation here suggested is less difficult to reconcile with the validity of induction than a regularity theory is. It is also hard to see how, if there is no necessary connection between cause and effect, the regularities in nature which we do as a matter of fact so frequently experience could be anything but unexplained coincidences more improbable than having all the trumps in one hand ten times running in a game of bridge.[9] It should be noted that this view of causation does not of itself necessarily involve

---

9. I have myself tried to justify the view of causation as logically necessary connection—I called it the "entailment theory of causation"—in my *Idealism*, chap. IV, sect. 3.

determinism, i.e., the view that every event is completely determined in all details by causes. Since, however, on even an indeterminist view causation plays a very large part in the world, the real would still have to be regarded as partaking at least to a very large extent of the character of logical system. (c) The proponents of the view were usually convinced by an examination of actual cases of argument that the criterion of truth is coherence in a system. From this, it would seem to follow that reality must be itself a coherent, i.e. logically connected system. (d) They may well have been influenced by the following fallacious argument, which was refuted by G. E. Moore.[10] Given the premises (1) A is related to B by r, (2) C is not related to B by r, it is logically impossible that (3) C could be A. It does not follow that, wherever these conditions are fulfilled, the nature of C is such that it is *intrinsically impossible* for *explain* it to be A. That would only be the case if the impossibility followed from (2) taken by itself, and it does not. It follows only from (1) and (2) together. Yet it may well have been the case that adherents of the internal theory of relations confused the true proposition that (1) and (2) jointly entail (3) with the different proposition that, wherever (1) is true, (2) by itself logically entails (3)—a proposition from which it would follow that, if A stands in a particular relation, it could not have failed to stand in that relation without being something other than itself, i.e. without self-contradiction.

Bradley's treatment of relations is somewhat different, though less so than one would expect from his phraseology. He does not say that relations are internal but that they are unreal.[11] However, he admits that the internal theory of relations comes very much nearer to being true than the opposite view, and truth is always for him a matter of degree.

The coherence theory was generally supported primarily by criticism of its rival, the correspondence theory, on the ground that we cannot compare our thoughts to reality to see whether they correspond. Our inability to make a comparison suggested the need for an internal criterion of truth, and the coherence theory was advanced to answer the need. The theory, moreover, was claimed to have been derived from a study of our actual procedure in science

---

10. "External and Internal Relations," in Moore's *Philosophical Studies*, chap. IX.
  11. v. below, p. 130.

and in thought generally. It was argued that of two hypotheses we always prefer the one which we think comes nearer to making a coherent system of our experience. Further, in order to account for our knowledge that what is true conforms to the coherence criterion, it was maintained that coherence should be taken as the definition and not only as the criterion of truth. This alone makes the theory definitely idealistic: a person who held that coherence was the criterion but did not hold that it was the definition of truth might be a realist. But we never arrive at a system of propositions which conforms perfectly to the coherence ideal. Truth then becomes a matter of degree, which is certainly paradoxical. Nor is it easy to see how the theory can do justice to the persistently brutal empirical character of so much of our knowledge. These circumstances have given rise to the chief difficulties for the theory. Most of its holders would, however, admit that for us at least it is coherence with experience which is the criterion, not bare coherence as such. They would further deny that we ever encountered in experience such a thing as the merely given as empirical fact, apart from its organization into a relatively coherent system by the work of thought. In this of course they follow Kant.

What has been said will have made it clear to the reader that "idealism" covers a great diversity of types of philosophical systems. Their variety is so great that I could not discuss them all here. The following classification may, however, be of some help to the reader. (1) There is the type which argues that physical objects involve mind, and since they are independent of *human* minds, therefore imply a divine mind, or that a divine mind is required to think the moral law or other universal laws which we cannot help recognizing as objective. (2) There are the "absolute idealists" who view the whole of reality as a *single experience* or mind, although they may differ in ascribing or not ascribing personality to this mind. (3) There is the idealism which makes reality consist of a *society* of spirits who are either very highly developed already, although they may not appear so now, time being unreal, or if time is real, will at least become so eventually. On this view, no single spirit holds the supreme position of God. (4) There is the "panpsychic" form of idealism according to which physical objects are the appearance of non-human but low grade minds or, rather, psychical entities. Just as animal minds are inferior to human, so these sub-minds are conceived as inferior to animal. This view may or may not be combined with theism. (5) There is the view according to which physical objects are just abstractions from human experience.

I have not in this introduction talked of ethics, because idealists as such have no special system of ethics. What is often called "idealist ethics" is merely the ethics of a particular school, and not by any means the ethics of all idealists. At the same time idealists may on the whole not unreasonably claim to have given a more careful consideration to the valuational aspect of things in their account of the cosmos than have the realists. They have usually thought this to be at any rate a very important partial clue to the nature of reality as such. But the most fundamental characteristic of the idealist school is the persistent determination of its members to try to interpret reality in terms of mind. Even if all such interpretations were to prove completely unfeasible, it is very desirable that there should always be some philosophers who make the attempt. The failure of such attempts is likely to be almost as instructive as their success. We are also apt, especially in the present age of material advance, to underestimate what is not obvious to the senses and underestimating the importance of mind is even more disastrous to civilization in the highest sense than underestimating the importance of matter. We may sum up the situation in the words of a well-balanced realist critic who has said some hard things of idealists in other contexts: "The characteristic fault of Idealism is to be unable to see the trees for the wood, and the characteristic fault of Realism is to be unable to see the wood for the trees. The great merit of Idealism is that it really has tried to do justice to the social, ethical, aesthetic and religious facts of the world. The great merit of Realism is that it really has tried to face in a patient and detailed way the problem of matter and of our perception of it. But neither of these activities is a substitute for the other; and a genuine Speculative Philosophy must combine the detailed study of the lower categories with the due recognition of the higher categories, and must try to reconcile the pervasiveness of the former with the apparently growing importance of the latter."[12]

---

12. C. D. Broad in *Contemporary British Philosophy*, ed. J. H. Muirhead, 1st Series, p. 99.

Selections

GEORGE BERKELEY

(1685-1753)

The passage selected from the *Principles of Human Knowledge* contains in outline Berkeley's attack on the belief in independent material things and concludes with his main argument for the existence of God. The argument against substance is omitted by me because it cannot be directed against all forms of realism, but only the particular one adopted by Locke. Berkeley's other argument for the existence of God, i.e., that physical things are independent of human minds and, being "ideas," must exist in a non-human mind, is not made explicit in the *Principles* but occurs in *The Three Dialogues between Hylas and Philonous.* This important idealist argument is also given in a passage taken from Rashdall (v. below, p. 203).

Of the Principles
of Human Knowledge

1. IT IS EVIDENT to any one who takes a survey of the *objects of human knowledge,* that they are either *ideas* actually imprinted on the senses; or else such as are perceived by attending to the passions and operations of the mind; or lastly, *ideas* formed by help of memory and imagination—either compounding, dividing, or barely representing those originally perceived in the aforesaid ways. By sight I have the ideas of light and colours, with their several degrees and variations. By touch I perceive hard and soft, heat and cold, motion and resistance; and of all these more and less either as to quantity or degree. Smelling furnishes me with odours; the palate with tastes; and hearing conveys sounds to the mind in all their variety of tone and composition.

And as several of these are observed to accompany each other, they come to be marked by one name, and so to be reputed as one

First published in 1710.

thing. Thus, for example, a certain colour, taste, smell, figure and consistence having been observed to go together, are accounted one distinct thing, signified by the name apple; other collections of ideas constitute a stone, a tree, a book, and the like sensible things; which as they are pleasing or disagreeable excite the passions of love, hatred, joy, grief, and so forth.

2. But, besides all that endless variety of ideas or objects of knowledge, there is likewise Something which knows or perceives them; and exercises divers operations, as willing, imagining, remembering, about them. This perceiving, active being is what I call *mind, spirit, soul,* or *myself.* By which words I do not denote any one of my ideas, but a thing entirely distinct from them, wherein they exist, or, which is the same thing, whereby they are perceived; for the existence of an idea consists in being perceived.

3. That neither our thoughts, nor passions, nor ideas formed by the imagination, exist without the mind is what everybody will allow. And to me it seems no less evident that the various sensations or ideas imprinted on the Sense, however blended or combined together (that is, whatever objects they compose), cannot exist otherwise than in a mind perceiving them. I think an intuitive knowledge may be obtained of this, by any one that shall attend to what is meant by the term *exist* when applied to sensible things. The table I write on I say exists; that is, I see and feel it: and if I were out of my study I should say it existed; meaning thereby that if I was in my study I might perceive it, or that some other spirit actually does perceive it. There was an odour, that is, it was smelt; there was a sound, that is, it was heard; a colour or figure, and it was perceived by sight or touch. This is all that I can understand by these and the like expressions. For as to what is said of the *absolute* existence of unthinking things, without any relation to their being perceived, that is to me perfectly unintelligible. Their *esse* is *percipi;* nor is it possible they should have any existence out of the minds or thinking things which perceive them.

4. It is indeed an opinion strangely prevailing amongst men, that houses, mountains, rivers, and in a word all sensible objects, have an existence, natural or real, distinct from their being perceived by the understanding. But, with how great an assurance and acquiescence soever this Principle may be entertained in the world, yet whoever shall find in his heart to call it in question, may,

if I mistake not, perceive it to involve a manifest contradiction. For, what are the forementioned objects but the things we perceive by sense? and what do we perceive besides our own ideas or sensations? and is it not plainly repugnant that any one of these, or any combination of them, should exist unperceived? . . .

6. Some truths there are so near and obvious to the mind that a man need only open his eyes to see them. Such I take this important one to be, viz. that all the choir of heaven and furniture of the earth, in a word all those bodies which compose the mighty frame of the world, have not any subsistence without a mind; that their *being* is to be perceived or known; that consequently so long as they are not actually perceived by me, or do not exist in my mind, or that of any other created spirit, they must either have no existence at all, or else subsist in the mind of some Eternal Spirit: it being perfectly unintelligible, and involving all the absurdity of abstraction, to attribute to any single part of them an existence independent of a spirit. [To be convinced of which, the reader need only reflect, and try to separate in his own thoughts the *being* of a sensible thing from its *being perceived.*]

7. From what has been said it is evident there is not any other Substance than *Spirit,* or that which perceives. But, for the fuller proof of this point, let it be considered the sensible qualities are colour, figure, motion, smell, taste, and such like, that is, the ideas perceived by sense. Now, for an idea to exist in an unperceiving thing is a manifest contradiction; for to have an idea is all one as to perceive: that therefore wherein colour, figure, and the like qualities exist must perceive them. Hence it is clear there can be no unthinking substance or *substratum* of those ideas.

8. But, say you, though the ideas themselves do not exist without the mind, yet there may be things like them, whereof they are copies or resemblances; which things exist without the mind, in an unthinking substance. I answer, an idea can be like nothing but an idea; a colour or figure can be like nothing but another colour or figure. If we look but never so little into our thoughts, we shall find it impossible for us to conceive a likeness except only between our ideas. Again, I ask whether those supposed *originals,* or external things, of which our ideas are the pictures or representations, be themselves perceivable or no? If they are, then *they* are ideas, and we have gained our point: but if you say they are not, I appeal

to any one whether it be sense to assert a colour is like something which is invisible; hard or soft, like something which is intangible; and so of the rest.

9. Some there are who make a distinction betwixt *primary* and *secondary* qualities. By the former they mean extension, figure, motion, rest, solidity or impenetrability, and number; by the latter they denote all other sensible qualities, as colours, sounds, tastes, and so forth. The ideas we have of these last they acknowledge not to be the resemblances of anything existing without the mind, or unperceived; but they will have our ideas of the *primary qualities* to be patterns or images of things which exist without the mind, in an unthinking substance which they call Matter. By Matter, therefore, we are to understand an inert, senseless substance, in which extension, figure, and motion do actually subsist. But it is evident, from what we have already shewn, that extension, figure and motion are only ideas existing in the mind, and that an idea can be like nothing but another idea; and that consequently neither they nor their archetypes can exist in an unperceiving substance. Hence, it is plain that the very notion of what is called *Matter* or *corporeal substance*, involves a contradiction in it. [Insomuch that I should not think it necessary to spend more time in exposing its absurdity. But, because the tenet of the existence of Matter seems to have taken so deep a root in the minds of philosophers, and draw after it so many ill consequences, I choose rather to be thought prolix and tedious than omit anything that might conduce to the full discovery and extirpation of that prejudice.]

10. They who assert that figure, motion, and the rest of the primary or original qualities do exist without the mind, in unthinking substances, do at the same time acknowledge that colours, sounds, heat, cold, and such-like secondary qualities, do not; which they tell us are sensations, existing in the mind alone, that depend on and are occasioned by the different size, texture, and motion of the minute particles of matter. This they take for an undoubted truth, which they can demonstrate beyond all exception. Now, if it be certain that those *original* qualities are inseparably united with the other sensible qualities, and not, even in thought, capable of being abstracted from them, it plainly follows that *they* exist only in the mind. But I desire any one to reflect, and try whether he can, by any abstraction of thought, conceive the extension and motion of a body without all other sensible qualities. For my own part, I see

evidently that it is not in my power to frame an idea of a body
extended and moving, but I must withal give it some colour or other
sensible quality, which is acknowledged to exist only in the mind.
In short, extension, figure, and motion, abstracted from all other
qualities, are inconceivable. Where therefore the other sensible qualities are, there must these be also, to wit, in the mind and nowhere
else. . . .

14. I shall farther add, that, after the same manner as modern
philosophers prove certain sensible qualities to have no existence
in Matter, or without the mind, the same thing may be likewise
proved of all other sensible qualities whatsoever. Thus, for instance,
it is said that heat and cold are affections only of the mind, and not
at all patterns of real beings, existing in the corporeal substances
which excite them; for that the same body which appears cold to
one hand seems warm to another. Now, why may we not as well
argue that figure and extension are not patterns or resemblances of
qualities existing in Matter; because to the same eye at different
stations, or eyes of a different texture at the same station, they
appear various, and cannot therefore be the images of anything
settled and determinate without the mind? Again, it is proved that
sweetness is not really in the sapid thing; because the thing remaining unaltered the sweetness is changed into bitter, as in case
of a fever or otherwise vitiated palate. Is it not as reasonable to
say that motion is not without the mind; since if the succession of
ideas in the mind become swifter, the motion, it is acknowledged,
shall appear slower, without any alteration in any external object?

15. In short, let any one consider those arguments which are
thought manifestly to prove that colours and tastes exist only in
the mind, and he shall find they may with equal force be brought
to prove the same thing of extension, figure, and motion. Though it
must be confessed this method of arguing does not so much prove
that there is no extension or colour in an outward object, as that
we do not know by sense which is the true extension or colour of
the object. But the arguments foregoing plainly shew it to be impossible that any colour or extension at all, or other sensible quality whatsoever, should exist in an unthinking subject without the
mind, or in truth that there should be any such thing as an outward object. . . .

18. But, though it were possible that solid, figured, moveable
substances may exist without the mind, corresponding to the ideas

we have of bodies, yet how is it possible for us to know this? Either
we must know it by Sense or by Reason. As for our senses, by them
we have the knowledge only of our sensations, ideas, or those things
that are immediately perceived by sense, call them what you will:
but they do not inform us that things exist without the mind, or
unperceived, like to those which are perceived. This the materialists
themselves acknowledge.—It remains therefore that if we have any
knowledge at all of external things, it must be by reason inferring
their existence from what is immediately perceived by sense. But [I
do not see] what reason can induce us to believe the existence of
bodies without the mind, from what we perceive, since the very
patrons of Matter themselves do not pretend there is any necessary
connexion betwixt them and our ideas? I say it is granted on all
hands (and what happens in dreams, frensies, and the like, puts it
beyond dispute) that it is possible we might be affected with all the
ideas we have now, though no bodies existed without resembling
them. Hence it is evident the supposition of external bodies is not
necessary for the producing our ideas; since it is granted they are
produced sometimes, and might possibly be produced always, in
the same order we see them in at present, without their concurrence.

19. But, though we might possibly have all our sensations without them, yet perhaps it may be thought easier to conceive and explain the manner of their production, by supposing external bodies
in their likeness rather than otherwise; and so it might be at least
probable there are such things as bodies that excite their ideas in
our minds. But neither can this be said. For, though we give the
materialists their external bodies, they by their own confession are
never the nearer knowing how our ideas are produced; since they
own themselves unable to comprehend in what manner body can
act upon spirit, or how it is possible it should imprint any idea in
the mind. Hence it is evident the production of ideas or sensations
in our minds, can be no reason why we should suppose Matter or
corporeal substances; since that is acknowledged to remain equally
inexplicable with or without this supposition. If therefore it were
possible for bodies to exist without the mind, yet to hold they do so
must needs be a very precarious opinion; since it is to suppose, without any reason at all, that God has created innumerable beings that
are entirely useless, and serve to no manner of purpose.

20. In short, if there were external bodies, it is impossible we
should ever come to know it; and if there were not, we might have

the very same reasons to think there were that we have now. Suppose—what no one can deny possible—an intelligence, without the help of external bodies, to be affected with the same train of sensations or ideas that you are, imprinted in the same order and with like vividness in his mind. I ask whether that intelligence hath not all the reason to believe the existence of Corporeal Substances, represented by his ideas, and exciting them in his mind, that you can possibly have for believing the same thing? Of this there can be no question. Which one consideration were enough to make any reasonable person suspect the strength of whatever arguments he may think himself to have, for the existence of bodies without the mind. . . .

22. I am afraid I have given cause to think I am needlessly prolix in handling this subject. For, to what purpose is it to dilate on that which may be demonstrated with the utmost evidence in a line or two, to any one that is capable of the least reflexion? It is but looking into your own thoughts, and so trying whether you can conceive it possible for a sound, or figure, or motion, or colour to exist without the mind or unperceived. This easy trial may perhaps make you see that what you contend for is a downright contradiction. Insomuch that I am content to put the whole upon this issue:—If you can but conceive it possible for one extended moveable substance, or in general for any one idea, or anything like an idea, to exist otherwise than in a mind perceiving it, I shall readily give up the cause. And, as for all that compages of external bodies you contend for, I shall grant you its existence, though you cannot either give me any reason why you believe it exists, or assign any use to it when it is supposed to exist. I say, the bare possibility of your opinions being true shall pass for an argument that it is so.

23. But, say you, surely there is nothing easier than for me to imagine trees, for instance, in a park, or books existing in a closet, and nobody by to perceive them. I answer, you may so, there is no difficulty in it. But what is all this, I beseech you, more than framing in your mind certain ideas which you call *books* and *trees,* and at the same time omitting to frame the idea of any one that may perceive them? But do not you yourself perceive or think of them all the while? This therefore is nothing to the purpose: it only shews you have the power of imagining, or forming ideas in your mind; but it does not shew that you can conceive it possible the objects of your thought may exist without the mind. To make out this, it is necessary that you conceive them existing unconceived or unthought

of; which is a manifest repugnancy. When we do our utmost to conceive the existence of external bodies, we are all the while only contemplating our own ideas. But the mind, taking no notice of itself, is deluded to think it can and does conceive bodies existing unthought of, or without the mind, though at the same time they are apprehended by, or exist in, itself. A little attention will discover to any one the truth and evidence of what is here said, and make it unnecessary to insist on any other proofs against the existence of *material substance*.

24. [Could men but forbear to amuse themselves with words, we should, I believe, soon come to an agreement in this point.] It is very obvious, upon the least inquiry into our own thoughts, to know whether it be possible for us to understand what is meant by the *absolute existence of sensible objects in themselves,* or *without the mind*. To me it is evident those words mark out either a direct contradiction, or else nothing at all. And to convince others of this, I know no readier or fairer way than to entreat they would calmly attend to their own thoughts; and if by this attention the emptiness or repugnancy of those expressions does appear, surely nothing more is requisite for their conviction. It is on this therefore that I insist, to wit, that the *absolute existence of unthinking things* are words without a meaning, or which include a contradiction. This is what I repeat and inculcate, and earnestly recommend to the attentive thoughts of the reader.

25. All our ideas, sensations, notions, or the things which we perceive, by whatsoever names they may be distinguished, are visibly inactive: there is nothing of power or agency included in them. So that one idea or object of thought cannot produce or make any alteration in another. To be satisfied of the truth of this, there is nothing else requisite but a bare observation of our ideas. For, since they and every part of them exist only in the mind, it follows that there is nothing in them but what is perceived: but whoever shall attend to his ideas, whether of sense or reflexion, will not perceive in them any power or activity; there is, therefore, no such thing contained in them. A little attention will discover to us that the very being of an idea implies passiveness and inertness in it; insomuch that it is impossible for an idea to do anything, or, strictly speaking, to be the cause of anything: neither can it be the resemblance or pattern of any active being, as is evident from Section 8. Whence it plainly follows that extension, figure, and motion cannot

be the cause of our sensations. To say, therefore, that these are the effects of powers resulting from the configuration, number, motion, and size of corpuscles, must certainly be false.

26. We perceive a continual succession of ideas; some are anew excited, others are changed or totally disappear. There is therefore, *some* cause of these ideas, whereon they depend, and which produces and changes them. That this cause cannot be any quality or idea or combination of *ideas,* is clear from the preceding section. It must therefore be a *substance;* but it has been shewn that there is no corporeal or material substance: it remains therefore that the cause of ideas is an incorporeal active substance or Spirit. . . .

IMMANUEL KANT

(1724-1804)

Kant's main line of argument for the kind of idealism he adopts is as follows: we can admit synthetic *a priori* propositions only if they are confined to appearances and are not taken to apply to reality. Our ability to anticipate *a priori* what is going to happen, as we do in mathematics and also in the case of a few other general principles like that of causality, can be explained only if this *a priori* knowledge depends on what we ourselves contributed to the organization of the data given in experience. Geometry is regarded by Kant as the study of space and arithmetic as a science which can be synthetic because it can at least be illustrated in terms of moments of time or dots in space. Thus to account for their *a priori* character and their applicability to the world he supposes that the mind in perceiving generates space and time and organizes the empirical content in terms of these. Kant expresses this by saying that space and time are *a priori* intuitions as opposed to the "manifold" given by sensation. The German word translated *intuition* (*Anschauung*) does not mean what "intuition" usually would in a modern writer, but approximately "perception," used in a wide enough sense to cover not only the perception of particular physical objects but the general form contributed by our faculty of perception. Only if we contribute the form ourselves can we say that everything we know will conform to it. If this is so an element in what we perceive without which the rest would be quite unrecognisable is always due to our mind and not to other things. From this Kant concluded that we can never know things as they are in themselves but only as they appear to us.

The second selection is taken from the central passage of the *Critique of Pure Reason,* the Transcendental Deduction of the Categories. In it Kant argues that all knowledge presupposes a synthesis by which the self makes a unity of its experience. The historical importance of the passage perhaps lies chiefly in the fact that it established once for all the principle that perception is not just an acceptance of given data. The synthesis presupposes in some sense self-identity, but Kant insists that this does not mean that the self can be asserted to have an inherent unity apart from its activity in unifying knowledge. So the transcendental unity of apperception, the unity of the subjective side of our experience, cannot be separated from the unified world of the objects of our knowledge and *vice versa*. The term "transcendental" applied to a deduction means that the deduction has resulted in evincing a necessary condition of our empirical knowledge.

The third selection gives Kant's proof of *causality* (the second analogy) by showing that we can distinguish subjective and objective succession only if the latter is necessarily determined. If he is right, it follows that all judgments asserting objective succession in time presuppose causality. To the sceptic who would ask whether we had any right to make objective judgments of any kind, Kant would reply that it cannot be disputed that at least we know the subjective order of our own apprehensions and this can be known only in contrast to a physical order. The latter is objective relatively to us as individuals, although it is not an order independent of all experience, but only the way in which things-in-themselves must appear to human beings. Another conclusion which Kant draws is that, since this is the only way of proving causality, we are not entitled to use it in arguments going beyond the sphere of actual and possible human experience, e.g., in order to prove God's existence.

The fourth selection gives the first and third antinomies and an outline of Kant's solution. The antinomies are intended by Kant partly to show that the idea of a world existing in space and time independently of experience is self-contradictory, partly to expose the unsoundness of the foundations of metaphysical arguments. The solution of the antinomies in general is that reality is neither finite nor infinite in space and time because it is not in space and time at all. As regards appearances they can be infinite only in the sense that we could always go on finding new ones. But the detailed solution of the two antinomies is different in principle. As regards the first Kant says that both thesis and antithesis are false; as regards the third he says they may both be true, the thesis of reality and the antithesis of appearances. Thus the world *may* depend timelessly on God and yet each event be also determined causally in another sense of "causation" (probably Kant means by this sense of "causation" regular sequence) by preceding events, so that there is no first cause in the series of appearances which constitutes the world. In this way Kant thought he could also provide the only possible solution for the problem of human freedom.

Kant's idealism is far more negative than Berkeley's, but the two philosophers agree in making physical objects inseparable from experience. Although in the *Critique of Pure Reason* Kant insists that we cannot have any theoretical knowledge of things in themselves (*noumena*) and so denies the possibility of theoretical metaphysics, he really believes in God on the strength of an ethical argument and only denies that this amounts to knowledge in the strict sense. In the fifth selection he tries to reconcile these two positions.

1.

How Is
Pure Mathematics Possible

§ 6. HERE IS a great and established branch of knowledge, encompassing even now a wonderfully large domain and promising an unlimited extension in the future. Yet it carries with it thoroughly apodeictical certainty, i.e., absolute necessity, which therefore rests upon no empirical grounds. Consequently it is a pure product of reason, and moreover is thoroughly synthetical. [Here the question arises:]

"How then is it possible for human reason to produce a cognition of this nature entirely *a priori?*"

Does not this faculty [which produces mathematics], as it neither is nor can be based upon experience, presuppose some ground of cognition *a priori*, which lies deeply hidden, but which might reveal itself by these its effects, if their first beginnings were but diligently ferreted out?

§ 7. But we find that all mathematical cognition has this peculiarity: it must first exhibit its concept in a visual form (*Anschauung*) and indeed *a priori*, therefore in a visual form which is not empirical, but pure. Without this mathematics cannot take a single step; hence its judgments are always visual, viz., "intuitive"; whereas philosophy must be satisfied with discursive judgments from mere concepts, and though it may illustrate its doctrines through a visual figure, can never derive them from it. This observation on the nature of mathematics gives us a clue to the first and highest condition of its possibility, which is, that some non-sensuous visualisation (called pure intuition, or *reine Anschauung*) must form its basis, in which all its concepts can be exhibited or constructed, *in concreto* and yet *a priori*. If we can find out this pure intuition and

---

This selection comprises the entire "First Part of the Fundamental Problem" of Kant's *Prolegomena to Any Future Metaphysics*. The *Prolegomena* was first published in 1783. All translations from the *Prolegomena* used in this book are by Paul Carus and are reprinted with the kind permission of The Open Court Publishing Company.

its possibility, we may thence easily explain how synthetical propositions *a priori* are possible in pure mathematics, and consequently how this science itself is possible. Empirical intuition [viz., sense-perception] enables us without difficulty to enlarge the concept which we frame of an object of intuition [or sense-perception], by new predicates, which intuition [i.e., sense perception] itself presents synthetically in experience. Pure intuition [viz., the visualization of forms in our imagination, from which every thing sensual, i.e., every thought of material qualities, is excluded] does so likewise, only with this difference, that in the latter case the synthetical judgment is *a priori* certain and apodeictical, in the former, only *a posteriori* and empirically certain; because this latter contains only that which occurs in contingent empirical intuition, but the former, that which must necessarily be discovered in pure intuition. Here intuition, being an intuition *a priori,* is *before all experience,* viz., before any perception of particular objects, inseparably conjoined with its concept.

§ 8. But with this step our perplexity seems rather to increase than to lessen. For the question now is, "How is it possible to intuite [in a visual form] anything *a priori?*" An intuition [viz., a visual sense-perception] is such a representation as immediately depends upon the presence of the object. Hence it seems impossible to intuite from the outset *a priori,* because intuition would in that event take place without either a former or a present object to refer to, and by consequence could not be intuition. Concepts indeed are such, that we can easily form some of them *a priori,* viz., such as contain nothing but the thought of an object in general; and we need not find ourselves in an immediate relation to the object. Take, for instance, the concepts of Quantity, of Cause, etc. But even these require, in order to make them understood, a certain concrete use—that is, an application to some sense-experience (*Anschauung*), by which an object of them is given us. But how can the intuition of the object [its visualization] precede the object itself?

§ 9. If our intuition [i.e., our sense-experience] were perforce of such a nature as to represent things as they are in themselves, there would not be any intuition *a priori,* but intuition would be always empirical. For I can only know what is contained in the object in itself when it is present and given to me. It is indeed even then incomprehensible how the visualizing (*Anschauung*) of a present thing should make me know this thing as it is in itself, as its properties cannot migrate into my faculty of representation. But even granting this possibility, a visualizing of that sort would not take place *a priori,* that is, before the object were presented to me; for without this latter fact no reason of a relation between my representation and the object can be imagined, unless it depend upon a direct inspiration.

Therefore in one way only can my intuition (*Anschauung*) anticipate the actuality of the object, and be a cognition *a priori,* viz.: if my intuition contains nothing but the form of sensibility, antedating in my subjectivity all the actual impressions through which I am affected by objects.

For that objects of sense can only be intuited according to this form of sensibility I can know *a priori.* Hence it follows: that propositions, which concern this form of sensuous intuition only, are possible and valid for objects of the senses; as also, conversely, that intuitions which are possible *a priori* can never concern any other things than objects of our senses.

§ 10. Accordingly, it is only the form of sensuous intuition by which we can intuite things *a priori,* but by which we can know objects only as they *appear* to us (to our senses), not as they are in themselves; and this assumption is absolutely necessary if synthetical propositions *a priori* be granted as possible, or if, in case they actually occur, their possibility is to be comprehended and determined beforehand.

Now, the intuitions which pure mathematics lays at the foundation of all its cognitions and judgments which appear at once apodeictic and necessary are Space and Time. For mathematics must first have all its concepts in intuition, and pure mathematics in pure intuition, that is, it must construct them. If it proceeded in any other way, it would be impossible to make any headway, for mathematics proceeds, not analytically by dissection of concepts, but synthetically, and if pure intuition be wanting, there is nothing in which the matter of synthetical judgments *a priori* can be given. Geometry is based upon the pure intuition of space. Arithmetic accomplishes its concept of number by the successive addition of units in time; and pure mechanics especially cannot attain its concepts of motion without employing the representation of time. Both representations, however, are only intuitions; for if we omit from the empirical intuitions of bodies and their alterations (motion) everything empirical, or belonging to sensation, space and time still remain, which are therefore pure intuitions that lie *a priori* at the basis of the empirical. Hence they can never be omitted, but at the same time, by their being pure intuitions *a priori,* they prove that they are mere forms of our sensibility, which must precede all empirical intuition, or perception of actual objects, and conformably to which objects can be known *a priori,* but only as they appear to us.

§ 11. The problem of the present section is therefore solved. Pure mathematics, as synthetical cognition *a priori,* is only possible by referring to no other objects than those of the senses. At the basis of their empirical intuition lies a pure intuition (of space and of time) which is *a priori.* This is possible, because the latter intuition is nothing but the mere form of sensibility, which precedes the actual appearance of the objects, in that it, in fact, makes them possible. Yet this faculty of intuiting *a priori* affects not the matter of the phenomenon (that is, the sense-element in it, for this constitutes that which is empirical), but its form, viz., space and time. Should any man venture to doubt that these are determinations adhering not to things in themselves, but to their relation to our sensibility, I should be glad to know how it can be possible to know the constitution of things *a priori,* viz., before we have any acquaintance with them and before they are presented to us. Such, however, is the case with space and time. But this is quite comprehensible as soon as both count for nothing more than formal conditions of our sensibility, while the objects count merely as phenomena; for then the form of the phenomenon, i.e., pure intuition, can by all means be represented as proceeding from ourselves, that is, *a priori.*

§ 12. In order to add something by way of illustration and confirmation, we need only watch the ordinary and necessary procedure of geometers. All proofs of the complete congruence of two given figures (where the one can in every respect be substituted for the other) come ultimately to this that they may be made to coincide; which is evidently nothing else than a synthetical proposition resting upon immediate intuition, and this intuition must be pure, or given *a priori,* otherwise the proposition could not rank as apodeictically certain, but would have empirical certainty only. In that case, it could only be said that it is always found to be so, and holds good only as far as our perception reaches. That everywhere space (which [in its entirety] is itself no longer the boundary of another space) has three dimensions, and that space cannot in any

way have more, is based on the proposition that not more than
three lines can intersect at right angles in one point; but this proposition cannot by any means be shown from concepts, but rests
immediately on intuition, and indeed on pure and *a priori* intuition,
because it is apodeictically certain. That we can require a line to
be drawn to infinity (*in indefinitum*), or that a series of changes
(for example, spaces traversed by motion) shall be infinitely continued, presupposes a representation of space and time, which can
only attach to intuition, namely, so far as it in itself is bounded by
nothing, for from concepts it could never be inferred. Consequently,
the basis of mathematics actually are pure intuitions, which make
its synthetical and apodeictically valid propositions possible. Hence
our transcendental deduction of the notions of space and of time
explains at the same time the possibility of pure mathematics. Without some such deduction its truth may be granted, but its existence
could by no means be understood, and we must assume "that everything which can be given to our senses (to the external senses in
space, to the internal one in time) is intuited by us as it appears to
us, not as it is in itself."

§ 13. Those who cannot yet rid themselves of the notion that
space and time are actual qualities inhering in things in themselves,
may exercise their acumen on the following paradox. When they
have in vain attempted its solution, and are free from prejudices at
least for a few moments, they will suspect that the degradation of
space and of time to mere forms of our sensuous intuition may
perhaps be well founded.

If two things are quite equal in all respects as much as can be
ascertained by all means possible, quantitatively and qualitatively,
it must follow, that the one can in all cases and under all circumstances replace the other, and this substitution would not occasion
the least perceptible difference. This in fact is true of plane figures
in geometry; but some spherical figures exhibit, notwithstanding a
complete internal agreement, such a contrast in their external relation, that the one figure cannot possibly be put in the place of the
other. For instance, two spherical triangles on opposite hemispheres,
which have an arc of the equator as their common base, may be
quite equal, both as regards sides and angles, so that nothing is to
be found in either, if it be described for itself alone and completed,
that would not equally be applicable to both; and yet the one cannot
be put in the place of the other (being situated upon the opposite

hemisphere). Here then is an internal difference between the two triangles, which difference our understanding cannot describe as internal, and which only manifests itself by external relations in space.

But I shall adduce examples, taken from common life, that are more obvious still.

What can be more similar in every respect and in every part more alike to my hand and to my ear, than their images in a mirror? And yet I cannot put such a hand as is seen in the glass in the place of its archetype; for if this is a right hand, that in the glass is a left one, and the image or reflection of the right ear is a left one, which never can serve as a substitute for the other. There are in this case no internal differences which our understanding could determine by thinking alone. Yet the differences are internal as the senses teach, for, notwithstanding their complete equality and similarity, the left hand cannot be enclosed in the same bounds as the right one (they are not congruent); the glove of one hand cannot be used for the other. What is the solution? These objects are not representations of things as they are in themselves, and as the pure understanding would cognize them, but sensuous intuitions, that is, appearances, the possibility of which rests upon the relation of certain things unknown in themselves to something else, viz., to our sensibility. Space is the form of the external intuition of this sensibility, and the internal determination of every space is only possible by the determination of its external relation to the whole space, of which it is a part (in other words, by its relation to the external sense). That is to say, the part is only possible through the whole, which is never the case with things in themselves, as objects of the mere understanding, but with appearances only. Hence the difference between similar and equal things, which are yet not congruent (for instance, two symmetric helices), cannot be made intelligible by any concept, but only by the relation to the right and the left hands which immediately refers to intuition.

REMARK I

Pure Mathematics, and especially pure geometry, can only have objective reality on condition that they refer to objects of sense. But in regard to the latter the principle holds good, that our sense representation is not a representation of things in themselves, but of the way in which they appear to us. Hence it follows that the propositions of geometry are not the results of a mere creation of our poetic imagination, and that therefore they cannot be referred with assurance to actual objects; but rather that they are necessarily valid of space, and consequently of all that may be found in space, because space is nothing else than the form of all external appearances, and it is this form alone in which objects of sense can be given. Sensibility, the form of which is the basis of geometry, is that upon which the possibility of external appearance depends. Therefore these appearances can never contain anything but what geometry prescribes to them.

It would be quite otherwise if the senses were so constituted as to represent objects as they are in themselves. For then it would not by any means follow from the conception of space, which with all its properties serves to the geometer as an *a priori* foundation, together with what is thence inferred, must be so in nature. The space of the geometer would be considered a mere fiction, and it would not be credited with objective validity, because we cannot see how things must of necessity agree with an image of them, which we make spontaneously and previous to our acquaintance with them. But if this image, or rather this formal intuition, is the essential property of our sensibility, by means of which alone objects are given to us, and if this sensibility represents not things in themselves, but their appearances: we shall easily comprehend, and at the same time indisputably prove, that all external objects of our world of sense must necessarily coincide in the most rigorous way with the propositions of geometry; because sensibility by means of its form of external intuition, viz., by space, the same with which the geometer is occupied, makes those objects at all possible as mere appearances.

It will always remain a remarkable phenomenon in the history of philosophy, that there was a time, when even mathematicians, who at the same time were philosophers, began to doubt, not of the accuracy of their geometrical propositions so far as they concerned space, but of their objective validity and the applicability of this concept itself, and of all its corollaries, to nature. They showed much concern whether a line in nature might not consist of physical points, and consequently that true space in the object might consist of simple [discrete] parts, while the space which the geometer has in his mind [being continuous] cannot be such. They did not recognise that this mental space renders possible the physical space, i.e., the extension of matter; that this pure space is not at all a quality of things in themselves, but a form of our sensuous faculty of representation; and that all objects in space are mere appearances, i.e., not things in themselves but representations of our sensuous intuition. But such is the case, for the space of the geometer is exactly the form of sensuous intuition which we find *a priori* in us, and contains the ground of the possibility of all external appearances (according to their form), and the latter must necessarily and most rigidly agree with the propositions of the geometer, which he draws not from any fictitious concept, but from the subjective basis of all external phenomena, which is sensibility itself. In this and no other way can geometry be made secure as to the undoubted objective reality of its propositions against all the intrigues of a shallow Metaphysics, which is surprised at them [the geometrical propositions], because it has not traced them to the sources of their concepts.

REMARK II

Whatever is given us as object, must be given us in intuition. All our intuition however takes place by means of the senses only; the understanding intuites nothing, but only reflects. And as we have just shown that the senses never and in no manner enable us to know things in themselves, but only their appearances, which are mere representations of the sensibility, we conclude that "all bodies, together with the space in which they are, must be considered nothing but mere representations in us, and exist nowhere but in our thoughts." You will say: Is not this manifest idealism?

Idealism consists in the assertion, that there are none but thinking beings, all other things, which we think are perceived in intuition, being nothing but representations in the thinking beings, to which no object external to them corresponds in fact. Whereas I say, that things as objects of our senses existing outside us are given, but we know nothing of what they may be in themselves, knowing only their appearances, i.e., the representations which they cause in us by affecting our senses. Consequently I grant by all means that there are bodies without us, that is, things which, though quite unknown to us as to what they are in themselves, we yet know by the representations which their influence on our sensibility procures us, and which we call bodies, a term signifying merely the appearance of the thing which is unknown to us, but not therefore less actual. Can this be termed idealism? It is the very contrary.

Long before Locke's time, but assuredly since him, it has been generally assumed and granted without detriment to the actual existence of external things, that many of their predicates may be said to belong not to the things in themselves, but to their appearances, and to have no proper existence outside our representation. Heat, color, and taste, for instance, are of this kind. Now, if I go farther, and for weighty reasons rank as mere appearances the remaining qualities of bodies also, which are called primary, such as extension, place, and in general space, with all that which belongs to it (impenetrability or materiality, space, etc.)—no one in the least can adduce the reason of its being inadmissible. As little as the man who admits colors not to be properties of the object in itself, but only as modifications of the sense of sight, should on that account be called an idealist, so little can my system be named idealistic, merely because I find that more, nay,

All the properties which constitute the intuition of a body belong merely to its appearance.

The existence of the thing that appears is thereby not destroyed, as in genuine idealism, but it is only shown, that we cannot possibly know it by the senses as it is in itself.

I should be glad to know what my assertions must be in order to avoid all idealism. Undoubtedly, I should say, that the representation of space is not only perfectly conformable to the relation which our sensibility has to objects—that I have said—but that it is quite similar to the object,—an assertion in which I can find as little meaning as if I said that the sensation of red has a similarity to the property of vermilion, which in me excites this sensation.

REMARK III

Hence we may at once dismiss an easily foreseen but futile objection, "that by admitting the ideality of space and of time the whole sensible world would be turned into mere sham." At first all philosophical insight into the nature of sensuous cognition was spoiled, by making the sensibility merely a confused mode of representation, according to which we still know things as they are, but without being able to reduce everything in this, our representation, to a clear consciousness; whereas proof is offered by us that sensibility consists, not in this logical distinction of clearness and obscurity, but in the genetical one of the origin of cognition itself. For sensuous perception represents things not at all as they are, but only the mode in which they affect our senses, and consequently by sensuous perception appearances only and not things themselves are given to the understanding for reflection. After this necessary corrective, an objection rises from an unpardonable and almost intentional misconception, as if my doctrine turned all the things of the world of sense into mere illusion.

When an appearance is given us, we are still quite free as to how we should judge the matter. The appearance depends upon the senses, but the judgment upon the understanding, and the only question is, whether in the determination of the object there is truth or not. But the difference between truth and dreaming is not ascertained by the nature of the representations, which are referred to objects (for they are the same in both cases), but by their connection according to those rules, which determine the coherence of the representations in the concept of an object, and by ascertaining whether they can subsist together in experience or not. And it is not the fault of the appearances if our cognition takes illusion for truth, i.e., if the intuition, by which an object is given us, is considered a concept of the thing or of its existence also, which the understanding can only think. The senses represent to us the paths of the planets as now progressive, now retrogressive, and herein is neither falsehood nor truth, because as long as we hold this path to be nothing but appearance, we do not judge of the objective nature of their motion. But as a false judgment may easily arise when the understanding is not on its guard against this subjective mode of representation being considered objective, we say they appear to move backward; it is not the senses however which must be charged with the illusion, but the understanding, whose province alone it is to give an objective judgment on appearances.

Thus, even if we did not at all reflect on the origin of our representations, whenever we connect our intuitions of sense (whatever they may contain), in space and in time, according to the rules of the coherence of all cognition in experience, illusion or truth will arise according as we are negligent or careful. It is merely a question of the use of sensuous representations in the understanding, and not of their origin. In the same way, if I consider all the representations of the senses, together with their form, space and time, to be nothing but appearances, and space and time to be a mere form of the sensibility, which is not to be met with in objects out of it, and if I make use of these representations in reference to possible experience only, there is nothing in my regarding them as appearances that can lead astray or cause illusion. For all that, they can correctly cohere according to rules of truth in experience. Thus all the propositions of geometry hold good of space as well as of all the objects of the senses, consequently of all possible experience, whether I consider space as a mere form of the sensibility, or as something cleaving to the things themselves. In the former case however I comprehend how I can know *a priori* these propositions concerning all the objects of external intuition. Otherwise, everything else as regards all possible experience remains just as if I had not departed from the vulgar view.

But if I venture to go beyond all possible experience with my notions of space and time, which I cannot refrain from doing if I proclaim them qualities inherent in things in themselves (for what should prevent me from letting them hold good of the same things, even though my senses might be different, and unsuited to them?), then a grave error may arise due to illusion, for this I would proclaim to be universally valid what is merely a subjective condition of the intuition of things and sure only for all objects of sense, viz., for all possible experience; I would refer this condition to things in themselves, and do not limit it to the conditions of experience.

My doctrine of the ideality of space and time, therefore, far from reducing the whole sensible world to mere illusion, is the only means of securing the application of one of the most important cognitions (that which mathematics propounds *a priori*) to actual objects, and of preventing its being regarded as mere illusion. For without this observation it would be quite impossible to make out whether the intuitions of space and time, which we borrow from no experience, and which yet lie in our representation *a priori,* are not mere phantasms of our brain, to which objects do not correspond, at least not adequately, and consequently, whether we have been able to show its unquestionable validity with regard to all the objects of the sensible world just because they are mere appearances.

Secondly, though these my principles make appearances of the representations of the senses, they are so far from turning the truth of experience into mere illusion, that they are rather the only means of preventing the transcendental illusion, by which metaphysics has hitherto been deceived, leading to the childish endeavor of catching at bubbles, because appearances, which are mere representations, were taken for things in themselves. Here originated the remarkable event of the antimony of Reason which I shall mention by and by, and which is destroyed by the single observation, that appearance, as long as it is employed in experience, produces truth, but the moment it transgresses the bounds of experience, and consequently becomes transcendent, produces nothing but illusion.

Inasmuch, therefore, as I leave to things as we obtain them by the senses their actuality, and only limit our sensuous intuition of these things to this, that they represent in no respect, not even in the pure intuitions of space and of time, anything more than mere appearance of those things, but never their constitution in themselves, this is not a sweeping illusion invented for nature by me. My protestation too against all charges of idealism is so valid and clear as even to seem superfluous, were there not incompetent judges, who, while they would have an old name for every deviation from their perverse though common opinion, and never judge of the spirit of philosophic nomenclature, but cling to the letter only, are ready to put their own conceits in the place of well-defined notions, and thereby deform and distort them. I have myself given this my theory the name of transcendental idealism, but that cannot authorise any one to confound it either with the empirical idealism of Descartes, (indeed, his was only an insoluble problem, owing to which he thought every one at liberty to deny the existence of the corporeal world, because it could never be proved satisfactorily), or with the mystical and visionary idealism of Berkeley, against which and other similar phantasms our Critique contains the proper antidote. My idealism concerns not the existence of things (the doubting of which, however, constitutes idealism in the ordinary sense), since it never came into my head to doubt it, but it concerns the sensuous representation of things, to which space and time especially belong. Of these [viz., space and time], consequently of all appearances in general, I have only shown, that they are neither things (but mere modes of representation), nor determinations belonging to things in themselves. But the word "transcendental," which with me means a reference of our cognition, i.e., not to things, but only to the cognitive faculty, was meant to obviate this misconception. Yet rather than give further occasion to it by this word, I now retract it, and desire this idealism of mine to be called critical. But if it be really an objectionable idealism to convert actual things (not appearances) into mere representations, by what name shall we call him who conversely changes mere representations to things? It may, I think, be called "dreaming idealism," in contradistinction to the former, which may be called "visionary," both of which are to be refuted by my transcendental, or, better, critical idealism.

2.

The Transcendental Deduction
of the Categories

TRANSITION TO THE TRANSCENDENTAL DEDUCTION
OF THE CATEGORIES

THERE ARE only two possible ways in which synthetic representations and their objects can establish connection, obtain necessary relation to one another, and, as it were, meet one another. Either the object alone must make the representation possible, or the representation alone must make the object possible. In the former case, this relation is only empirical, and the representation is never possible *a priori*. This is true of appearances, as regards that [element] in them which belongs to sensation. In the latter case, representation in itself does not produce its object in so far as *existence* is concerned, for we are not here speaking of its causality by means of the will. None the less the representation is *a priori* determinant of the object, if it be the case that only through the representation is it possible to *know* anything *as an object*. Now there are two conditions under which alone the knowledge of an object is possible, first, *intuition*, through which it is given, though only as appearance; secondly, *concept*, through which an object is thought corresponding to this intuition. It is evident from the above that the first condition, namely, that under which alone objects can be intuited, does actually lie *a priori* in the mind as the formal ground of the objects. All appearances necessarily agree with this formal condition of sensibility, since only through it can they appear, that is, be empirically intuited and given. The question now arises

This selection comprises the beginning of §14 from Chapter II, Section 1 of the "Transcendental Analytic" and the whole of Section 2 of the same chapter of the *Critique of Pure Reason*. The latter is given in the version contained in the first edition. I have used the first rather than the second edition because it is clearer and in certain respects more explicit. *The Critique of Pure Reason* was first published in 1781.

All selections from the *Critique of Pure Reason* are taken from the Kemp Smith translation and are reproduced with the kind permission of St. Martin's Press, Inc., and the translator.

whether *a prori* concepts do not also serve as antecedent conditions under which alone anything can be, if not intuited, yet thought as object in general. In that case all empirical knowledge of objects would necessarily conform to such concepts, because only as thus presupposing them is anything possible as *object of experience*. Now all experience does indeed contain, in addition to the intuition of the senses through which something is given, a *concept* of an object as being thereby given, that is to say, as appearing. Concepts of objects in general thus underlie all empirical knowledge as its *a priori* conditions. The objective validity of the categories as *a priori* concepts rests, therefore, on the fact that, so far as the form of thought is concerned, through them alone does experience become possible. They relate of necessity and *a priori* to objects of experience, for the reason that only by means of them can any object whatsoever of experience be thought. . . .

THE *A Priori* GROUNDS OF THE POSSIBILITY OF EXPERIENCE

That a concept, although itself neither contained in the concept of possible experience nor consisting of elements of a possible experience, should be produced completely *a priori* and should relate to an object, is altogether contradictory and impossible. For it would then have no content, since no intuition corresponds to it; and intuitions in general, through which objects can be given to us, constitute the field, the whole object, of possible experience. An *a priori* concept which did not relate to experience would be only the logical form of a concept, not the concept itself through which something is thought.

Pure *a priori* concepts, if such exist, cannot indeed contain anything empirical; yet, none the less, they can serve solely as *a priori* conditions of a possible experience. Upon this ground alone can their objective reality rest.

If, therefore, we seek to discover how pure concepts of understanding are possible, we must enquire what are the *a priori* conditions upon which the possibility of experience rests, and which remain as its underlying grounds when everything empirical is abstracted from appearances. A concept which universally and adequately expresses such a formal and objective condition of experience would be entitled a pure concept of understanding. Certainly, once I am in possession of pure concepts of understanding, I can think objects which may be impossible, or which, though perhaps in themselves possible, cannot be given in any experience. For in the connecting of these concepts something may be omitted which yet necessarily belongs to the condition of a possible experience (as in the concept of a spirit). Or, it may be, pure concepts are extended further than experience can follow (as with the concept of God). But the *elements* of all modes of *a priori* knowledge, even of capricious and incongruous fictions, though they cannot, indeed, be derived from experience, since in that case they would not be knowledge *a priori,* must nonetheless always contain the pure *a priori* conditions of a possible experience and of an empirical object. Otherwise nothing would be thought through them, and they themselves, being without data, could never arise even in thought.

The concepts which thus contain *a priori* the pure thought involved in every experience, we find in the categories. If we can prove that by their means alone an object can be thought, this will be a sufficient deduction of them, and will justify their objective validity. But since in such a thought more than simply the faculty of thought, the understanding, is brought into play, and since this faculty itself, as a faculty of *knowledge* that is meant to relate to objects, calls for explanation in regard to the possibility of such relation, we must first of all consider, not in their empirical but in their transcendental constitution, the subjective sources which form the *a priori* foundation of the possibility of experience.

If each representation were completely foreign to every other, standing apart in isolation, no such thing as knowledge would ever arise. For knowledge is [essentially] a whole in which representations stand compared and connected. As sense contains a manifold in its intuition, I ascribe to it a synopsis. But to such synopsis a synthesis must always correspond; receptivity can make knowledge possible only when combined with spontaneity. Now this spontaneity is the ground of a threefold synthesis which must necessarily be found in all knowledge; namely, the *apprehension* of representations as modifications of the mind in intuition, their *reproduction* in imagination, and their *recognition* in a concept. These point to three subjective sources of knowledge which make possible the understanding itself —and consequently all experience as its empirical product.

The deduction of the categories is a matter of such extreme difficulty, compelling us to penetrate so deeply into the first grounds of the possibility of our knowledge in general, that in order to avoid the elaborateness of a complete theory, and yet at the same time to omit nothing in so indispensable an enquiry, I have found it advisable in the four following passages rather to prepare than to instruct the reader. Systematic exposition of these elements of the understanding is first given in Section 3, immediately following. The reader must not therefore be deterred by obscurities in these earlier sections. They are unavoidable in an enterprise never before attempted. They will, as I trust, in the section referred to, finally give way to complete insight.

1. THE SYNTHESIS OF APPREHENSION IN INTUITION

Whatever the origin of our representations, whether they are due to the influence of outer things, or are produced through inner causes, whether they arise *a priori,* or being appearances have an empirical origin, they must all, as modifications of the mind, belong to inner sense. All our knowledge is thus finally subject to time, the formal condition of inner sense. In it they must all be ordered, connected, and brought into relation. This is a general observation which, throughout what follows, must be borne in mind as being quite fundamental.

Every intuition contains in itself a manifold which can be represented as a manifold only in so far as the mind distinguishes the time in the sequence of one impression upon another; for each representation, *in so far as it is contained in a single moment,* can never be anything but absolute unity. In order that unity of intuition may arise out of this manifold (as is required in the representation of space) it must first be run through, and held together. This act I name the *synthesis of apprehension,* because it is directed immediately upon intuition, which does indeed offer a manifold, but a manifold which can never be represented as a manifold, and as contained *in a single representation,* save in virtue of such a synthesis.

This synthesis of apprehension must also be exercised *a priori,* that is, in respect of representations which are not empirical. For without it we should never have *a priori* the representations either of space or of time. They can be produced only through the synthesis of the manifold which sensibility presents in its original receptivity. We have thus a pure synthesis of apprehension.

2. THE SYNTHESIS OF REPRODUCTION IN IMAGINATION

It is a merely empirical law, that representations which have often followed or accompanied one another finally become associated, and so are set in a relation whereby, even in the absence of the object, one of these representations can, in accordance with a fixed rule, bring about a transition of the mind to the other. But this law of reproduction presupposes that appearances are themselves actually subject to such a rule, and that in the manifold of these representations a coexistence or sequence takes place in conformity with certain rules. Otherwise our empirical imagination would never find opportunity for exercise appropriate to its powers, and so would remain concealed within the mind as a dead and to us unknown faculty. If cinnabar were sometimes red, sometimes black, sometimes light, sometimes heavy, if a man changed sometimes into this and sometimes into that animal form, if the country on the longest day were sometimes covered with fruit, sometimes with ice and snow, my empirical imagination would never find opportunity when representing red color to bring to mind heavy cinnabar. Nor could there be an empirical synthesis of reproduction, if a certain name were sometimes given to this, sometimes to that object, or were one and the same thing named sometimes in one way, sometimes in another, independently of any rule to which appearances are in themselves subject.

There must then be something which, as the *a priori* ground of a necessary synthetic unity of appearances, makes their reproduction possible. What that something is we soon discover, when we reflect that appearances are not things in themselves, but are the mere play of our representations, and in the end reduce to determinations of inner sense. For if we can show that even our purest *a priori* intuitions yield no knowledge, save in so far as they contain a combination of the manifold such as renders a thoroughgoing synthesis of reproduction possible, then this synthesis of imagination is likewise grounded, antecedently to all experience, upon *a priori* principles; and we must assume a pure transcendental synthesis of imagination as conditioning the very possibility of all experience. For experience as such necessarily presupposes the reproducibility of appearances. When I seek to draw a line in thought, or to think of the time from one noon to another, or even to represent to myself some particular number, obviously the various manifold representations that are involved must be apprehended by me in thought one after the other. But if I were always to drop out of thought the preceding representations (the first parts of the line, the antecedent parts of the time period, or the units in the order represented), and did not reproduce them while advancing to those that follow, a complete representation would never be obtained: none of the above-mentioned thoughts, not even the purest and most elementary representations of space and time, could arise.

The synthesis of apprehension is thus inseparably bound up with the synthesis of reproduction. And as the former constitutes the transcendental ground of the possibility of all modes of knowledge whatsoever—of those that are pure *a priori* no less than of those that are empirical—the reproductive synthesis of the imagination is to be counted among the transcendental acts of the mind. We shall therefore entitle this faculty the transcendental faculty of imagination.

3. THE SYNTHESIS OF RECOGNITION IN A CONCEPT

If we were not conscious that what we think is the same as what we thought a moment before, all reproduction in the series of representations would be useless. For it would in its present state be a new representation which would not in any way belong to the act whereby it was to be gradually generated. The manifold of the representation would never, therefore, form a whole, since it would lack that unity which only consciousness can impart to it. If, in counting, I forget that the units, which now hover before me, have been added to one another in succession, I should never know that a total is being produced through this successive addition of unit to unit, and so would remain ignorant of the number. For the concept of the number is nothing but the consciousness of this unity of synthesis.

The word "concept" might of itself suggest this remark. For this unitary consciousness is what combines the manifold, successively intuited, and thereupon also reproduced, into one representation. This consciousness may often be only faint, so that we do not connect it with the act itself, that is, not in any direct manner with the *generation* of the representation, but only with the outcome [that which is thereby represented]. But notwithstanding these variations, such consciousness, however indistinct, must always be present; without it, concepts, and therewith knowledge of objects, are altogether impossible.

At this point we must make clear to ourselves what we mean by the expression "an object of representations." We have stated above that appearances are themselves nothing but sensible representations, which, as such and in themselves, must not be taken as objects capable of existing outside our power of representation. What, then, is to be understood when we speak of an object corresponding to, and consequently also distinct from, our knowledge? It is easily seen that this object must be thought only as something in general $= x$, since outside our knowledge we have nothing which we could set over against this knowledge as corresponding to it.

Now we find that our thought of the relation of all knowledge to its object carries with it an element of necessity; the object is viewed as that which prevents our modes of knowledge from being haphazard or arbitrary, and which determines them *a priori* in some definite fashion. For in so far as they are to relate to an object, they must necessarily agree with one another, that is, must possess that unity which constitutes the concept of an object.

But it is clear that, since we have to deal only with the manifold of our representations, and since that x (the object) which corresponds to them is nothing to us—being, as it is, something that has to be distinct from all our representations—the unity which the object makes necessary can be nothing else than the formal unity of consciousness in the synthesis of the manifold of representations. It is only when we have thus produced synthetic unity in the manifold of intuition that we are in a position to say that we know the object. But this unity is impossible if the intuition cannot be generated in accordance with a rule by means of such a function of synthesis as makes the reproduction of the manifold *a priori* necessary, and renders possible a concept in which it is united. Thus we think a triangle as an object, in that we are conscious of the combination of three straight lines according to a rule by which such an intuition can always be represented. This *unity of rule* determines all the manifold, and limits it to conditions which make unity of apperception possible. The concept of this unity is the representation of the object $= x$, which I think through the predicates, above mentioned, of a triangle.

All knowledge demands a concept, though that concept may, indeed, be quite imperfect or obscure. But a concept is always, as regards its form, something universal which serves as a rule. The concept of body, for instance, as the unity of the manifold which is thought through it, serves as a rule in our knowledge of outer appearances. But it can be a rule for intuitions only in so far as it represents in any given appearances the necessary reproduction of their manifold, and thereby the synthetic unity in our consciousness of them. The concept of body, in the perception of something outside us, necessitates the representation of extension, and therewith representations of impenetrability, shape, etc.

All necessity, without exception, is grounded in a transcendental condition. There must, therefore, be a transcendental ground of the unity of consciousness in the synthesis of the manifold of all our intuitions, and consequently also of the concepts of objects in general, and so of all objects of experience, a ground without which it would be impossible to think any object for our intuitions; for this object is no more than that something, the concept of which expresses such a necessity of synthesis.

This original and transcendental condition is no other than *transcendental apperception*. Consciousness of self according to the determinations of our state in inner perception is merely empirical, and always changing. No fixed and abiding self can present itself in this flux of inner appearances. Such consciousness is usually named *inner sense,* or *empirical apperception.* What has *necessarily* to be represented as numerically identical cannot be thought as such through empirical data. To render such a transcendental presupposition valid, there must be a condition which precedes all experience, and which makes experience itself possible.

There can be in us no modes of knowledge, no connection or unity of one mode of knowledge with another, without that unity of consciousness which precedes all data of intuitions, and by relation to which representation of objects is alone possible. This pure original unchangeable consciousness I shall name *transcendental apperception.* That it deserves this name is clear from the fact that even the purest objective unity, namely, that of the *a priori* concepts (space and time), is only possible through relation of the intuitions to such unity of consciousness. The numerical unity of this apperception is thus the *a priori* ground of all concepts, just as the manifoldness of space and time is the *a priori* ground of the intuitions of sensibility.

This transcendental unity of apperception forms out of all possible appearances, which can stand alongside one another in one experience, a connection of all these representations according to laws. For this unity of consciousness would be impossible if the mind in knowledge of the manifold could not become conscious of the identity of function whereby it synthetically combines it in one knowledge. The original and necessary consciousness of the identity of the self is thus at the same time a consciousness of an equally necessary unity of the synthesis of all appearances according to concepts, that is, according to rules, which not only make them necessarily reproducible but also in so doing determine an object for their intuition, that is, the concept of something wherein they are necessarily interconnected. For the mind could never think its identity in the manifoldness of its representations, and indeed think this identity *a priori,* if it did not have before its eyes the identity of its act, whereby it subordinates all synthesis of apprehension (which is empirical) to a transcendental unity, thereby rendering possible their interconnection according to *a priori* rules.

Now, also, we are in a position to determine more adequately our concept of an *object* in general. All representations have, as representations, their object, and can themselves in turn become objects of other representations. Appearances are the sole objects which can be given to us immediately, and that in them which relates immediately to the object is called intuition. But these appearances are not things in themselves; they are only representations, which in turn have their object—an object which cannot itself be intuited by us, and which may, therefore, be named the non-empirical, that is, transcendental object = *x.*

The pure concept of this transcendental object, which in reality throughout all our knowledge is always one and the same, is what can alone confer upon all our empirical concepts in general relation to an object, that is, objective reality. This concept cannot contain any determinate intuition, and therefore refers only to that unity which must be met with in any manifold of knowledge which stands in relation to an object. This relation is nothing but the necessary unity of consciousness, and therefore also of the synthesis of the manifold, through a common function of the mind, which combines it in one representation. Since this unity must be regarded as necessary *a priori* —otherwise knowledge would be without an object—the relation to a transcendental object, that is, the objective reality of our empirical knowledge, rests on the transcendental law, that all appearances, in so far as through them objects are to be given to us, must stand under those *a priori* rules of synthetical unity whereby the interrelating of these appearances in empirical intuition is alone possible. In other words, appearances in experience must stand under the conditions of

the necessary unity of apperception, just as in mere intuition they
must be subject to the formal conditions of space and of time. Only
thus can any knowledge become possible at all.

4. PRELIMINARY EXPLANATION OF THE POSSIBILITY OF THE CATEGORIES, AS KNOWLEDGE *A Priori*

There is one single experience in which all perceptions are represented as in thoroughgoing and orderly connection, just as there is
only one space and one time in which all modes of appearance and
all relation of being or not being occur. When we speak of different
experiences, we can refer only to the various perceptions, all of
which, as such, belong to one and the same general experience. This
thoroughgoing synthetic unity of perceptions is indeed the form of
experience; it is nothing else than the synthetic unity of appearances
in accordance with concepts.

Unity of synthesis according to empirical concepts would be altogether accidental, if these latter were not based on a transcendental
ground of unity. Otherwise it would be possible for appearances to
crowd in upon the soul, and yet to be such as would never allow
of experience. Since connection in accordance with universal and
necessary laws would be lacking, all relation of knowledge to objects
would fall away. The appearances might, indeed, constitute intuition
without thought, but not knowledge; and consequently would be for
us as good as nothing.

The *a priori* conditions of a possible experience in general are
at the same time conditions of the possibility of objects of experience.
Now I maintain that the categories, above cited, are nothing but the
conditions of thought in a possible experience, just as space and time
are the conditions of intuition for that same experience. They are
fundamental concepts by which we think objects in general for appearances, and have therefore *a priori* objective validity. This is
exactly what we desired to prove.

But the possibility, indeed the necessity, of these categories rests
on the relation in which our entire sensibility, and with it all possible
appearances, stand to original apperception. In original apperception
everything must necessarily conform to the conditions of the thoroughgoing unity of self-consciousness, that is, to the universal functions
of synthesis, namely, of that synthesis according to concepts in which
alone apperception can demonstrate *a priori* its complete and necessary identity. Thus the concept of a cause is nothing but a synthesis

(of that which follows in the time-series, with other appearances) *according to concepts;* and without such unity, which has its *a priori* rule, and which subjects the appearances to itself, no thoroughgoing, universal, and therefore necessary, unity of consciousness would be met within the manifold of perceptions. These perceptions would not then belong to any experience, consequently would be without an object, merely a blind play of representations, less even than a dream.

All attempts to derive these pure concepts of understanding from experience, and so to ascribe to them a merely empirical origin, are entirely vain and useless. I need not insist upon the fact that, for instance, the concept of a cause involves the character of necessity, which no experience can yield. Experience does indeed show that one appearance customarily follows upon another, but not that this sequence is necessary, nor that we can argue *a priori* and with complete universality from the antecedent, viewed as a condition, to the consequent. But as regards the empirical rule of *association,* which we must postulate throughout when we assert that everything in the series of events is so subject to rule that nothing ever happens save in so far as something precedes it on which it universally follows— upon what, I ask, does this rule, as a law of nature, rest? How is this association itself possible? The ground of the possibility of the association of the manifold, so far as it lies in the object, is named the *affinity* of the manifold. I therefore ask, how are we to make comprehensible to ourselves the thoroughgoing affinity of appearances, whereby they stand and *must* stand under unchanging laws?

On my principles it is easily explicable. All possible appearances, as representations, belong to the totality of a possible self-conscious-ness. But as self-consciousness is a transcendental representation, numerical identity is inseparable from it, and is *a priori* certain. For nothing can come to our knowledge save in terms of this original apperception. Now, since this identity must necessarily enter into the synthesis of all the manifold of appearances, so far as the synthesis is to yield empirical knowledge, the appearances are subject to *a priori* conditions, with which the synthesis of their apprehension must be in complete accordance. The representation of a universal condition according to which a certain manifold can be posited in uniform fashion is called a *rule,* and, when it *must* be so posited, a *law.* Thus all appearances stand in thoroughgoing connection according to neces-sary laws, and therefore in a transcendental affinity, of which the empirical is a mere consequence.

That nature should direct itself according to our subjective ground of apperception, and should indeed depend upon it in respect of its conformity to law, sounds very strange and absurd. But when we consider that this nature is not a thing in itself but is merely an aggregate of appearances, so many representations of the mind, we shall not be surprised that we can discover it only in the radical faculty of all our knowledge, namely, in transcendental apperception, in that unity on account of which alone it can be entitled object of all possible experience, that is, nature. Nor shall we be surprised that just for this very reason this unity can be known *a priori,* and therefore as necessary. Were the unity given in itself independently of the first sources of our thought, this would never be possible. We should not then know of any source from which we could obtain the synthetic propositions asserting such a universal unity of nature. For they would then have to be derived from the objects of nature themselves; and as this could take place only empirically, none but a merely accidental unity could be obtained, which would fall far short of the necessary interconnection that we have in mind when we speak of nature.

3.

Principle of Succession in Time, in Accordance with the Law of Causality

All alterations take place in conformity with the law of the connection of cause and effect.

PROOF

(THE PRECEDING PRINCIPLE has shown that all appearances of succession in time are one and all only *alterations,* that is, a successive being and not-being of the determinations of substance which abides; and therefore that the being of substance as following on its not-being, or its not-being as following upon its being cannot be admitted—in other words, that there is no coming into being or passing away of substance itself. Still otherwise expressed the principle is, that *all change (succession) of appearances is merely alteration.* Coming into being and passing away of substance are not alterations of it, since the concept of alteration presupposes one and the same object as existing with two opposite determinations, and therefore as abiding. With this preliminary reminder, we pass to the proof.)

I perceive that appearances follow one another, that is, that there is a state of things at one time the opposite of which was in the preceding time. Thus I am really connecting two perceptions in time. Now connection is not the work of mere sense and intuition, but is here the product of a synthetic faculty of imagination, which determines inner sense in respect of the time-relation. But imagination can connect these two states in two ways, so that either the one or the other precedes in time. For time cannot be perceived in itself, and what precedes and what follows cannot, therefore, by relation to it, be empirically determined in the object. I am conscious only that my imagination sets the one state before and the other after,

---

This selection is taken from the "Second Analogy." It occurs in Chapter II of Book II of the Transcendental Analytic of the *Critique of Pure Reason.*

not that the one state precedes the other in the object. In other words, the *objective relation* of appearances that follow upon one another is not to be determined through mere perception. In order that this relation be known as determined, the relation between the two states must be so thought that it is thereby determined as necessary which of them must be placed before, and which of them after, and that they cannot be placed in the reverse relation. But the concept which carries with it a necessity of synthetic unity can only be a pure concept that lies in the understanding, not in perception; and in this case it is the concept of the *relation of cause and effect,* the former of which determines the latter in time, as its consequence—not as in a sequence that may occur solely in the imagination (or that may not be perceived at all). Experience itself—in other words, empirical knowledge of appearances—is thus possible only in so far as we subject the succession of appearances, and therefore all alteration, to the law of causality; and, as likewise follows, the appearances, as objects of experience, are themselves possible only in conformity with the law.

The apprehension of the manifold of appearance is always successive. The representations of the parts follow upon one another. Whether they also follow one another in the object is a point which calls for further reflection, and which is not decided by the above statement. Everything, every representation even, in so far as we are conscious of it, may be entitled object. But it is a question for deeper inquiry what the word "object" ought to signify in respect of appearances when these are viewed not in so far as they are (as representations) objects, but only in so far as they stand for an object. The appearances, in so far as they are objects of consciousness simply in virtue of being representations, are not in any way distinct from their apprehension, that is, from their reception in the synthesis of imagination; and we must therefore agree that the manifold of appearances is always generated in the mind successively. Now if appearances were things in themselves, then since we have to deal solely with our representations, we could never determine from the succession of the representations how their manifold may be connected in the object. How things may be in themselves, apart from the representations through which they affect us, is entirely outside our sphere of knowledge. In spite, however, of the fact that the appearances are not things in themselves, and yet are what alone can be given to us to know, in spite also of the fact that their representation in apprehension is always successive, I have to show what sort of a connection in time belongs to the manifold in the appearances themselves. For instance, the apprehension of the manifold in the appearance of a house which stands before me is successive. The question then arises, whether the manifold of the house is also in itself successive. This, however, is what no one will grant. Now immediately I unfold the transcendental meaning of my concepts of an object, I realise that the house is not a thing in itself, but only an appearance, that is, a representation, the transcendental object of which is unknown. What, then, am I to understand by the question: how the manifold may be connected in the appearance itself, which yet is nothing in itself? That which lies in the successive apprehension is here viewed as representation, while the appearance which is given to me, notwithstanding that it is nothing but the sum of these representations, is viewed as their object; and my concept, which I derive from the representations of apprehension, has to agree with it. Since truth consists in the agreement of knowledge with the object, it will at once be seen that we can here inquire only regarding the formal conditions of empirical truth, and that appearance, in contradistinction to the representations of apprehension, can be represented as an object distinct from them only if it stands under a rule which distinguishes it from every other apprehension and necessitates some one particular mode of connection of the manifold. The object is *that* in the appearance which contains the condition of this necessary rule of apprehension.

Let us now proceed to our problem. That something happens, *i.e.,* that something, or some state which did not previously exist, comes to be, cannot be perceived unless it is preceded by an appearance which does not contain in itself this state. For an event which should follow upon an empty time, that is, a coming to be preceded by no state of things, is as little capable of being apprehended as empty time itself. Every apprehension of an event is therefore a perception that follows upon another perception. But since, as I have above illustrated by reference to the appearance of a house, this likewise happens in all synthesis of apprehension, the apprehension of an event is not yet thereby distinguished from other apprehensions. But, as I also note, in an appearance which contains a happening (the preceding state of the perception we may entitle A, and the succeeding B) B can be apprehended only as following upon A; the perception A cannot follow upon B but only precede it. For

instance, I see a ship move down stream. My perception of its lower
position follows upon the perception of its position higher up in the
stream, and it is impossible that in the apprehension of this appearance the ship should first be perceived lower down in the stream and
afterwards higher up. The order in which the perceptions succeed
one another in apprehension is in this instance determined, and to
this order apprehension is bound down. In the previous example of
a house my perceptions could begin with the apprehension of the
roof and end with the basement, or could begin from below and end
above; and I could similarly apprehend the manifold of the empirical
intuition either from right to left or from left to right. In the series
of these perceptions there was thus no determinate order specifying
at what point I must begin in order to connect the manifold empirically. But in the perception of an event there is always a rule that
makes the order in which the perceptions (in the apprehension of
this appearance) follow upon one another a *necessary* order.

In this case, therefore, we must derive the *subjective succession* of
apprehension from the *objective succession* of appearances. Otherwise the order of apprehension is entirely undetermined, and does not
distinguish one appearance from another. Since the subjective succession by itself is altogether arbitrary, it does not prove anything
as to the manner in which the manifold is connected in the object.
The objective succession will therefore consist in that order of the
manifold of appearance according to which, *in conformity with a
rule,* the apprehension of that which happens follows upon the apprehension of that which precedes. Thus only can I be justified in
asserting, not merely of my apprehension, but of appearance itself,
that a succession is to be met within it. This is only another way
of saying that I cannot arrange the apprehension otherwise than in
this very succession.

In conformity with such a rule there must lie in that which
precedes an event the condition of a rule according to which this
event invariably and necessarily follows. I cannot reverse this order,
proceeding back from the event to determine through apprehension
that which precedes. For appearance never goes back from the succeeding to the preceding point of time, though it does indeed stand
in relation to *some* preceding point of time. The advance, on the
other hand, from a given time to the determinate time that follows
is a necessary advance. Therefore, since there certainly is something

that follows [*i.e.* that is *apprehended* as following], I must refer it necessarily to something else which precedes it and upon which it follows in conformity with a rule, that is, of necessity. The event, as the conditioned, thus affords reliable evidence of some condition, and this condition is what determines the event. . . .

4.
The Antinomies of Pure Reason

FIRST CONFLICT OF THE TRANSCENDENTAL IDEAS

THESIS

The world has a beginning in time, and is also limited as regards space.

PROOF

If we assume that the world has no beginning in time, then up to every given moment an eternity has elapsed, and there has passed away in the world an infinite series of successive states of things. Now the infinity of a series consists in the fact that it can never be completed through successive synthesis. It thus follows that it is impossible for an infinite world-series to have passed away, and that a beginning of the world is therefore a necessary condition of the world's existence. This was the first point that called for proof.

As regards the second point, let us again assume the opposite, namely, that the world is an infinite given whole of co-existing things. Now the magnitude of a quantum which is not given in intuition[1] as within certain limits, can be thought only through the synthesis of its parts, and the totality of such a quantum only through a synthesis that is brought to comple-

ANTITHESIS

The world has no beginning, and no limits in space; it is infinite as regards both time and space.

PROOF

For let us assume that it has a beginning. Since the beginning is an existence which is preceded by a time in which the thing is not, there must have been a preceding time in which the world was not, *i.e.*, an empty time. Now no coming to be of a thing is possible in an empty time, because no part of such a time possesses, as compared with any other, a distinguishing condition of existence rather than of non-existence; and this applies whether the thing is supposed to arise of itself or through some other cause. In the world many series of things can, indeed, begin; but the world itself cannot have a beginning, and is therefore infinite in respect of past time.

As regards the second point, let us start by assuming the opposite, namely, that the world in space is finite and limited, and consequently exists in an empty space which is unlimited. Things will therefore not only be related *in space* but also

---

These selections are taken from Chapter II of Book II of the Transcendental Dialectic of the *Critique of Pure Reason*.

1. An indeterminate quantum can be intuited as a whole when it is such that though enclosed within limits we do not require to construct its totality through measurement, that is, through the successive synthesis of its parts. For the limits, in cutting off anything further, themselves determine its completeness.

tion through repeated addition of unit to unit.[2] In order, therefore, to think, as a whole, the world which fills all spaces, the successive synthesis of the parts of an infinite world must be viewed as completed, that is, an infinite time must be viewed as having elapsed in the enumeration of all co-existing things. This, however, is impossible. An infinite aggregate of actual things cannot therefore be viewed as a given whole, nor consequently as simultaneously given. The world is, therefore, as regards extension in space, not infinite, but is enclosed within limits. This was the second point in dispute.

related *to space.* Now since the world is an absolute whole beyond which there is no object of intuition, and therefore no correlate with which the world stands in relation, the relation of the world to empty space would be a relation of it to no *object.* But such a relation, and consequently the limitation of the world by empty space, is nothing. The world cannot, therefore, be limited in space; that is, it is infinite in respect of extension.[3]

. . . .

THIRD CONFLICT OF THE TRANSCENDENTAL IDEAS

THESIS

Causality in accordance with laws of nature is not the only causality from which the appearances of the world can one and all be derived. To explain these appearances it is necessary to assume that there is also another causality, that of freedom.

ANTITHESIS

There is no freedom; everything in the world takes place solely in accordance with laws of nature.

2. The concept of totality is in this case simply the representation of the completed synthesis of its parts; for, since we cannot obtain the concept from the intuition of the whole—that being in this case impossible—we can apprehend it only through the synthesis of the parts viewed as carried, at least in idea, to the completion of the infinite.

3. Space is merely the form of outer intuition (formal intuition). It is not a real object which can be outwardly intuited. Space, as prior to all things which determine (occupy or limit) it, or rather which give an empirical intuition in accordance with its form, is, under the name of absolute space, nothing but the mere possibility of outer appearances in so far as they either exist in themselves or can be added to given appearances. Empirical intuition is not, therefore, a composite of appearances and space (of perception and empty intuition). The one is not the correlate of the other in a synthesis; they are connected in one and the same empirical intuition as matter and form of the intuition. If we attempt to set one of these two factors outside the other, space outside all appearances, there arise all sorts of empty determinations of outer intuition, which yet are not possible perceptions. For example, a determination of the relation of the motion (or rest) of the world to infinite empty space is a determination which can never be perceived, and is therefore the predicate of a mere thought-entity.

PROOF

Let us assume that there is no other causality than that in accordance with laws of nature. This being so, everything which *takes place* presupposes a preceding state upon which it inevitably follows according to a rule. But the preceding state must itself be something which has taken place (having come to be in a time in which it previously was not); for if it had always existed, its consequence also would have always existed, and would not have only just arisen. The causality of the cause through which something takes place is itself, therefore, something that has *taken place,* which again presupposes, in accordance with the law of nature, a preceding state and its causality, and this in similar manner a still earlier state, and so on. If, therefore, everything takes place solely in accordance with laws of nature, there will always be only a relative and never a first beginning, and consequently no completeness of the series on the side of the causes that arise the one from the other. But the law of nature is just this, that nothing takes place without a cause *sufficiently* determined *a priori.* The proposition that no causality is possible save in accordance with laws of nature, when taken in unlimited universality, is therefore self-contradictory; and this cannot, therefore, be regarded as the sole kind of causality.

We must, then, assume a causality through which something takes place, the cause of which is not itself determined, in accordance with necessary laws, by another cause antecedent to it, that is to say, an *absolute spontaneity* of the cause, whereby a series of appear-

PROOF

Assume that there is freedom in the transcendental sense, as a special kind of causality in accordance with which the events in the world can have come about, namely, a power of absolutely beginning a state, and therefore also of absolutely beginning a series of consequences of that state; it then follows that not only will a series have its absolute beginning in this spontaneity, but that the very determination of this spontaneity to originate the series, that is to say, the causality itself, will have an absolute beginning; there will be no antecedent through which this act, in taking place, is determined in accordance with fixed laws. But every beginning of action presupposes a state of the not yet acting cause; and a *dynamical* beginning of the action, if it is also a first beginning, presupposes a state which has no *causal* connection with the preceding state of the cause, that is to say, in nowise follows from it. Transcendental freedom thus stands opposed to the law of causality; and the kind of connection which it assumes as holding between the successive states of the active causes renders all unity of experience impossible. It is not to be met with in any experience, and is therefore an empty thought-entity.

In nature alone, therefore, [not in freedom], must we seek for the connection and order of cosmical events. Freedom (independence) from the laws of nature is no doubt a liberation from compulsion, but also from the guidance of all rules. For it is not permissible to say that the *laws* of freedom enter into the causality exhibited in the course

ances, which proceeds in accordance with laws of nature, begins *of itself*. This is transcendental freedom, without which, even in the [ordinary] course of nature, the series of appearances on the side of the causes can never be complete.

of nature, and so take the place of natural laws. If freedom were determined in accordance with laws, it would not be freedom; it would simply be nature under another name. Nature and transcendental freedom differ as do conformity to law and lawlessness. Nature does indeed impose upon the understanding the exacting task of always seeking the origin of events ever higher in the series of causes, their causality being always conditioned. But in compensation it holds out the promise of thoroughgoing unity of experience in accordance with laws. The illusion of freedom, on the other hand, offers a point of rest to the inquiring understanding in the chain of causes, conducting it to an unconditioned causality which begins to act of itself. This causality is, however, blind, and abrogates those rules through which alone a completely coherent experience is possible.

* * * * * * * * * * * *

CRITICAL SOLUTION OF THE COSMOLOGICAL CONFLICT OF REASON WITH ITSELF

The whole antinomy of pure reason rests upon the dialectical argument: If the conditioned is given, the entire series of all its conditions is likewise given; objects of the senses are given as conditioned; therefore, etc. Through this syllogism, the major premise of which appears so natural and evident, as many cosmological ideas are introduced as there are differences in the conditions (in the synthesis of appearances) that constitute a series. The ideas postulate absolute totality of these series; and thereby they set reason in unavoidable conflict with itself. We shall be in a better position to detect what is deceptive in this pseudo-rational argument, if we first correct and define some of the concepts employed in it.

In the first place, it is evident beyond all possibility of doubt, that if the conditioned is given, a regress in the series of all its conditions is *set us as a task*. For it is involved in the very concept of the conditioned that something is referred to a condition, and if this condition is again itself conditioned, to a more remote condition, and so through all the members of the series. The above proposition is thus analytic, and has nothing to fear from a transcendental criticism. It is a logical postulate of reason, that through the understanding we follow up and extend as far as possible that connection of a concept with its conditions which directly results from the concept itself.

Further, if the conditioned as well as its condition are things in themselves, then upon the former being given, the regress to the latter is not only *set as a task,* but therewith already really *given.* And since this holds of all members of the series, the complete series of the conditions, and therefore the unconditioned, is given therewith, or rather is presupposed in view of the fact that the conditioned, which is only possible through the complete series, is given. The synthesis of the conditioned with its condition is here a synthesis of the mere understanding, which represents things *as they are,* without considering whether and how we can obtain knowledge of them. If, however, what we are dealing with are appearances—as mere representations appearances cannot be given save in so far as I attain knowledge of them, or rather attain them in themselves, for they are nothing but empirical modes of knowledge—I cannot say, in the same sense of the terms, that if the conditioned is given, all its conditions (as appearances) are likewise given, and therefore cannot in any way infer the absolute totality of the series of its conditions. The *appearances* are in their apprehension themselves nothing but an empirical synthesis in space and time, and are given only in *this synthesis.* It does not, therefore, follow, that if the conditioned, in the [field of] appearance, is given, the synthesis which constitutes its empirical condition is given therewith and is presupposed. This synthesis first occurs in the regress, and never exists without it. What we can say is that a *regress* to the conditions, that is, a continued empirical synthesis, on the side of the conditions, is enjoined or *set as a task,* and that *in this regress* there can be no lack of given conditions. . . .

If it be said that all bodies have either a good smell or a smell that is not good, a third case is possible, namely, that a body has no smell at all; and both the conflicting propositions may therefore be false. If, however, I say: all bodies are either good-smelling or not good-smelling (*vel sauveolens vel non suaveolens*), the two judgments are directly contradictory to one another, and the former only is false, its contradictory opposite, namely, that some bodies are not good-smelling, comprehending those bodies also which have no smell at all. Since, in the previous opposition (*per disparata*), smell, the contingent condition of the concept of the body, was not removed by the opposed judgment, but remained attached to it, the two judgmens were not related as *contradictory* opposites.

If, therefore, we say that the world is either infinite in extension or is not infinite (*non est infinitus*), and if the former proposition is false, its contradictory opposite, that the world is not infinite, must be true. And I should thus deny the existence of an infinite world, without affirming in its place a finite world. But if we had said that the world is either infinite or finite (non-infinite), both statements might be false. For in that case we should be regarding the world in itself as determined in its magnitude, and in the opposed judgment we do not merely remove the infinitude, and with it perhaps the entire separate existence of the world, but attach a determination to the world, regarded as a thing actually existing in itself. This assertion may, however, likewise be false; the world may not be given as a thing in itself, nor as being in its magnitude either infinite or finite. I beg permission to entitle this kind of opposition *dialectical,* and that of contradictories *analytical.* Thus of two dialectically opposed judgments both may be false; for the one is not a mere contradictory of the other, but says something more than is required for a simple contradiction.

If we regard the two propositions, that the world is infinite in magnitude and that it is finite in magnitude, as contradictory opposites, we are assuming that the world, the complete series of appearances, is a thing in itself that remains even if I suspend the infinite or the finite regress in the series of its appearances. If, however, I reject this assumption, or rather this accompanying transcendental illusion, and deny that the world is a thing in itself, the contradictory opposition of the two assertions is converted into a merely dialectical opposition. Since the world does not exist in itself, independently of the regressive series of my representations, it exists *in itself* neither as an *infinite* whole nor as a *finite* whole. It exists only in the empirical regress of the series of appearances, and is not to be met with as something in itself. If, then, this series is always conditioned, and therefore can never be given as complete, the world is not an unconditioned whole, and does not exist as such a whole, either of infinite or of finite magnitude.

What we have here said of the first cosmological idea, that is, of the absolute totality of magnitude in the [field of] appearance, applies also to all the others. The series of conditions is only to be met with in the regressive synthesis itself, not in the [field of] appearance viewed as a thing given in and by itself, prior to all regress. We must therefore say that the number of parts in a given appearance is in itself neither finite nor infinite. For an appearance is not something existing in itself, and its parts are first given in and through the regress of the decomposing synthesis, a regress which is never given in absolute completeness, either as finite or as infinite. This also holds of the series of subordinated causes, and of the series that proceeds from the conditioned to unconditioned necessary existence. These series can never be regarded as being in themselves in their totality either finite or infinite. Being series of subordinated *representations,* they exist only in the dynamical regress, and prior to this regress can have no existence in themselves as self-subsistent series of things.

Thus the antinomy of pure reason in its cosmological ideas vanishes when it is shown that it is merely dialectical, and that it is a conflict due to an illusion which arises from our applying to appearances that exist only in our representations, and therefore, so far as they form a series, not otherwise than in a successive regress, that idea of absolute totality which holds only as a condition of things in themselves. From this antinomy we can, however, obtain, not indeed a dogmatic, but a critical and doctrinal advantage. It affords indirect proof of the transcendental ideality of appearances—a proof which ought to convince any who may not be satisfied by the direct proof given in the Transcendental Aesthetic. This proof would consist in the following dilemma. If the world is a whole existing in itself, it is either finite or infinite. But both alternatives are false (as shown in the proofs of the antithesis and thesis respectively). It is therefore also false that the world (the sum of all appearances) is a whole existing in itself. From this it then follows that appearances in general are nothing outside our representations—which is just what is meant by their transcendental ideality.

This remark is of some importance. It enables us to see that the

proofs given in the fourfold antinomy are not merely baseless decep-
tions. On the supposition that appearances, and the sensible world
which comprehends them all, are things in themselves, these proofs
are indeed well-grounded. The conflict which results from the propositions thus obtained shows, however, that there is a fallacy in this
assumption, and so leads us to the discovery of the true constitution
of things, as objects of the senses. While the transcendental dialectic
does not by any means favour scepticism, it certainly does favour
the sceptical method, which can point to such dialectic as an example
of its great services. For when the arguments of reason are allowed
to oppose one another in unrestricted freedom, something advan-
tageous, and likely to aid in the correction of our judgments, will
always accrue, though it may not be what we set out to find. . . .

*Explanation of the Cosmological Idea of Freedom in its connection
    with Universal Natural Necessity.*

. . . That everything which happens has a cause, is a law of nature.
Since the causality of this cause, that is, the *action* of the cause, is
antecedent in time to the effect which has *ensued* upon it, it cannot
itself have always existed, but must have *happened,* and *among the
appearances* must have a cause by which it in turn is determined.
Consequently, all events are empirically determined in an order of
nature. Only in virtue of this law can appearances constitute a *nature*
and become objects of experience. This law is a law of the understanding, from which no departure can be permitted, and from which
no appearance may be exempted. To allow such exemption would be
to set an appearance outside all possible experience, to distinguish it
from all objects of possible experience, and so to make of it a mere
thought-entity, a phantom of the brain.

This would seem to imply the existence of a chain of causes which
in the regress to their conditions allows of no *absolute totality.* But
that need not trouble us. The point has already been dealt with in
the general discussion of the antinomy into which reason falls when
in the series of appearances it proceeds to the unconditioned. Were
we to yield to the illusion of transcendental realism, neither nature
nor freedom would remain. The only question here is this:—Admitting
that in the whole series of events there is nothing but natural necessity, is it yet possible to regard one and the same event as being in

one aspect merely an effect of nature and in another aspect an effect due to freedom; or is there between these two kinds of causality a direct contradiction?

Among the causes in the [field of] appearance there certainly cannot be anything which could begin a series absolutely and of itself. Every action, [viewed] as appearance, in so far as it gives rise to an event, is itself an event or happening, and presupposes another state wherein its cause is to be found. Thus everything which happens is merely a continuation of the series, and nothing that begins of itself is a possible member of the series. The actions of natural causes in the time-sequence are thus themselves effects; they presuppose causes antecedent to them in the temporal series. An *original* act, such as can by itself bring about what did not exist before, is not to be looked for in the causally connected appearances.

Now granting that effects are appearances and that their cause is likewise appearance, is it necessary that the causality of their cause should be exclusively empirical? May it not rather be, that while for every effect in the [field of] appearance a connection with its cause in accordance with the laws of empirical causality is indeed required, this empirical causality, without the least violation of its connection with natural causes, is itself an effect of a causality that is not empirical but intelligible? This latter causality would be the action of a cause which, in respect of appearances, is original, and therefore, as pertaining to this faculty, not appearance but intelligible; although it must otherwise, in so far as it is a link in the chain of nature, be regarded as entirely belonging to the world of sense.

The principle of the causal connection of appearances is required in order that we may be able to look for and to determine the natural conditions of natural events, that is to say, their causes in the [field of] appearance. If this principle be admitted, and be not weakened through any exception, the requirements of the understanding, which in its empirical employment sees in all happenings nothing but nature, and is justified in so doing, are completely satisfied; and physical explanations may proceed on their own lines without interference. These requirements are not in any way infringed, if we assume, even though the assumption should be a mere fiction, that some among the natural causes have a faculty which is intelligible only, inasmuch as its determination to action never rests upon empirical conditions, but solely on grounds of understanding. We must, of course, at the same time be able to assume that the *action* of these causes *in the* [*field of*] *appearance* is in conformity with all the laws of empirical causality. In this way the acting subject, as *causa phaenomenon,* would be bound up with nature through the indissoluble dependence of all its actions, and only as we ascend from the empirical object to the transcendental should we find that this subject, together with all its causality in the [field of] appearance, has in its *noumenon* certain conditions which must be regarded as purely intelligible. For if in determining in what ways appearances can serve as causes we follow the rules of nature, we need not concern ourselves what kind of ground for these appearances and their connection may have to be thought as existing in the transcendental subject, which is empirically unknown to us. This intelligible ground does not have to be considered in empirical enquiries; it concerns only thought in the pure understanding; and although the effects of this thought and action of the pure understanding are to be met with in the appearances, these appearances must none the less be capable of complete causal explanation in terms of other appearances in accordance with natural laws. We have to take their strictly empirical character as the supreme ground of explanation, leaving entirely out of account their intelligible character (that is, the transcendental cause of their empirical character) as being completely unknown, save in so far as the empirical serves for its sensible sign.

Let us apply this to experience. Man is one of the appearances of the sensible world, and in so far one of the natural causes the causality of which must stand under empirical laws. Like all other things in nature, he must have an empirical character. This character we come to know through the powers and faculties which he reveals in his actions. In lifeless, or merely animal, nature we find no ground for thinking that any faculty is conditioned otherwise than in a merely sensible manner. Man, however, who knows all the rest of nature solely through the senses, knows himself also through pure apperception; and this, indeed, in acts and inner determinations which he cannot regard as impressions of the senses. He is thus to himself, on the one hand phenomenon, and on the other hand, in respect of certain faculties the action of which cannot be ascribed to the receptivity of sensibility, a purely intelligible object. We entitle these faculties understanding and reason. The latter, in particular, we distinguish in a quite peculiar and especial way from all empirically conditioned powers. For it views its objects exclusively in the light of ideas, and in accordance with them determines the understanding, which then proceeds to make an empirical use of its own similarly pure concepts.

That our reason has causality, or that we at least represent it to ourselves as having causality, is evident from the *imperatives* which in all matters of conduct we impose as rules upon our active powers. *"Ought"* expresses a kind of necessity and of connection with grounds which is found nowhere else in the whole of nature. The understanding can know in nature only what is, what has been, or what will be. We cannot say that anything in nature *ought to be* other than what in all these time-relations it actually is. When we have the course of nature alone in view, *"ought"* has no meaning whatsover. It is just as absurd to ask what ought to happen in the natural world as to ask what properties a circle ought to have. All that we are justified in asking is: what happens in nature? what are the properties of the circle?

This *"ought"* expresses a possible action the ground of which cannot be anything but a mere concept; whereas in the case of a merely natural action the ground must always be an appearance. The action to which the *"ought"* applies must indeed be possible under natural conditions. These conditions, however, do not play any part in determining the will itself, but only in determining the effect and its consequences in the [field of] appearance. No matter how many natural grounds or how many sensuous impulses may impel me to *will,* they can never give rise to the *"ought,"* but only to a willing which, while very far from being necessary, is always conditioned; and the *"ought"* pronounced by reason confronts such willing with a limit and an end—nay more, forbids or authorises it. Whether what is willed be an object of mere sensibility (the pleasant) or of pure reason (the good), reason will not give way to any ground which is empirically given. Reason does not here follow the order of things as they present themselves in appearance, but frames for itself with perfect spontaneity an order of its own according to ideas, to which it adapts the empirical conditions, and according to which it declares actions to be necessary, even although they have never taken place, and perhaps never will take place. And at the same time reason also presupposes that it can have causality in regard to all these actions, since otherwise no empirical effects could be expected from its ideas. . . .

5.

The Limits of Human Reason and
the Notion of the Supreme Being

... WE HAVE ABOVE (§ § 33,34) indicated the limits of reason with regard to all cognition of mere creations of thought. Now, since the transcendental ideas have urged us to approach them, and thus have led us, as it were, to the spot where the occupied space (viz., experience) touches the void (that of which we can know nothing, viz., noumena), we can determine the bounds of pure reason. For in all bounds there is something positive (e.g., a surface is the boundary of corporeal space, and is therefore itself a space, a line is a space, which is the boundary of the surface, a point the boundary of the line, but yet always a place in space), whereas limits contain mere negations. The limits pointed out in those paragraphs are not enough after we have discovered that beyond them there still lies something (though we can never cognize what it is in itself). For the question now is, What is the attitude of our reason in this connection of what we know with what we do not, and never shall, know? This is an actual connection of a known thing with one quite unknown (and which will always remain so), and though what is unknown should not become the least more known—which we cannot even hope— yet the notion of this connection must be definite, and capable of being rendered distinct.

We must therefore accept an immaterial being, a world of understanding, and a Supreme Being (all mere noumena), because in them only, as things in themselves, reason finds that completion and satisfaction, which it can never hope for in the derivation of appearances from their homogeneous grounds, and because these actually have reference to something distinct from them (and totally heterogenous), as appearances always presuppose an object in itself, and therefore suggest its existence whether we can know more of it or not.

But as we can never cognize these beings of understanding as they are in themselves, that is, definitely, yet must assume them as regards

This selection is taken from the *Prolegomena to any Future Metaphysics* (§57).

the sensible world, and connect them with it by reason, we are at least able to think this connection by means of such concepts as express their relation to the world of sense. Yet if we represent to ourselves a being of the understanding by nothing but pure concepts of the understanding, we then indeed represent nothing definite to ourselves, consequently our concept has no significance; but if we think it by properties borrowed from the sensuous world, it is no longer a being of understanding, but is conceived as an appearance, and belongs to the sensible world. Let us take an instance from the notion of the Supreme Being.

Our deistic conception is quite a pure concept of reason, but represents only a thing containing all realities, without being able to determine any one of them; because for that purpose an example must be taken from the world of sense, in which case we should have an object of sense only, not something quite heterogeneous, which can never be an object of sense. Suppose I attribute to the Supreme Being understanding, for instance; I have no concept of an understanding other than my own, one that must receive its perceptions (*Anschauung*) by the senses, and which is occupied in bringing them under rules of the unity of consciousness. Then the elements of my concept would always lie in the appearance; I should however by the insufficiency of the appearance be necessitated to go beyond them to the concept of a being which neither depends upon appearance, nor is bound up with them as conditions of its determination. But if I separate understanding from sensibility to obtain a pure understanding, then nothing remains but the mere form of thinking without perception (*Anschauung*), by which form alone I cognize nothing definite, and consequently no object. For that purpose I should conceive another understanding, such as would directly perceive its objects, but of which I have not the least notion; because the human understanding is discursive, and can [not directly perceive, it can] only cognise by means of general concepts. And the very same difficulties arise if we attribute a will to the Supreme Being; for we have this concept only by drawing it from our internal experience, and therefore from our dependence for satisfaction upon objects whose existence we require; and so the notion rests upon sensibility, which is absolutely incompatible with the pure concept of the Supreme Being.

Hume's objections to deism are weak, and affect only the proofs, and not the deistic assertion itself. But as regards theism, which depends on a stricter determination of the concept of the Supreme

Being which in deism is merely transcendent, they are very strong, and as this concept is formed, in certain (in fact in all common) cases irrefutable. Hume always insists, that by the mere concept of an original being, to which we apply only ontological predicates (eternity, omnipresence, omnipotence), we think nothing definite, and that properties which can yield a concept *in concreto* must be superadded; that it is not enough to say, it is Cause, but we must explain the nature of its causality, for example, that of an understanding and of a will. He then begins his attacks on the essential point itself, i.e., theism, as he had previously directed his battery only against the proofs of deism, an attack which is not very dangerous to it in its consequences. All his dangerous arguments refer to anthropomorphism, which he holds to be inseparable from theism, and to make it absurd in itself; but if the former be abandoned, the latter must vanish with it, and nothing remain but deism, of which nothing can come, which is of no value, and which cannot serve as any foundation to religion or morals. If this anthropomorphism were really unavoidable, no proofs whatever of the existence of a Supreme Being, even were they all granted, could determine for us the concept of this Being without involving us in contradictions.

If we connect with the command to avoid all transcendent judgments of pure reason, the command (which apparently conflicts with it) to proceed to concepts that lie beyond the field of its immanent (empirical) use, we discover that both can subsist together, but only at the boundary of all lawful use of reason. For this boundary belongs as well to the field of experience, as to that of the creations of thought, and we are thereby taught, as well, how these so remarkable ideas serve merely for marking the bounds of human reason. On the one hand they give warning not boundlessly to extend cognition of experience, as if nothing but the world remained for us to cognize, and yet, on the other hand, not to transgress the bounds of experience, and to think of judging about things beyond them, as things in themselves.

But we stop at this boundary if we limit our judgment merely to the relation which the world may have to a Being whose very concept lies beyond all the knowledge which we can attain within the world. For we then do not attribute to the Supreme Being any of the properties in themselves, by which we represent objects of experience, and thereby avoid dogmatic anthropomorphism; but we attribute them to his relation to the world, and allow ourselves a symbolic anthropomorphism, which in fact concerns language only, and not the object itself.

If I say that we are compelled to consider the world, as if it were the work of a Supreme Understanding and Will, I really say nothing more, than that a watch, a ship, a regiment, bears the same relation to the watchmaker, the shipbuilder, the commanding officer, as the world of sense (or whatever constitutes the substratum of this complex of appearances) does to the Unknown, which I do not hereby cognize as it is in itself, but as it is for me or in relation to the world, of which I am a part.

GEORG WILHELM FRIEDRICH HEGEL

(1770-1831)

I have tried without success to find a passage or passages in Hegel which would be both sufficiently general and sufficiently intelligible for publication in a book of this kind.[1] I have finally been driven to evade the difficulty by selecting passages from commentators which give one more of an idea and a much clearer idea of his philosophy than could be obtained from Hegel himself, at least in any extracts of a manageable length. They at the same time express the characteristic point of view of the school which dominated most British and at least much American philosophy during the last years of the nineteenth century, a school definitely inspired by Hegel.

The idealism of Hegel and those influenced by him has commonly been described as "objective" in opposition to the "subjective idealism" of Berkeley. It insists rather that reality is in certain aspects at least a rational system than that the *esse* of physical objects is or involves *percipi*. However, as will appear at certain points in the first selection, it also involves the argument that to be intelligible the world must be essentially related to the mind that knows it. Hegel's main aim in his dialectic is to sketch the logical structure and pattern of development of reality, mind, human life and civilization. It is quite impossible to sum up here the long, complicated process of argument in the *Logic*, passing through dozens of categories to its consummation in the notion of spirit. A summary of the account of the different stages of human consciousness in the *Phenomenology* is attempted by Royce in the second selection.

Hegel and the Unity of Opposites

By EDWARD CAIRD

. . . An *absolute* distinction by its very nature would be self-contradictory, for it would cut off all connection between the things it distinguished. It would annihilate the relation implied in the distinc-

---

These selections are taken from Caird's book *Hegel*, Chapters VII and VIII, published in 1891.

1. Similar difficulties have prevented the inclusion of any selections from Fichte and Schelling.

tion, and so it would annihilate the distinction itself. If, therefore, we say that everything—every intelligible object or thought as such —must be differentiated from all others, yet we must equally say that no object or thought can be absolutely differentiated; in other words, differentiated so as to exclude any identity or unity which transcends the difference. An absolute difference is something which cannot exist within the intelligible world, and the thought which attempts to fix such a difference is unconscious of its meaning. If it could succeed, it would, *ipso facto,* commit suicide. We can stretch the bow to the utmost point consistent with its not breaking, but if we go an inch further, it ceases to be stretched at all. We can embrace in one thought the widest antagonism consistent with the unity of thought itself, but an antagonism inconsistent with that unity is unthinkable, for the simple reason that, when the unity disappears, the antagonism also disappears with it.

If then the world, as an intelligible world, is a world of distinction, differentiation, individuality, it is equally true that in it, as an intelligible world, there are no absolute separations or oppositions, no antagonisms which cannot be reconciled. All difference presupposes a unity, and is itself, indeed, an expression of that unity; and if we let it expand and develop itself to the utmost, yet ultimately it must exhaust itself, and return into the unity. This is all that Hegel means when he, as is often asserted, "denies the validity of the laws of identity and contradiction." All he denies, in fact, is their *absolute* validity. "Every finite thing is itself, and no other." True, Hegel would answer, but with a *caveat.* Every finite thing, by the fact that it is finite, has an essential relation to that which limits it, and thus it contains the principle of its destruction in itself. It is therefore, in this sense, a self-contradictory existence, which at once is itself and its other, itself and not itself. It is at war with itself, and its very life-process is the process of its dissolution. In an absolute sense, it cannot be said *to be,* any more than *not to be.* "Every definite thought, by the fact that it is definite, excludes other thoughts, and especially the opposite thought." True, Hegel would answer, but with a *caveat.* Every definite thought, by the fact that it is definite, has a necessary relation to its negative, and cannot be separated from it without losing its own meaning. In the very definiteness with which it affirms itself, therefore, is contained the proof that its affirmation is not absolute. If we fix our attention upon it, to the exclusion of its negative, if we try to hold it to itself alone, it disappears. To maintain it and do it full justice is already to go beyond it. Hence we are obliged to modify the assertion, that every definite thought absolutely excludes its negative, and to admit that, in this point of view, it also includes or involves it. It is, and it is not, itself, for it contains in itself its own negation. If we are to reassert it again, it can only be so far as we combine it with its negative in a higher thought, in which, therefore, it is partly denied and partly affirmed.

Thus neither things nor thoughts can be treated as simply self-identical—as independent or atomic existences, which are related only to themselves. They are essentially parts of a whole, or stages in a process, and as such they carry us beyond themselves, the moment we clearly understand them. Nor can we escape from this conclusion by saying that it is merely a subjective illusion, and that the objects really remain, though our mind passes from the one to the other. In regard to thoughts, this is obviously a subterfuge; for the thought is not something different from the process which our minds go through in apprehending it—it *is* that process. And in regard to "things," the distinction is equally inapplicable; for what we are considering is the conditions essential to the intelligible, as such, and the "things" of which we speak must be at least intelligible, since they exist for our intelligence. The truth therefore is, that definiteness, finitude, or determination, as such, though they have an affirmative or positive meaning, also contain or involve in themselves their own negation. There is a community or unity between them and their opposites, which overreaches their difference or opposition, though it does not by any means exclude that difference or opposition *in its proper place, and within its proper limits*. Of any definite existence or thought, therefore, it may be said with quite as much truth that it *is not,* as that it *is,* its own bare self. This appears paradoxical, only because we are accustomed to think that the whole truth about a thing can be expressed once for all in a proposition; and here we find that two opposite propositions can be asserted with equal truth. The key, however, to the difficulty is, that neither the assertion nor the denial, nor even both together, exhaust all that is to be said. To know an object, we must follow the process of its existence, in which it manifests all that is in it, and so by that very manifestation exhausts itself, and is taken up as an element into a higher existence. . . .

. . . "The intelligible world is relative to the intelligence." This principle, which was expressed by Kant, but of which Kant, by his distinctions of phenomenon and noumenon, reason and faith, evaded the full meaning, is taken in earnest by Hegel. He is therefore forced to deny the absoluteness even of those antagonisms which have been conceived to be altogether insoluble: for any absolute antagonism would ultimately imply an irreconcilable opposition between the intelligence and its object. In other words, it would imply that the intelligence is *not* the unity which is presupposed in all the differences of things, and which, therefore, through all these differences, returns to itself. The essential unity of all things with each other and with the mind that knows them, is the adamantine circle within which the strife of opposites is waged, and which their utmost violence of conflict cannot break. No fact, which is in its nature incapable of being explained or reduced to law,—no law, which it is impossible ever to recognize as essentially related to the intelligence that apprehends it,—can be admitted to exist in the intelligible universe. No absolute defeat of the spirit,—no defeat that does not contain the elements of a greater triumph,—can possibly take place in a world which is itself nothing but the realization of spirit.

In a sense, this principle may be said to be incapable of proof, since a proof of it would already presuppose it. But a disproof of it would do so equally. And scepticism, when it brings this very result to light—in other words, when in its own necessary development it destroys itself—gives all the proof of it that is necessary. The self-contradiction of absolute scepticism makes us conscious of the unity of thought and things, of being and knowing, as an ultimate truth, which yet is not an assumption, because all belief and unbelief, all assertion and denial, alike presuppose it. . . .

. . . "Being and not-Being are identical." This mysterious utterance of Hegel, round which so much controversy has waged, and which has seemed to many but a caprice of metaphysic run mad, may now be seen to have a serious meaning. It does not mean that Being and not-Being are not also distinguished; but it does mean that the distinction is not absolute, and that if it is made absolute, at that very moment it disappears. The whole truth, therefore, cannot be expressed either by the simple statement that Being and not-Being are identical, or by the simple statement that they are different. But the consideration of what these abstractions are in themselves when we isolate them from each other,—just as a scientific man might isolate a special element in order to find the essential relativity or energy that lies in it,—shows that their truth is not *either* their identity *or* their difference, but is their *identity in difference*. But one who has apprehended this thought has already risen above the abstractions whose unity in difference he has seen. He is like the scientific man who has discovered an identity of principle connecting phenomena between which formerly he had seen no essential relation. By such discovery the mere external view of them as different things, related only by adjacent place or time, has disappeared, and the one phenomenon has become the counterpart or complementary aspect of the other. In like manner, the thinker who has fully seen into the correlativity of given opposites has reached a new attitude of thought in regard to them. They have become for him inseparable elements of a higher unity, which is now seen to be organic or vital. Or the whole thought is seen to be a process through certain phases, each of which necessitated the other, and by the unity of which it—the whole thought—is constituted. Nor does the movement stop here. The whole thought reached in this way has again its opposite or negative, which it at once excludes and involves, and the process may be repeated in regard to it, with the result of reaching a still higher unity, a more complex thought, in which it and its opposite are elements. And so on, through ever-widening sweep of differentiation and integration, 'till the whole body of thought is seen in its organic unity and development, every fibre of it alive with relation to the whole in which it is a constituent element.

Has the process which has just been described a natural beginning and end? If it be true that self-consciousness includes or involves in it all the categories, it is obvious that the end is in the full *definition* of self-consciousness—i.e., the full analysis or differentiation of all the contents of the idea of self-consciousness, and their integration in that idea, as the unity of them all. And, on the other hand, its beginning must obviously be in the simplest and most abstract category,—which, as we have seen, is the category of Being,—the category by which a thing is referred to itself, *as if* it had no relation to other things or to the mind. And the process which connects the beginning with the end is just the gradual revelation of these two relativities,—to things and to the mind,—which are implicit or presupposed, but not explicit or consciously present, in our first immediate attitude of thought. The *first* main division of logic, then, will have to do with the categories in which, as yet, relativity is not expressed; categories like Being, Quality, Quantity, which, though they involve, do not immediately suggest, any relation of the object to which they are applied to any other object. The *second* main division will have to do with categories such as Essence and Existence, Force and Expression, Substance and Accident, Cause and Effect, which force us to go beyond the object with which we are dealing, and to connect it with other objects, or at least with something that is not immediately presented to us in the perception of it. And the *last* main division will have to do with categories, such as those of final cause and organic unity, by which the object is characterized as related to intelligence, or as having in it that self-determined nature of which the intelligence is the highest type; or to put it otherwise, it will have to do with categories by which the object is determined as essentially Being, or having in it, an ideal unity which is reached and realized in and through all the manifoldness of its existence. The general argument of the *Logic,* when we pursue it through all these stages, therefore is this: that reality,—which at first is present to us as the Being of things which are regarded as standing each by itself, determined in quality and quantity, but as having no necessary relations to each other,—comes in the process of thought to be known as an endless aggregate of essentially related and transitory existences, each of which exists only as it determines and is determined by the others, according to universal laws,—and finally, is discovered to lie in a world of objects, each and all of which exist only in so far as they exist for intelligence, and in so far as intelligence is revealed or realized in them. And that, indeed, is the movement of thought by which the reality of things is disclosed, is proved by the demonstration that the categories of *Being,*—used in the first attitude of thought, which corresponds to our simplest and most unsophisticated consciousness of things,—when fully understood and reasoned out, necessarily lead us to the categories of Relation, employed in the second attitude of thought, which corresponds generally to the scientific or reflective consciousness; and that these in turn, when fully comprehended and pressed to their consequences, necessarily pass into the categories of *Ideal Unity,* or, as it is sometimes expressed, "the notion,"—categories used in the third stage of consciousness, which corresponds to philosophy. Science is the *truth* of common-sense, because the points of view from which the former considers the world, include and transcend the points of view from which it is regarded by the latter; and philosophy is the *truth* of science for the same reason, because it is science and something more. This something more, however, in each case is not merely something externally added to what went before; it is a vital growth from it,—a transformation which takes place in it, by reason of latent forces that are already present. In this way self-consciousness—the last category or point of view—is seen to sum up and interpret all that went before; for while, like our first immediate consciousness of things, it is a direct assertion of independent Being—and while, like reflection, it includes difference and relation,—it goes beyond both in so far as it expresses the integration of differences—a relation of elements which, though opposed, are yet identified. . . .

Hegel's "Phenomenology of Mind"

By Josiah Royce

IF WE TURN TO THE STUDY of the special phases through which consciousness passes, as these are depicted in the *Phaenomenologie,* we find that the defects of the imperfect phases are such as, according to the doctrine, tend of themselves to make clear the structure of the absolute consciousness. For as you have just heard, the imperfections of the finite are all of them aspects of the complete expression of the infinite or perfect self or Absolute. Let us enumerate, then, some of these defects as they come out in the course of the book. The lower stages of consciousness, whether individual or social, may first be viewed as divided into two types. They are stages where the finite subject, or knower of the process in question, is either too exclusively theoretical or too exclusively practical in his attitude towards his life and towards his world. The Absolute alone combines in one both of these aspects. In finite life the too exclusively practical stages may be described as in general "blind." Those who are confined to these stages are active, earnest, enthusiastic, fanatical, hopeful or heroic. But they do not rightfully grasp what it is they are trying to do. The too exclusively theoretical stages of consciousness may be described as relatively "empty." One looks on the world, but finds in it little of significance, of the ideal, of the valuable. One becomes skeptical. One mercilessly exposes the contradictions of his own abstract conceptions. One thinks; but one has so far not learned to live.

From another point of view the lower stages are distinct from the absolute consciousness. The finite self finds its world, whether this be theoretical or practical, as if it were something foreign. It fails to recognize its own unity with its world. Viewed theoretically, its facts then appear accidental or unexplained, or as if due to mysterious power. Viewed practically, the world seems to the mind uncanny or hostile. The finite self is not at home. It becomes a wanderer. It

---

These selections are taken from Royce', *Lectures on Modern Idealism,* Lectures VII and VIII, a book first published in 1919. They are reprinted with the kind permission of Yale University Press.

sees its destiny elsewhere. Perhaps it is in the desert, guided only by the pillar of cloud by day and by fire by night. Perhaps it is amongst its foes who must be defeated. Perhaps, like Kant, it is dealing with the mysterious thing in itself. However the foreign world appears, the defect is that the self here does not recognize this world as its own. Or again, although on higher stages it may be thoroughly sure, as heroic and confident reformers are sure, that its world is its own and truly belongs to it, or as Hegel expresses it, is *an sich,* the self, the subject, does not yet see how this is true. Obviously the defective stages may here be, as we have said, either theoretical or practical. They may also be either individual or social. Israel in the wilderness, which Hegel himself does not mention as an illustration, would stand for a society whose world is foreign and whose laws are, consequently, supposed to be merely an ideal legislation for a future commonwealth.

But the imperfect life of the finite self may be characterized in still another way. In general the finite stages of consciousness are those in which the subject assumes some special form—is, as Hegel often says, *bestimmt,* that is determined to a particular way of living or of thinking. Dialectical considerations, then, always insure that over against this special form of self-consciousness, and in so far contemporaneous with it, there must be other opposed forms of subjectivity. These opposed forms of subjectivity are, then, to any one of the determinate subjects, his enemies. And so the world assumes the type which we characterized a moment ago. From this point of view finite life appears not merely as a passing away of each stage but as a conflict upon each stage with its own enemies, who are after all identical in nature with itself.

The imperfect stages of finite consciousness may be also viewed thus: The self, anticipating its own absolute calling and destiny, confident that it does know the world, may try to express the still unclear consciousness of its absoluteness either by affirming itself as this ego, this person, or on the other hand, by sacrificing all its personality and surrendering itself to a vague Absolute. In other words, the self may be thus a conscious individualist, or a self-abnegating mystic. In its social forms, this opposition between two imperfect types of self-consciousness would be expressed, for instance, in anarchy on the one hand and despotism on the other. That is, the theory of society might be founded on the maxim, Everyone for himself; or it might be founded on the maxim, All are subject to one.

Whether individual or social, this type of finite imperfection is found exemplified all the way through the series of stages.

If one contrast with these types of imperfection the type of an absolute consciousness, of the consciousness that views itself, and rightly views itself, as world-possessor and as self-possessor, this fulfilled self of the absolute knowledge must, according to Hegel, possess the following characteristics:

(1) It must be a union of theoretical and practical consciousness. It must see only what is its own deed, and must do nothing except what it understands. Precisely this, according to Hegel, is what occurs, to be sure in a highly abstract form, in the philosophical theory of the categories such as he afterwards embodied in his logic. For the categories of the Hegelian logic are at once pure thoughts and pure deeds.

(2) The absolute consciousness must be that of a self which is conscious of objects without going beyond its consciousness to find them. Such a consciousness, Hegel views as in the abstract realizable in a philosophical system.

(3) Somewhat more important still is the consideration that the Absolute must be a self that by virtue of its inmost principle appears to itself as an interrelated unity of selves without being the less one self. From this point of view Hegel calls the Absolute, *Geist.* Spirit in its complete sense is a consciousness, for which the individual exists only in social manifestation and expression, so that an individual apart from other individuals is meaningless, and so that the relations of individuals have been so completely expressed that each finds his being in all the others and exists in perfect unity with them. In his later sytem of philosophy this view of the nature of spirit lies at the foundation of Hegel's interpretation of the positive theory both of society and of religion. In the *Phaenomenologie,* the highest form of spirit which appears concretely expressed in the life of humanity is the form assumed by the church, in so far as the church is in possession of a perfectly rational religion. The Holy Spirit, identical with and present in the true life of the church, is for Hegel, in the *Phaenomenologie,* the living witness to this essentially social character of the absolute consciousness. That there appears considerable doubt whether the church as Hegel conceives it in this book is precisely identical with any one of the forms which the Christian church has assumed, is a consideration which does not here further concern us.

(4) Possibly the most notable feaure of the absolute conscious-

ness is that which unites completely finite and infinite. It saves its absoluteness by assuming special embodiments. Hegel always laid very great stress upon this thesis. It is a failure to grasp it which has so often made the religious conception of the deity what Hegel regards as abstract and relatively fruitless. To conceive God as first perfect by Himself and then, so to speak, capriciously creating a world of imperfection, this is not to conceive the divine consciousness as it is; it is perfect through the infinite imperfections of its finite expressions, and through the fact that these imperfections are nevertheless unified in its complete life. In the *Phaenomenologie,* this view is repeatedly insisted upon, and is expressed in connection with that phase of consciousness which Hegel calls the forgiveness of sin.

The thesis, then, in terms of which Hegel defines his Absolute is that the absolute self is aware of itself as a process involving an inner differentiation into many centers of selfhood. Each one of these centers of selfhood is, when viewed as a particular center and taken in its finitude, theoretically self-contradictory, practically evil. On the other hand, each of these finite expressions of the self is theoretically true, in so far as it represents the Universal and is related thereto; and it is practically justified, in so far as it aims at the Universal in deed and in spirit. In the religious consciousness of the forgiveness of sin, the Absolute, both as forgiving infinite and as forgiven finite, reaches this consciousness in a form which expresses the absolute process. The absolute process is, however, further expressible, apart from such images and allegories. To Hegel's mind it is inseparably associated with religion in the form of a philosophical or scientific consciousness. This philosophical consciousness explains, justifies, makes clear the existence of finitude, actuality, imperfection, sin. In the form of the dialectical method, philosophy emphasizes that contradictory and imperfect expression is necessary to the life of the infinite. In assigning to each special category its place, exhibiting its defect, and justifying this defect by its place in the whole system, philosophy expresses in the form of a rational consciousness what the religious consciousness discovers in the form of the union of the finite and infinite through the forgiveness of sin.

I turn from this indication of a very remarkable attempt to solve the problems of that time and of this type of philosophy, to a mention of some of the special illustrations. Let us confine ourselves for the moment to illustration of individual rather than of social types of consciousness. The first *Gestalt* of individual consciousness which Hegel considers is, as we said at the last time, the savage consciousness of the warrior, practically viewing himself as the only real self in the world, boasting his prowess as such, and consequently seeking to destroy whatever pretentious fellow may attempt falsely to be the self. It is because of the assurance, dim of course and purely practical, on the part of each man that he is the Absolute—it is because of this that the universal war of all against all appears. This primitive state of universal war, a conception which Hegel in so far accepts from the seventeenth-century theories of human nature, is to his mind a phase of human nature as transient as it is irrational. The reason for this transiency lies in the fact that killing a man proves nothing, except that the victor, in order to prove himself to be the self, needs still another man to kill, and is therefore essentially a social being. Even head hunting implies dependence upon one's neighbor who is good enough to furnish one more head for the hunter. Let one note this element of mutuality, and mere destruction gives way to a higher form of social consciousness. This higher stage of individual self-realization is reached in the still primitive type of society which is represented by the master and his slave. The master essentially recognizes that he needs somebody else in order that this other may prove him, the master, to be the self. The best proof that I am the self, so the master thinks, is given when another is subject to my will. Because he is another, and in so far a self, he by contrast assures me of my own selfhood; for with Hegel, as with Schelling, individual self-consciousness is a social contrast effect. For after all, I can only know myself as this individual if I find somebody else in the world, by contrast with whom I recognize who I am. But the master essentially hopes to prove himself to be the true self, by making the slave his mere organ, the mirror of his own functions, his will objectified. The world of the master and slave is therefore explicitly two-fold, and is not like the world of the head-hunting warriors, the world in which each man lived only by denying that the other had any right to live. The slave, to be sure, has no rights, but he has his uses, and he teaches me, the master, that I am the self. Unfortunately, however, for the master, the master hereby becomes dependent upon the slave's work. The master after all is merely the onlooker and is self only so far as he sees the other at work for him. The master's life is therefore essentially lazy and empty. Of the two, the faithful slave after all comes much nearer to

genuine selfhood. For self-consciousness is practical, is active, and
depends upon getting control of experience. The slave, so Hegel says,
works over, reconstructs the things of experience. Therefore by his
work he, after all, is conquering the world of experience, is making
it the world of the self, is becoming the self. The slave is potentially,
or in embryo—is *an sich,* as Hegel would say—the self-respecting
man, who in the end must become justly proud of the true mastery
that his work gives him. Let this essential character of the slave,—
the fact that he, as worker, is the only true man in this primitive
society—let this fact come to his own consciousness, and the self
becomes transformed from slavery to a higher phase of consciousness. This new phase is represented in Hegel's account, curiously
enough, by a form which in history appears as a stage of philosophical
consciousness, namely, by stoicism.

Stoicism, however, is here viewed in its practical, and not in
its theoretical, aspects as a doctrine of the world. Practically stoicism
is the attitude of the man who regards all things with which he deals
as necessarily subject to his own reason, whether he can control them
physically or not; because he has found that the self, through its own
rational ideal, needs no slaves, no conquest at war, to prove its independence. He is still a member of a society, but it is now an ideal
society, composed of the stoic and of his ideal, Reason, his guide.
Through the discipline of life the stoic has become entirely indifferent
to whether he is master or slave. Whether on the throne or in chains
or in service, the self, and just the individual self, is self-possessed
if it ideally declares itself so to be. Its social relation, its relation to
another is now simply its relation to its own ideal. I and my reason
constitute the world. The dialectical defect of the stoic's position is
that the actual world of the stoic's life—the world of activity, of
desire, of interest—is meanwhile going on in its own accidental way.
The self in order to attain independence has resigned all definite
plans of control over fortunes. Its concrete life is therefore empty.
If it hereupon becomes aware of this fact it turns from the stoic into
the skeptic, and learns to doubt even its own present ideal. Hegel
here has in mind the practical aspect of the forms of older ancient
skepticism, which undertook to retain the term of rational self-
consciousness by a reflection upon the vanity of all special doctrines,
ideals, dogmas, assurances, concerning common life. The skeptic, a
Diogenes in a tub, proves his independence by destroying convictions, by being entirely indifferent to conventions, by being essentially

restless, and merely dialectical. The result of a thoroughgoing adoption of this point of view is that life gets the sort of vanity which has been well suggested to our own generation by Fitzgerald's wonderful paraphrase of the Omar Khayyam stanzas. The self is now indeed free, but life is vain; and the world has once more fallen, seemingly in a hopeless way, into chaos. The *Weltgeist,* recognizing its failure so far to win its own, must once more transmigrate.

Hereupon Hegel introduces as the next *Gestalt* of individual consciousness a very remarkable one entitled, "The Unhappy Consciousness." That the consciousness of the Omar Khayyam stanzas is unhappy we shall all remember. And that this unhappiness results from skepticism concerning the worth of every concrete human life, is also obvious. What Hegel notes is the substantial identity between a consciousness which is unhappy for this reason, and the consciousness which, like that expressed in well-known devotional books, such as *The Imitation of Christ,* or in the practical life of solitary religious devotees of all faiths, views its unhappiness as due to its estrangement from a perfection of life, which ought to be its own but which in this world of conflicting motives and transient actvities seems hopelessly remote. Whether you express your unhappy consciousness in purely skeptical or in devout form, that is, with emphasis upon a cynical or upon a mystical attitude, is to a certain degree a matter of accident. But of course the devotional expression is the deeper one and looks more in the direction in which the solution of the problem, according to Hegel, is to be found. The unhappy consciousness is therefore depicted in its religious form, and with a constant use of metaphors derived from mediaeval Christianity. In fact Hegel is here unquestionably treating one aspect of the religious consciousness. It is however very notable, and characteristic of the method of the *Phaenomenologie* that Hegel does not regard this form of consciousness as a genuine expression of religion in its wholeness. Religion as such appears in the *Phaenomenologie* as a social and not as an individual life. The unhappy consciousness is here expressly what William James would call a variety of religious experience; it is not a concrete form of religion. It may appear in connection with the most varied phases of faith. Viewed, so to speak, metaphysically, it involves a distinctly individual interpretation of one's relation to the universe. That which the unhappy consciousness seeks, can therefore indeed be named God. It might also be named just Peace, or the Ideal Self. . . .

. . . Hegel depicts this form of individual self-consciousness with a rather excessive detail but with a very profound insight into the sentimentality, the hopelessness, and the genuine meaning of the entire process. The dialectic situation depends upon the pathetic fact that the unhappy consciousness always actually has its salvation close at hand, but is still forbidden by its own presuppositions to accept that salvation. What it seeks is nothing whatever but an inner self-confidence, which it apparently ought to win by a mere resolution—an act of manly will. Yet, by hypothesis, it is estranged from every resolute inner self-consciousness, since it conceives all good solely as belonging to its object, the Changeless. It prays to the Changeless, it longs for the Changeless. It tries to see its Lord face to face. But it always finds, says Hegel, only the empty sepulchre whence the Lord has been taken away. "Nay, if I find the Holy Grail itself, it too will fade and crumble into dust."

Under these circumstances, however, the consciousness in question does indeed learn to make a transition, which is in so far positive and which is due to taking over the lesson that the slave learned from the master. After all, the very emptiness of the sepulchre shows that if the Lord is not there he is arisen. Seek not the living among the dead. One's seeking must become an activity; one must do something even as the risen Lord does. And so the mere sentiment of the first stage of this unhappy consciousness changes into service. But the service is not a control of natural phenomena; it is not essentially any social business. It is the doing of what is pleasing in the sight of the Changeless; it is the life of self-sacrifice as such—the self-chastisement of the devotee. But once more the division recurs. What is done is, after all, but the transient deed of a poor sinner. The Changless, the perfect, cannot be realized hereby. One's work is but vain. One's righteousness is as rags. The true self is not satisfied. One's best work gets all its value, (when it gets any value at all), from the fact that the foreign and changeless self somehow kindly inspires this deed of righteousness and permits the poor sinner to do something for his Lord. But the doer himself still remains worthless, whatever he does. He wishes to be meet for the master's service, but after all he is but a broken and empty vessel, and this is all that he has to offer for the master's service. And under these circumstances the only hope must indeed come from the other side. After all, the changeless self is concerned in the salvation of this poor sinner, makes its own sacrifice for him, permits communion with the Changeless, gradually sanctifies the poor soul through the higher life, means in the end to bring the imperfect into union with itself. *Quantus labor ne sit cassus,* and so at length perhaps, through self-discipline, self-abnegation, endless self-chastisement, the imperfect self does come to some consciousness of a new and sanctified and redeemed nature. The Changeless perchance has come to live in it. It has now become, through the ineffable grace of the Changeless, the instrument of the divine.

But hereupon, for the unhappy consciousness the enemy appears, as Hegel says, in his worst form. The former self-abnegation changes into spiritual pride. The sanctified person becomes the home of vanity, and needs a constantly renewed casting down into the depths of humility, until this very pride in its own expertness in the art of self-humiliation becomes the inspiring principle of its life. It becomes intensely overcareful as to every detail of its fortunes and of its functions. Its existence is one of painful conscientiousness, of fruitless dreariness. And yet, after all, if it could only reflect, it would see that through its despair it has already found the essential experience. For what it has essentially discovered is that if a man will reasonably submit himself to the conditions of the true life, he must attain, through activity, a genuine unity with his ideal world. In other words, the unhappy consciousness is simply seeking in its lonesomeness what the civilized man is finding in his concrete relations, not to the enemies whom he kills, nor to the slaves whom he controls, nor to the abstract ideals that he follows, but to the humane life in which he finds his place. Whenever consciousness reaches, says Hegel, a stage of genuine reason, it becomes sure of itself and rests from the vain labors of all this suspicious self-questioning. It finds indeed a new field of work, and of intense and absorbing work, but not the labor of conquering these fantastic spiritual foes. It becomes assured that the practically humane life is, in meaning, one with the whole of reality. The unhappy consciousness, however, can in and for itself never recognize this fact. It will not wake up to its own truth. . . .

. . . The types of consciousness which here immediately follow, are depicted with a marvelous union of sympathetic detail and of merciless dialectic perculiarly characteristic of Hegel. They are, one might say, renaissance types of character—ethical and not theoretical—interpreted, however, from the point of view which German romanticism had determined. Common to them all is the explicit recognition that without actively pursuing its ideal in a world of life, in a world of objective fortune, in an organized and social order, the self cannot win its own place, cannot be a self at all. Common to them all is the further fact that the self, despite this recognition, tries to center this acknowledged social world about just that individual man in whom the self, by chance, conceives itself, in each new incarnation, to be embodied. The conception of the social universe is thus, each time, characteristically that of vigorous and ambitious youth, confident that in him the absolute ideal has found an incarnation, nowhere else attained. "I will show you, O world, that you are my own," he says. Yet he speaks not as the savage. He is the civilized youth, with powers, talents, training, and a love of emulation. He must conquer his world; but he knows that he needs a world to conquer, and is so far dependent. Not the killing of his enemies, but spiritual mastery of the universe is his aim. Moreover, he has behind him, in essence although perhaps not in memory, the experience of the unhappy consciousness. A merely sentimental and lonely religion seems to him vanity. He is beyond all that. For the time, he has no religion whatever. He is not afraid of life. He sets out to win and to enjoy. He recognizes that the truth of things is the human, the social truth. But he is resolved that whatever any man can experience, possess, attain, is by right his, so far as his ideal demands such possession.

He begins this sort of life by taking form as Faust. The Faust-ideal in question is due to so much of that poem as was at this time known to Hegel, and is not the Faust-ideal that Goethe later taught us to recognize as his own. Hegel conceives the Faust of the poem, as it was then before him, simply as the pleasure seeker longing for the time when he can say, "O moment stay, thou art so fair." The outcome of Faust's quest, as far as it goes, is for Hegel the discovery that the passing moment will neither stay nor be fair; so that the world where one seeks merely the satisfaction of the moment, proves rather to be the foreign world of a blind necessity. This necessity, in the guise of cruel fate, ruthlessly destroys everything that has seemed, before the moment of enjoyment, so entrancing. Pleasure seeking means, then, the death of whatever is desirable about life; and Hegel foresees, for Faust himself, so far as just his incarnation of the *Geist* can go, no escape from the fatal circle. At all events, the self is not to be found in this life of lawless pursuit of that momentary control over life which is conceived as pleasure. Such is Hegel's reading of the first part of Faust. He entitles the sketch, "Pleasure and Destiny."

The next form or incarnation of our hero is entitled, "The Law of the Heart." In making the transition from the pleasure-seeking consciousness with its inevitable discovery of a world of blind necessity, where every pleasure fades, Hegel shows a very fine comprehension of tendencies which the romantic movement had already notably exemplified, and which it was, in later literature, still further to exemplify. For the lesson of the defeated and romantic pleasure seeker's experience is indeed not, in strong and free natures, mere repentance, nor yet a mere reversion to the "unhappy consciousness." Hegel does not send his disillusioned worldling back to the cloister. The lesson rather is the discovery that the hero had been really seeking, not pleasure as such at all, but something so potent, so full of appeal to his heart that he would be as ready to die as to live for such an ideal; something in brief that could fill him with enthusiasm and devotion. . . .

. . . This transformation of the love of pleasure into the longing for a passionate ideal, is something much deeper than mere remorse. The outcome of the search for the satisfying moment of experience is the discovery of the law that all passes away and turns into the sere and yellow leaf. The lesson is that if one adopts this very law as one's own, if one scorns delight and lives laborious days, simply because all else fades, while the inmost desire of the heart may outlast all transient contentment, then one is nearer to one's own true expression. Choose your ideal then, choose it anyhow, and be ready to die for it. Then for the first time you learn how to live. Living means having something dear enough to fill the heart.

Thus Hegel suggests his diagnosis of the remarkable transition from passionate pleasure seeking to vehement self-surrender which is so notable in romantic periods and in youthful idealism.

The next type, the hero of the "law of the heart," hereupon appears as an enthusiast for an ideal—what ideal is indeed indifferent except so far as his own mere feeling is his guide. His heart tells him that this *is* his ideal. He is ready to die for it. That is enough. He has found himself. All about him, of course, is the vain world of the people who do not comprehend this ideal. But the hero is an altruist. His heart beats high for the good of mankind. What mankind needs is to learn of his ideal. He is therefore a reformer, a prophet of humanity, one of whom, as his own heart infallibly tells him, the world is not worthy. He is good enough, nevertheless, to be ready to save this so far ruined world. . . .

. . . Since in a similar fashion all other hearts, if once awakened, are laws unto themselves, the realm of such a company of romantic reformers is a renewal, upon a higher level, of the primal warfare of all against all. It is a world of mad prophets, each the fool of his own vanity. . . .

. . . The result of the dialectic of these successive types is so far obvious. The individual in order to come to himself needs a world, and a social one, to win over and to control. But control can only be won through self-surrender. Hence the individual needs a world where he may find something to which he can devote himself as to an objective truth—something quite definite which he can serve unhesitatingly so as to be free from the querulousness of the restless reformer, and free too from the idle vanity of the knight-errant. The true world must become for me the realm of my life task, of my work, of my objectively definite and absorbing pursuit. Only so can I truly come to myself and to my own. Is not then, after all, the artist who pursues art for art's sake, the scholar, who loves learning just for learning's sake, the man, in brief, who is completely given over to a laborious calling just for the sake of the absorbing consciousness which accompanies this calling—is not such a man, at length, in possession of the true form of self-consciousness? My work, my calling, my life task—this I pursue not because I wish for mere pleasure, but because I love the work. Moreover, this task is indeed the law of my heart; but I do not seek to impose it upon all other men. I leave them free to choose their life tasks. Nor is my calling merely an object of sentiment. I view it as a worthy mode of self-expression. Meanwhile, unlike the knight-errant, I do not pretend to be the one virtuous representative of my calling, who as such is reforming the base world. No, in my calling, I have my colleagues who work with me in a common cause. This cause (*die Sache*) is ours. Here, then, are the conditions of an ideal society. Here subject and object are at least, it might seem, upon equal terms. We who pursue a common calling exist as servants of our *Sache;* and this cause—our science, our art, our learning, our creating process, whatever it be—this exists by virtue of our choice, and of our work. Meanwhile, if this is not your calling, you must not ask, as from without, what this "cause" of ours is good for. Our art is just for art's sake; our learning is its own reward. Our cause is indeed objective; we serve it; we sacrifice for it; but it is its own excuse for being. If you want to attain the right type of self-consciousness, find such a cause, make it yours, and then serve it. . . .

. . . In explaining the dialectic of this type of consciousness Hegel shows all the skill of the reflective man who is confessing the only too natural defects incident to his own calling. And no reader can doubt the thoroughness of the confession. For no sentimental dreamer of the foregoing romantic types fares worse under Hegel's dissection than does the type of the scholar or the artist who defies the self in terms of the "cause," and who thereupon can say nothing better of the "cause" than that it is its own excuse for being. Such an ideal Hegel finds wholly accidental and capricious, and shrewdly notes that what the scholars and artists in question really mean by their pretended devotion to the "cause" is that they are fond of displaying their wits to one another and of showing their paces and of winning applause, and with a touch of the old savagery about them are also fond of expressing contempt for the failures of other men. . . .

. . . Yet, once again, the result of this dialectic is positive. The ideal of the intellectual animals is in fact a sound one. Their hypocrisy lies merely in pretending to have found this ideal in art for art's sake, or in learning for learning's sake. Suppose that there indeed is a task which is not arbitrarily selected by me as my task, and then hypocritically treated as if it were the universal task which I impersonally serve. Suppose that the genuine task is one forced upon us all by our common natural and social needs. This then will be *"die Sache,"* our work, our life, whether we individually admit the fact or not. Against the magnitude of this common task, the individual's service will then indeed be as nothing, and the individual, when he notes this, may frankly admit the fact without any hypocritical posing. On the other hand, this task will furnish for each man his only possible true self-expression in terms of human action. Is there such a task, such a *Sache?* Hegel replies in effect: Yes, the consciousness of a free people, of a *Volk,* of an organized social order, will constitute such an expression of selfhood. To each of its loyal citizens, the state whose life is that of such a people will be his objective self. This his true self then assigns to the individual his private task, his true cause, gives dignity and meaning to his personal virtues, fills his heart with a patriotic ideal, and secures him the satisfactions of his natural life. Here at last in this con-

sciousness of a free people, we have—no longer crude self-consciousness, no longer lonely seeking of impossible ideals, and no
longer the centering of the world about the demands of any one
individual. In this consciousness of a free people each individual
self is in unity with the spirit of the entire community. And herewith the world of the *Geist* begins. All the previous forms were
abstractions, fragments of life, bits of self-hood. In history they
appear as mere differentiations within some form of the life of the
Geist—as mere phases of individual life which involve, as it were,
a sleep and a forgetting of the unity upon which all individual life
is based. An organized social order is the self for each one of its
loyal subjects. The truth of the individual is the consciousness of
the people to which he loyally belongs. . . .

The skeptical discovery that the state appears to exist simply
as the embodiment of the selfish will of its subjects, and that loyal
professions are mere cloaks for individual greed, the growth of a
corrupt use of political power even by virtue of the growth of the
general social intelligence, the conflict of the social classes—these
are phases in the great process of the cultivation which the social
mind gives to itself. These phases culminate in the consciousness
which the Enlightenment of the eighteenth century represents. Society is indeed necessary, but it exists solely for the sake of forming,
nourishing, and cultivating, free individuals. Utility is the sole test
of social truth. All that is real exists simply in order to make men
happy. Whatever principle underlies this world-process is an unknowable Supreme Being. Visibly true is only this, that what tends
to the greatest good of the greatest number of individual men is
alone justified. This, then, is what we have been seeking. This is
wisdom's last social word. Away with all arbitrary laws and sovereign powers. Away with loyalty to anything but the common rights
of all men. We are all free and equal. The *Geist* has been transformed
into the multitude of free and equal individuals. Let the people
come to their own.

Herewith, then, comes the Revolution, the absolute freedom—
and the Terror. For the horde of individuals thus let loose are whatever they happen to be. The will of all is indeed to be done. But
who shall do it? The sovereign ruler? But the sovereign is dead. The
representatives of the people? But these are now free individuals,
with no loyalty that they can any longer define in rational terms.
The only way for them to become conscious of the universal will is

to express their own will. They mean of course to do whatever brings the greatest happiness to the greatest number. But they have now no test of what is thus to be universally useful except what is furnished by the light of their own personal experience. Their subjective decision they therefore impose upon all others. Thus they become a faction, appear as public enemies, and are overthrown. Society has returned to primitive anarchy, and exists once more as the war of all against all. . . .

. . . And Hegel hereupon depicts, in terms derived from Kant and Fichte, what he now calls the moral theory of the universe of the spirit. Upon this stage the mind, still aware of its essentially social destiny, now undertakes to define the reality as a certain eternal and ideal order which is valid for all rational being—the city of God, whose constitution never passes away. This higher and eternal realm, where the moral autonomy of every free agent is guaranteed even by virtue of his acceptance of a moral law that he conceives as binding for all rational beings, is as true as it is shadowy and full of antithesis. On earth this ideal moral order can never be realized, for on earth we see only phenomena. . . .

. . . But still another form of this moral theory of reality remains. Perhaps the spirit is actually realized not through what we accomplish, but by the simple fact that, on the highest levels we intend to be rational. Perhaps the readiness is all. Perhaps the triumph of the self in its world simply takes the form of a ceaseless determination, in spite of failure and of finitude, to *aim* at the highest, at complete self-expression, at unity. Perhaps the curtain is the picture; perhaps the will is the deed; and perhaps in the end the spirit, like a higher sort of "intellectual animal," contents itself with merely saying, "I have accomplished nothing, but at least I have tried my best." So to conceive the solution is to take the position of some of Hegel's contemporaries, to whom, as formerly to Lessing, the search for the truth is all that can be viewed as accessible or as really worthy. This, in fact, is curiously near to Hegel's own form of Absolutism; but is also curiously remote from it.

For if, at least, it is the pure intent to be reasonable that constitutes reasonableness, if the whole life of the spirit, individual and social, exists only as an aim, an idea, an attitude, a purpose, still one has to remember, as one looks back over this long story of error and defeat, that every deed in which the self was expressed was, in its measure, a falling away from its own intent—was an expression of illusion, was a finite mistake, and, if conscious, was a sin against the ideal.

What consciousness so far learns, then, is that finite defect, error, sin, contradiction, is somehow of the very nature of the self, even when the self seeks and means the highest. Every effort to find and to express the perfect self is *ipso facto* a lapse into imperfection. The pure self cannot be expressed without impurity. The rational self cannot be expressed without irrationality. The absolute purpose, to be the self and to be one with one's own world, is realizable only through a continual inner conflict and a constant transcending of finite failures.

To see this, however, is also to see that it is not in the failures themselves, but in the transcending of them that the true life of the spirit—of the self—comes to be incorporated. And Hegel here expresses this by saying that it is not the consciousness of sin but the consciousness of the forgiveness of sin that brings us to the threshold of understanding why and how the true self needs to be expressed, i.e., through a process of the conscious overcoming of the defects of its own stages of embodiment, through a continual conquest over self-estrangements that are meanwhile inevitable, but never final.

To give this very view of the nature of the self, and of the relation between perfection and imperfection, finitude and the infinite—to give this view a genuine meaning, we must turn to that still higher form of the social consciousness which is historically embodied in religion.

Religion may be defined, so Hegel says, as the consciousness of the Absolute Being. In other words religion is not, like the foregoing, the effort of one who, beginning with his own individual self-consciousness as the center of his universe, tries to find the place of this individual self in his world. Religion is rather the consciousness which is seeking to express what the Absolute Being, the universe, really is, although, to be sure, religion is inevitably an interpretation of the Absolute Being as seen from the point of view of the inquiring self.

In history, religion has appeared as an attitude of the social consciousness towards the world. Religion is, for Hegel, an interpretation of the world by the social self, and by the individual man only in so far as he identifies himself with the social self. That is, the nation or the church or humanity has a religion. The individual man comes to a consciousness of his religion through his community with his nation or his church or with humanity. Religion as a purely private and personal experience could only consist of such forms as the unhappy consciousness has already exemplified.

The early forms of religion define the universe in terms of powers of nature. The unconscious idealism of the primitive mind appears in the fact that these powers tend from the outset to be conceived as living powers, which, in order that they may be viewed as sufficiently foreign and mysterious, are often typified by animals. Gradually the consciousness grows that human activity is needed in order that by suitable monuments, by vast constructions due to the worshippers themselves, the nature of the world-fashioning intelligence may be at once fittingly honored and, through imitation, portrayed. The result is seen in the vast architectural religion of Egypt, of whose true nature Hegel, when he wrote this book, had indeed small knowledge. Greek religious thought, conceiving its deities in human form, came nearer to a knowledge of the true relation of the Absolute and the finite being. The result was the religion of art, wherein the divine is portrayed by representing ideal types of human beings. But art, in humanizing the divine, inevitably tends also to humanize itself. In tragic poetry the gods gradually give place to mortal heroes; and poetry becomes consciously an imitation of human life. Comedy completes the process of this humanization. Man, who started to portray the gods, portrays, and in the end mercilessly criticizes, merely men; and the ancient religion dissolves itself in a humanistic skepticism. There are no gods. There are only men. The individual selves are all. This is the anarchical stage of religion.

But the world itself remains—mysterious, all-powerful, objective, the dark realm that this skepticism cannot pierce. The mythical personifications have turned into human fancies. Man remains on one side, the Absolute on the other. The one is self-conscious; but the other is the hidden source of self-consciousness, hopeless, baffling, overwhelming in its vastness. What form of conception can portray the now seemingly impenetrable essence of this Absolute, from which we creatures of a day seem to be now sundered as mere outer shells of meaningless finitude?

There remains one form of the religious consciousness untried. It is, at this point in human history, ready to come to life. In a highly dramatic passage Hegel now depicts how, about the birth-place of this new form of consciousness, there gather, like the wise men from the East, some of the most significant of the *Gestalten* so far represented: Stoicism is there, proclaiming the dignity of the self as the universal reason, but knowing not who the self is; the unhappy consciousness is there, seeking its lost Lord; the social spirit of the ancient state is there, lamenting the loss of its departed spirit: all these forms wait and long for the new birth. And the new birth comes thus: That it is the faith of the world that the Absolute, even as the Absolute that was hidden, has now revealed itself as an individual man, and has become incarnate.

This faith then holds not that an accidental individual man is all, but that the essential Absolute reveals itself as man, and this is the first form of the Christian consciousness.

This form too must pass away. This visible Lord must be hidden again in the heavens. For sense never holds fast the Absolute. There remains the consciousness, first that the Spirit of God is ever present in his church, and then that the church knows—although indeed under the form of allegories—how the Absolute Being is complete in himself only in so far as he expresses himself in a world which endlessly falls away from him into finitude, sin, darkness, and error, while he as endlessly reconciles it to himself again, living and suffering in individual form in order that, through regaining his union with his own Absolute Source, he may draw and reconcile all things to himself.

This, says Hegel, is the allegory of which philosophy is the truth.

ARTHUR SCHOPENHAUER

(1788-1860)

As is well known, Schopenhauer differs from most other idealists in his pessimistic view of life. This is connected with his idea that the dominant factor is an irrational will. In this he finds the essence not only of ourselves but of physical nature. The will seeks to maintain its own existence, though it would on Schopenhauer's pessimistic view be more rational to seek non-existence. We are perpetually restless and unhappy since we do not act except as a result of painful desire, and the moment a desire is fulfilled it gives way either to another desire or to satiety and boredom. (This one exception is the alleviation to be found in aesthetic enjoyment.)

On the Possibility of Knowing
the Thing in Itself

. . . WHAT IS *knowledge?* It is primarily and essentially *idea.* What is *idea?* A very complicated *physiological* process in the brain of an animal, the result of which is the consciousness of a *picture* there. Clearly the relation between such a picture and something entirely different from the animal in whose brain it exists can only be a very indirect one. This is perhaps the simplest and most comprehensible way of disclosing the *deep gulf between the ideal and the real.* This belongs to the things of which, like the motion of the earth, we are not directly conscious; therefore the ancients did not observe it, just as they did not observe the motion of the earth. Once pointed out, on the other hand, first by Descartes, it has ever since given philosophers no rest. But after Kant had at last proved in the most thorough manner the complete diversity of the ideal and the real, it was an attempt, as bold as it was absurd, yet per-

---

This selection is from Vol. II of *The World as Will and Idea,* Supplements to the Second Book, Ch. XVIII. The translation is by R. B. Haldane and John Kemp. *The World as Will and Idea* was first published in 1819

fectly correctly calculated with reference to the philosophical public in Germany, and consequently crowned with brilliant results, to try to assert the *absolute identity* of the two by dogmatic utterances, on the strength of a pretended intellectual intuition. In truth, on the contrary, a subjective and an objective existence, a being for self and a being for others, a consciousness of one's own self, and a consciousness of other things, is given us directly, and the two are given in such a fundamentally different manner that no other difference can compare with this. About himself every one knows directly, about all others only very indirectly. This is the fact and the problem. . . .

. . . If, however, it should be said: "The perception is itself the knowledge of the thing in itself: for it is the effect of that which is outside us, and as this *acts,* so it *is*: its action is just its being"; to this we reply: (1) that the law of causality, as has been sufficiently proved, is of subjective origin, as well as the sensation from which the perception arises; (2) that at any rate time and space, in which the object presents itself, are of subjective origin; (3) that if the being of the object consists simply in its action, this means that it consists merely in the changes which it brings about in others; therefore itself and in itself it is nothing at all. Only of *matter* is it true, as I have said in the text, and worked out in the essay on the principle of sufficient reason, that its being consists in its action, that it is through and through only causality, thus is itself causality objectively regarded; hence, however, it is also nothing in itself, but as an ingredient in the perceived object, is a mere object, a mere abstraction, which for itself alone can be given in no experience. It will be fully considered later on in a chapter of its own. But the perceived object must be something *in itself,* and not merely something *for others.* For otherwise it would be altogether merely idea, and we would have an absolute idealism, which would ultimately become theoretical egoism, with which all reality disappears and the world becomes a mere subjective phantasm. If, however, without further question, we stop altogether at the *world as idea,* then certainly it is all one whether I can explain objects as ideas in my head or as phenomena exhibiting themselves in time and space; for time and space themselves exist only in my head. In this sense, then, an identity of the ideal and the real might always be affirmed; only, after Kant, this would not be saying anything new. Besides this, however, the nature of things and of the phenomenal world would clearly not thereby be exhausted; but with it we would always remain still upon the ideal side. The *real* side must be someting *toto genere* different from *the world as idea,* it must be that which things are in *themselves;* and it is this entire diversity between the ideal and the real which Kant has proved in the most thorough manner.

Locke had denied to the senses the knowledge of things as they are in themselves; but Kant denied this also to the perceiving *understanding,* under which name I here comprehend what he calls the *pure* sensibility, and, as it is given *a priori,* the law of causality which brings about the empirical perception. Not only are both right, but we can also see quite directly that a contradiction lies in the assertion that a thing is known as it is in and for itself, *i.e.,* outside of knowledge. For all knowing is, as we have said, essentially a perceiving of ideas; but my perception of ideas, just because it is mine, can never be identical with the inner nature of the thing outside me. The being in and for itself, of everything, must necessarily be *subjective;* in the idea of another, however, it exists just as necessarily as *objective*—a difference which can never be fully reconciled. For by it the whole nature of its existence is fundamentally changed; as objective it presupposes a foreign subject, as whose idea it exists, and, moreover, as Kant has shown, has entered forms which are foreign to its own nature, just because they belong to that foreign subject, whose knowledge is only possible by means of them. If I, absorbed in this reflection, perceive, let us say lifeless bodies, of easily surveyed magnitude and regular, comprehensible form, and now attempt to conceive this spatial existence, in its three dimensions, as their being in itself, consequently as the existence which to the things is subjective, the impossibility of the thing is at once apparent to me, for I can never think those objective forms as the being to which the things is subjective, rather I become directly conscious that what I there perceive is only a picture produced in my brain, and existing only for me as the knowing subject, which cannot constitute the ultimate, and therefore subjective, being in and for itself even of these lifeless bodies. But, on the other hand, I must not assume that even these lifeless bodies exist only in my idea, but, since they have inscrutable qualities, and, by virtue of these, activity, I must concede to them a *being in itself* of some kind. But this very inscrutableness of the properties, while, on the one hand, it certainly points to something which exists independently of our knowledge, gives also, on the other hand, the empirical proof that our knowledge, because it consists simply in *framing ideas* by means of subjective forms, affords us always mere *phenomena,* not the true being of things. This is the explanation of the fact that in all that we know there remains hidden from us a certain something, as quite inscrutable, and we are obliged to confess that we cannot thoroughly understand even the commonest and simplest phenomena. For it is not merely the highest productions of nature, living creatures, or the *complicated* phenomena of the unorganized world that remain inscrutable to us, but even every rock-crystal, every iron-pyrite, by reason of its crystallographical, optical, chemical, and electrical properties, is to the searching consideration and investigation an abyss of incomprehensibilities and mysteries. This could not be the case if we knew things as they are in themselves; for then at least the simpler phenomena, the path to whose qualities was not barred for us by ignorance, would necessarily be thoroughly comprehensible to us, and their whole being and nature would be able to pass over into our knowledge. Thus it lies not in the defectiveness of our acquaintance with things, but in the nature of knowledge itself. For if our perception, and consequently the whole empirical comprehension of the things that present themselves to us, is already essentially and in the main determined by our faculty of knowledge, and conditioned by its forms and functions, it cannot but be that things exhibit themselves in a manner which is quite different from their own inner nature, and therefore appear as in a mask, which allows us merely to assume what is concealed beneath it, but never to know it; hence, then, it gleams through as an inscrutable mystery, and never can the nature of anything entire and without reserve pass over into knowledge; but much less can any real thing be construed *a priori,* like a mathematical problem. Thus the empirical inscrutableness of all natural things is a proof *a posteriori* of the ideality and merely phenomenal-actuality of their empirical existence.

According to all this, upon the path of *objective knowledge,* hence starting from the *idea,* one will never get beyond the idea, *i.e.,* the phenomenon. One will thus remain at the outside of things, and will never be able to penetrate to their inner nature and investigate what they are in themselves, *i.e.,* for themselves. So far I agree with Kant. But, as the counterpart of this truth, I have given prominence to this other truth, that we are not merely the *knowing subject,* but, in another aspect, we ourselves also belong to the inner nature that is to be known, *we ourselves are the thing in itself;* that therefore a *way from within* stands open for us to that inner nature belonging to things themselves, to which we cannot penetrate *from without,* as it were a substerranean passage, a secret alliance, which as if by treachery, places us at once within the fortress which it was impossible to take by assault from without. The thing in itself can, as such, only come into consciousness quite directly, in this way, that *it is itself conscious of itself*: to wish to know it objectively is to desire something contradictory. Everything objective is idea, therefore appearance, mere phenomenon of the brain.

Kant's chief result may in substance be thus concisely stated: "All conceptions which have not at their foundation a perception in space and time (sensuous intuition), that is to say then, which have not been drawn from such a perception, are absolutely empty, *i.e.,* give no knowledge. But since now perception can afford us only *phenomena,* not things in themselves, we have also absolutely no knowledge of things in themselves." I grant this of everything, with the single exception of the knowledge which each of us has of his own *willing*: this is neither a perception (for perception is spatial) nor is it empty; rather it is more real than any other. Further, it is not *a priori,* like merely formal knowledge, but entirely *a posteriori;* hence also we cannot anticipate it in the particular case, but are hereby often convicted of error concerning ourselves. In fact, our *willing* is the one opportunity which we have of understanding from within any event which exhibits itself without, consequently the one thing which is known to us *immediately,* and not, like all the rest, merely given in the idea. Here, then, lies the datum which alone is able to become the key to everything else, or, as I have said, the single narrow door to the truth. Accordingly, we must learn to understand nature from ourselves, not conversely ourselves from nature. What is known to us immediately must give us the explanation of what we know only indirectly, not conversely. Do we perhaps understand the rolling of a ball when it has received an impulse more thoroughly than our movement when we feel a motive? Many may imagine so, but I say it is the reverse. Yet we shall attain to the knowledge that what is essential in both the occurrences just mentioned is identical; although identical in the same way as the lowest audible note of harmony is the same as the note of the same name ten octaves higher.

Meanwhile it should be carefully observed, and I have always kept it in mind, that even the inward experience which we have of our own will by no means affords us an exhaustive and adequate knowledge of the thing in itself. This would be the case if it were entirely an immediate experience; but it is effected in this way: the will, with and by means of the corporization, provides itself also with an intellect (for the sake of its relations to the external world), and through this now knows itself as will in self-consciousness (the necessary counterpart of the external world); this knowledge therefore of the thing in itself is not fully adequate. First of all, it is bound to the form of the idea, it is apprehension, and as such falls asunder into subject and object. For even in self-consciousness the I is not absolutely simple, but consists of a knower, the intellect, and a known, the will. The former is not known, and the latter does not know, though both unite in the consciousness of an I. But just on this account that the I is not thoroughly *intimate* with itself, as it were transparent, but is opaque, and therefore remains a riddle to itself, thus even in inner knowledge there also exists a difference between the true being of its object and the apprehension of it in the knowing subject. Yet inner knowledge is free from two forms which belong to outer knowledge, the form of *space* and the form of *causality,* which is the means of effecting all sense-perception. On the other hand, there still remains the form of *time,* and that of being known and knowing in general. Accordingly in this inner knowledge the thing in itself has indeed in great measure thrown off its veil, but still does not yet appear quite naked. In consequence of the form of time which still adheres to it, every one knows his will only in its successive *acts,* and not as a whole, in and for itself; therefore no one knows his character *a priori,* but only learns it through experience and always incompletely. But yet the apprehension, in which we know the affections and acts of our own will, is far more immediate than any other. It is the point at which the thing in itself most directly enters the phenomenon and is most closely examined by the knowing subject; therefore the event thus intimately known is alone fitted to become the interpreter of all others.

For in every emergence of an act of will from the obscure depths of our inner being into the knowing consciousness a direct transition occurs of the thing in itself, which lies outside time, into the phenomenal world. Accordingly the act of will is indeed only the closest and most distinct *manifestation* of the thing in itself; yet it follows from this that if all other manifestations or phenomena could be known by us as directly or inwardly, we would be obliged to assert

them to be that which the will is in us. Thus in this sense I teach
that the inner nature of everything is *will,* and I call will the thing
in itself. Kant's doctrine of the unknowableness of the thing in itself
is hereby modified to this extent, that the thing in itself is not only
absolutely and from the very foundation knowable, that yet by far
the most immediate of its phenomena, which by this immediateness
is *toto genere* distinguished from all the rest, represents it for us;
and accordingly we have to refer the whole world of phenomena
to that one in which the thing itself appears in the very thinnest of
veils, and only still remains phenomenon in so far as my intellect,
which alone is capable of knowledge, remains ever distinguished
from me as the willing subject, and moreover does not even in *inner*
perfection put off the form of knowledge of *time.*

Accordingly, even after this last and furthest step, the question
may still be raised, what that will, which exhibits itself in the world
and as the world, ultimately and absolutely is in itself? *i.e.,* what it
is, regarded altogether apart from the fact that it exhibits itself as
will, or in general *appears, i.e.,* in general is *known.* This question
can never be answered: because, as we have said, becoming known
is itself contradictory of being in itself, and everything that is known
as such is only phenomenal. But the possibility of this question shows
that the thing in itself, which we know most directly in the will, may
have, entirely outside all possible phenomenal appearance, ways of
existing, determinations, qualities, which are absolutely unknowable and incomprehensible to us, and which remain as the nature
of the thing itself, when, as is explained in the fourth book, it has
voluntarily abrogated itself as *will,* and has therefore retired altogether from the phenomenon, and for our knowledge, *i.e.,* as regards
the world of phenomena, has passed into empty nothingness. If the
will were simply and absolutely the thing in itself this nothing would
also be *absolute,* instead of which it expressly presents itself to us
as there only *relative.*

I now proceed to supplement with a few considerations pertinent
to the subject the exposition given both in our second book and
in the work *Ueber den Willen in der Natur,* of the doctrine that what
makes itself known to us in the most immediate knowledge as will
is also that which objectifies itself at different grades in all the phenomena of this world; and I shall begin by citing a number of psychological facts which prove that first of all in our own consciousness the will always appears as primary and fundamental, and

throughout asserts its superiority to the intellect, which, on the other hand, always presents itself as secondary, subordinate, and conditioned. This proof is the more necessary as all philosophers before me, from the first to the last, place the true being or the kernel of man in the *knowing* consciousness, and accordingly have conceived and explained the I, or, in the case of many of them, its transcendental hypostasis called soul, as primarily and essentially *knowing,* nay, *thinking,* and only in consequence of this, secondarily and derivatively, as *willing.* This ancient and universal radical error, must before everything be set aside, and instead of it the true state of the case must be brought to perfectly distinct consciousness. Since, however, this is done here for the first time, after thousands of years of philosophizing, some fullness of statement will be appropriate. The remarkable phenomenon, that in this most essential point all philosophers have erred, nay, have exactly reversed the truth, might, especially in the case of those of the Christian era, be partly explicable from the fact that they all had the intention of presenting man as distinguished as widely as possible from the brutes, yet at the same time obscurely felt that the difference between them lies in the intellect, not in the will; whence there arose unconsciously within them an inclination to make the intellect the essential and principal thing, and even to explain volition as a mere function of the intellect. Hence also the conception of a soul is not only inadmissible, because it is a transcendent hypostasis, as is proved by the *Critique of Pure Reason,* but it becomes the source of irremediable errors, because in its "simple substance" it establishes beforehand an indivisible unity of knowledge and will, the separation of which is just the path to the truth. That conception must therefore appear no more in philosophy, but may be left to German doctors and physiologists, who, after they have laid aside scalpel and spattle, amuse themselves by philosophizing with the conceptions they received when they were confirmed. They might certainly try their luck in England. The French physiologists and zootomists have (till lately) kept themselves free from that reproach.

The first consequence of their common fundamental error, which is very inconvenient to all these philosophers, is this: since in death the knowing consciousness obviously perishes, they must either allow death to be the annihilation of man, to which our inner being is opposed, or they must have recourse to the assumption of a continued existence of the knowing consciousness, which requires a strong faith, for his own experience has sufficiently proved to every one the thorough and complete dependence of the knowing consciousness upon the brain, and one can just as easily believe in digestion without a stomach as in a knowing consciousness without a brain. My philosophy alone leads out of this dilemma, for it for the first time places the true being of man not in the consciousness but in the will, which is not essentially bound up with consciousness, but is related to consciousness, *i.e.*, to knowledge, as substance to accident, as something illuminated to light, as the string to the resounding-board, and which enters consciousness from within as the corporeal world does from without. Now we can comprehend the indestructibleness of this, our real kernel and true being, in spite of the evident ceasing of consciousness in death, and the corresponding non-existence of it before birth. For the intellect is as perishable as the brain whose product or rather action it is. But the brain, like the whole organism, is the product of the phenomenon, in short, the subordinate of the will, which alone is imperishable.

THOMAS HILL GREEN

(1836-1882)

Green's main argument is as follows: Everything that exists involves relations. Relations can exist only for a mind. Therefore everything depends on the mind. The reason for inferring a single mind on which the whole universe depends as opposed to a form of polytheism is that everything is related to everything else and in Green's philosophy A can be related to B only if they are both present to the same mind. The argument will recall Berkeley's to the reader but differs from his in that (a) it stresses thought rather than sense-perception and (b) it holds there are relations between human minds and not only between physical objects. This argument would directly establish the dependence of physical objects as well as of human minds on God, while Berkeley could not draw this conclusion in the case of human minds without supplementary considerations. However Green insists that, since we are ourselves thinkers, we are not only the objects of the divine thought like physical things but also its manifestations or modes. In the latter capacity it transcends altogether the natural order and everything that is in time.

The Spiritual Principle
in Knowledge and in Nature

. . . THE READER is probably acquainted with Kant's dictum that "the understanding makes nature." It gives no doubt a somewhat startling expression to the revolution in philosophy which Kant believed himself to have introduced, and which he compared to the change effected by the Copernican theory in men's conception of the relative positions of the earth and the sun. When we inquire, however, into the precise sense in which Kant used the expression, we find that its meaning is subject to a qualification which testifies to the difficulty experienced by Kant himself in carrying out the

This selection is from Chapter I of Green's *Prolegomena to Ethics,* which was first published in 1883.

doctrine which the words seem to convey. *"Macht zwar der Verstand die Natur, aber er schafft sie nicht."* The understanding "makes" nature, but out of a material which it does not make. That material, according to Kant, consists in phenomena or "data" of sensibility, given under the so-called forms of intuition, space and time. This apparent ascription of nature to a twofold origin—an origin in understanding in respect of its form as a nature, as a single system of experience; an origin elsewhere in respect of the "matter" which through the action of understanding becomes a nature—cannot but strike us as unsatisfactory. Perhaps it may not be a doctrine in which we can permanently acquiesce, but meanwhile it represents fairly enough on its two sides the considerations which on the one hand lead us to regard nature as existing only in relation to thought, and those on the other which seem obstinately opposed to such a view.

To say with Kant that the understanding is the principle of objectivity, that only through understanding is there for us an objective world, is sure to seem at first sight the extreme of perversity. We have come to think of the understanding as specially an agency of our own, and of the objective world as specially that which is presented to us independently of any such agency; as that which we find and do not make, and by which we have to correct the fictions of our own minds. When we ask, however, whether any impression is or represents anything "real and objective," what exactly does the question mean, and how do we set about answering it? It is not equivalent to a question whether a feeling is felt. Some feeling must be felt in order to the possibility of the question being raised at all. It is a question whether a given feeling is what it is taken to be; or, in other words, whether it is related as it seems to be related. It may be objected indeed that, though *some* feeling or other must be felt in order to give any meaning to the question as to the objectivity of the impression or its correspondence with reality, yet still this question may and often is true; but a particular feeling is a feeling related in a certain way, and the question whether a particular feeling is really felt is always translatable into the form given—Is a feeling, which is undoubtedly felt, really related as some one thinking about it takes it to be? If an engine-driver, under certain conditions, permanent with him or temporary, "sees a signal wrong," as we say, his disordered vision has its own reality just as much as if he saw right. There are relations between combinations of moving particles on the one side and his visual organs on the other, between the present state of the latter and certain determining conditions, between the immediate sensible effect and the secondary impressions which it in turn excites, as full and definite—with sufficient inquiry and opportunity, as ascertainable—as in any case of normal vision. There is as much reality in the one case as in the other, but it is not the same reality: *i.e.*, it does not consist in the same relations. The engine-driver mistakes the effect of one set of relations for that of another, one reality for another, and hence his error in action. He may be quite innocent of a scientific theory of vision, but he objectifies his sensations. He interprets them as related in a certain way, and as always the same in the same relations; or, to use an equivalent but more familiar expression, as signs of objects from which he distinguishes his feelings and by which he explains them. Were this not the case, his vision might be normal or abnormal, but he would be incapable of mistaking one kind of reality for another since he would have no conception of reality at all.

The terms "real" and "objective," then, have no meaning except for a consciousness which presents its experiences to itself as determined by relations, and at the same time conceives a single and unalterable order of relations determining them, with which its temporary presentation, as each experience occurs, of the relations determining it may be contrasted. For such a consciousness, perpetually altering its views of the relations determining any experience under the necessity of combining them in one system with other recognized relations, and for such a consciousness only, there is significance in the judgment that any experience seems to be so and so, *i.e.*, to be related in a certain way, but really is otherwise related. We shall have afterwards to consider the question whether the consciousness, for which alone this contrast of the real and the apparent is possible, has anything to do with the establishment of the relations in which it conceives reality to consist—whether the conception of reality has any identity with the act by which reality is constituted. But even if this latter question is waived or answered in the negative, there will still be an important sense in which understanding, or consciousness as acting in the manner described, may be said to be the principle of objectivity. It will be through it that there is *for us* an objective world; through it that we *conceive* an order of nature, with the unity of which we must reconcile our interpretations of phenomena, if they are to be other than "subjective" illusions. . . .

. . . "May it [consciousness] not be a product of *previous* events?" If it is so, a series of events of which there is no conscious experience must be supposed to produce a consciousness of another series. On any other supposition the difficulty is only postponed. For if the series of events which produces a certain consciousness of other events is one of which there *is* a consciousness, this consciousness, not being explicable as the product of the events of which it is the consciousness, will have in turn to be referred to a prior series of events; and ultimately there will be no alternative between the admission of a consciousness which is not a product of events at all and the supposition stated—the supposition that the primary consciousness of events results from a series of events of which there is no consciousness. But this supposition, when we think of it, turns out to be concatenation of words to which no possible connection of ideas corresponds. It asserts a relation of cause and effect, in which the supposed cause lacks all the characteristics of a cause. It may be questioned whether we can admit anything as a cause which does not explain its supposed effect, or is not equivalent to the conditions into which the effect may be analyzed. But granting that we may, a cause must at least be that to which experience testifies as the uniform antecedent of the effect. Now a series of events of which there is no consciousness is certainly not a set of conditions into which consciousness can be analyzed. And as little can it be an antecedent uniformly associated with consciousness in experience, for events of which there is no consciousness cannot be within experience at all.

It seems necessary, then, to admit that experience, in the sense of a consciousness of events as a related series—and in no other sense can it help to account for the knowledge of an order of nature —cannot be explained by any natural history, properly so called. It is not a product of a series of events. It does not arise out of materials other than itself. It is not developed by a natural process out of other forms of natural existence. Given such a consciousness, the scientific conception of nature, no less than the everyday distinction between fact and fancy, between objective reality and subjective illusion, can be exhibited as a development of it, for there is an assignable element of identity between the two. But between the consciousness itself on the one hand, and on the other anything determined by the relations under which a nature is presented to consciousness, no process of development, because no community, can really be traced. Nature, with all that belongs to it, is a process of change: change on a uniform method, no doubt, but change still. All the relations under which we know it are relations in the way of change or by which change is determined. But neither can any process of change yield a consciousness of itself, which, in order to be a consciousness of the change, must be equally present to all stages of the change; nor can any consciousness of change, since the whole of it must be present at once, be itself a process of change. There may be a change into a state of consciousness of change, and a change out of it, on the part of this man or that; but within the consciousness itself there can be no change, because no relation of before and after, of here and there, between its constituent members—between the presentation, for instance, of point A and that of point B in the process which forms the object of the consciousness.

From the above considerations thus much at any rate would seem to follow: that a form of consciousness, which we cannot explain as of natural origin, is necessary to our conceiving an order of nature, an objective world in fact from which illusion may be distinguished. In other words, an understanding—for that term seems to fit as any other to denote the principle of consciousness in question—irreducible to anything else, "makes nature" for us, in the sense of enabling us to conceive that there is such a thing. Now that which the understanding thus presents to itself consists, as we have seen, in certain relations regarded as forming a single system. The next question, then, will be whether understanding can be held to "make nature" in the further sense that it is the source, or at any rate a condition, of there being these relations. If it cannot, we are left in the awkward position of having to suppose that, while the conception of an order of nature on the one side, and that order itself on the other, are of different and independent origin, there is yet some unaccountable pre-established harmony through which there comes to be such an order corresponding to our conception of it. This indeed might be urged as a reason for seeking some way of escape from the conclusion at which we have just arrived. But before we renew an attempt which has often been made and failed, let us see whether the objections to the other alternative—to the view that the understanding which presents an order of nature to us is in principle one with an *God ?* understanding which constitutes that order itself—have really the cogency which common sense seems to ascribe to them. . . .

. . . Let us consider how we stand. We have rejected the question, What is or constitutes the real? as intrinsically unmeaning, because it could only be answered by a distinction which would imply that there was something unreal. The question arises, we have seen, out of an abstraction from our constant inquiry into the real nature of this or that particular appearance or event—an inquiry in which we always seek for an unchanging relation between these and certain other conditions. The complete determination of an event it may be possible for our intelligence to arrive at. There may always remain unascertained conditions which may render the relation between an appearance and such conditions of it as we know, liable to change. But that there *is* an unalterable order of relations, if we could only find it out, is the presupposition of all our inquiry into the real nature of appearances; and such unalterableness implies their inclusion in one system which leaves nothing outside itself. Are we then entitled to ask—and if so, are we able to answer—the further question, What is implied in there being such a single, all-inclusive, system of relations? or, What is the condition of its possibility? If this question can be answered, the condition ascertained will be the condition of there being a nature and of anything being real, in the only intelligible sense that we can attach to the words "nature" and "real." It would no doubt still be open to the skeptic, should this result be attained, to suggest that the validity of our conclusion, upon our own showing, depends upon there really being such an order of nature as our quest of knowledge supposes there to be, which remains unproven. But as the skeptic, in order to give his language a meaning, must necessarily make the same supposition— as he can give no meaning to reality but the one explained—his suggestion that there really may not be such an order of nature conveys nothing at all.

First, then, is there any meaning in the question just put? Having set aside as unmeaning the question, What is the real? can we be entitled to ask, What is implied in there being a nature of things? If the former question would have been answerable only on the self-contradictory supposition of there really being something other than the real from which it could be distinguished, will not the latter in like manner be only answerable on the equally impossible supposition of there being something outside the nature of things, outside the one all-inclusive system of relations, by reference to which this nature of system can be explained? To this we reply that the question stated is or is not one that can be fitly asked, according as the conception of nature, of a single all-inclusive system of relations, is or is not that one can stand alone, is or is not one that requires something else to render it intelligible. To suppose that this "something else," if nature were found unthinkable without it, is related to those conditions, of which the relation to each other forms the system of nature, in the same way in which these are related to each other, would no doubt be in contradiction with our account of this system as one and all-inclusive. It could not therefore be antecedent to an invariable sequent, or as one body to another outside it. But there would be no contradiction in admitting a principle which renders all relations possible, and is itself determined by none of them, if, on consideration of what is needed to constitute a system of relations, we found such a principle to be requisite.

This, then, is the consideration which we have now to undertake. Relation to us is such a familiar fact that we are apt to forget that it involves all the mystery, if it be a mystery, of the existence of many in one. Whether we say that a related thing is one in itself, manifold in respect of its relations, or that there is one relation between manifold things, *e.g.,* the relation of mutual attraction between bodies— and one expression or the other we must employ in stating the simplest facts—we are equally affirming the unity of the manifold. Abstract the many relations from the one thing, and there is nothing. They, being many, determine or constitute its definite unity. It is not the case that it first exists in its unity, and then is brought into various relations. Without the relations it would not exist at all. In like manner the one relation is a unity of the many things. They, in their manifold being, make the one relation. If these relations really exist, there is a real unity of the manifold, a real multiplicity of that which is one. But a plurality of things cannot of themselves unite in one relation, nor can a single thing of itself bring itself into a multitude of relations. It is true, as we have said, that the single things are nothing except as determined by relations which are the negation of their singleness, but they do not therefore cease to be single things. Their common being is not something into which their several existences disappear. On the contrary, if they did not survive in their singleness, there could be no relation between them—nothing but a blank featureless identity. There must, then, be something other than the manifold things themselves, which combines them without effacing their severalty.

With such a combining agency we are familiar as our intelligence. It is through it that the sensation of the present moment takes a character from comparison with the sensation of a moment ago, and that the occurrence, consisting in the transition from one to the other, is presented to us. It is essential to the comparison and to the character which the sensations acquire from the comparison, essential, too, to their forming an observable event or succession, that one should not be fused with the other, that the distinct being of each should be maintained. On the other hand, in the relation to which their distinctness is thus necessary they are at the same time united. But if it were not for the action of something which is not either of them or both together, there would be no alternative between their separateness and their fusion. One might give place to the other, or both together might be combined into a third; but a unity in which their distinctness is preserved could not be constituted without the relating act of an intelligence which does not blend with either.

The above is an instance of relation between sensations which, as brought into relation by intelligence, become sensible objects or events. But the same or an analogous action is necessary to account for any relation whatever—for a relation between material atoms as much as any other. Either then we must deny the reality of relations altogether and treat them as fictions of our combining intelligence; or we must hold that, being the product of our combining intelligence, they are yet "empirically real" on the ground that our intelligence is a factor in the real of experience; or if we suppose them to be real otherwise than merely as for us, otherwise than in the "cosmos of our experience," we must recognize as the condition of this reality the action of some unifying principle analogous to that of our understanding. . . .

. . . There are difficulties enough, no doubt, in the way of accepting such a form of "idealism," but they need not be aggravated by misunderstanding. It is simply misunderstood if it is taken to imply either the reduction of facts to feelings—impressions and ideas, in Hume's terminology—or the obliteration of the distinction between illusion and reality. The reduction of facts to relations is the very reverse of their reduction to feelings. No feeling, as such or as felt, is a relation. We can only suppose it to be so through confusion between it and that fact of its occurrence which is no doubt related to other facts, but, as so related, is not felt. Even a relation between feelings is not itself a feeling or felt. A feeling can only be felt as successive to another feeling, but the terms of a relation, as we have seen, even though the relation be one of suc-

cession, do not succeed one another. In order to constitute the
relation they must be present together; so that, to constitute a
relation between feelings, there must be something other than the
feelings for which they are equally present. The relation between
the feelings is not felt, because it is only for something that distinguishes itself from the feelings that it can subsist. It is our
cognizance of the successiveness or transitoriness of feelings that
makes us object intuitively to any idealism which is understood to
imply an identification of the realities of the world with the feelings
of men. Facts, we are sure, are in some way permanent. They are
not "like the bubble on the fountain," a moment here, then "gone,
and for ever." But if they were feelings as we feel them, they would
be so. They would not be "stubborn things"; for as each was felt
it would be done with. They would not form a world to which we
have to adapt ourselves; for in order to make a world they must
coexist, which feelings, as we feel them, do not.

But the idealism which interprets facts as relations, and can
only understand relations as constituted by a single spiritual principle, is chargeable with no such outrage on common sense. On the
contrary, its very basis is the consciousness of objectivity. Its whole
aim is to articulate coherently the conviction of there being a world
of abiding realities other than, and determining, the endless flow of
our feelings. The source of its differences from ordinary realism
lies in its being less easily satisfied in its analysis of what the existence of such a world implies. The mere statement that facts are
not feelings, that things are not ideas, that we can neither feel nor
think except contingently upon certain functions of matter and
motion being fulfilled, does not help us to understand what facts
and things, what matter and motion, are. It does not enable us,
when we seek to understand these expressions, to give them any
meaning except such as is derived from experience, and, if from
experience, then from relations that have their being only for an
intelligent consciousness. . . .

FRANCIS HERBERT BRADLEY

(1846-1924)

Bradley's principal book, *Appearance and Reality,* starts with an attempt to show that all the concepts with which we work are self-contradictory. The most important argument here is that against relations given in Selection 1. If it is valid, it discloses a self-contradiction in all our thought, since human thought is, as Bradley admits, relational throughout. The conclusion is not so serious as it sounds because he holds that, although all our judgments are strictly false, they are also all partly true and differ immensely in the degree by which they fall short of complete truth. We can, he holds, make some judgments which, though not wholly true, are as true as any judgment could be. The criticism of Bradley's argument against relations by James Cook Wilson, a distinguished realist, is also included in this book (pp. 285-88). The criticism was, I think, widely accepted (I accepted it in my own book *Idealism*), but I do not now think it quite to the point. Bradley is not, I think, intending to dispose of all rival views of relations by the infinite regress argument, but only of one which consists in treating the relation as itself a third term. In that case a new relation would be required to link it to its terms and so on *ad infinitum*. The arguments against the alternative views which reduce relations to a kind of qualities are summed up in the footnote reproduced on p. 133. Certainly, if relations are to be reduced to anything else, they must be reduced either to terms or to qualities. And it seems that this cannot be done without self-contradiction. The usual reply of the realist would be that the concept of relation is unique and cannot be reduced to any other. It is only by treating a relation as something else that we get into a position where we need another relation to connect it to its terms. If it is really a relation it does not need something else to relate itself to them any more than a sound chain needs another chain to attach it to each of the things which it chains together thus giving rise to an infinite regress which would make it impossible to chain anything. Bradley's answer would be that the realist account is unintelligible: we cannot understand what a relation is, he would say, without defining it and explaining how it follows from and so holds together its terms.

In the second Selection Bradley develops his argument as to the positive nature of reality. He argues that our very condemnation of our concepts as self-contradictory presupposes that reality has the positive character of self-consistency, since otherwise self-contradictoriness could not be a ground for saying something was unreal. Partly because of his argument against relations and partly because of his conviction that nothing could be understood fully apart from everything else, he further maintains that reality cannot consist of a number of different independent things but must partake of the nature of a closely knit system. To the obvious objection that even statements like this presuppose the reality of relations he would reply that they are indeed not absolutely true, but that truth is a matter of degree and they are as true statements as any we could make. Of course, like anybody else, Bradley is obliged to use relational terms himself, and he would admit that some are much less inadequate than others. He insists, however, that, although we cannot ourselves replace relational terms, they do not do full justice to the unity of the real. In order even to relate two different elements in the real we have to separate them when they are not really separated, for a relation implies the distinctness of its terms. Further, Reality must somehow include all those things he had pronounced appearances, since appearances are after all something. How then can they be self-contradictory? Bradley's answer is that, as so included, they are radically different from what they are as taken apart. We only found them self-contradictory because, owing to the inevitable limitations of our thinking, we had to take them apart. We know that the self-contradiction must be transcended in some way, though we cannot see how. Bradley further by a characteristically idealist argument tries to show that there is nothing in reality but experience.

In the third Selection Bradley argues that reality is perfect in a valuational sense on the ground that otherwise it could not be even intellectually coherent—a bold conclusion but one on which absolute idealists really insisted and which brings him much nearer to the religious point of view than might perhaps appear from certain other aspects of his thought. He holds that, though the religious concept of the Absolute as personal is not ultimately true, it is nearer to being so than even the concepts of science, and that the degree of reality of things is ultimately in proportion to their value. The radical difference between anything as it is for us on our partial view and the same thing as it is for the Absolute is used by him elsewhere to show that the problem of evil may be soluble. This does not, however, mean that evil for Bradley is just an illusion. All appearances, even the most evil ones, are part of the real. But the very same thing which for us, who see it by itself, is evil, could still be justified in reality as necessary for a greater good.

Selection 4 is included as the chief statement in English of the type of idealist view which bases ethics on social institutions rather than on the individual conscience, and which has been made the excuse for such perverted dogmas as that the State can do no wrong and for the excesses of nationalism and militarism. Fortunately, in English-speaking countries it has, as far as I know, been put forward by important writers only in a relatively moderate form. In regard to Bradley's own exposition we must remember that he is here expressly intending only to give one side of the case and that he supplements it in the succeeding chapter, entitled "Ideal Morality." We need not deny that what he says does express the essence of one very important side of ethics. The earlier part of the selection is a characteristic expression of the view which takes literally the doctrine of common objective universals in particulars, interpreting it as meaning that different things really have parts of their being in common, so that identity and diversity are not absolute but relative. Such a view supports a form of monism.

1.

Relation and Quality

. . . TO FIND qualities without relations is surely impossible. In the field of consciousness, even when we abstract from the relations of identity and difference, they are never independent. One is together with, and related to, one another, at the least—in fact, always to more than one. Nor will an appeal to a lower and undistinguished state of mind, where in one feeling are many aspects, assist us in any way. I admit the existence of such states without any relation, but I wholly deny there the presence of qualities. For if these felt aspects, while merely felt, are to be called qualities proper, they are so only for the observation of an outside observer. And then for him they are given *as* aspects—that is, together with relations. In short, if you go back to mere unbroken feeling, you have no relations and no qualities. But if you come to what is distinct, you get relations at once.

I presume we shall be answered in this way. Even though, we shall be told, qualities proper cannot be discovered apart from relations, that is no real disproof of their separate existence. For we are well able to distinguish them and to consider them by themselves. And for this perception certainly an operation of our minds is required. So far, therefore, as you say, what is different must be distinct, and, in consequence, related. But the relation does not really belong to the reality. The relation has existence only for us, and as a way of our getting to know. But the distinction, for all that, is based upon differences in the actual; and these remain when our relations have fallen away or have been removed.

This selection is from Chapter III of the second edition of *Appearance and Reality*, a book first published in 1893.

Such an answer depends on the separation of product from process, and this separation seems indefensible. The qualities, as distinct, are always made so by an action which is admitted to imply relation. They are made so, and, what is more, they are emphatically kept so. And you cannot ever get your product standing apart from its process. Will you say, the process is not essential? But that is a conclusion to be proved, and it is monstrous to assume it. Will you try to prove it by analogy? It is possible for many purposes to accept and employ the existence of processes and relations which do not affect specially the inner nature of objects. But the very possibility of so distinguishing in the end between inner and outer, and of setting up the inner as absolutely independent of all relation, is here in question. Mental operations such as comparison, which presuppose in the compared qualities already existing, could in no case prove that these qualities depend on no relations at all. But I cannot believe that this is a matter to be decided by analogy, for the whole case is briefly this. There is an operation which, removing one part of what is given, presents the other part in abstraction. This result is never to be found anywhere apart from a persisting abstraction. And, if we have no further information, I can find no excuse for setting up the result as being fact without the process. The burden lies wholly on the assertor, and he fails entirely to support it. The argument that in perception one quality must be relative, is hardly worth mentioning. What is more natural than for qualities always to have come to us in some conjunction, and never alone?

We may go further. Not only is the ignoring of the process a thing quite indefensible—even if it blundered into truth—but there is evidence that it gives falsehood. For the result bears internally the character of the process. The manyness of the qualities cannot, in short, be reconciled with their simplicity. Their plurality depends on relation, and, without that relation, they are not distinct. But, if not distinct, then not different, and therefore not qualities. . . .

. . . We have found that qualities, taken without relations, have no intelligible meaning. Unfortunately, taken together with them, they are equally unintelligible. They cannot, in the first place, be wholly resolved into the relations. You may urge, indeed, that without distinction no difference is left; but, for all that, the differences will not disappear into the distinction. They must come to it, more or less, and they cannot wholly be made by it. I still insist that for thought what is not relative is nothing. But I urge, on the other hand, that nothings cannot be related, and that to turn qualities in relation into mere relations is impossible. Since the fact seems constituted by both, you may urge, if you please, that either one of them constitutes it. But if you mean that the other is not wanted, and that relations can somehow make the terms upon which they seem to stand, then, for my mind, your meaning is quite unintelligible. So far as I can, relations must depend upon terms, just as much as terms upon relations. And the partial failure, now manifest, of the Dialectic Method seems connected with some misapprehension on this point.

Hence the qualities must be, and must *also* be related. But there is hence a diversity which falls inside each quality. Each has a double character, as both supporting and being made by the relation. It may be taken as at once condition and result, and the question is as to how it can combine this variety. For it must combine the diversity, and yet it fails to do so. *A* is both made, and is not made, what it is by relation; and these different aspects are not each the other, nor again is either *A*. If we call its diverse aspects a and a, then *A* is partly each of these. As a it is the difference on which distinction is based, while as a it is the distinctness that results from connection. *A* is really both somehow together as *A* (a — a). But *without* the use of a relation it is impossible to predicate this variety of *A*. And, on the other hand, *with* an integral relation *A*'s unity disappears, and its contents are dissipated in an endless process of distinction. *A* at first becomes a in relation with a, but these terms themselves fall hopelessly asunder. We have got, against our will, not a mere aspect, but a new quality a, which itself stands in a relation; and hence (as we saw before with *A*) its content must be manifold. As going into the relation it itself is a^2, and as resulting from the relation it itself is a^2. And it combines, and yet cannot combine, these adjectives. We, in brief, are led by a principle of fission which conducts us to no end. Every quality in relation has, in consequence, a diversity within its own nature, and this diversity cannot immediately be asserted of the quality. Hence the quality must exchange its unity for an internal relation. But, thus set free, the diverse aspects, because each something in relation, must each be something also beyond. This diversity is fatal to the internal unity of each; and it demands a new relation, and so on without limit. In short, qualities in a relation have turned

out as unintelligible as were qualities without one. The problem
from both sides has baffled us.

3. We may briefly reach the same dilemma from the side of
relations. They are nothing intelligible, either with or without their
qualities. In the first place, a relation without terms seems mere
verbiage; and terms appear, therefore, to be something beyond
their relation. At least, for myself, a relation which somehow
precipitates terms which were not there before, or a relation which
can get on somehow without terms, and with no differences beyond
the mere ends of a line of connection, is really a phrase without
meaning. It is, to my mind, a false abstraction, and a thing which
loudly contradicts itself; and I fear that I am obliged to leave the
matter so. As I am left without information, and can discover with
my own ears no trace of harmony, I am forced to conclude to a
partial deafness in others. And hence a relation, we must say,
without qualities is nothing.

But how the relation can stand to the qualities is, on the other
side, unintelligible. If it is nothing to the qualities, then they are
not related at all; and, if so, as we saw, they have ceased to be
qualities, and their relation is a nonentity. But if it is to be something to them, then clearly we now shall require a new connecting
relation. For the relation hardly can be the mere adjective of one
or both of its terms; or, at least, as such it seems indefensible.[1]
And, being something itself, it does not itself bear a relation to the
terms, in what intelligible way will it succeed in being anything to
them? But here again we are hurried off into the eddy of a hopeless
process, since we are forced to go on finding new relations without
end. The links are united by a link, and this bond of union is a
link which also has two ends; and these require each a fresh link
to connect them with the old. The problem is to find how the
relation can stand to its qualities; and this problem is insoluble.
If you take the connection as a solid thing, you have got to show,
and you cannot show, how the other solids are joined to it. And,
if you take it as a kind of medium or unsubstantial atmosphere, it
is a connection no longer. You find, in this case, that the whole

---

1. The relation is not the adjective of one term, for, if so, it does not relate.
Nor for the same reason is it the adjective of each term taken apart, for then again
there is no relation between them. Nor is the relation their common property,
for then what keeps them apart? They are now not two terms at all, because not
separate. And within this new whole, in any case, the problem of inherence would
break out in an aggravated form. But it seems necessary to work all this out in
detail.

question of the relation of the qualities (for they certainly in some way *are* related) arises now outside it, in precisely the same form as before. The original relation, in short, has become a nonentity, but, in becoming this, it has removed no element of the problem.

I will bring this chapter to an end. It would be easy, and yet profitless, to spin out its argument with ramifications and refinements. And for me to attempt to anticipate the reader's objections would probably be useless. I have stated the case, and I must leave it. The conclusion to which I am brought is that a relational way of thought—any one that moves by the machinery of terms and relations—must give appearance, and not truth. It is a makeshift, a device, a mere practical compromise, most necessary, but in the end most indefensible. We have to take reality as many, and to take it as one, and to avoid contradiction. We want to divide it, or to take it, when we please, as indivisible; to go as far as we desire in either of these directions, and to stop when that suits us. And we succeed, but succeed merely by shutting the eyes, which if left open would condemn us; or by a perpetual oscillation and a shifting of the ground, so as to turn our back upon the aspect we desire to ignore. But when these inconsistencies are forced together, as in metaphysics they must be, the result is an open and staring discrepancy. And we cannot attribute this to reality; while, if we try to take it on ourselves, we have changed one evil for two. Our intellect, then, has been condemned to confusion and bankruptcy, and the reality has been left outside uncomprehended. Or rather, what is worse, it has been stripped bare of all distinction and quality. It is left naked and without a character, and we are covered with confusion. . . .

2.

The General Nature of Reality

THE RESULT of our First Book has been mainly negative. We have taken up a number of ways of regarding reality, and we have found that they are all vitiated by self-discrepancy. The reality can accept not one of these predicates, at least in the character in which so far they have come. We certainly ended with a reflection which promised something positive. Whatever is rejected as appearance is, for that very reason, no mere nonentity. It cannot bodily be shelved and merely got rid of, and, therefore, since it must fall somewhere, it must belong to reality. To take it as existing somehow and somewhere in the unreal, would surely be quite meaningless. For reality must own and cannot be less than appearance, and that is the one positive result which, so far, we have reached. But as to the character which, otherwise, the real possesses, we at present know nothing; and a further knowledge is what we must aim at through the remainder of our search. . . .

. . . Is there an absolute criterion? This question, to my mind, is answered by a second question: How otherwise should we be able to say anything at all about appearance? For through the last Book, the reader will remember, we were for the most part criticizing. We were judging phenomena and we were condemning them, and throughout we proceeded as if the self-contradictory could not be real. But this was surely to have and to apply an absolute criterion. For consider: you can scarcely propose to be quite passive when presented with statements about reality. You can hardly take the position of admitting any and every nonsense to be truth, truth absolute and entire, at least so far as you know. For, if you think at all so as to discriminate between truth and falsehood, you will find that you cannot accept open self-contradiction. Hence to think is to judge, and to judge is to criticize, and to criticize is to use a criterion of reality. And surely to doubt this would be mere blindness or confused self-deception. But, if so, it is clear that, in re-

---

This selection is from Chapters XIII and XIV of *Appearance and Reality*.

jecting the inconsistent as appearance, we are applying a positive knowledge of the ultimate nature of things. Ultimate reality is such that it does not contradict itself; here is an absolute criterion. And it is proved absolute by the fact that, either in endeavoring to deny it, or even in attempting to doubt it, we tacitly assume its validity.

One of these essays in delusion may be noticed briefly in passing. We may be told that our criterion has been developed by experience, and that therefore at least it may not be absolute. But why anything should be weaker for having been developed is, in the first place, not obvious. And, in the second place, the whole doubt, when understood, destroys itself. For the alleged origin of our criterion is deliberated to us by knowledge which rests throughout on its application as an absolute test. And what can be more irrational than to try to prove that a principle is doubtful, when the proof through every step rests on its unconditional truth? . . .

. . . Reality is one in this sense that it has a positive nature exclusive of discord, a nature which must hold throughout everything that is to be real. Its diversity can be diverse only so far as not to clash, and what seems otherwise anywhere cannot be real. And, from the other side, everything which appears must be real. Appearance must belong to reality, and it must therefore be concordant and other than it seems. The bewildering mass of phenomenal diversity must hence somehow be at unity and self-consistent; for it cannot be elsewhere than in reality, and reality excludes discord. Or again we may put it so: the real is individual. It is one in the sense that its positive character embraces all differences in an inclusive harmony. And this knowledge, poor as it may be, is certainly more than bare negation or simple ignorance. So far as it goes, it gives us positive news about absolute reality.

Let us try to carry this conclusion a step further on. We know that the real is one; but its oneness so far, is ambiguous. Is it one system, possessing diversity as an adjective; or is its consistency, on the other hand, an attribute of independent realities? We have to ask, in short, if a plurality of reals is possible, and if these can merely coexist so as not to be discrepant? Such a plurality would mean a number of things not dependent on each other. On the one hand they would possess somehow the phenomenal diversity, for that possession, we have seen, is essential. And, on the other hand, they would be free from external disturbance and from inner discrepancy. After the inquiries of our First Book the possibility of such reals hardly calls for discussion. For the internal states of each give rise to hopeless difficulties. And, in the second place, the plurality of the reals cannot be reconciled with their independence. I will briefly resume the arguments which force us to this latter result.

If the Many are supposed to be without internal quality, each would forthwith become nothing, and we must therefore take each as being internally somewhat. And, if they are to be plural, they must be a diversity somehow coexisting together. Any attempt again to take their togetherness as unessential seems to end in the unmeaning. We have no knowledge of a plural diversity, nor can we attach any sense to it, if we do not have it somehow as one. And, if we abstract from this unity, we have also therewith abstracted from the plurality, and are left with mere being.

Can we then have a plurality of independent reals which merely coexist? No, for absolute independence and coexistence are incompatible. Absolute independence is an idea which consists merely in one-sided abstraction. It is made by an attempted division of the aspect of several existences from the aspect of relatedness; and these aspects, whether in fact or thought, are really indivisible. . . .

Our result so far is this. Everything phenomenal is somehow real; and the absolute must at least be as rich as the relative. And, further, the Absolute is not many; there are no independent reals. The universe is one in this sense that its differences exist harmoniously within one whole, beyond which there is nothing. Hence the Absolute is, so far, an individual and a system, but, if we stop here, it remains but formal and abstract. Can we then, the question is, say anything about the concrete nature of the system?

Certainly, I think, this is possible. When we ask as to the matter which fills up the empty outline, we can reply in one word, that this matter is experience. And experience means something much the same as given and present fact. We perceive, on reflection, that to be real, or even barely to exist, must be to fall within sentience. Sentient experience, in short, is reality, and what is not this is not real. We may say, in other words, that there is no being or fact outside of that which is commonly called psychical existence. Feeling, thought, and volition (any groups under which we class psychical phenomena) are all the material of existence, and there is no other material, actual or even possible. This result in its general form seems evident at once; and, however serious a step we now seem to have taken, there would be no advantage

at this point in discussing it at length. For the test in the main lies
ready to our hand, and the decision rests on the manner in which
it is applied. I will state the case briefly thus. Find any piece of
existence, take up anything that one could possibly call a fact, or
could in any sense assert to have being, and then judge if it does
not consist in sentient experience. Try to discover any sense in
which you can still continue to speak of it, when all perception and
feeling have been removed; or point out any fragment of its matter,
any aspect of its being, which is not derived from and is still not
relative to this source. When the experiment is made strictly, I can
myself conceive of nothing else than the experienced. Anything, in
no sense felt or perceived, becomes to me quite unmeaning. And
as I cannot try to think of it without realizing either that I am not
thinking at all, or that I am thinking of it against my will as being
experienced, I am driven to the conclusion that for me experience
is the same as reality. The fact that falls elsewhere seems, in my
mind, to be a mere word and a failure, or else an attempt at self-
contradiction. It is a vicious abstraction whose existence is meaningless nonsense and is therefore not possible.

This conclusion is open, of course, to grave objection, and must
in its consequences give rise to serious difficulties. I will not attempt to anticipate the discussion of these, but before passing on,
will try to obviate a dangerous mistake. For, in asserting that the
real is nothing but experience, I may be understood to endorse a
common error. I may be taken first to divide the percipient subject
from the universe; and then, resting on that subject, as on a thing
actual by itself, I may be supposed to urge that it cannot transcend
its own states. Such an argument would lead to impossible results,
and would stand on a foundation of faulty abstraction. To set up
the subject as real independently of the whole, and to make the
whole into experience in the sense of an adjective of that subject
seems to me indefensible. And when I contend that reality must be
sentient, my conclusion almost consists in the denial of this fundamental error. For if, seeking for reality, we go to experience, what
we certainly do *not* find is a subject or an object, or indeed any
other thing whatever, standing separate on its own bottom. What
we discover rather is a whole in which such distinctions can be
made, but in which divisions do not exist. And this is the point on
which I insist, and it is the very ground on which I stand, when I
urge that reality is sentient experience. I mean that to be real is to

be indissolubly one thing with sentience. It is to be something which comes as a feature and aspect within one whole of feeling, something which, except as an integral element of such sentience, has no meaning at all. And what I repudiate is the separation of feeling from the felt, or of the desired from desire, or of what is thought from thinking, or the division—I might add—of anything from anything else. Nothing is ever so presented as real by itself, or can be argued so to exist without demonstrable fallacy. And in asserting that the reality is experience, I rest throughout on this foundation. You cannot find fact unless in unity with sentience, and one cannot in the end be divided from the other, either actually or in idea. But to be utterly indivisible from feeling or perception, to be an integral element in a whole which is experienced, this surely is itself to *be* experience. Being and reality are, in brief, one thing with sentience; they can neither be opposed to, nor even in the end distinguished from it.

I am well aware that this statement stands in need of explanation and defense. This will, I hope, be supplied by succeeding chapters, and I think it better for the present to attempt to go forward. Our conclusion, so far, will be this, that the Absolute is one system, and that its contents are nothing but sentient experience. It will hence be a single and all-inclusive experience, which embraces every partial diversity in concord. For it cannot be less than appearance, and hence no feeling or thought, of any kind, can fall outside its limits. And if it is more than any feeling or through which we know, it must still remain more of the same nature. It cannot pass into another region beyond what falls under the general head of sentience. For to assert that possibility would be in the end to use words without a meaning. We can entertain no such suggestion except as self-contradictory, and as therefore impossible. . . .

3.

The Perfection of the Absolute

IF WE UNDERSTAND by perfection a state of harmony with pleasure, there is no direct way of showing that reality is perfect. For, so far as the intellectual standard at present seems to go, we might have harmony with pain and with partial dissatisfaction. But I think the case is much altered when we consider it otherwise, and when we ask if on another ground such harmony is possible. The intellect is not to be dictated to; that conclusion is irrefragable. But is it certain, on the other hand, that the mere intellect can be self-satisfied, if other elements of our nature remain not contented? Or must we not think rather that indirectly any partial discontent will bring unrest and imperfection into the intellect itself? If this is so, then to suppose any imperfection in the Absolute is inadmissible. To fail in any way would introduce a discord into perception itself. And hence, since we have found that, taken perceptively, reality is harmonious, it must be harmonious altogether, and must satisfy our whole nature. Let us see if on this line we can make an advance.

If the Absolute is to be theoretically harmonious, its elements must not collide. Idea must not disagree with sensation, nor must sensations clash. In every case, that is, the struggle must not be a mere struggle. There must be a unity which it subserves, and a whole, taken in which it is a struggle no longer. How this resolution is possible we may be able to see partly in our subsequent chapters, but for the present I would insist merely that somehow it must exist. Since reality is harmonious, the struggle of diverse elements, sensations or ideas, barely to qualify the self-same point must be precluded. But, if idea must not clash with sensation, then there cannot in the Absolute be unsatisfied desire or any practical unrest. For in these there is clearly an ideal element not concordant with presentation but struggling against it, and, if you remove this discordance, then with it all unsatisfied desire is gone. In order for such a desire, even in its lowest form, to persist, there must (so far as I can see)

This selection is from Chapter XIV of *Appearance and Reality*.

[140]

be an idea qualifying diversely a sensation and fixed for the moment in discord. And any such state is not compatible with theoretical harmony. . . .

. . . When we pass from the conditions to the effects of painful feeling, we are on surer ground. For in our experience the result of pain is disquietude and unrest. Its main action is to set up change, and to prevent stability. There is authority, I am aware, for a different view, but, so far as I see, that view cannot be reconciled with facts. This effect of pain has here a most important bearing. Assume that in the Absolute there is a balance of pleasure, and all is consistent. For the pains can condition those processes which, as processes, disappear in the life of the whole; and these pains can be neutralized by an overplus of pleasure. But if you suppose, on the other hand, a balance of pain, the difficulty becomes at once insuperable. We have postulated a state of harmony, and, together with that, the very condition of instability and discord. We have in the Absolute, on one side, a state of things where the elements cannot jar, and where in particular idea does not conflict with presentation. But with pain on the other side we have introduced a main-spring of change and unrest, and we thus produce necessarily an idea not in harmony with existence. And this idea of a better and of a non-existing condition of things must directly destroy theoretical rest. But, if so, such an idea must be called impossible. There is no pain on the whole, and in the Absolute our whole nature must find satisfaction. For otherwise there is no theoretical harmony, and that harmony we saw must certainly exist. I shall ask in our last chapter if there is a way of avoiding this conclusion, but for the present we seem bound to accept it as true. We must not admit the possibility of an Absolute perfect in apprehension yet resting tranquilly in pain. The question as to actual evidence of defect in the universe will be discussed in Chapter xvii; and our position so far is this. We cannot argue directly that all sides of our nature must be satisfied, but indirectly we are led to the same result. For we are forced to assume theoretical satisfaction; and to suppose that existing one-sidedly, and together with practical discomfort, appears inadmissible. Such a state is a possibility which seems to contradict itself. It is a supposition to which, if we cannot find any ground in its favor, we have no right. For the present at least it is better to set it down as inconceivable.

And hence, for the present at least, we must believe that reality satisfies our whole being. Our main wants—for truth and life, and

for beauty and goodness—must all find satisfaction. And we have
seen that this consummation must somehow be experience, and be
individual. Every element of the universe, sensation, feeling, thought
and will, must be included within one comprehensive sentience. And
the question which now occurs is whether really we have a positive
idea of such sentience. Do we at all know what we mean when we
say that it is actual?

Fully to realize the existence of the Absolute is for finite beings
impossible. In order thus to know we should have to be, and then
we should not exist. This result is certain, and all attempts to avoid
it are illusory. But then the whole question turns on the sense in
which we are to understand "knowing." What is impossible is to
construct absolute life in its detail, to have the specific experience in
which it consists. But to gain an idea of its main features—an idea
true so far as it goes, though abstract and incomplete—is a different
endeavor. And it is a task, so far as I see, in which we may succeed.
For these main features, to some extent, are within our own experience; and again the idea of their combination is, in the abstract,
quite intelligible. And surely no more than this is wanted for a
knowledge of the Absolute. It is a knowledge which of course differs enormously from the fact. But it is true, for all that, while it
respects its own limits; and it seems fully attainable by the finite
intellect.

I will end this chapter by briefly mentioning the sources of such
knowledge. First, in mere feeling, or immediate presentation, we
have the experience of a whole. This whole contains diversity, and,
on the other hand, is not parted by relations. Such an experience,
we must admit, is most imperfect and unstable, and its inconsistencies
lead us at once to transcend it. Indeed, we hardly possess it as more
than that which we are in the act of losing. But it serves to suggest
to us the general idea of a total experience, where will and thought
and feeling may all once more be one. Further, this same unity, felt
below distinctions, shows itself later in a kind of hostility against
them. We find it in the efforts made both by theory and practice, each
to complete itself and so to pass into the other. And, again, the relational form, as we saw, pointed everywhere to a unity. It implies a
substantial totality beyond relations and above them, a whole endeavoring without success to realize itself in their detail. Further, the
ideas of goodness, and of the beautiful, suggest in different ways the
same result. They more or less involve the experience of a whole

beyond relations though full of diversity. Now, if we gather (as we can) such considerations into one, they will assuredly supply us with a positive idea. We gain from them the knowledge of a unity which transcends and yet contains every manifold appearance. They supply not an experience but an abstract idea, an idea which we make by uniting given elements. And the mode of union, once more in the abstract, is actually given. Thus we know what is meant by an experience, which embraces all divisions, and yet somehow possesses the direct nature of feeling. We can form the general idea of an absolute experience in which phenomenal distinctions are merged, a whole become immediate at a higher stage without losing any richness. Our complete inability to understand this concrete unity in detail is no good ground for our declining to entertain it. Such a ground would be irrational, and its principle could hardly everywhere be adhered to. But if we can realize at all the general features of the Absolute, if we can see that somehow they come together in a way known vaguely and in the abstract, our result is certain. Our conclusion, so far as it goes, is real knowledge of the Absolute, positive knowledge built on experience, and inevitable when we try to think consistently. . . .

4.

My Station and Its Duties

LET US TAKE a man, an Englishman as he is now, and try to point
out that, apart from what he has in common with others, apart from
what he has in common with others, apart from his sameness with
others, he is not an Englishman—nor a man at all; that if you take
him as something by himself, he is not what he is. Of course we do
not mean to say that he can not go out of England without disap-
pearing, nor, even if all the rest of the nation perished, that he
would not survive. What we mean to say is, that he is what he is
because he is a born and educated social being, and a member of
an individual social organism; that if you make an abstraction of
all this, which is the same in him and in others, what you have left
is not an Englishman, nor a man, but some I know not what residuum, which never has existed by itself, and does not so exist. If
we suppose the world of relations, in which he was born and bred,
never to have been, then we suppose the very essence of him not
to be; if we take that away, we have taken him away; and hence
he now is not an individual, in the sense of owing nothing to the
sphere of relations in which he finds himself, but does contain those
relations within himself as belonging to his very being; he is what
he is, in brief, so far as he is what others also are.

But we shall be cut short here with an objection. "It is impossible," we shall be told, "that two men should have the same thing
in common. You are confusing sameness and likeness." I say in
answer that I am not, and that the too probable objector I am
imagining probably knows the meanings of neither one word nor the
other. But this is a matter we do not intend to stay over, because it
is a metaphysical question we cannot discuss, and which, moreover,
we cannot be called on to discuss. We cannot be called on to
discuss it, because we have to do again here with sheer assertion,
which either is ignorant of or ignores the critical investigation of
the subject, and which, therefore, has no right to demand an answer.

These selections are from the essay "My Station and Its Duties" which forms
Chapter IV of *Ethical Studies*, a work first published in 1876.

We allude to it merely because it has become a sort of catchword
with "advanced thinkers." All that it comes to is this; first identity
and diversity are assumed to exclude one another, and therefore,
since diversity is a fact, it follows that there is no identity. Hence a
difficulty; because it has been seen long ago, and forces itself upon
every one, that denial of all identity brings you into sharp collision
with ordinary fact, and leads to total scepticism; so, to avoid this,
while we yet maintain the previous dogma, "resemblance" is brought
in—a concept which (I suppose I need not add) is not analyzed
or properly defined, and so does all the better. Against these assertions I shall put some others: viz. that identity and diversity, sameness and difference, imply one another, and depend for their meaning
on one another; that mere diversity is nonsense, just as mere
identity is also nonsense; that resemblance or likeness, strictly speaking, falls not in the objects, but in the person contemplating (liken-
ing, *vergleichend*); that "is A really like B?" does not mean "does
it seem like?" It may mean "would it seem like to everybody?," but
it generally means "is there an objective identity? Is there a point
or points the same in both, whether any one sees it or not?" We do
not talk of cases of "mistaken likeness"; we do not hang one man
because he is "exactly like" another, or at least we do not wish to
do so. We are the same as we were, not merely more or less like.
We have the same faith, hope, and purpose, and the same feelings
as another man has now, as ourselves had at another time—not
understanding thereby the numerical indistinguishedness of particular states and moments, but calling the feelings one and the same
feeling, because *what* is felt is the same, and not merely like. In
short, so far is it from being true that "sameness" is really "likeness,"
that it is utterly false that two things are really and objectively
"like," unless that means "more or less the same." So much by way
of counter assertion; and now let us turn to our facts.

The "individual" man, the man into whose essence his community with others does not enter, who does not include relation to
others in his very being, is, we say, a fiction, and in the light of facts
we have to examine him. Let us take him in the shape of an English
child as soon as he is born; for I suppose we ought not to go further
back. Let us take him as soon as he is separated from his mother,
and occupies a space clear and exclusive of all other human beings.
At this time, education and custom will, I imagine, be allowed to
have not as yet operated on him or lessened his "individuality."

But is he now a mere "individual," in the sense of not implying in his being identity with others? We can not say that, if we hold to the teaching of modern physiology. Physiology would tell us, in one language or another, that even now the child's mind is no passive "tabula rasa"; he has an inner, a yet undeveloped nature, which must largely determine his future individuality. What is this inner nature? Is it particular to himself? Certainly not all of it, will have to be the answer. The child is not fallen from heaven. He is born of certain parents who come of certain families, and he has in him the qualities of his parents, and, as breeders would say, of the strains from both sides. Much of it we can see, and more we believe to be latent, and, given certain (possible or impossible) conditions, ready to come to light. On the descent of mental qualities, modern investigation and popular experience, as expressed in uneducated vulgar opinion, altogether, I believe, support one another, and we need not linger here. But if the intellectual and active qualities do descend from ancestors, is it not, I would ask, quite clear that a man may have in him the same that his father and mother had, the same that his brothers and sisters have? And if any one objects to the word "same," I would put this to him. If, concerning two dogs allied in blood, I were to ask a man, "Is that of the same strain or stock as this?" and were answered, "No, not the same, but similar," should I not think one of these things, that the man either meant to deceive me, or was a "thinker," or a fool? . . .

. . . We see the child has been born at a certain time of parents of a certain race, and that means also of a certain degree of culture. It is the opinion of those best qualified to speak on the subject, that civilization is to some not inconsiderable extent hereditary; that aptitudes are developed, and are latent in the child at birth; and that it is a very different thing, even apart from education, to be born of civilized and of uncivilized ancestors. These "civilized tendencies," if we may use the phrase, are part of the essence of the child: he would only partly (if at all) be himself without them; he owes them to his ancestors, and his ancestors owe them to society. The ancestors were made what they were by the society they lived in. If in answer it be replied, "Yes, but individual ancestors were prior to their society," then that, to say the least of it, is a hazardous and unproved assertion, since man, so far as history can trace him back, is social; and if Mr. Darwin's conjecture as to the development of man from a social animal be received, we must say that man has never been anything but social, and society never was made by individual men. Nor, if the (baseless) assertion of the priority of individual men were allowed, would that destroy our case; for certainly our more immediate ancestors were social; and, whether society was manufactured previously by individuals or not, yet in their case it certainly was not so. They at all events have been so qualified by the common possessions of social mankind that, as members in the organism, they have become relative to the whole. If we suppose then that the results of the social life of the race are present in a latent and potential form in the child, can we deny that they are common property? Can we assert that they are not an element of sameness in all? Can we say that the individual is this individual, because he is exclusive, when, if we deduct from him what he includes, he loses characteristics which make him himself, and when again he does include what the others include, and there-fore does (how can we escape the consequence?) include in some sense the others also, just as they include him? By himself, then, what are we to call him? I confess I do not know, unless we name him a theoretical attempt to isolate what can not be isolated; and that, I suppose, has, out of our heads, no existence. But what he is really, and not in mere theory, can be described only as the specifi-cation or particularization of that which is common, which is the same amid diversity, and without which the "individual" would be so other than he is that we could not call him the same. . . .

. . . Let us now in detail compare the avantages of our present view with the defects of "duty for duty's sake." The objections we found fatal to that view may be stated as follows: (1) The universal was abstract. There was no content which belonged to it and was one with it; and the consequence was, that either nothing could be willed, or what was willed was willed not because of the universal, but capriciously. (2) The universal was "subjective." It certainly gave itself out as "objective," in the sense of being independent of this or that person, but still it was not real in the world. It did not come to us as what *was* in fact, it came as what in itself merely was to be, an inner notion in moral persons, which, at least perhaps, had not the power to carry itself out and transform the world. And self-realization, if it means will, does mean that we, in fact, do put ourselves forth and see ourselves actual in outer existence. Hence, by identifying ourselves with that which has not necessarily this existence, which is not master of the outer world, we can not secure our self-realization; since, when we have identified ourselves with the end, the end may still remain a mere inner end which does not accomplish itself, and so does not satisfy us. (3) The universal left a part of ourselves outside it. However much we tried to be good, however determined we were to make our will one with the good will, yet we never succeeded. There was always something left in us which was in contradiction with the good. And this we saw was even necessary, because morality meant and implied this contradiction, unless we accepted that form of conscientiousness which consists in the simple identification of one's conscience with one's own self (unless, i.e., the consciousness of the relation of my private self to myself as the good self be degraded into my self-consciousness of my mere private self as the good self); and this cannot be, if we are in earnest with morality. There thus remains a perpetual contradiction in myself, no less than in the world, between the "is to be" and the "is," a contradiction that can not be got rid of without getting rid of morality; for, as we saw, it is inherent in morality. The man cannot realize himself in himself as moral, because the conforming of his sensuous nature to the universal would be the radical suppression of it, and hence not only of himself, but also of the morality which is constituted by the relation of himself to the universal law. The man then cannot find self-realization in the morality of pure duty; because (1) he cannot look on his subjective self as the realized moral law; (2) he cannot look on the objective world as the realization of the moral law; (3) he cannot realize the moral law at all, because it is defined as that which has no particular content, and therefore no reality; or, if he gives it a content, then it is not the law he realizes, since the content is got not from the law, but from elsewhere. In short, duty for duty's sake is an unsolved contradiction, the standing "is to be," which, therefore, because it is to be, is *not*; and in which, therefore, since it is *not,* he cannot find himself realized nor satisfy himself.

These are serious defects: let us see how they are mended by "my station and its duties." In that (1) the universal is concrete; (2) it is objective; (3) it leaves nothing of us outside it.

(1) It is concrete, and yet not given by caprice. Let us take the latter first. It is not given by caprice; for, although within certain limits I may chose my station according to my own liking, yet I and every one else must have some station with duties pertaining

to it, and those duties do not depend on our opinion or liking. Certain circumstances, a certain position, call for a certain course. How I in particular know what my right course is, is a question we shall recur to hereafter—but at present we may take it as an obvious fact that in my station my particular duties are precribed to me, and I have them whether I wish to or not. And secondly, it is concrete. The universal to be realized is no abstraction, but an organic whole; a system where many spheres are subordinated to one sphere, and particular actions to spheres. This system is real in the detail of its functions, not out of them, and lives in its vital processes, not away from them. The organs are always at work for the whole, the whole is at work in the organs. And I am one of the organs. The universal then which I am to realize is the system which penetrates and subordinates to itself the particulars of all lives, and here and now in my life has this and that function in this and that case, in exercising which through my will it realizes itself as a whole, and me in it.

(2) It is "objective"; and this means that it does not stand over against the outer world as mere "subject" confronted by mere "object." In that sense of the words it is neither merely "objective" nor merely "subjective"; but it is that real identity of subject and object, which, as we have seen, is the only thing that satisfies our desires. The inner side does exist, but it is no more than the inside; it is one factor in the whole, and must not be separated from the other factor; and the mistake which is made by the morality which confines itself to the individual man, is just this attempt at the separation of what cannot be separated. The inner side certainly is a fact, and it can be distinguished from the rest of the whole; but it really is one element of the whole, depends on the whole for its being, and cannot be divided from it. Let us explain. The moral world, as we said, is a whole, and has two sides. There is an outer side, systems and institutions, from the family to the nation; this we may call the body of the moral world. And there must also be a soul, or else the body goes to pieces; every one knows that institutions without the spirit of them are dead. In the moral organism this spirit is in the will of the organs, as the will of the whole which, in and by the organs, carries out the organism and makes it alive, and which also (and this is the point to which attention is requested) is, and must be felt or known, in each organ as his own inward and personal will. It is quite clear that a nation is not strong without

public spirit, and is not public-spirited unless the members of it are public-spirited, i.e., feel the good of the public as a personal matter, or have it at their hearts. . . .

. . . To be moral, I must will my station and its duties; that is, I will to particularize the moral system truly in a given case; and the other side to this act is, that the moral system wills to particularize itself in a given station and functions, i.e., in my actions and by my will. In other words, my moral self is not simply mine; it is not an inner which belongs simply to me; and further, it is not a mere inner at all, but it is the soul which animates the body and lives in it, and would not be the soul if it had not a body and *its* body. The objective organism, the systematized moral world, is the reality of the moral will; my duties on the inside answer to due functions on the outside. There is no need here for a pre-established or a postulated harmony, for the moral whole is the identity of both sides; my private choice, so far as I am moral, is the mere form of bestowing myself on, and identifying myself with, the will of the moral organism, which realizes in its process both itself and myself. Hence we see that what I have to do I have not to force on a recalcitrant world; I have to fill my place—the place that waits for me to fill it; to make my private self the means, my life the sphere and the function of the soul of the whole, which thus, personal in me, externalizes both itself and me into a solid reality, which is both mine and its.

(3) What we come to now is the third superiority of "my station and its duties." The universal which is the end, and which we have seen is concrete and does realize itself, does also more. It gets rid of the contradiction between duty and the "empirical" self; it does not in its realization leave me for ever outside and unrealized.

In "duty for duty's sake" we were always unsatisfied, no nearer our goal at the end than at the beginning. There we had the fixed antithesis of the sensuous self on one side and a nonsensuous moral ideal on the other—a standing contradiction which brought with it a perpetual self-deceit, or the depressing perpetual confession that I am not what I ought to be in my inner heart, and that I never can be so. Duty, we thus saw, was an infinite process, an unending "not-yet"; a continual "not" with an everlasting "to be," or an abiding "to be" with a ceaseless "not."

From this last peevish enemy we are again delivered by "my station and its duties." There I realize myself morally, so that not only what ought to be in the world is, but I am what I ought to be, and find so my contentment and satisfaction. If this were not the case, when we consider that the ordinary moral man is self-contented and happy, we should be forced to accuse him of immorality, and we do not do this; we say he most likely might be better, but we do not say that he is bad, or need consider himself so. Why is this? It is because "my station and its duties" teaches us to identify others and ourselves with the station we fill; to consider that as good, and by virtue of that to consider others and ourselves good too. It teaches us that a man who does his work in the world is good, notwithstanding his faults, if his faults do not prevent him from fulfilling his station. It tells us that the heart is an idle abstraction; we are not to think of it, nor must we look at our insides, but at our work and our life, and say to ourselves, Am I fulfilling my appointed function or not? Fulfill it we can, if we will: what we have to do is not so much better than the world that we cannot do it; the world is there waiting for it; my duties are my rights. On the one hand, I am not likely to be much better than the world asks me to be; on the other hand, if I can take my place in the world I ought not to be discontented. Here we must not be misunderstood; we do not say that the false self, the habits and desires opposed to the good will, are extinguished. Though negated, they never are all of them entirely suppressed, and cannot be. Hence, we must not say that any man really does fill his station to the full height of his capacity; nor must we say of any man that he cannot perform his function better than he does, for we all can do so, and should try to do so. We do not wish to deny what are plain moral facts, nor in any way to slur them over.

How then does the contradiction disappear? It disappears by my identifying myself with the good will that I realize in the world, by my refusing to identify myself with the bad will of my private self. So far as I am one with the good will, living as a member in the moral organism, I am to consider myself real, and I am not to consider the false self real. That cannot be attributed to me in my character of member in the organism. Even in me the false existence of it has been partly suppressed by that organism; and, so far as the organism is concerned, it is wholly suppressed, because contradicted in its results, and allowed no reality. Hence, not existing for the organism, it does not exist for me as a member thereof; and only as a member thereof do I hold myself to be real. And yet this is not justification by faith, for we not only trust, but see, that despite our faults the moral world stands fast, and we in and by it. It is like faith, however, in this, that not merely by thinking ourselves, but by willing ourselves as such, can we look on ourselves as organs in a good whole, and so ourselves good. And further, the knowledge that as members of the system we are real, and not otherwise, encourages us more and more to identify ourselves with that system; to make ourselves better, and so more real, since we see that the good is real, and that nothing else is.

Or, to repeat it, in education my self by habituation has been growing into one with the good self around me, and by my free acceptance of my lot hereafter I consciously make myself one with the good, so that, though bad habits cling to and even arise in me, yet I can not but be aware of myself as the reality of the good will. That is my essential side; my imperfections are not, and practically they do not matter. The good will in the world realizes itself by and in imperfect instruments, and in spite of them. The work is done, and so long as I will my part of the work and do it (as I do), I feel that, if I perform the function, I *am* the organ, and that my faults, if they do not matter to my station, do not matter to me. My heart I am not to think of, except to tell by my work whether it is in my work, and one with the moral whole; and if that is so, I have the consciousness of absolute reality in the good because of and by myself, and in myself because of and through the good; and with that I am satisfied, and have no right to be dissatisfied.

The individual's consciousness of himself is inseparable from the knowing himself as an organ of the whole; and the residuum falls more and more into the background, so that he thinks of it, if at all, not as himself, but as an idle appendage. For his nature now is not distinct from his "artificial self." He is related to the living moral system not as to a foreign body; his relation to it is "too inward even for faith," since faith implies a certain separation. It is no other-world that he cannot see but must trust to: he feels himself in it, and it in him; in a word, the self-consciousness of himself *is* the self-consciousness of the whole in him, and his will is the will which sees in him its accomplishment by him; it is the free will which knows itself as the free will, and, as this, beholds its realization and is more than content.

BERNARD BOSANQUET

(1848-1923)

Bosanquet's philosophy is similar to Bradley's but has a much less negative emphasis than *Appearance and Reality*. Selection 1 gives an idea of Bosanquet's wide view of logic, standing in striking contrast to the formalized and abstract logic one finds in logical textbooks from Aristotle to the most advanced logicians of the present day. This is further elucidated in Selection 2, which is chosen as giving a good idea of the coherence theory of truth, although this term is not used there. Selection 3 is important as a defense of the internal theory of relations. Selection 4 shows in its more moderate form the tendency of absolute idealists to exalt the state and is therefore selected as an example of a political philosophy with which "idealism" (though by no means all idealists) has been specially associated in the past.

1.
Life and Philosophy

PHILOSOPHY, I take it, is its own criterion. No experience of life, nor any partial aspect of knowledge, can be more to it than a suggestion or a stimulus. Nevertheless, since experience in the broad sense is all we have, our work as students of philosophy must take its form and colour from what we have most deeply made our own in life; or indeed it might be as true to say that what we have most deeply made our own in life has been selectively determined by the same leanings and impulses which our philosophy has expressed.

Thus, being asked for some account of my philosophy, and believing that if it ever could have interest for anyone, that interest would surely be absent from any brief abstract or bird's-eye view

This essay was Bosanquet's contribution to the first series of *Contemporary British Philosophy* (ed. J. H. Muirhead). It is here reprinted by the kind permission of George Allen and Unwin Ltd., London, and the Macmillan Co., New York. *Contemporary British Philosophy* was first published in 1924, the year after Bosanquet's death.

of what I have tried my best to exhibit always in concrete detail, I
am going, in the present paper, to say something about the things
which I have most deeply made my own, or, in a word, have cared
for most in life, attempting to indicate throughout their respective
functions as theoretical impulses in my work. Of course it may be
said: "This is autobiography, not philosophy; what is it doing here?"
But what I mean is not exactly autobiography; it is referring one's
theories to the needs which drove him to them; needs partly springing from life and from current experience, partly again from the
previous theory of others. I am sure such an account would interest
me in connection with anyone whose thought I at all value; and it
seems to me my best chance of explaining my own attitude in a
small space so as to interest anyone else.

On this line I will begin without further preface, and will do the
best I can.

1. A friend, a very competent philosopher, told me the other
day that he had been greatly helped in understanding my social and
political theory by having paid a visit to my old home on a large
Northumbrian farm. It is a place where for several generations
there has reigned a practice of business efficiency together with a
spirit of cordial co-operation and neighborly kindness. As Huxley
once said—I quote from memory: "In teaching a boy science you
should let him feel the pull of the magnet for himself," so it seems
to me that a constant habituation, from childhood up, to the feeling of the co-operative will and to what Miss Follett calls "the art
of living together," is a sound starting-point for social theory. After
such a habituation the doctrine of the real social will, for example,
comes to one as the recognition of an obvious and solid fact; and
the difficulties which are raised on the ground of counter-volitions,
tensions, and lacunæ in its formation, seem to be nothing but what
you expect in speaking of a will at all. "Where, in particular, are
you to find the actual social will?" Well, where in particular are
you to find your actual will or mine? Only in the several successive
and distinct decisions of every day, hour, or minute? Surely this is
to abandon the idea of a man's will. What you can say, and all you
can say, is: "When one lives with him, and has learned to act and
feel with him, one sees that on the whole this is what he wants and
what he sticks to." And for a social body, if you have in yourself
any social habit at all, you can say this much at least, and often
more. For the social spirit is more fully expressed, because of the

needs of external co-operation, than the private will. It is indeed the completer fact in which the private will finds form and stability.

And so with "the art of living together." To have been accustomed to it from day to day, and to the constant discussion and consideration of its failures and its successes and their respective reasons, is a leading which, "when the principle comes," as Plato says, introduces you to a world of problems, intricate and arduous enough in all conscience, but one of which the secret is after all in the main an open secret—the concrete unity of life as it is lived, overriding abstractions like bare pleasure or duty, for example, or like the meaningless opposition of mere egoism and altruism.

When things of this kind, the will and the art, have taken their place in the basis of life as rooted interests, they continue to develop their effect throughout the practical and theoretical elements of the environment, such as are suggested for my own lifetime by the names of T. H. Green, Arnold Toynbee, and C. S. Loch; so that any scepticism which takes the line that such things are not solid realities and ruling elements in the world, simply falls dead, as if it were denying that steam or electricity can do work. For a student, then, to draw out their nature as given in social and political life, to place them in relation with other forms of spiritual being, and to exhibit the comparatively incoherent and artificial nature of those doctrines "of the first look" on which individualism and its pseudo-liberty and pseudo-sovereignty rest becomes a compelling and inevitable task. And it is a task which readily connects itself with other endeavors to exhibit truth and reality in the light of the criterion which is the positive non-contradictory whole.

2. Another early experience was of great significance to me, just when I was beginning to reflect critically on the New Testament narrative. I was persuaded, I suspect for the good of my soul, to go to hear at a chapel in London the distinguished preacher, Dr. Moorhouse, afterwards Bishop of Manchester. After discussing some of the current criticisms on the New Testament story, the preacher broke forth with extreme emotion: "But what are all these reasonings to me? I *know* that these things are true." I left the chapel with two convictions firmly fixed in my mind, convictions which seemed then to have become explicit, but which, of course, had long been forming themselves. The first was that such a speaker evidently had hold of an experience which brought him strength and inspiration. The second was that this experience could not conceivably be what

he seemed to me to identify it with (here I may have misjudged him, but I am clear as to the impression I carried away at the time), viz. an assurance that certain events in history had actually taken place.

Convictions like these, once more, adopted into the basis of thought, called one in principle to the task of interpreting such experiences. If they did not indicate facts in history, what did they indicate? Plainly, it seemed, there were values in life, and accessible values; but it was possible to look for them in the wrong place. And where ought one to look for them? The need of a criterion to distinguish the accident from the essence became obvious; and this being so, the notion of "the real thing," that in the experience which affirmed and maintained itself with power, what drew the rest with it and held it in place, in short, of the whole as a criterion, could not be far off.

3. In groping among the connected problems thus forced upon the mind, one came perpetually across a current phrase—"the other world." Even to enumerate the multiple forms of this conception, and its antithesis, would demand a considerable space. Their common essence lay in the connection or opposition of value and remoteness.

In this context two theoretical influences, closely allied to one another, made themselves emphatically felt, and one experience which was at that crisis almost new to me. The theoretical impulses were those of Plato and Hegel: the relatively new experience was that of æsthetic value.

Plato, in particular, came as a revelation; not as confirming the dualism of "this" world and "the other," but because, against one's hazy expectation, and in opposition to the current and more or less popular legends of his meaning, it was so plain and obvious that his true passion was for the unity of things and, as guides to its nature, for science and goodness. Relativity and appearance, indeed, were not left out; but the amazing point, in contrast with the Plato of everyday acceptation, was the way in which they came in. If his main passion was for the unity of the universe, it was no less a passion for analyzing, as relative to the impotence of finite minds, the varying levels of the actual scenes and experiences in which they severally and particularly live. His hunger for science and his passion for goodness obviously meant that "the other world" was not in its nature remote, but became here and now for you if you could see it and live it; and the two passions coincided in the vision of the universe as that which alone could satisfy the whole intelligence and the total desire. The law of value, as he laid it down for all time, "that which is filled with the more real, is more really filled," together with his doctrine of the increasing concreteness and vital stability of the higher experiences, made an end of dualism in principle, though fragments of dualistic formulæ might float in the ocean of his thought undissolved for the moment.

More particularly, the doctrine of the divine spirit as present in the human society, inherited from Plato by Christianity, and interpreting and insisting upon social education and habituation as that of which I previously spoke, completed in principle the reconciliation of "the other world" with "this"; and when Hegel told us, in so many words, that the object-matter of philosophy was never anything abstruse and remote, but always something concrete and in the highest sense present, the ghost of the other world was finally laid, as in Plato it had been laid in principle.

Only it was to be borne in mind that its otherness was not spoken of without a reason. You could and often did live in a world intellectually, morally, and æsthetically mean and horrible, and because of this it was desirable and indeed indispensable to see and feel in its whole intensity the contrast with the "other" world, which yet, to apply St. Paul's expression, "was not another."

4. A new experience which reinforced and further interpreted the sense of socio-political unity, and the vision of cosmic unity as postulated by science and goodness, was, as I said, the æsthetic experience.

The genuineness of such experience in those who are not specially endowed for its reception is apt to be held doubtful. On this point, so far as it touches the philosophical student's right to comment upon the significance of beauty, I will make just three short observations. First, it appears to me that recent instructed opinion, while rightly intolerant of spurious æsthetic sentiment and gossip, is willing to concede a serious value to the simple love of beauty in unpretending minds. All who go far with William Morris are bound, I think, to such an attitude. And secondly, I would urge that the world of poetry, which is in some ways free from the technical conditions, which in the specialized arts demand special endowments almost physical in nature, is not to be treated as outside and alien to "art"; but rather exhibits the essence of art at once in its hightest and in its most accessible forms. A lover of poetry is not disqualified for æsthetic experience though he were blind and deaf. And thirdly, what perhaps would have been by itself enough to say, people should take our suggestions on their merits, as they find them. It is absolutely and totally impossible to predict how much truth this or that mind may get from a given basis in experience. It is the great test of minds; and yet there is in it also an element of luck. You cannot tell till you try.

Now this æsthetic experience has a prerogative bearing on the meaning with which we recognize "another world." It gives us a present world, a world which is even one with the world we live in, but yet is twice-born, is at once its own truest self and the profoundest revelation that itself can convey. Words like these, indeed, must even weaken the experience they indicate. We all know it in fact, whether or no we care to describe it in general language. We know that it takes us into a new world, which is the old at its best. In this aspect the æsthetic experience has a profound speculative interest, and after coming under the influence, first of Ruskin, and then, and most especially, of William Morris, I was led to trace its operation on the passage from Kant's antitheses to the concrete and objective ideas by which, in the last decade of the eighteenth century, the beginnings of nineteenth-century philosophy took form. In beauty we have the meeting-point of Nature and Freedom, Kant has said in effect. In beauty man is free without ceasing to be sensuous; or again, poetry and art have two conditions: they must arise above the actual and remain within the sensuous. These are the sayings of Schiller; and it was the unity thus recognized of the universal with the particular, of freedom with necessity, of the spiritual with the natural, which in Hegel's judgment, passed into the principle of knowledge and existence in Schelling's philosophy, which was the first fully to recognize the absolute stand-point, and recognized it in this synthesis. Here the whole apparatus of traditional dualism became in principle once and forever obsolete. This world and the other, the *a posteriori* and the *a priori,* the natural and the supernatural, with all their family, taken as signifying antithetical realms of being and experience, were for the future idle tales.

But at the same time, as we urged in speaking of Plato, the significance at which they had really aimed was not abolished but intensified, and the opposition between the worlds of truth, beauty and goodness, and those of falsehood, ugliness and evil acquired a new poignancy from being referred to a common root in the spiritual life.

And the paradox of beauty has a further suggestion, to which we shall return. It is not so very far from the essence of the beautiful as interperted in the sentences cited above to the essence of religious faith which has been described as "rising into another world while remaining here."

5. Yet another aspect in which reality presents itself as a concrete unity replacing antithetical abstractions, helped to carry forward my thought in the direction just indicated. Attention had been intensely focussed in England on the Hedonistic controversy, especially in connection with John Stuart Mill's *Utilitarianism* and Henry Sidgwick's *Methods of Ethics*. For many of us the publication of Mr. F. H. Bradley's *Ethical Studies* in 1876—T. H. Green's conceptions being known at the time to his students through his lectures, but not yet made public in a treatise—was an epoch-making event, not merely as restating and concluding the discussion of Hedonism, but because of a philosophical significance which far transcended that particular subject-matter. And I confess that so far as my knowledge of subsequent English theory carries me, it still appears to me surprising that the strictly philosophical implications of this work have not produced a more complete transformation, not merely of ethical doctrine, but of the entire interpretation and stand-point from which the permanent value of Kantian ethics can be and ought to be approached. It appears to me absolutely plain that by developing the conception of "law universal" into that of a concrete system, embodied in the actual whole of existing institutions, and yet furnishing through its particulars a content in which the universal end lives and grows within the individual will, a meaning is given to the Kantian ethical idea which Kant very likely would have disowned, but which really satisfies the theoretical demand which his system recognized but failed to meet. From the same line of thought, in connection with the factors insisted on above, we get suggestions for dealing with the demand involved in the Thing-in-itself or the Noumenon, restoring to the latter term its true and Platonic meaning of that which is most fully and determinately experienced, and superseding the ridiculous usage in which "what is understood" had become almost equivalent to "what cannot be known." Here, again, the ghost of the other world is laid, and the concrete universal of experience is established as the typical reality.

But the implication takes us yet further, and the incompleteness of the moral stand-point involves an appeal to the religious experience. This, as we saw just now, is akin in its meeting of extremes to the æsthetic attitude, and is the province in which the antithesis of this world and the other is the most poignant and fundamental experience, and its transcendence is the deepest need of man.

From this study of the religious experience, as from the treatment of ethics proper in the same volume, I should have expected a greater effect upon contemporary philosophy than it appears to have produced. Partly its influence must have been diminished by the fact that it soon passed out of print and has remained inaccessible to most students ever since. One constantly observes that arguments and ideas derived from it appear unfamiliar to most writers of the day, and when reproduced by others, even if favourably received, are received as novelties. Partly, too, I am convinced that the book, though brilliantly written, suffered from the excess of thought and experience which it contained. It is to most books on philosophy like Dickens or Meredith to most novels; a page of it would dilute into a hundred of any other. At this point I have in mind especially the fundamental contrast between the moral and the religious attitude, according to which morality lies essentially in a recognition of the "ought-to-be" which is not (the *sollen,* the *dover essere*), and therefore involves an individualistic conception of perfectibility (individualistic, because its whole point is the relation of the ought-to-be to the individual will) in particular finite spirits throughout a temporal progression. While religion, implying as a subordinate feature all that morality can imply of duty and self-improvement, is understood to lie essentially in a union by faith and will with a real supreme perfection in which finite imperfection, though actual, is felt to be transcended and abolished. The very widespread influence of the ethical culture movement and a progressive temper akin to it, throughout our higher civilization, appears to me to show that the philosophical lesson typically inherent in the argument to which I am referring has not at all been mastered by the enlightenment of to-day; and that, in the latter's lofty aspiration to a pure humanistic ethic, it has lost hold of the truth which had been won by religion in the ancient doctrine for which justification was essentially by faith. Mysticism, on the other side, keeps alive the genuine insight; but mysticism in its full contention is not everyone's affair, and it is distressing to see the central and sober realities of religion divided between the ethical and the mystical extremes, in each of which, taken apart, there is an inherent tendency to extravagance. Compare Benedetto Croce with Jakob Böhme, and ask yourself if a reasonable man could sit down with either. Certainly, compared with these, the "Concluding Remarks" of *Ethical Studies* embody, in my judgment, a view as much deeper than the one as it is saner than the other.

6. All the above modes of experience, which in so many ways have proved their attraction for the mind, are linked together in a central enthusiasm when our attention is thoroughly focussed on thought as the determination of reality, and on logic as the theory of thought.

Current experience may be stimulating through its negations no less than its affirmations; and of all the platitudes by which it has from my mind's first awakening driven me to rebellion, none were more superficial than those implied in the phrases "pure thought" and "mere logic" or "merely logical," whether employed by the professed friends of reason or its acknowledged foes. If, indeed, pure thought were taken to mean genuine thinking, as contrasted with irrelevant associative transition, that might serve well enough, and would fairly coincide with the meaning which I shall ascribe below to what can genuinely be called "logic" and "logical." But pure thought as an ideal, whether imputed or accepted, of thinking which has learned nothing from the universe and in no way determines it by affirmation, exhibits itself to my mind as the very type of impotence and self-contradiction, false alike as an imputation by the foes of reason, and as an aspiration of its would-be friends.

Thought, as I understand the matter, is always an affirmation about reality through the process of particular minds. Its conception is correlative to that of reality. If you ask what reality is, you can in the end say nothing but that it is the whole which thought is always endeavouring to affirm. And if you ask what thought is, you can in the end say nothing but that it is the central function of mind in affirming its partial world to belong to the real universe. Thought which deals with no given, and constructs no order is a *res nihili*. Thus it is an incomplete description even to qualify thought as we did just now, by the term "function of mind," without calling attention to its other aspects as the self-revelation of reality. The "I think," of which so much has been heard, is on one side a deceptive phrase. It would avoid misapprehension if we were rather to

say (Mr. Russell has suggested it, and I have urged what amounts
to the same point): "It thinks in me" or "my world in me takes the
shape that———." As Green said long ago, the essence of thought is
not a mental faculty, but in the objective order of things. We bring
the two sides together if we say it is the control exercised by reality
over mental process.

The same thing in principle with the fallacious idea of "pure
thought" is the popular conception of "logic," "mere logic," "a
merely logical contradiction," "the strictly logical application of a
principle." Our great and splendid neighbour across the Channel
believes itself to be especially endowed with a logical genius, and
we believe ourselves to believe it also, and with a significantly proud
self-depreciation we say of ourselves by contrast that we are not a
logical nation, that we do not love logic; that England—was it not
Disraeli who told us so, and did he say "England" or in general
terms "a nation"?—"is not governed by logic but by rhetoric." So
that it seemed to me "like a sober man among drunkards" when
Dr. McTaggart with his indomitable courage declared that "no man
ever went about to break logic, but in the end logic broke him."
What we Englishmen believe in, then, I hold, after all is logic, complete, concrete and solid inference, and it is this which we sometimes
contrast with the "merely logical," or the "purely logical contradiction." We feel the full nauseousness of modern superficial sentiment on this point when we read in a clever article that "men are
busied to-day in lifting the jewel of human vision out of the mire
of logic." The writer might reply—I hope he would—that the logic
on which he pours contempt is just the "mere logic" which I am
repudiating, and that therefore he is making the same point as
myself, in obedience to Plato's magnificent educational revelation,
and not, as his words suggest, in angry caricature directed against
it. But I am afraid he cannot really mean that. His language may
be aimed against formalism; but I feel pretty sure he is unaware
that formalism is not the essence of logic.

To me, then, this whole conception of "mere logic" was from
the first repulsive. It drove me in the opposite direction. To me,
from the first, logic was no isolated discipline reposing on axioms
and principles peculiar to itself, but was simply the clear perception
of the way in which, through their connection and co-operation,
the natures that compose the universe frame and mold the assertions which constitute our thought. A contradiction, for example,

I took to mean, as explained by Plato, a collision in which different elements of experience attempt to occupy the same place in the same system. By a "logical" contradiction I understood not something different from this, some play of formulæ by themselves, but any such collision distinctly apprehended in its typical conditions, and, if fully stated, in the typical modifications of them by which it might be removed. The logical adherence to a principle did not mean the literal and unconsidering endeavour to apply it everywhere by itself, down to the bitter end—this would be *a*logical. It meant the appreciation of it in all its bearings, as arising from its necessary implication, when fully considered, in some living individual reality. The universal, the very life and spirit of logic, did not mean a general predicate, but the plastic unity of an inclusive system. The syllogism itself, in its central paradox typical of all inference, the new springing necessarily from the old, represented, if Ruskin is right, in the work of the early painter of the Spanish chapel at Santa Maria Novella in Florence, by the living and leafy spray, thus ranks itself as the identification of our mind with the very growing-point of thought, the leaping and vital flame by which a whole system exhibits its concentrated life within a single focus, creating a something which is at once the old in the new and the new in the old.

Thus it always appeared to me that of all silly superficialities the opposition of logic to feeling was the silliest. Plato's principle seemed so obvious and so inevitable, that it takes the whole object to elicit the whole mind. And as Aristotle told us in his *Æsthetic,* no object is a whole which is not logically coherent. This is one of the truths which is always admitted, and never applied. The emotional absorbing or carrying power which belongs to great ideas, great characters, great works of art, is measured by the depth and spread of their roots and sources in reality; and this again is measured by their logical power, their power to develop and sustain coherence with the whole. It is a blundering rejoinder to say that bare consistency is a poor ideal, and a fraud upon reality; bare consistency is bare because it is slight and shallow. The incoherence of great creations and great characters is a coherence with the profounder things; and the profounder things are the things that more thoroughly penetrate the real.

Thus, in the genuine logic, which embodies the natural impulse to seek truth and reality in what satisfies the more complex demand,

we have "the whole" operating explicitly as the criterion. Implicit
in all the modes of experience which attracted us throughout, it is
now considered in its own typical manifestations, in which the idea
of system, the spirit of the concrete universal, in other words, of
individuality, is the central essence. From the first my delight was
in the successive shapes in which this essence had embodied its
advance, as the exhibition of the comprehensive and coherent character of the whole, and of the interconnecting modes of implication,
known as inference, by which the world of fact and truth made its
elements available for the supplementation of one another by way
of development and correction.

I will illustrate the superior effectiveness of such a conception
to that which acquiesces in the traditional formulæ, first, from the
difficulty which arises owing to the possible ambiguity of the middle
term in every syllogism.

> A deadly poison is one that kills
> Arsenic is a deadly poison
> . . . Arsenic kills.

Of course the conclusion, read as a universal statement, is bad. The
middle term in the major premise is read as implying a fatal dose
with the conditions necessary to its action. In the minor premise it
may just as well be taken to omit these particulars, and merely to
qualify "arsenic" as "combustible" qualifies "wood." And such ambiguity seems inevitable. You could always, though not always with
equal plausibility, put a double sense on the middle term. You could
always say that to preserve a single sense in it, it must be specially
interpreted.

But this trouble merely comes of working with bare formulæ in
their text-book shape, to which no one would think of restricting
himself in a serious inquiry. You would have the same difficulty in
any argument reduced to a detached formula. The formula of the
syllogism, for all that, is quite sound. But of course it is only a
beginning. You cannot guard against all misapprehensions in a
couple of sentences. For a serious conclusion you must cover a large
area of investigation; and you must exhibit all your reasons or conditions or middle terms in graduated series, so that where one
meaning leaves off another begins, and the whole ground is covered,
each nexus being linked to its special and appropriate consequence
and explicitly distinguished at every frontier where it passes into

any other. Then, of course, "deadly poison" would be one of a series of characters determined in quantity and quality, and all together laying down precisely the conditions of fatal administration continuously with those which exclude it. You would have in place of a nexus merely named by a general name a concrete system of concomitant variations. And of course in the use of common language and common sense something approaching to such a system is presupposed. You supply in your mind the typical conditions which are obviously intended to be assumed in the statement.

When this is done, either implicitly as in common sense or explicitly as in science, there is no room for your middle term to go wrong. The exhibition of the relevant system holds the particulars in their right places. It is like the point which I believe is now recognized about the inheritance even of Mendelian characters. *All* inheritance whatever is conditional on environment. There is no absolute or abstract heredity. An organism cannot develop any character except under conditions which it can develop itself. Thus, also, of course, we assume common sense in the interpretation of current language. We must postulate, in interpreting, the conditions which a statement is obviously intended to imply.

A kindred advantage is obtained in the treatment of error. If we understand the judgment as an isolated relation, apart from its connection with knowledge as a whole, the treatment of error becomes—what we see in Mr. Russell's *Analysis of Mind,* p. 272. If words take their meaning from facts, each to each, every fact being equally taken as a fact, and if the objective reference of propositions, which are true or false, is derived from the meanings of words by putting them together, then *prima facie* no proposition can be false whose words have meanings. And you have to introduce such a metaphor as pointing to or away from the fact to explain the existence of false propositions.

But if the matter is regarded with reference to the whole system of knowledge, we see that facts are differently considered when asserted as realities and when entertained as mere meanings of words. In the former case they are taken as elements in the real world; in the latter they are attended to each for itself, out of relation to the whole system. So considered, they are not treated as actual facts, but as possibilities. They are isolated by the fact that we ignore the conditions under which alone they can belong to reality; and, thus isolated, we call them possibilities, because not in a position to be actually or unconditionally affirmed, though we know that under some conditions or other it would be right to affirm them. For ultimately, even ideas which are thus merely entertained, are in some sense or other taken as representing facts which belong to reality. Thus there is room for a proposition which has a meaning and yet is false, viz., when a fact which is the meaning of an idea entertained as merely possible (conditional) is asserted as actual (unconditionally asserted). Possibilities are the source of the false objectives which we are told are not to be found. I believe I was the first to use in English the term objective reference, precisely in order to make the distinction which Mr. Russell's use of it confounds: the distinction between meaning and truth, between that "objective reference" which is the meaning of a word conditionally predicable, and the "affirmation" made by a proposition which predicates unconditionally. Error arises then quite simply, when the whole of knowledge, as present, through insufficient determination leaves alternatives possible, and there is therefore nothing to save us from affirming one which the reality, if more fully known, would be seen to exclude. The selection of the alternative we assert, its conditions not being fully known, must be held *prima facie* for us a matter of chance; and unquestionably there is room for the case insisted on by a certain view, that moral perversity has much to do—some say everything to do—with error. We are in a lacuna of the determining system, and anything may turn the scale.

I cannot think the difficulty about error would be felt as much as it is, if we brought to bear on it our common sense and our most trivial everyday experience. I find simple and obvious examples every hour of the day. It, again, is a favourite province of observation, which has greatly influenced my theory. I come in from a walk, and cannot find my handkerchief. I am sure I put it back in my pocket. "No doubt; but was it not your overcoat pocket?" I want to take my black pencil out of my pocket; I pull out a small smooth cylinder two inches long, but it is my blue pencil. I go to the electric switches to turn the downstairs light on, and I turn the upstairs light off. Always there is some point clear and settled; but under it there are varying possibilities, alternative cases, and between these my present consciousness has nothing to decide it. I may not even know or recollect at the moment that there is an alternative. Of course we must remember that the error, when being made, seems truth; and I may take it *faute de mieux,* because I can see no better alternative. Thus, What is freedom? You are sure you mean by it a state in which you can assert yourself. But if your thought has not taken you beyond this, then you may jump at the alternatives under it which first comes to hand. "It is absence of restraint." And you may never hit on the further alternative which the reality further pursued would give you. "It is capacity meeting opportunity." The reservoir of possible error, then, so to speak, is that of facts whose conditions are partially or very slightly known, the storehouse of possible alternatives. Every general name suggests a number of them, cases possible starting from it alone. Is a round square intelligible? Why, yes, *prima facie*. We know "round" and we know "square." And formally, therefore, we may try to treat "square" as a possible alternative under "round," or vice versa. And so the phrase designates a problem which we can attempt, though we cannot solve it.

All this follows from the graduated dependence of every so-called "fact" on the whole system of reality as present in knowledge. Error rests simply on inadequate determination within a system, which leaves alternative possibilities open, i.e., dependent on unknown conditions.

7. This recognition of the spirit of logic as the essential criterion of value and reality throughout experience, in accordance with the principle that it takes the whole reality to elicit the whole mind, was for me intensified from the first by a strong repugnance, in the moral and religious field, to finding freedom in anything that savored of chance or caprice. "Necessity is laid upon me" seemed in all the higher walks of life, in conduct, in religious unity, in art, and in love, to be the utterance which the human soul at its fullest stretch demanded and embodied. It was a trivial and external reinforcement of this conviction, but so far significant, to reflect how hopeless and inconceivable would be freedom of thought or action in a world where chance prevailed—and if admitted at all it must prevail, for how be warned of its intervention here or there?—that is, where process showed a solution of continuity, and synthetic unity was severed. One could not but observe how deeply, in confirmation of the full doctrine of life-mind in Plato and Aristotle, the roots of intelligence sink into the foundations of nature, and how, as the behaviourist tells us to-day, the salient features of thought, the habits which exhibit the simplest operation of what will be the logical universal, are traceable in organic beings long before they

reveal themselves in explicit consciousness. It seemed plain throughout that the basis and character of freedom lay not in simple initia-
tions but in an equipment capable of embodying extraordinarily
delicate responses to extraordinarily varied environments, and that
it is on capacities of such a nature that the possibility of self-
realization in the universe was and essentially must be founded.
Thus for freedom as for truth and reality, freedom in society, in
morals, and in all action and expression, once more the condition
and criterion was the participation in the whole, by union with which
alone the finite spirit could become what it had in it to be.

What then is the true method of moral self-determination in
which freedom is realized? It is an application, often instinctive and
unconscious, of the criterion we have been discussing. Its motto is
in a single sentence, "To be equal to the situation"—to realize,
that is, the organized consciousness, the tradition, so to speak, of
the self as a whole, in action which deals with practical problems as
sound theory deals with such as are theoretical. Its object is to
realize the greatest value, as the theorist's is to realize the greatest
truth. This we see in the simple phrase of Xenophon's Socrates, noting the failure of the incontinent man, "He does not attend to the
most important things"; or, as we should say, he is not guided by
a true sense of values. This idea of study and habituation in the art
of living is essential to the understanding of Socrates' conception of
"knowledge of the good," which gives goodness the whole force of
an overmastering professional enthusiasm comparable to that of
the trained craftsman, so that habit is involved in the idea from the
very first, and it is the root of Aristotle's conception of moral education, essentially one with that of Socrates as described in the
Republic, instead of being, as is often supposed, its opposite. The
identification of goodness with the trained and formed character,
skilled and enthusiastic in realizing the ideal self which is the whole,
has always been my delight; and I hold any intellectualistic interpretation of Socrates' and Plato's meaning to be an anachronism and
a blunder. But I cannot go further into this matter here.

8. So far, I venture to think, the character of experience as a
revelation of the world of values is pretty clear. It rests, in every
special aspect, on ideal experiment, that is to say, on the experienced
satisfaction which we attain, in proportion as in any form of living
we find ourselves for the moment beyond the field of contradiction.

And so far the conclusion to a real and absolute world of values rests on the suggestive force of these special experiences.

The question now presses upon us whether we can carry the matter further. Can we understand or appreciate the world of eternal values in its character as a whole? Have we any experience which stands to the theory of its ultimate nature as the special experiences were found to stand to the theories of beauty, of ethics, or of religion?

It seems plain that we can have no such experience completely. To possess completely the world of eternal values would obviously involve a total realization and solution of contradictions incompatible with the self-revelation of the universe through particular beings. Our inference to any total perfection must be what might be called a matter of concomitant variations, resting on the impossibility of closing the ideal advance, that is, of drawing a line where the argument and the experience of value can go no further. And we must notice the fundamental importance of being in earnest with these variations. I have noted above the passionate vehemence of Plato's belief in the multiplicity, as well as in the unity, which is actual in the universe. For it is all a question of the experience of spirits; and while in one sense nothing can be more actual than its gradations, yet in another it is all of the same stuff, penetrated with a symbolism embodying its fundamental unity, and pointing to a single spirit which runs through it all. I am not forcing upon Plato a modern idealism; I am only saying what is to me perfectly plain, that where grades of life and vision are presented as correlative to grades of mind, there is an obvious basis and presumption for the idea that in an ultimate sense the whole means more than it appears either in the imperfect souls or to them.

I was asking, then, whether we could put our finger on any special experience which aids us in conceiving the totality of the universe as a being in which reality coincides with value, according to the glimpses which everyday living has been shown to afford us. And from this point of view it seems natural to turn to the current phrase above mentioned which exhibits strikingly the endorsement unconsciously set upon our conception of reality by the popular mind in its most active and various pursuits. The highest praise, perhaps, is felt to be conveyed by it in any and every topic of experience, when it judges of anything it cares for—a game, a speech, a policy,

a play or a fight, a poem or piece of music, a great religion or a great
character—that in it you have "the real thing."

I suppose that, in its everyday use, this expression has two
grades of meaning. The expert in a game or sport means by it, I
imagine, that the thing is being done as that particular thing ought
to be done—it belongs to the best of its kind. The more romantic
critic may use it of love, or religion, or poetry, and then he will be
beginning to mean not merely that it belongs to the best of its kind,
but that it is the best thing in life. For me, if I may end with the
method with which I began, the expression has always possessed a
special fascination. It combines so many aspects, all of them good.
It is what holds water, what is strong, and what has stability, what
is durable and permanent, what is alive and comes of itself, the
whole object which calls out the whole mind, in a word, what *satisfies*. This is the logical character present in all the great experiences,
in æsthetic and religious experience no less than in that which is
explicitly logical and metaphysical.

Why should this strength and poignancy of the real thing—the
touch of the essential flame—bring close to us the absolute? I suppose, because its quality, being the most indubitable of experiences,
is also uniquely and intimately in positive feeling what the term
absolute expresses by a more negative approach. "The real thing,"
we saw, concentrates strength and value in itself. It supersedes all
else. When you have it, you have what in wanting anything, you
want, or in believing anything, you believe in. It has swallowed all
contradictions, and you can bring against it nothing from outside—
there is nothing to bring. This is what, from the negative approach,
the absolute says for itself. "I am all that there is—all the being
and the value. You want nothing but me, and nothing beyond me
can so much as be conceived."

Here in "the real thing" we experience the positive quality of
the absolute, and at least begin to understand its power and right
to be all that is. The intrinsic connection of reality and values becomes here transparent to us.

Thus, in this experience, we possess on the one side the characteristic quality of the absolute: on the other, the ground of its
totality, the meaning of its absoluteness.

One word more on our experience of "the real thing." It suggests
not only value at its height, but unity at its simplest. As in the
middle region of practice and business, so in the middle region of

reflection and critical common sense, we tend to sharp distinctions and would-be absolute divisions. But as in the deepest experience so in the simplest—the primitive experience which underlies and supports all other—we are in a world which is wholly one both with itself and with ourself. As in visible Nature, we are told today, there are no lines, so in felt experience there are no divisions. As the unity of the human race is not confined to the names that live in history, so the unity of the universe is not confined to the peaks where life touches its top. We live, it has been said long ago, and well repeated by Alexander in the last year or two, a planetary and telluric life as well as one that is animal and human, and this, our indistinctness from our world, is always with us in our feeling. Thus we begin with unity; it never leaves us; it accents itself as life grows full and strong; and again, perhaps, no less characteristically, as it is descending towards repose. In our simplest being, as in our highest activity, "the real thing" comes to us as an absolute—not exactly as a one, only because a one implies another.

9. There is difficulty, no doubt, in maintaining our vision of the absolute throughout the middle region of conflict and division in which we principally live. But what has always pressed upon my mind is the extent of the things which we directly possess. We possess the rare moments, and we possess the simple universal feeling; we possess also, throughout, the criterion which lives in all experience, the spirit and essence of the whole. The whole, it is plain, is such as on the one hand to include change, and on the other hand not to break away from totality. Totality expresses itself in value, which is, as we have seen, the concentration and focus of reality in its essence as real, as a positive center which is a solution of contradictions, and so far as at any point it asserts itself in experience, a satisfaction which rests on the tensions which are harmonized at that point. This has been to me, throughout, the direct and obvious teaching of life, when looked at as comprehensively as I knew how; and I will only add one word as to the difficulties, which also experience obviously presents. They consist, in principle, of extreme cases, whether for theory or practice; and against extreme cases, I have always strongly felt, it is a fair method to set cases no less extreme, in which parallel difficulties are solved. What man has done, man, I believe, may do, and of the evils which *prima facie* amaze and confound our ideas and our emotional nature, there are none, it seems to me, unparalleled by such as even we can see to be

intrinsic and essential in the highest conceivable values. For this insight we need no more than, for instance, genuinely to realize what is implied in love. Or, what is ultimately the same thing: Why does the most exalted enjoyment as yet freely created by man take the form of poetical tragedy? What would be the basis of our life if all that enables us to care for these things were torn away?

"My philosophy," then, is the theoretical fabric to the construction of which (adopting, of course, almost wholly what I have learned from others) my experience, as above indicated, has driven me. New ideas necessarily appear, or old ones reappear, as the whole reveals more of itself; but remembering that philosophy must above all things keep its head, and deal with all the sides of life, and not let itself be upset just by this or that, I find it hard to believe that, as the totality which is its own criterion, it will find the new in the main irreconcilable with the old.

2.

The General Nature of Implication

IN ATTEMPTING to ascertain the ultimate basis of Inference, it will be well to begin by noting the peculiar nature of the fact which makes knowledge, in principle, irrefragable. This fact may be expressed in different forms; but its underlying character is perhaps best accented by saying that we find it a contradiction in terms to repudiate knowledge as a whole. Denial is a form of knowing, no less than affirmation, and can be applied, as experiment shows directly, only within the whole of knowledge, and not to the whole as such. . . .

And a general doubt will be found open to the same objections as a general denial. It must, that is, and yet cannot, offer itself on the basis of some knowledge of that reality the knowledge of which it declines to accept. A man can, of course, adopt an attitude of general doubt in the sense that he pronounces himself to have found no certainty which satisfies him, and that as a personal resolve he has made up his mind to abandon theoretical inquiry. But he cannot support his position by reasoning without founding it upon some conviction which amounts to an assumption of knowledge as to the kind of thing that can be known. . . .

. . . Thus it would seem to be a natural assumption that in establishing the details of our knowledge we transfer the character of certainty which we primarily recognize in the province of truth as a whole, to the several matters which we progressively establish within it. And a general consideration which merely embodies this presumption might be rendered by some such formulas as "This or nothing," which, empirically speaking, we do often make use of in representing the grounds of a conviction. The essence of an inference then would be in showing of any suggested assertion that unless we accepted it, our province of truth would as a whole be taken from us. It is through such a conception, with the explana-

This selection is from Chapter I of *Implication and Linear Inference* (Macmillan and Company, 1920). It is reprinted with the kind permission of Mrs. Ellen Bosanquet.

tions and modifications which it obviously demands, that I shall attempt to unite under a single point of view some recent contributions to the theory of Inference. . . .

Thus it follows from the nature of implication that every inference involves a judgment based on the whole of reality, though referring only to a partial system which need not even be actual. You cannot draw a conclusion *from* a mere and pure supposition, Though you may draw one which explicitly refers to such a supposition and nothing more. Every assertion, when its explicit condition is discounted, asserts absolutely of reality as a whole. This is the claim which truth makes *ab initio,* that you must either affirm this proposition or deny the whole of experience. Apprehend this partial system—so an inference from a supposition says—as continuous with the real universe, and reality being what it is, so and so must result. Without this reference you do not even know that reality is noncontradictory of itself.

By way of anticipation, and to arouse interest if possible in the idea of a principle pervading the region of contingent inference and insight which is the same as that operative in *a priori* thought or necessary matter, I wll add some commonplace examples of everyday reasoning, stated so as to illustrate the analogy I am suggesting. I do not propose to discuss them at the present stage. In every case there is a definite given complex, the individual nature of which, considered together with the system of reality, gives rise to special conclusions.

According to the British Constitution, the king can only act through his ministers; and therefore in and subject to that special complex, "the king can do no wrong."

In the human circulating system the blood is driven through an intricate system of elastic tubes, therefore in that system there must be a powerful force-pump in continuous operation.

In a good electrical installation, a fuse will be blown before any conducting wire can be overheated.

In a country with large foreign trade, if you want to fix prices, you must control imports.

"Where there is no property, there is no injustice" (Locke). Here the nature of the system within which the inference is to hold good is perhaps inadequately defined.

In a body like that of any higher animal the separation of the head from the trunk must be fatal to life.

In such a body vitality must one day give way before the forces
which obstruct it.

Or the analogy may even be seen in examples where the system
of content suggests no necessity in the conclusions—in the connection of fact with fact, say, as cause and effect, but where nevertheless
the "circumstantial evidence"—say, the interpretation of a whole
complex of facts, as necessitated by the nature of causality—forces
an external necessity upon a conjunction of brute circumstances.

On the basis of the given connection of circumstances he was the
possible murderer and no one else was.

Considering what is demonstrated and what excluded, i.e., the
given system, it follows that the excision of the thyroid gland dulls
the intelligence.

Considering testimony causes and results there can be no doubt
that Charles I. was beheaded.

This latter set of examples anticipates later discussions. I will
now return to the cases of simpler *a priori* apprehension or inference.

Considering then the arithmetical and geometrical examples of
apprehended connections within systems, we ought, if our suggestion
is warranted, to have before us, in their case, the nerve of inference
quite naked. What is it? Is our vision of it a mere intuition in the
mystic sense; something that defies analysis?

Its necessity is certainly not reducible to subsumption under
general formulae which can be arranged as schedules, dictating the
arrangement of data and the type of conclusion after syllogistic
fashion. Nevertheless, there are some general features which can be
noted.

a. In the first place, these complexes, the spatial triangle plus the
construction necessary to exhibit this or that among its properties,
and the arithmetical system, are typical of the nature of true wholes.
I use this cumbrous expression, in preference to saying that they are
true wholes, because their character of wholeness is bought at the
price of a very extreme simplicity and the omission of nearly all the
responsiveness that characterizes for example an organic whole. Still,
such as they are, they bear the features of genuine wholes, in which
no part nor characteristic is indifferent to any other; or perhaps it
would be better to speak more moderately, and to say that there
is no part nor characteristic which does not affect a number of others
quite different from itself. But, owing to the imperfection which in
some degree clings to all but the very highest conceivable kinds of

systems, there are features and modifications of features which are completely indifferent to each other—*e.g.*, the magnitude of a triangle and the comparative magnitude of its several angles.

Still, in a very great measure, the connection, as we said, lies naked before us. The three angles of a triangle are together equal to two right angles. If it is equilateral, it is equiangular, and *vice versa*. If a side is lengthened *ceteris paribus,* the opposite angle is enlarged. So too in the numerical system. Alter the value of any combination, and some correlatives, and ultimately the whole system, must be altered. If 1 is 5, 2 is 10. All is relevant to all. There is something in each which runs through every point in the system, and makes each of them, though apparently unique and peculiar, respond to every other, and vary, though in its own individual manner, yet correspondingly to the variations of other points or traits. Complexes, in so far as they present this character, are true "wholes" or "universals." You can tell from the modification in which one feature of them is given in what modification another feature, though quite dissimilar in character, must be given at the same time. The essence of its nature lies, to repeat it in a sentence, in being a system with different features or properties, such that without being at all similar or repetitions of each other they present variations connected by law, and therefore the variation of one is an index to the variation of others. Such laws are to be seen in simple forms in Euclid's theorems which develop the properties of triangles or in the statements of the multiplication table.

b. In the second place, the connection with one another of such factors or elements within a system—let us call them terms and relations—might in some cases be causal, but obviously it is not so always. It is most adequately expressed by the word implication. Within a given complex, a system of terms and relations, so far as it possesses the unity of a true universal, the presence or absence of certain terms in certain modifications enables us to be sure that certain other terms in certain determinate forms will be present or absent. Thus, if our suggestion is right, the fundamental principle of inference will be implication. This is the general name for the relation which exists between one term or relation within a universal, or connected system of terms and relations, and the others, so far as their respective modifications afford a clue to one another. . . .

. . . All inference, then, is within a connected system, and consists in reading off the implications which this system, construed as one with the whole of knowledge so far as relevant, imposes upon some of its terms. The inference is founded upon some acceptance of the joint system so arising. Its necessity may be expressed, as we say, in the formula "This or nothing." There is a given complex as starting-point, whether fact or supposition makes no difference. Construed along with the ordered whole of our experience, it affirms a certain result, and this result, its implication, you must admit *as* its implication, so long as you affirm the ordered whole to be real. You cannot escape from the implication as such by pointing out that you do not affirm as a fact the complex which is your starting-point. On the contrary, you may decide to deny it as a fact just because its implication is inevitable. If the joint system has been rightly read, which we must assume, you could only annul the implication by ceasing to affirm the system of reality within which you are judging it to hold. If you have judged the relation rightly, you would in the end, in attempting to annul your judgment, have to deny the Law of Contradiction. That is to say, an implication rightly judged is guaranteed by the whole system of reality. If you deny it, you leave nothing standing. . . .

3.
The Doctrine of Relevant Relations

. . . "THE WORLD is a world of many things, with relations which are not to be deduced from a supposed nature or scholastic essence of the related things. In this world, whatever is complex is composed of related simple things. There is no identity in difference, there is identity and there is difference, and complexes may have some elements identical and some different, but we are no longer obliged to say of any pair of objects that may be mentioned that they are both identical and different."[1]

The core of the view, as is well known, is the rejection of what have been called "internal relations," i.e., relations grounded in the nature of the related terms; and the assertion of mere external relations, i.e., as I understand that there is no reason why relations should be so grounded.[2] The phrase "internal relations" seems to me not quite satisfactory, as suggesting relations between parts within a given term. At least the view which to me appears reasonable would be better expressed by some such term as "relevant relations," i.e., relations which are connected with the properties of their terms, so that any alteration of relations involves an alteration of properties, and vice versa.

The following reasons for accepting a doctrine of relevant relations appear to me to be unimpeached.

(1) In a large proportion of cases the relevancy of the relations to the properties of the related terms involves a community of kind. You cannot have a spatial relation between terms which are not in

---

This selection is from Chapter IX of the 2nd edition of *Logic*, Vol. II, a book first published in 1888. It is reprinted with the kind permission of The Clarendon Press, Oxford.

1. Russell, *Philosophical Essays*, p. 169. I do not think it is maintained on our part that relations can be deduced from the properties of single terms which are in relation. I understand the point of interest to be that you cannot explain one term of a complex without explaining the rest. Every complex, it must be remembered, has a special quality of its own, and every member of it has a quality relative to this; see i, pp. 139-40.
2. *Op. cit.*, p. 161. It would be important to know if it is maintained that relations cannot be so grounded, because then we could ask for the author's explanation of the more obvious cases in which they appear to be so.

space. You cannot have a moral relation between terms which are not members of a moral world. Why is it absurd to ask for the distance from London Bridge to one o'clock? Surely because the one term is in space and the other in time. This is not a general argument that if the relation were other the terms would be other, from which any possible conclusion might follow. It is an analytic determination of a common positive element on which both property and relation depend.

(2) There is further no case in which on philosophical scrutiny the relevancy of relations to properties is not perceptible. I do not say that the relation can be reduced to a fact about the one object only together with a fact about the other object only. The point of the relevancy of relations, as I understand it, is that each of two or more terms can only be understood if all are understood. "Father" and "Son" is a vulgar traditional instance. But I do not see that it is not a sound one. And in every case, I think, the basis of such a necessity can be shown. This or that observer may not possess the knowledge or the acuteness required to formulate the element which changes with the relation in precise detail. But it can always be shown what sort of thing must be relevant to the relation. So much so, that I cannot think this to be really and totally denied of so-called external relations. And I will pass on to a point of view which raises this question.

(3) Relations are true of their terms. They express their positions in complexes, which positions elicit their behavior, their self-maintenance in the world of things. This is really the all-important argument. And I cannot believe that if the doctrine of mere external relations were completely stated, we should not find the same thing admitted by it, in one way or another. If the relations make no difference to the terms, it follows that things do not react or behave with reference to the complexes to which they belong. Yet if Charles I had died in his bed, he would have died in a different bodily attitude from that in which he died on the scaffold.

I do not understand relations to be adjectives of their terms. They are not adjectives because they involve other terms which are as substantive as any of which we might be inclined to pronounce them adjectives. Relations cannot be reduced to qualities, nor qualities to relations. Relations are just the way in which discursive thought represents the unity of terms which it cannot make adjectives of one another. As Mr. Bradley has said that they are a *modus vivendi* between predicates of the same subject whose unity we cannot really construe to ourselves, so it might be said they are a *modus vivendi* between terms in the same universe, of whose unity in the imperfection of our experience, the same is true.

None of the objections which have been put forward appear to me to touch these points.

I quite understand that on the doctrine offered to us Identity in Difference must go. And I quite see for myself that it must go "in the end," that is to say, in any experience for which objects are self-contained, and cease to transcend themselves. What our pluralist realists are grasping at is therefore justly anticipated. Undoubtedly the Real is self-complete and self-contained. But I insist on the words "in the end" because it is their repudiation of them that I take to be the root of their failure. They are the extreme Absolutists. They are not content to have the Absolute "in the end," as we more modestly claim it, not meaning after a lapse of time, but in so far as what are fragments for us point out to us a completion beyond them. And there is surely a difference of completeness in different experiences. But they will have the Absolute here and now; and to make it handy and adaptable for everyday use they split it into little bits. A universe of tiny Absolutes; that is really what they offer us. But if any of these Absolutes imply any term beyond themselves their absolutism breaks down. And we have tried to show that in all relations this is the case. . . .

4.
The Function of the State

I WISH TO PRESENT a brief positive account of the theory of the state as I understand it, more particularly with reference to the state in its external relations, and the conditions essential to federations or a world-state.

It seems to me that much misconception is prevalent as to the views which in fact great philosophers have held upon this problem. But I do not wish to raise mere questions in the history of philosophy, but to meet the issue as it seems to me to stand to-day. The ideas which I express are therefore my own, in the sense that no one else is responsible for the form I give them. But, to the best of my judgment, they represent the Greek tradition as renewed by Hegel and by English thought.

In considering any problem affecting the state I take the primary question to be how self-government is possible. For anything which interferes with the possibility of self-government destroys altogether the conditions of true government. The answer is drawn, I take it, from the conception of the general will, which involves the existence of an actual community, of such a nature as to share an identical mind and feeling. There is no other way of explaining how a free man can put up with compulsion and even welcome it.

Here then we have the universal condition of legitimate outward authority. City-state, Nation-state, Commonwealth, Federation, World-state, it makes no difference. Behind all force there must be a general will, and the general will must represent a communal mind. All other contrivances for government are external and tyrannical.

1. This is the reason of the unique relation between the state and the individual which is caricatured by critics as state absolutism. Of course the state is not the ultimate end of life. The ultimate end, if we avoid religious phraseology, which would probably furnish the truest expression of it, is surely the best life. I understand by the

This selection is from Chapter XIII of Bosanquet's book *Social and International Ideals* (Macmillan and Co., London, 1917). It is here reprinted with the kind permission of Mrs. Ellen Bosanquet.

state the power which, as the organ of a community, has the function of maintaining the external conditions necessary to the best life. These conditions are called rights. They are the claims recognized by the will of a community as the *sine qua non* of the highest obtainable fulfillment of the capacities for the best life possessed by its members.

Now the relation between the state and the individual is the external equivalent of that between the community and the individual. And it is a unique relation, because there is no other body that bears the same relation to the individual's will as that community which is represented by a state in the external world.

This can be said with as much precision as human affairs admit, because there is reason to expect that the community which organises itself as a state will be for every group the largest body which possesses the unity of experience necessary for constituting a general will. There is, as we shall see, no other body at all comparable with it in intensity of unity. "A national purpose is the most unconquerable and victorious of all things on earth." And the individual's private will, we must bear in mind, is certainly and literally a part of the communal will. There is no other material of which his will can be made. If he rejects the communal will in part, he rejects it on the basis of what it is in him, not from any will of his own which has a different source. This is the ground of the duty of rebellion.

This unique relation between the individual and the community which the state represents—it may be a nation or any other community—is what seems to me to dominate the whole problem. It is further determined when we add the consideration that the state is an organ of action in the external world. In this sphere, which is its special sphere as an organ exercising force, it may really be called absolute, that is, if power extending to life and death and complete disposal of property can be called absolute. This does not mean that it is the whole end of life, nor that it is the only object of loyalty. It means, as I understand it, that, being the special organ of arrangement in the external world, corresponding to that particular community whose will *is* our own will when most highly organised, it has the distinctive function of dictating the final adjustment in matters of external action. This is the only sense in which I have called it absolute, and the ground is obvious and simple. It lies in the tendency of the world of action to bring into collision factors which, apart from action, might never conflict. However purely non-political two associations may be, and however cosmopolitan, if they

claim the same funds or the same building they must come before a
power which can adjust the difference without appeal. And if such
a power were not single in respect of them, obviously there could
be no certainty of adjustment without a conflict between the two
or more powers which might claim jurisdiction. Cases like that supposed are frequent, of course, with churches.

Thus there are two connected points, which, I think, the critics
confuse under the names of absolutism. One is the power of the
state as sustainer of all adjustments in the world of external action,
on the ground which has just been explained. The other is the unique
relation to the individual of such a community as is at present exemplified by his nation-state, because it represents, as nothing else in
the world does, that special system of rights and sentiments, the
complement of his own being, which the general will of his group
has formed a state to maintain.

It is the result, I take it, of these two grounds of unity cooperating, that in times of stress the state, as the organ of the community,
will suspend or subject to conditions any form of intercourse between
its members and persons or associations within or without its territory, and will require any service that it thinks fit from any of its
members. It does, in Mr. Bradley's words, "with the moral approval
of all what the explicit theory of scarcely one will morally justify."
That it does not exercise such powers to anything like the same degree
in ordinary times, and that it recognizes the rights of conscience even
in times of stress, flows from the fact that its primary end is the
maintenance of rights, and it will override no right by force where
an adjustment is possible compatible with the good life of the whole.
And of this possibility it is the sole judge. What it permits, it permits
by reason of its end, and no theory can stand which will not justify
in principle its habitual action in times of stress.

2. "The state," as I understand the words, is a phrase framed in
the normal way, to express that one is dealing with the members of
a class strictly according to the connotation of the class-name. If a
plural noun is used, there can be no certainty whether we are speaking of the characteristics which belong to the class-members as such,
or of circumstances which may occur in each of them for independent
reasons. "The state," in a word, is a brief expression for "states *qua*
states." I confess that I am a good deal surprised that nearly all
recent critics have stumbled, as it seems to me, in this simple matter
of interpretation. Would they find the same difficulty in the title of

a book on "the heart" or "the steam-engine"? It would be urged, perhaps, that a heart does not imply other hearts, but that a state does imply other states; but if the thing implies other things its name implies the reference to them.

And, indeed, the whole *raison d'être* of our theory is to show why, and in what sense, there must be states wherever there are groups of human beings, and to explain for what reasons men are distinguished into separate adjacent political bodies instead of forming a single system over the whole earth's surface.

Our theory has told us, for example, that states represent differentiations of the single human spirit (Hegel), whose extent and intensity determine and are determined by territorial limits. They are members, we are told by Plato and Hegel, of an ethical family of nations, so far, at least, as the European world is concerned; they are characterized—it is Mazzini's well-known doctrine—by individual missions or functions which furnish for every state its distinctive contribution to human life. They have a similar task to achieve, each within its territory allotted by history, so Green argues, and the more perfectly each of them attains its proper object of giving free scope to the capacities of all persons living on a certain range of territory, the easier it is for others to do so. Obviously they are cooperating units. This is throughout the essence of the theory.

Now it is not, I think, unfair to point out that my critics, dealing unguardedly with "states" and not with "the state" or with "states *qua* states," have on the whole founded their account of states not upon what they are, so far as states, but just upon what, *qua* states, they are not; upon defects which appear unequally in the several communities, consisting in those evils which the organization of the state exists in order to remove, and does progressively remove in so far as true self-government is attained. Such evils are war, exploitation within or without, class privilege, arbitrary authority, discontent directing ambitions to foreign conquest and to jealousy of other states, the doctrine that one state's gain is *ipso facto* another's loss.

3. Space and time do not permit me to discuss, what I should be interested in discussing at some length, the continuous relations which extend beyond the frontiers of individual states, their importance compared with that of other continuities which are co-extensive with the area of the states and constituent of them, and why it is

necessary to recognize, in spite of the former, separate sovereign political units which undoubtedly, while imperfect, tend to break down at the frontier, in a regrettable way, the continuities which pass beyond it. Broadly speaking, the reason lies, I take it, in the exceptionally intense unity and concreteness of certain group-minds, in which innumerable continuities coincide, while other continuities, which extend beyond the group, nevertheless do not coincide with any marked rival unity.

4. It follows from our theory, as we saw, that the normal relation of states is cooperative. Their influence on each other's structure and culture is mainly a question of wants and materials. The characteristic dealing with them depends after all upon the national mind, as we see in the contrast of Athens and Sparta, the two leading states of one and the same civilization. It is a curious fallacy in the disparagement of the state that the recognition of a debt to foreign culture has been pushed so far as to suggest that nothing great originates in any state because everything is imported from some other.

Further, it follows that the maintenance of this normal relation, or its attainment where unattained, depends on the right discharge by states of their internal function—the maintenance of rights as the conditions of good life. War, as Plato showed, is not of the essence of states, but has its causes in their internal disease and distraction, leading to policies of "expansion." Therefore, in this sense, to begin with, we want more of the state and not less. In order to reinforce the organization of rights by other states, the main thing it has to do is to complete its own. This fundamental truth none of the critics seem to have observed, and to have emphasized it appears to me a very great merit in our philosophy. The fundamental principle is that states *qua* states are—"the state" is—the human mind doing the same work in different localities with different materials. Obviously, in so far as it succeeds, its efforts assist each other.

5. Thus every state as such—that is, "the state"—is "the guardian of a whole moral world," maintaining the peculiar contribution of its community to the total of human life and of human mind. We shall see why this double expression is necessary. And it is very important to observe that this moral world includes a whole distinctive attitude to life and humanity. It is an attitude *of* the community, but *to* the world. Thus you cannot get away from it. All individuals

share it, more or less, and every relation of the group, external or internal, is brought to a meeting point within their consciousness, and elicits a response from it.

It is easy to discern how such guardianship on the part of bodies so highly individualized, so deeply conscious of a function and as yet so imperfectly organized, may lead, from time to time, to differences which can only be resolved by force. It is a profound mistake, I am convinced, to direct the moral of the present calamity against the communal sense of a function and a mission; against, in a word, the belief that a community has a conscience. Yet this belief is the root of the doctrine caricatured under the name of state absolutism. It seems to me foolish to take a hostile attitude to a general truth because it displays the root of serious evils. For, indeed, what displays their root is the only indication of the remedy. The true moral is, surely, not that a community should have no overmastering purpose, no consciousness of a mission and no conscience, but simply that its conscience should as far as possible be enlightened. Enlightened consciences, I venture to assume, cannot bring actions into conflict. But, being internally ill organized, and correspondingly biassed and unenlightened, communities enter into conflicts from time to time with their whole heart and soul, just because they *have* consciences and *have* moral worlds to guard. It happens naturally to them as to private persons that they throw their whole sense of right into what is wrong. In order to produce a disastrous collision, we must bear in mind, the aspirations of two communities need not be in conflict at every point. It is like two trains running side by side, where an encroachment of an inch is enough to produce a calamity. Aspirations may be irreconcilable in practice which have a very large factor of agreement. This factor is the ground for hope, which consists in their being, after all, aspirations of communities which possess reason and conscience. Reconciliation of them by harmonious adjustment, though impracticable at certain moments, is never inconceivable.

Now it is surely plain that no power on earth can deal with such a cause of conflict, except something that enables the biassed and erroneous factors of the conflicting claims to be eliminated. And this can never be done by external force, but must mainly depend on a better organization of rights by every state at home, with a consequent correction of its ambitions and outlook on the world. A healthy state is not militant.

But the mischief is, that the popular mind, observing that the present trouble has arisen through aspirations in others which we pronounce perverse, is inclined to attribute to a false philosophy the whole conception of national aspirations as representing the conscience of a people and its overmastering sense of duty. Men do not reflect that precisely such aspirations are determining their own group-action at every step. They say, as our critics are saying, that the theory of the unity of a people in the moral consciousness of a pre-eminent duty, and the principle of its expression through an organ supreme in practical life, are absolutism, and ought to be weakened or abandoned. The unique obligation of the private person to the community as incomparably the fullest representative of himself is to be put on a level with isolated abstract obligations arising in the course of this or that special relation, although it is on the communal mind that the task of harmonizing them must ultimately fall. In short, the whole moral status and moral being of the community is to be indefinitely but considerably lowered.

All this seems to me to point exactly the wrong way. We all know, in modern society more especially, that we pay for the existence of great organizing agencies by the possibility of their conflicting. But that does not make us desire to weaken them; it makes us desire to amplify their members' faith in them, and to get them to do their work more completely. The remedy for disorganization is not less organization, but more. All organization, of course, brings a concurrent risk of conflict. You bring claims together, and you find points which for the moment cannot be adjusted. It is a flat contradiction to maintain that the state is morally responsible, and also that it must not face an actual conflict where its conscience is concerned. Even within the community, where obligations to the common will are so high and so determinate, the conscientious objector will follow his conscience to the end, and if we believe him to be sincere we all respect him for it. Why should the community, an individual in a far deeper sense than the citizen, being the nearest approach to a true individual that exists upon the earth, be expected not to follow its conscience? The clause on which I have just insisted is, as Rousseau pointed out, the fundamental issue. The point to be remembered is that the individual only has his individuality through the social consciousness. The nearer he approaches to being himself the more he approaches identification with the communal mind. This mind can only be expressed as what the individual would be if he possessed in completeness all that his actual consciousness implies regarding group-life. If he sees reason to rebel, it is still as a social duty. It cannot be in virtue of some right of his own, as he would be, *per impossibile,* apart.

No doubt, when there is strife between communities, a wrong is being committed somewhere. But the way to right it is not for the conscientious group to make a rule of yielding on points which it holds fundamental to its function.

Now I think that the critics of our theory speak uncertainly here. Is our fault in saying that the community which asserts itself through the state *is* a moral being, and *has* a conscience, or is not a moral being and has not a conscience? They seem to me in effect to say both at once. But only one can be true.

It is clear, I think, that we are accused of denying the moral responsibility of the community which has the state for its organ. But it can hardly be doubted that we are also accused of putting this moral responsibility much too high. Thus the critics find themselves driven to treat the community which is a state as a mere association of individuals, which cannot possess an organic moral conscience nor general will. Though in one passage disclaiming individualism, the argument breathes its spirit. If you call the state an association, you speak the language of individualism, and still more so, if you speak of individual rights which can be asserted against it, and of the individual judgment as ultimate. To call it an "association" is contrary, I think, both to usage and to truth. The word is, I presume, employed intentionally as paradoxical and aggressive.

It is really, then, the moral being and moral responsibility of the state which we affirm, and which the main attack desires to undermine. The opposite suggestion, that we do not recognize the moral responsibility of the members of a group for its action, is, as we shall see, a mere misconception, derived from the fact that we observe the moral action of a community not to be capable of being criticized by the method of comparison with that of an individual.

The unique position of the state springs, as I said at starting, from the fact that it is molded, as no mere association is, by and for the special task of maintaining in a certain territory the external conditions of good life as a whole. Its territorial area adjusts itself to that unity of communal experience which is most favorable to the maintenance of an organized will, so that it tends to cover the largest area within which, for a certain group, the conditions of such an experience exist. . . .

JOSIAH ROYCE

(1855-1916)

Royce is the chief American absolute idealist. His argument for idealism in Selection 2 is one of the most important. It will be seen that he takes a much more personal view of the Absolute than Bradley or Bosanquet.

1.
Object and Idea

. . . OBJECT AND IDEA, viewed as entities, are twain. Realism began by saying so. So much is nominated in the bond. The realist shall have his pound of flesh, although we can grant him indeed not one drop of blood for all his world. By the original hypothesis either any individual idea, or *o,* the object of that idea, could without contradiction be conceived as changing, or as vanishing, without any logically necessary change in the other member of the pair. Therefore, according to what we have now shown to be the case with any two independent realities, the idea of *o* and *o,* as real beings, not only have, as first defined, no connection with each other, but they can never get any possible linkage or relation. All their connections are nominal. As idea, the idea was said to have *o* for its object. But the idea is an entity. It can have nothing to do with the other entity *o.* These two are not in the same space, nor in the same time, nor in the same natural order, nor in the same spiritual order. They have nothing in common, neither quality nor worth, neither form nor content, neither truth nor meaning. No causality links them. If you say so, you again use mere names. No will genuinely can relate them. That they appear to have connections is simply a matter of false seeming. Our original definition called the one of them an idea relating to the object *o.* We now know that

This selection is from Lecture III of Royce's book, *The World and the Individual,* 1st series, first published in 1900.

[189]

such an expression was a mere name. The idea has assumed as idea an obligation that as independent entity it cannot pay. It has no true relation with o, and o has no community with the idea. To speak of any being not o itself as if it were really an idea of o, is as if you spoke of the square root of an odor, or of the logarithm of an angel. For idea and object are two real beings. Their irrevocable sundering no new definition of their essence can now join again. For reality, in this doctrine, is independent of all definitions that could be made after the fact. Relations that could link the two entities would merely prove to be new independent beings other than either of them.

Nor is this all. The idea here in question is any idea or opinion. O is any object. Now a realist's own theory is an idea or opinion. And the world was to be his object. Our perfectly general result, true of all ideas, applies of course to the group of ideas called the realistic theory. As an entity, the realist is an independent being. His ideas, as part of his being, can have nothing to do with any object that exists independently of himself or themselves. The realistic theory, then, as we now know, by its own explicit consequences, and just because its real objects are totally independent of its ideas, has nothing to do with any independently real object, and has no relation to the independent external world that its own account defines. Nor can it ever come to get such a relation. No realist, as he himself now must consistently maintain, either knows any independent being, or has ever, in idea, found himself related to one, or has ever made any reference to such a being, or has ever formed or expressed an opinion regarding one, or, in his own sense of the word "real," really believes that there is one.

And thus, suddenly at one stroke, the entire realistic fabric, with all those "suns and milky ways" to which Schopenhauer, in a famous passage, so prettily referred, vanishes,—leaving not a wrack, not even a single lonely Unknowable, behind. For an Unknowable, too, would be an independent real object. Our present idea of it would have to refer to this object, if it were real; and no idea, as we know, can refer to any independent reality, since in order for such reference to be itself real, two irrevocably sundered beings would have to destroy the chasm whose presence is determined by their own very essence. . . .

2.
The Nature of Truth

THE THESIS of our antinomy is as follows: There seems to be, in the object of an idea, just in so far as it is the object of that specific idea, no essential character which is not predetermined by the purpose, the internal meaning, the conscious intent, of that idea itself.

For consider: An object, as we have seen, has two relations to an idea. The one is the relation that constitutes it the object meant by that idea. The other is the sort of correspondence that is to obtain between object and idea. As to the first of these two: An object is not the object of a given idea merely because the object causes the idea, or impresses itself upon the idea as the seal impresses the wax. For there are objects of ideas that are not causes of the ideas which refer to these objects, just as there are countless cases where my ideas are supposed to have causes, say physiological or psychological causes, of which I myself never become conscious at all, as my objects. Nor is the object the object of a given idea merely because, from the point of view of an external observer, who looks from without upon idea and object, and compares them, the idea resembles the object. For the sort of correspondence to be demanded of the idea is determined by itself, and this correspondence cannot be judged merely from without. Again, my idea of my own past experiences may resemble your past experiences, in case you have felt as I have felt, or have acted in any way as I have acted. Yet when my ideas, in a moment of reminiscence, refer to my own past, and have that for their object, they do not refer to your past, nor to your deeds and sorrows, however like my own these experiences of yours may have been. One who, merely comparing my ideas and your experiences, said that because of the mere likeness I must be thinking of your past as my object, would, therefore, err, if it was my own past of which I was thinking. Neither such a relation as causal connection nor such a relation as mere similarity is, then, sufficient to identify an object as the object of a given idea.

This selection is from Lecture VII of *The World and the Individual*, first series.

Nor yet can any other relation, so far as it is merely supposed to be seen from without, by an external observer, suffice to identify any object as the object of a given idea. For suppose that any such relation, merely observed from without, were regarded as finally sufficient to constitute an object the object of a given idea. I care not what this relation may be. Call it what you will. As soon as you define such a relation from without, and declare that the idea has an object by virtue of that relation to this object, I shall merely ask: Did the idea itself intend and select that relation as the relation in which its purposed object was to stand to the idea? If you answer "No," then I take my stand beside the idea, and shall persist in demanding by what right you thus impose the relation in question upon the idea as the relation rightly characterizing its object. For the idea, in seeking for truth, does not seek for your aims, so far as you are a merely external observer. The idea is selective. It seeks its own. It attends as itself has chosen. It desires in its own way. If you, having somehow first finished and established your own definition of Being, choose to regard the idea and its object as entities in your own supposed world, then, indeed, you can talk, from your own point of view, of the various real relations of these entities, precisely as a psychologist does when he discusses the origin or the results of ideas. But just now we are not first presupposing that we know what the Being of the object is apart from the idea, and what the Being of the idea is apart from the object. We are trying, in advance of a finished conception of the Being of the object, to define the essential relation that makes an object the object of that particular idea. And as the idea, precisely so far as it intends truth at all, is through and through a selection, a choosing of an object, I ask what reason you can have to say that the object is the object of the idea, unless you observe somehow that the idea chooses for itself this object.

But now if you reply, "Yes, the relation of object to idea, here in question, is the one chosen by the idea," then you admit the essential point. The relation to the object is so far predetermined by the idea. Hence, as we have now seen, the object of the idea is predetermined, both as to what object it is, and as to how it is to correspond to the idea, through the choice made by the idea itself. The object, precisely in so far as it is object of that idea, seems thus to be altogether predetermined. In brief, the object and the idea of that object appear to be related as Hamlet in the play is related to

the intent of Shakespeare, or as creation and creative purpose in
general arc related. Hamlet is what Shakespeare's idea intends him
to be. The object is what it is because the idea means it to be the
object of just this idea. And so much may suffice for our thesis.

But the antithesis runs: No finite idea predetermines, in its object, exactly the character which, when present in the object, gives
the idea the desired truth. For observe, first, that the object of a
true finite idea, such as our idea of the world or of space, is in any
case something other than the mere idea itself. And the truth of the
idea depends upon a confirmation of the idea through the presence
and the characters of this other,—the object. Now error is certainly
possible in finite ideas. For some finite ideas are false. And that this
last assertion itself is true, is not only a matter of common opinion,
but can be proved by the very counterpart of the Augustinian argument about *Veritas.* For if there could be no error, then the customary
assertion that ideas can err, i.e., our well-known common-sense conviction that error is possible, would be itself an error, and this result
would involve a self-contradiction. Or again, were no error possible,
there would be no truth, since then the assertion that there is no truth
would itself be no error, or would itself be true. This, again, would be
a contradiction. Or finally, if error were impossible, any and every account of Being or truth, of ideas and of objects, of the world or of nothing at all, would be equally true, or in other words, no truth would ever
be defined. For truth we define by its contrast with the error that
it excludes. So some ideas certainly can and do err in as far as they
undertake to be ideas of objects. Ideas can then fail of their desired
correspondence with their intended objects, just because these objects are indeed other than themselves. But the error of an idea is
always a failure to win the intended aim of the idea, precisely in so
far as the idea sought truth. Hence, as no purpose can simply and
directly consist in willing or intending its own defeat, it is plain that
an idea, precisely in so far as it can turn out to be an erroneous
idea, can intend what its object forbids it to carry out, and can mean
what its object excludes; while in so far as the object thus refutes
the idea, the object contains what the idea did not purpose, and
was unable to predetermine. In brief, the very Possibility of Error,
the absolutely certain truth that some ideas give false accounts of
their own objects, shows that some objects contain what is opposed
to the intent of the very ideas that refer to these objects. And so the
antithesis is proved.

In view of this apparent antinomy, how is the idea related to its object? How is error possible? What is truth? The answer to these questions,—the solution to all our previous difficulties,—is in one respect so simple, that I almost fear, after this so elaborate preparation, to state it, lest by its very simplicity it may disappoint. Yet I must first state it, abstractly, and perhaps unconvincingly, and then illustrate it as I close the present discussion, leaving to a later lecture its fuller development. The idea, I have said, *seeks its own. It can be judged by nothing but what it intends.* Whether I think of God or of yesterday's events, of my own death, or of the destiny of mankind, of mathematical truth, or of physical facts, of affairs of business, or of Being itself, it is first of all what I mean, and not what somebody merely external to myself might desire me to mean, that both gives me an object, and determines for me the standard of correspondence to the object whereby I must be judged. Moreover, my idea is a cognitive process only in so far as it is, at the same time, a voluntary process, an act, the partial fulfilment, so far as the idea consciously extends, of a purpose. The object meant by the idea is the object because it is willed to be such, and the will in question is the will that the idea embodies. And that is why Realism proved to be impossible; that is why the Independent Beings were self-contradictory concepts; that, too, is why the resignation of all definite purpose which Mysticism required of our ideas was impossible without a failure to define Being as any but a mere Nothing. And every definition of truth or of Being must depend upon a prior recognition of precisely this aspect of the nature of ideas. . . .

. . . But now, in order that we may also take account of our former problem about the determinateness and individuality attributed to Being, let us add yet one further consideration: Whenever an idea of any grade aims at truth, it regards its object as other than itself, and that the object shall be thus other than itself is even a part of what the idea means and consciously intends. But as a will seeking its own fulfilment, the idea so selects the object, that, if the idea has a perfectly definite meaning and truth at all, this object is to be a precisely determinate object, *such that no other object could take its place as the object of this idea.* And in spite of the fact that the object is such solely by the will of the idea, the idea undertakes submissively to be either true or false when compared with that object.

Now the obvious way of stating the whole sense of these facts is to point out that what the idea always aims to find in its object is *nothing whatever but the idea's own conscious purpose or will, embodied in some more determinate form* than the idea by itself alone at this instant consciously possesses. When I have an idea of the world, my idea is a will, *and the world of my idea is simply my own will itself determinately embodied.*

And what this way of stating our problem implies may first be illustrated by any case where, in doing what we often call "making up our minds," we pass from a vague to a definite state of will and of resolution. In such cases we begin with perhaps a very indefinite sort of restlessness, which arouses the question, "What is it that I want? What do I desire? What is my real purpose?" To answer this question may take a long time and much care; and may involve many errors by the way, errors, namely, in understanding our own purpose. Such search for one's own will often occupies, in the practical life of youth, some very anxious years. Idleness, defective modes of conduct, self-defeating struggles without number, fickle loves that soon die out, may long accompany what the youth himself all the while regards as the search for his own will, for the very soul of his own inner and conscious purposes. In such cases one may surely err as to one's intent. The false or fickle love is a sort of transient dream of the coming true love itself. The transient choice is a shadow of the coming true choice. But how does one's own real intent, the object at such times of one's search, stand related to one's present and ill-defined vague restlessness, or imperfectly conscious longing. I answer, one's true will, one's genuine purpose, one's object here sought for, can be nothing whatever but one's present imperfect conscious will in some more determinate form. What one has, at such times, is the will of the passing moment,— an internal meaning, consciously present as far as it goes. And now it is this will and no other that one seeks to bring to clearer consciousness. But what other, what external meaning, what fact beyond, yes, what object, is the goal of this quest? I answer, nothing whatever in heaven or in earth but this present imperfect, internal meaning rendered more determinate, less ambiguous in its form, less a general longing, more a precisely united and determinate life. And this, once rendered perfectly determinate, would be what the man in question calls "My life according to my conscious will."

Well, this case of the vague purpose that one seeks, not to

abandon, but to get present to the moment's consciousness in another, that is a more explicit and precise, form, and if possible, in
what would finally prove to be an absolutely determinate form,—
this case, I insist, is typical of every case where an idea seeks its
object. *In seeking its object, any idea whatever seeks absolutely
nothing but its own explicit, and, in the end, complete, determination as this conscious purpose, embodied in this one way. The complete content of the idea's own purpose is the only object of which
the idea can ever take note. This alone is the Other that is sought.* . . .

. . . We are ready, now that we have defined both object and
truth, to assert, as our Fourth and final Conception of Being, this,
that *What is, or what is real, is as such the complete embodiment,
in individual form and in final fulfilment, of the internal meaning of
finite ideas.*

To later lectures must be left both the fuller development and
the further defense of this conception of Being. But our argument
in its favor is, in its foundation, already before you. Being is something Other than themselves which finite ideas seek. They seek
Being as that which, if at present known, would end their doubts.
Now Being is not something independent of finite ideas, nor yet a
merely immediate fact that quenches them. These were our results
when we abandoned Realism and Mysticism. Being involves the
validity of ideas. That we learned from critical Rationalism. Yet
mere validity, mere truth of ideas, cannot be conceived as a bare
universal fact. We wanted to find its concreter content, its finally
determinate form. We have carefully studied this form. No finite
idea can have or conform to any object, save what its own meaning
determines, or seek any meaning or truth but its own meaning and
truth. Furthermore, a finite idea is as much an instance of will as
it is a knowing process. In seeking its own meaning, it seeks then
simply the fuller expression of its own will. Its only Other is an
Other that would more completely express it. Its object proves
therefore to be, as proximate finite object, any fuller determination
whatever of its own will and meaning. But as final object, the idea
can have only its final embodiment in a complete and individual
form. This final form of the idea, this final object sought when we
seek Being, is (1) a complete expression of the internal meaning
of the finite idea with which, in any case, we start our quest; (2)
a complete fulfilment of the will or purpose partially embodied in
this idea; (3) an individual life for which no other can be substituted.

Now in defining this complete life, in which alone the finite idea, as a passing thrill of conscious meaning, can find the genuine object that it means fully embodied, we have so far still used many expressions derived from the conception of mere validity. We have spoken of what this life would be *if it were* completely present. But, having used these forms of expression as mere scaffolding, at the close we must indeed observe afresh that all validity, as an incomplete universal conception, needs another, to give it final meaning. If there is validity, there is then an object more than merely valid which gives the very conception of validity its own meaning. All that we learned before. It was that very defect of the third conception which sent us looking for the sense in which there can be an object of any idea.

We have now defined what this object is. It is an individual life, present as a whole, *totum simul,* as the scholastics would have said. This life is at once a system of facts, and the fulfilment of whatever purpose any finite idea, in so far as it is true to its own meaning, already fragmentarily embodies. This life is the completed will, as well as the completed experience, corresponding to the will and experience of any one finite idea. In its wholeness the world of Being is the world of individually expressed meanings,—an individual life, consisting of the individual embodiments of the wills represented by all finite ideas. Now *to be,* in the final sense, means to be just such a life, complete, present to experience, and conclusive of the search for perfection which every finite idea in its own measure undertakes whenever it seeks for any object. We may therefore lay aside altogether our *ifs* and *thens,* our *validity* and our other such terms, when we speak of this final concept of Being. What is, is for us no longer a mere Form, but a Life; and in our world of what was before mere truth the light of individuality and of will have finally begun to shine. The sun of true Being has arisen before our eyes. . . .

3.

The Struggle with Evil

. . . In all this, my own struggle with evil, wherein lies my comfort? I answer—my true comfort can never lie in my temporal attainment of my goal. For it is my first business, as a moral agent, and as a servant of God, to set before myself a goal that, in time, simply cannot be attained. Woe unto them that are at ease in Zion. Yes, woe unto them, for they are essentially self-contradictory in the blindness of their self-assertion. They assert that they win peace in their temporal doings; but temporal peace is a contradiction in terms. We approach such peace nearest of all when we have least of ideal significance in our consciousness. We attain it only in deep sleep, while the restlessly beating heart suggests that nature is even then dissatisfied with and in every present state of what men call our organism; but while we, as mere finite human individuals, will nothing, think nothing, and for just that time are nothing. Whoever is awake, is content with the present precisely in so far as the world means little to him. The more the world means, at any moment, to our consciousness, the more we go onward towards some goal. The more then are we discontent with the instant.

Our comfort cannot, therefore, be at once significant, and yet a matter of purely temporal experience. Wherein, then, can comfort truly be found? I reply, in the consciousness, first, that the ideal sorrows of our finitude are identically God's own sorrows, and have their purpose and meaning in the divine life as such significant sorrows; and in the assurance, secondly, that God's fulfilment in the eternal order—a fulfilment in which we too, as finally and eternally fulfilled individuals, share,—is to be won, not as the mystic supposed, without finitude and sorrow, but through the very bitterness of tribulation, and through overcoming the world. In being faithful to our task we, too, are temporally expressing the triumph whereby God overcomes in eternity the temporal world and its tribulations.

I say, our sorrows are identically God's own sorrows. This con-

This selection is from Lecture IX of *The World and the Individual*, 2nd series, first published in 1901. It is here reprinted with the kind permission of Mr. Josiah Royce, the author's grandson.

sequence flows directly from our Idealism. And we accept this consequence heartily. It contains the only ground for a genuine Theodicy. The Absolute knows all that we know, and knows it just as we know it. For not one instant can we suppose our finite experience first "absorbed" or "transmuted" and then reduced, in an ineffable fashion, to its unity in the divine life. The eternal fulfilment is not won by ignoring what we find present to ourselves when we sorrow, but by including this our experience of sorrow in a richer life. And, on the other hand, nothing in our life is external to the divine life. As the Absolute is identically our whole Will expressed, our experience brought to finality, our life individuated, so, on the other hand, we are the divine as it expresses itself here and now; and no item of what we are is other than an occurrence within the whole of the divine existence. In our more ideal sorrows we may become more clearly aware of *how* our intention, our plan, our meaning, is one with the divine intent, and *how* our experience is a part of the life through which God wins in eternity his own. And the comfort of this clearer insight lies precisely here:—I sorrow. But the sorrow is not only mine. This same sorrow, just as it is for me, is God's sorrow. And yet, since my will is here also, and consciously, one with the divine Will, God who here, in me, aims at what I now temporally miss, not only possesses, in the eternal world, the goal after which I strive, but comes to possess it even through and because of my sorrow. Through this, my tribulation, the Absolute triumph, then, is won. Moreover, this triumph is also eternally mine. In the Absolute I am fulfilled. Yet my very fulfilment, and God's, implies, includes, demands, and therefore can transcend, this very sorrow.

For now, secondly, I assert, even in all this, that the divine fulfilment in eternity can be won only through the sorrows of time. For, as a fact, we ourselves, even in our finitude, know that the most significant perfections include, as a part of themselves, struggle, whereby opposing elements, set by this very struggle into contrast with one another, become clearly conscious. Such perfections also include suffering, because in the conquest over suffering all the nobler gifts of the Spirit, all the richer experiences of life, consist. As there is no courage without a dread included and transcended, so in the life of endurance there is no conscious heroism without the present tribulations in whose overcoming heroism consists. There is no consciousness of strength without the presence of that resistance

which strength alone can master. Even love shows its glory as love
only by its conquest over the doubts and estrangements, the absences
and the misunderstandings, the griefs and the loneliness, that love
glorifies with its light amidst all their tragedy. In a world where there
was no such consciousness as death suggests to us mortals, love
would never consciously know the wealth and the faithfulness of its
own deathless meaning. Whoever has not at some time profoundly
despaired, knows not the blessed agony of rising from despair and
of being more than the demonic powers that are wrecking his life.
Art, which in its own way often gives us our brief glimpses of the
eternal order, delights to display to us all this dignity of sorrow.
The experience of life, amidst all the chaos of our present form of
consciousness, brings home to us this great truth that the perfection
of the Spirit is a perfection through the including and transcending
of sorrow,—and brings it home in a form that leaves us no doubt
that unless God knows sorrow, he knows not the highest good, which
consists in the overcoming of sorrow. . . .

4.

The Reality of Absolute Experience

. . . GRANT HYPOTHETICALLY, if you choose, for a moment, that there is no universal experience as a concrete fact, but only the hope of it, the definition of it, the will to win it, the groaning and travail of the whole of finite experience in the search for it, in the error of believing that it is. Well, what will that mean? This ultimate limitation, this finally imprisoned finitude, this absolute fragmentariness and error, of the actual experience that aims at the absolute experience when then there is no absolute experience at which to aim—this absolute finiteness and erroneousness of the real experience, I say, will itself be a fact, a truth, a reality, and, as such, just the absolute truth. But this supposed ultimate truth will exist for whose experience? For the finite experience? No, for although our finite experience knows itself to be limited, still, just as in so far as it is finite, it cannot know that there is no unity beyond its fragmentariness. For if any experience actually knew (that is, actually experienced) itself to be the whole of experience, it would have to experience how and why it was so. And if it knew this, it would be *ipso facto* an absolute, i.e., a completely self-possessed, experience, for which there was no truth that was not, as such, a datum,—no ideal of a beyond that was not, as such, judged by the facts to be meaningless, —no thought to which a presentation did not correspond, no presentation whose reality was not luminous to its comprehending thought. Only such an absolute experience could say with assurance: "Beyond my world there is no further experience actual." But if, by hypothesis, there is to be no such an experience, but only a limited collection of finite experiences, the question returns: The reality of this final limitation, the existence of no experience beyond the broken mass of finite fragments—this is to be a truth—but for whose experience is it to be a truth? Plainly, in the supposed case, it will be a truth nowhere presented—a truth for

This selection is from Chapter VII of Royce's book *The Conception of God*, first published in 1897.

nobody. But, as we saw before, to assert any absolute reality as real is simply to assert an experience—and, in fact, just insofar as the reality is absolute, an absolute experience—for which this reality exists. To assert a truth as more than possible is to assert the concrete reality of an experience that knows this experience. Hence—and here, indeed, is the conclusion of the whole matter—the very effort hypothetically to assert that the whole world of experience is a world of fragmentary and finite experience is an effort involving a contradiction. Experience must constitute, in its entirety, one self-determined and consequently absolute and organized whole.

Otherwise put: All concrete or genuine, and not barely possible truth is, as such, a truth somewhere experienced. This is the inevitable result of the view with which we started when we said that without experience there is no knowledge. For truth *is,* so far as it is *known.* Now, this proposition applies as well to the totality of the world of finite experience as it does to the parts of that world. There must, then, be an experience to which is present the constitution (i.e., the actual limitation and narrowness) of all finite experience, just as surely as there is such a constitution. That there is nothing at all beyond this limited constitution must, as a fact, be present to this final experience. But this fact that the world of finite experience has no experience beyond it could not be present, as a fact, to any but an absolute experience which knew all that is or that genuinely can be known; and the proposition that a totality of finite experience could exist without there being an absolute experience thus proves to be simply self-contradictory. . . .

HASTINGS RASHDALL

(1858-1924)

This passage quoted from a popular work gives one of the best statements of the Berkeleian type of argument for God's existence. Its author is not an absolute idealist and does not equate God with reality as a whole, though making everything dependent on God. This of course has always been the orthodox Christian view, though not necessarily combined with philosophical idealism.

The Idealist Argument
for the Existence of God

. . . IN THE EXPERIENCE which the plain man calls seeing or touching there is always present another thing. Even if we suppose that he is justified in saying "I touch matter," there is always present the "I" as well as the matter. It is always and inevitably matter-mind that he knows. Nobody ever can get away from this "I," nobody can ever see or feel what matter is like apart from the "I" which knows it. He may, indeed, infer that this matter exists apart from the "I" which knows it. He may infer that it exists, and may even go as far as to assume that, apart from his seeing or touching or anybody else's seeing or touching, matter possesses all those qualities which it possesses for his own consciousness. But this is inference, and not immediate knowledge. And the validity or reasonableness of the inference may be disputed. How far it is reasonable or legitimate to attribute to matter as it is in itself the qualities which it has for us must depend upon the nature of those qualities. Let us then go on to ask whether the qualities which constitute matter as we know it are qualities which we can reasonably or

This selection is from Rashdall's book, *Philosophy and Religion*, Lecture I. It was first published in 1909 by Duckworth Ltd., London, with whose kind permission it is here reprinted.

even intelligibly attribute to a supposed matter-in-itself, to matter
considered as something capable of existing by itself altogether apart
from any kind of conscious experience.

In matter, as we know it, there are two elements. There are
certain sensations, or certain qualities which we come to know by
sensation, and there are certain relations. Now, with regard to the
sensations, a very little reflection will, I think, show us that it is
absolutely meaningless to say that matter has the qualities implied
by these sensations, even when they are not felt, and would still
possess them, even supposing it never had been and never would
be felt by anyone whatever. In a world in which there were no eyes
and no minds, what would be the meaning of saying that things are
red or blue? In a world in which there were no ears and no minds,
there would clearly be no such thing as sound. This is exactly the
point at which Locke's analysis stopped. He admitted that the "secondary qualities"—colors, sounds, tastes—of objects were really
not in the things themselves but in the mind which perceives them.
What existed in the things was merely a power of producing these
sensations in us, the quality in the thing being not in the least like
the sensations which it produces in us: he admitted that this power
of producing a sensation was something different from, and totally
unlike, the sensation itself. But when he came to the primary qualities—solidarity, shape, magnitude and the like—he supposed that
the qualities in the thing were exactly the same as they are for our
minds. If all mind were to disappear from the Universe, there would
henceforth be no red and blue, no hot and cold; but things would
still be big or small, round or square, solid or fluid. Yet, even with
these "primary qualities," the reference to mind is really there just
as much as in the case of the secondary qualities; only the fact is
not quite so obvious. And one reason for this is that these primary
qualities involve, much more glaringly and unmistakably than the secondary, something which is not *mere* sensation—something which
implies thought and not mere sense. What do we mean by solidity,
for instance? We mean partly that we get certain sensations from
touching the object—sensations of touch and sensations of what is
called the muscular sense, sensations of muscular exertion and of
pressure resisted. Now, so far as that is what solidity means, it is
clear that the quality in question involves as direct a reference to
our subjective feelings as the secondary qualities of color and
sound. But something more than this is implied in our idea of

solidity. We think of external objects as occupying space. And spaciality cannot be analyzed away into mere feelings of ours. The feelings of touch which we derive from an object come to us one after the other. No mental reflection upon sensations which come one after the other in time could ever give us the idea of space, if they were not spacially related from the first. It is of the essence of spaciality that the parts of the object shall be thought of as existing side by side, outside one another. But this side-by-sideness, this outsideness, is after all a way in which the things present themselves to a mind. Space is made up of relations; and what is the meaning of relations apart from a mind which relates, or *for* which the things are related? If spaciality were a quality of the thing in itself, it would exist no matter what became of other things. It would be quite possible, therefore, that the top of this table should exist without the bottom; yet everybody surely would admit the meaninglessness of talking about a piece of matter (no matter how small, be it an atom or the smallest electron conceived by the most recent physical speculation) which had a top without a bottom, or a right-hand side without a left. This space-occupying quality which is the most fundamental element in our ordinary conception of matter is wholly made up of the relation of one part of it to another. Now can a relation exist except for a mind? As it seems to me, the suggestion is meaningless, Relatedness only has a meaning when thought of in connection with a mind which is capable of grasping or holding together both terms of the relation. The relation between point A and point B is not *in* point A or *in* point B taken by themselves. It is all in the "between": "betweenness" from its very nature cannot exist in any one point of space or in several isolated points of space or things in space; it must exist only in some one existent which holds together and connects those points. And nothing, as far as we can understand, can do that except a mind. Apart from mind there can be no relatedness: apart from relatedness no space: apart from space no matter. It follows that apart from mind there can be no matter. . . .

. . . If there is nothing in matter, as we know it, which does not obviously imply mind, if the very idea of matter is unintelligible apart from mind, it is clear that matter can never have existed without mind.

What then, it may be asked, of the things which no human eye has ever seen or even thought of? Are we to suppose that a new

planet comes into existence for the first time when first it sails into
the telescope of the astronomer, and that Science is wrong in inferring that it existed not only before that particular astronomer
saw it, but before there were any astronomers or other human or
even animal intelligences upon this planet to observe it? Did the
world of Geology come into existence for the first time when some
eighteenth-century geologist first suspected that the world was more
than six thousand years old? Are all those ages of past history, when
the earth and the sun were but nebulae, a mere imagination, or did
that nebulous mass come into existence thousands or millions of
years afterwards when Kant or Laplace first conceived that it had
existed? The supposition is clearly self-contradictory and impossible.
If Science be not a mass of illusion, this planet existed millions of
years before any human—or, so far as we know, any animal minds
—existed to think its existence. And yet I have endeavoured to show
the absurdity of supposing that matter can exist except for a mind.
It is clear, then, that it cannot be merely for such minds as ours that
the world has always existed. Our minds come and go. They have
a beginning; they go to sleep; they may, for aught that we can immediately know, come to an end. At no time does any one of them,
at no time do all of them together, apprehend all that there is to be
known. We do not create a Universe; we discover it piece by piece,
and after all very imperfectly. Matter cannot intelligibly be supposed
to exist apart from Mind: and yet it clearly does not exist merely
for *our* minds. Each of us knows only one little bit of the Universe:
all of us together do not know the whole. If the whole is to exist at
all, there must be some one mind which knows the whole. The mind
which is necessary to the very existence of the Universe is the mind
that we call God. . . .

GEORGE HOLMES HOWISON

(1834-1916)

Howison provides a good example of a still more pluralistic type of idealism which yet allows a place for God. His argument for God, whose existence he holds to be entailed by the existence of finite minds, is however less clear than his argument given in Selection 2 that each finite mind necessarily involves others because we can only be conscious of our self-identity in contrast to different persons.

1.
The Eternal Republic

... TO PUT THE THEORY of the present book in a clearer light, its chief points had best be summarised one by one. They may be stated as follows:

I. All existence is either (1) the existence of *minds,* or (2) the existence of *the items and order of their experience;* all the existences known as "material" consisting in certain of these experiences, with an order organised by the self-active forms of consciousness that in their unity constitute the substantial being of a mind, in distinction from its phenomenal life.

II. Accordingly, Time and Space, and all that both "contain," owe their entire existence to the essential correlation and coexistence of minds. This coexistence is not to be thought of as either their simultaneity or their contiguity. It is not at all spatial, nor temporal, but must be regarded as simply *their logical implication of each other in the self-defining consciousness of each.* And this recognition of each other as all alike self-determining, renders *their coexistence a moral order.*

III. These many minds, being in this mutual recognition of

This selection is from the Preface to the first edition of Howison's book, *The Limits of Evolution and Other Essays,* which was published in 1901. The selections from this work are reprinted with the kind permission of the University of California Press.

[207]

their moral reality the determining ground of all events and all mere "things," form the eternal (i.e. unconditionally real) world; and by a fitting metaphor, consecrated in the usage of ages, they may be said to constitute the "City of God." In this, all the members have the equality belonging to their common aim of fulfilling their one Rational Ideal; and God, the fulfilled Type of every mind, the living Bond of their union, reigns in it, not by the exercise of power, but solely by light; not by authority, but by reason; not by efficient, but by final causation,—that is, simply by being the impersonated Idea of every mind.

IV. The members of this Eternal Republic have no origin but their purely logical one of reference to each other, including thus their primary reference to God. That is, in the literal sense of the word, they have no origin at all—no source in *time* whatever. There is nothing at all, prior to them, out of which their being arises; they are not "things" in the chain of efficient causation. They simply *are,* and together constitute the eternal order.

V. Still, they exist only in and through their mutually thought correlation, their eternal "City," and out of it would be non-existent. But through their thought-reciprocity with each other, God being included in the circle, they are the ground of all literally originated, all temporal and spatial existences.

VI. Hence, relatively to the natural world, they are free, in the sense of being in control of it: so far from being bound *by* it and its laws, they are the very source of all the law there is or can be in it. Relatively to God also, and to each other, all minds other than God are free, in the still higher sense that nothing but their own light and conviction determines their actions toward each other or toward God. This freedom belongs to every one of them in their total or eternal reality, be it burdened and obscured as it may in the world of their temporal experience; and its intrinsic tendency must be to fulfil itself in this external world also.

VII. This Pluralism held in union by reason, this World of Spirits, is thus the genuine *Unmoved One that moves all Things.* Not the solitary God, but the whole World of Spirits including God, and united through recognition of him, is the real "Prime Mover" of which since the culmination of Greek philosophy we have heard so much. Its oneness is not that of a single inflexible Unit, leaving no room for freedom in the many, for a many that is really many, but is the oneness of uniting harmony, of spontaneous cooperation, in which every member, from inner initiative, from native contemplation of the same Ideal, joins in moving all things changeable toward the common goal.

VIII. This movement of things changeable toward the goal of a common Ideal is what we have in these days learned to call the process of Evolution. The World of Spirits, as the ground of it, can therefore neither be the product of evolution nor in any way subject to evolution; except that in the case of minds other than God, who have their differentiation from him in a side of their being which is in one aspect contradictory of their Ideal, this sense-world of theirs is by its very nature, in its conjunction with their total nature, under the law of return toward the essential Ideal. In this world of sense, this essentially incomplete and tentative world of experience, evolution must therefore reign universally; but beyond this world of phenomena it cannot go. Every mind has an eternal reality that did not arise out of change, and that cannot by change pass away.

IX. These several conceptions, founded in the idea of the World of Spirits as a circuit of moral relationship, carry with them a profound change in our habitual notions of the creative office of God. Creation, so far as it can be an office of God toward other spirits, is not an *event*—not an act causative and effective in *time*. It is not an *occurrence*, dated at some instant in the life of God, after the lapse of aeons of his solitary being. God has no being subject to time, such as we have; nor is the fundamental relation which minds bear to him a temporal relation. So far as it concerns minds, then, *creation must simply mean the eternal fact that God is a complete moral agent,* that his essence is just a perfect CONSCIENCE—the immutable recognition of the world of spirits as having each a reality as inexpugnable as his own, as sacred as his own, with rights to be revered; supremely, the right of self-direction from personal conviction. This immutable perfection of the moral recognition by God, let it be repeated, is the living Bond in the whole world of spirits. Did it not exist, did God not exist, there would be, there could be, no such world; there could be no other spirit at all. *Real creation,* then, *means such an eternal dependence of other souls upon God that the non-existence of God would involve the non-existence of all souls, while his existence is the essential supplementing Reality that raises them to reality; without him, they would be but void names and bare possibilities.* Thus in the Divine office designated "Creation," exactly as in that denoted by "Redemption"

or "Regeneration," the word is a metaphor; but in the one case as
in the other, it symbolises a reality eternal and essential, of a significance no less than stupendous.

X. The key to the whole view is found in its doctrine concerning
the *system* of causation. It reduces Efficient Cause from that supreme
place in philosophy which this has hitherto held, and gives the highest, the organising place to Final Cause instead. Final cause becomes
now not merely the guiding and regulative, but actually the ground-
ing and constitutive principle of real existence; all the other causes,
Material, Formal, Efficient, become its *derivatives* as well as the
objects of its systematizing control. A philosophy is thus presented
in which the Ideal is indeed central and determining, and therefore
real, and the measure of all other reality; a philosophy that, for the
first time, might with accuracy be named Absolute Idealism, did not
the title Personal express its nature still better. . . .

2.

Human Immortality

. . . I MUST NOT DELAY you with prolonged or intricate proofs that the real nature of Time is such as I have described, though such proofs are indeed numerous and prolific. It is enough for our purposes tonight to call attention, first, to the simple fact that we cannot rationally entertain the proposition that there is, or can be, no Time,—which shows that the consciousness of Time is inseparable from our essential being; in other words, is intrinsic in it. Secondly, let us attend to the more significant fact, that we are conscious of Time as a unity at once absolutely complete and also infinite, and cannot be conscious of it except with these characters,— which shows that it cannot have come to us by transfer or communication. For if it did come in this way, then, in the first place, it must have a history, and a limit of history to date, quite as all else that comes so has; and this would mean that it must be thought as finite in quantity, as well as an incomplete unity capable of increase. And, in the second place, its coming in this heroic fashion is itself unstatable and unthinkable, except in terms of Time itself; and this shows that the pretended empirical explanation requires the preemployment of the thing whose origin it would clear up,— all the light the explanation gives, it borrows from the very thing it pretends to explain.

Time is therefore inevitably brought home to the *soul* as its real source, and our convinced judgment confesses the consciousness of Time to be a consciousness *a priori;* that is, an *act* of the soul, of the individual mind, in the spontaneous unity of its existence. It is seen to be a changeless *principle of relation,* by which the active-conscious self connects the times of experience into the serial order which we call sequence or succession, and blends the two concomitant series, physical and psychic, into the single whole that expresses the self's own unity.

So a sufficiently strict interpretation of the modern psychological

This selection is from Chapter VI of *The Limits of Evolution.*

doctrine, instead of merely making materialism give way, and yield place for a chance and hope that we *may* be immortal,—instead of simply leaving room for the imperishable eternity of the universal *mother sea* of Mind,—lays sure the foundations for a certainty that we *each* belong to the eternal world, not simply to the world of shifting and transient experience. It provides for *our* selves, for each of them individually, a place in the world not merely of consequences and mediated *effects,* but of primary and unmediated *causes.* Hence it gives us assurance that death no more than any other event in experience is our end and close, but that we survive it, ourselves the springs that organise experience. It shows us possessed, intrinsically, of the very roots and sources of perception, not merely of its experienced fact, and so presents us as possessed of power to rise beyond the grave—yes, in and through the very act of death— into new worlds of perception. . . .

. . . We sometimes hear it objected to the foregoing line of proof, that it comes quite short of any immortality which a rational being can value. It can establish nothing, the objectors say, but the indestructible power of staying on, merely in a world of sense-perception.

The objection is pertinent, and would be serious were our *a priori* consciousness completely summed up in furnishing the conditions sufficient for a world of sense-perception only, and for self-preservative action in such a world. But the objection vanishes as soon as we realize that our argument, properly judged, rests upon the spontaneous character of the organising cognition as a source, not upon what happens to be the contents to which, for brevity's sake, we have thus far confined our attention in making out the fact of this spontaneous mental life. The truth is, our *a priori* cognition is not confined to these conditions of mere perception; it goes, on the contrary, and with still clearer evidence, to the region of our guiding ideals—to the True, to the Beautiful, to the Good. These all-controlling ideals are not only the goal of the sense-perceptive or experiencing spirit, but are actively constituent in the soul's primary being. The same reasoning that leads us to conclude Time, Space and Causation, the conditions of sense-perceptive life, to be structural in our active primal being, leads quite as unavoidably, and more directly, to the higher conclusion that the three ideals are also structural in it, and still more profoundly. By their very ideality

they conclusively refer themselves to our spontaneous life: nothing
ideal can be derived from experience, just as nothing experimental
is ever ideal.

The worth-imparting ideals, then, are, by virtue of the active
and indivisible unity of our person, in an elemental and inseparable
union with the root-principles of our perceptive life. Proof of our
indestructible sourcefulness for such percipient life is therefore *ipso
facto* proof that these ideals will reign everlastingly in and over that
life. Once let us settle that we are inherently capable of everlasting
existence, we are then assured of the highest worth of our existence
as measured by the ideals of Truth, of Beauty, and of Good, since
these and their effectually directive operation in us are insured by
their essential and constitutive place in our being.

'Tis but a surface-view of human nature which gives the impression that the argument to immortality from our *a priori* powers
leads to nothing more than bare continuance. What it really leads
to, is the continuance of a being whose most intimate nature is
found, not in the capacity of sensory life, but in the power of setting
and appreciating *values,* through its still higher power of determining its ideals. For such a nature to continue, is to continue in the
gradual development of all that makes for worth.

Not only does this follow from the general fact that all conscious being—at any rate, all human conscious life—takes hold
a priori upon worth of every sort, but it can be made still plainer
by considering for a moment just what the *a priori* cognition of
Worth is, when taken in its highest aspect—the aspect of good will,
or morality. The consciousness of self is intrinsically *personal*—the
consciousness of a society—of being in essential and inseparable
relation with other selves. That a mind is conscious of itself as a
self, means at the least that it discriminates itself *from* others, but
therefore that it also refers its own defining conception *to* others,—
is in relation *with* them, as unquestionably as it is in the relation
of differing *from* them. It cannot even *think* itself, except in this
relatedness to *them;* cannot at all *be,* except as a member of a
reciprocal society. Thus the logical roots of each mind's very being
are exactly this recognition of itself through its recognition of others,
and the recognition of others in its very act of recognising itself.
Hence moral life is not only primordial in the nature of mind, but
what we commonly call a *moral* consciousness, as if we would

thereby divide it permanently from the rest of consciousness, and count this remainder mere knowledge or mere aesthetic discernment as the case may be, turns out to be in fact and in truth the primary logical spring of all other possible consciousness. So profoundly and so immovably is this deepest Fountain of value and worth in-seated in our being.

J. M. ELLIS McTAGGART

(1866-1925)

Howison conceived reality as a society of spirits; McTaggart takes a further step towards pluralism in that he, unlike Howison, does not think it necessary to suppose the existence of a supreme spirit, God. The order of the universe, he thinks, is adequately explained as the result of the harmony between the finite spirits of which it is the appearance. McTaggart is the last British philosopher of any importance to have produced a system of metaphysics mainly *a priori*. It is certainly a highly paradoxical system. He claims by elaborate argument to have established that most of the things we seem to perceive are unreal, that reality is (approximately) a society of spirits loving each other, and even that the only reality is love. He claims also to have justified the conclusion that we are immortal and will all eventually (*sub specie temporis*) attain a state in which we no longer misperceive ourselves but are conscious of our true nature. This is a state of great bliss and an almost unmixed good. His philosophy, even though it denies the existence of God, is thus capable of providing much of the satisfaction given by religious belief. The argument is far too long and complicated to admit of summarization here, but a selection is given from McTaggart's own summary of his conclusions (Selection 1). His main argument for the unreality of time, which has no reference to infinity and thus differs from those usually employed, is given in Selection 2.

1.

An Ontological Idealism

. . . I PASS TO A POSITION which is very vital to my system—the position that no substance is simple. It is possible that a substance is simple in some of its dimensions, but it could not be simple in all of them. This proposition appears to me to be self-evident and

This selection is taken from Chapter XI of McTaggart's book *Philosophical Studies*, edited after McTaggart's death by S. V. Keeling. It was published in 1934 by Edward Arnold & Co., London, with whose kind permission it is here reprinted.

ultimate. I do not, therefore, attempt to defend it by direct arguments, though I believe that it is possible, by various explanations, to remove certain objections which might naturally be made to it.

Every substance, therefore, will have an infinite number of sets of parts. When two sets are such that no part in the second falls within more than one part of the first, while at least one part of the first set contains two or more parts of the second, I call the first set Precedent to the second, and the second Sequent to the first.

But now a difficulty arises. When the occurrence of the quality X determines intrinsically the occurrence of either the quality Y or the quality Z, but does not intrinsically determine whether it shall be Y or Z which does occur, let us say that X Presupposes the one of the two, Y or Z, which does actually occur. X may have more than one presupposition, and two of them may be such that when one of them is fixed to one of the alternatives, it implies the fixing of the other to one of the alternatives. Let us define the Total Ultimate Presupposition of X as being the aggregate of all the presuppositions of X after all those have been removed, the fixing of which is implied in the fixing of any of those which remain.

It is clear that whatever has a presupposition must have a total ultimate presupposition. But I maintain that it can be demonstrated that the sufficient descriptions of the members of any set of parts of a substance, would, except on one condition, have a presupposition without a total ultimate presupposition, which is absurd. The one condition on which this could be avoided must therefore be true. And that condition is that there must be some description of any substance, A, which implies sufficient descriptions of the members of all its sets of parts which are sequent to some given set of parts.

I think that there is only one way in which this result can be attained. Let A have a set of parts, B and C. Let it be true, in the first place, that each of these parts has a set of parts corresponding to each set of parts of A. In the second place, let it be true that the correspondence is of the same sort throughout, and that it is such that a certain sufficient description of C, which includes the fact that it is in this relation to *some* part of B, will determine a sufficient description of the part of B in question. And in the third place, let it be true that the correspondence is such that, when one determinant is part of another determinant, then any part determined by the first will be part of a part determined by the second.

I write B!C for that part of B which corresponds to C, and

B!C!D for that part of B which corresponds to that part of C which corresponds to D, and so on. I call such correspondence a Determining Correspondence, since by it, with the help of sufficient description of B and C, we can determine a sufficient description of B!C. I speak of C as the Determinant of B!C, and of B!C as the Determinate of C, or as determined by C. I say that B!C!D is Directly Determined by C!D, and Indirectly Determined by D. I call A a Primary Whole, and B a Primary Part. I call B!C a Secondary Part of the First Grade, B!C!D a Secondary Part of the Second Grade, and so on.

If the conditions mentioned above are fulfilled, it follows that sufficient descriptions of the primary parts will determine sufficient descriptions of parts of parts of A through an infinite series. We shall then have fulfilled the only condition, by fulfilling which it is possible to escape from the contradiction which would otherwise be involved in the infinite divisibility of substance. And as there seems no other theory which would fulfil this condition, I hold that we are entitled to regard the theory of determining correspondence as true, and to assert that the universe consists of one or more primary wholes, which, again, consist of primary parts, whose further parts are determined by determining correspondence.

It is not necessary, in order to establish determining correspondence, that each primary part should have parts corresponding to *all* the primary parts in its primary whole. It might have parts corresponding only to a certain number of them—e.g., to B and C, when the primary whole contained B, C, D, and E. Nor is it necessary that every primary part should be a determinant at all—though, of course, every primary part must be a determinate.

If, as I believe, causation is to be defined as a relation of intrinsic determination between the occurrence of existing qualities, it follows that determining correspondence is a causal relation, and, consequently, that a network of causal relations spreads through every primary part of the universe, though it does not follow that the occurrence of *every* existing quality is causally determined.

Determining correspondence also involves a classification of the content of the universe—into primary wholes, primary parts, secondary parts of the first grade, of the second grade, and so on. It can be shown that this classification is based on qualities which are of fundamental importance, and it may therefore be called the **Fundamental System of the Universe**.

In order that the secondary parts may be differentiated by determining correspondence, it is necessary that the primary parts should be differentiated independently of determining correspondence. This could happen in several ways. It might happen by a difference in original qualities, or by a difference in the sort of relations in which they stand to other things. Or, again, it might happen by a difference in the terms to which they stood in certain relations —though this last method of differentiation could not be the only method applicable to all primary parts, since that would involve a vicious infinite.

I now pass to the second part of my philosophy—as yet unpublished[1]—in which the results obtained in the first part will be applied to those general characteristics which empirical observation tells us are, or appear to be, true of various parts of the existent. In this part of the system it is impossible to hope for the absolute demonstration of positive results. The most that we can do is to show that certain empirically-known characteristics will meet the *a priori* requirements of the first part, and that no other characteristic which we know or can imagine will do so. But this will not assure us that the universe does possess these characteristics. For there may be others, which we have never experienced or imagined, which could also satisfy the *a priori* requirements. And it may be these latter which are found in part or all of the existent. But although we cannot attain absolute demonstration here, we may, I think, attain reasonable certainty. (With negative results we may be able to reach absolute demonstration. If we are certain *a priori* that nothing with the quality *x* can be real, we can be certain that any empirically-known characteristic, which involves the quality *x*, cannot be true of reality.)

It seems to me that one-empirically-known characteristic which cannot really belong to anything that exists is the characteristic of Time. I can only briefly summarize the argument which leads me to this conclusion. It is: that nothing can be really in time unless it really forms a series of Past, Present, and Future (which may be called an A series), as well as a series of Earlier and Later (which may be called a B series). But the A series involves a contradiction. For every term of it is both past, present, and future. And, on the other hand, the three predicates are incompatible. But, again, we

---

1. This "second part" occupies Vol. II of *The Nature of Existence* (Note by S. V. Keeling).

cannot regard the time series as totally erroneous. The terms which appear to us as a temporal series connected by the relation "earlier than," really do form a non-temporal series connected by another relation. (This I call the C series. It follows from what I have said that things are really in a C series, but not really in any A or B series.)

We must also, I think, hold that nothing which exists can have the quality of being matter. My positive reason for holding this conclusion is that it appears impossible for anything which has the quality of materiality to have that determining correspondence between its parts which we have seen that all substances must have. This conclusion, however, can be supported by showing (as I have endeavoured to show in the third chapter of *Some Dogmas of Religion*) that the positive arguments put forward for the existence of matter are untenable.

It also seems inevitable that we should reject the reality of sense-data—I do not mean that we must deny that we have objects which we perceive, but that we must hold that those objects have not the nature which is usually connoted by the name, sense-data. The ground for this assertion is, again, that nothing which has the quality of being a sense-datum can have determining correspondence between its parts. This position, like that of the unreality of time, involves that perception is sometimes erroneous. (I use Perception to mean the direct awareness of any substance.) The unreality of matter does not involve erroneous perception, since we never perceive anything as being material, though we judge it to be material.

What, then, shall we say about spirit? What, in the first place, do we mean by spirit? I should say that spirituality is the quality of having content—in the sense previously defined—all of which is content of one or more selves. I should say that the quality of being a self is a simple quality which is known to me because I perceive —in the strict sense of the word—one substance as possessing it. This substance is myself.

With regard to selves, I hold, further, that a self can be conscious without being self-conscious, and that it is possible for a self not to be self-conscious. I also hold that it is impossible for one self to be part of another self, or for two selves to have any common part.

The activities which spirits have, or appear *prima facie* to have, are perceptions, awareness of characteristics, judgments, assumptions (the *Annahmen* of Meinong), images, volitions, and emotions. By perceptions, as I have said, I mean the awareness of any substance. But, since we can base judgments as to the characteristics of substances on our perceptions of those substances, we must conclude that, although we cannot perceive *that* the substance A has the characteristic X, we can perceive the substance A *as having* the characteristic X.

There are three propositions about perception for which, I think, good reasons can be given. The first is that there is no intrinsic impossibility in a self perceiving another self, or a part of another self. The second is that a perception is part of a percipient self. The third is that a perception of the part of a whole *can* be part of a perception of that whole.

Then it follows that perception could be a relation of determining correspondence. We might have a primary whole, all of whose primary parts were selves, each of whom perceived all or some of the selves in the primary whole, and also perceived all the parts of each self it perceived. And it might be the case that each self had only one perception of each perception, and that he had no other contents but these perceptions. And in this case sufficient descriptions would be determined, within each self, of parts within parts to infinity. For each part would be sufficiently described by the description that it was the perception which a given self had of a given self, or of a given perception within a given self. In order that this should be the case, it would be necessary that each self should have a sufficient description which did not depend on determining correspondence. Such a description might be based either on qualitative or quantitative differences between the selves (or both), combined possibly with differences in relations.

It can be shown, further, that, while perception can thus give us determining correspondence, neither judgments, assumptions, images, nor awareness of characteristics can do so. There must be some substances whose parts admit of determination to infinity by determining correspondence. For there can be no substance which does not meet this requirement, and we know that there are some substances. Only three sorts of substance appear to be given us in experience—matter, sense-data, and spirit. We do not know, and we cannot imagine, any others. We have seen that no substance can really be matter or sense-data. This does not absolutely prove that all substances, or any substances, are spirits. For perhaps some, or all, substances are of some other nature which we do not know and cannot imagine. But although we have not here any absolute demonstration, we have, I think, good reason to believe that all reality is spiritual—in other words, that nothing exists except selves, groups of selves, and parts of selves.

What, then, about volition and emotion? I hold, in accordance with a view suggested by Dr. Moore, that a desire or an emotion is primarily a cogitation of the object of desire or emotion, which has the further quality—ultimate, and irreducible to any other sort of quality—which makes it a desire or an emotion. I hold that perceptions, which are cogitations, can be volitions and emotions.

Each of us has a perception of at least one other self. And I think that good reason can be shown for concluding that the relation in which a self stands to a self which it perceives is a relation of love —the percipient self loving the perceived self. By love I mean what is generally meant by the word—an emotion felt by one person towards another person.

This is the fact which decides all other emotions. If I love A, I shall regard myself with reverence, because I love him. If I indirectly perceive B, by perceiving A's perception of him, then, since I love A, and A loves B, I shall regard B with a feeling which may be distinguished from love by calling it affection. And I shall regard with complacency the parts of selves whom I regard with love, self-reverence, or affection.

There remains volition. Our perceptions cannot be ungratified volitions, since their objects exist. But are they gratified volitions, or not volitions at all? This question is answered by our last result. We cannot but acquiesce in the existence of what we regard with love, self-reverence, affection, or complacency; and the essence of volition is acquiescence.

If our conclusions are correct, the universe consists of selves, arranged in one or more primary wholes, whose whole content consists in their perceptions of themselves and of each other—perceptions which have emotional and volitional qualities such as those in our present experience, but, there is reason to believe, much more intense in quantity than they are in our present experience. Are such selves immortal? If we take immortality to mean endless existence in time—and I think it should be taken in this way—it is clear that selves cannot be really immortal, since they are not really in time. But the question still remains whether, when they appear *sub specie temporis,* their lives will appear as having or not having an end in time.

If the universe—the whole of that which exists—is of this nature can it include a self who is God? I use "God" to designate a being who is a self, who is good, and whose power is such that, whether he does or does not create all other selves, his volition can profoundly affect them.

It is clear to begin with that there can be no one who is really the creator of the universe, since the created must be in time, even if the creator could be timeless, and since nothing is in time. Nor could there even be a being who, *sub specie temporis,* appeared as a creator. For this there are three reasons. In the first place, both God and the other selves would be primary parts, and they could not be dependent on God in any way in which God was not dependent on them. In the second place, God's volitions respecting them, like all volitions of all primary selves, would be cogitatively perceptions, and therefore they would depend on their objects, and not their objects on them. In the third place, I think that it can be proved that, *sub specie temporis,* all selves begin simultaneously, so that God could not appear to be prior to the other selves in time.

The first and third of these objections do not apply to the view that God, while not creating the rest of the universe, controls it, but the second objection would apply to this hypothesis alone.

But, it might be said, it is certainly the case that the volitions of selves do appear to affect the state of the rest of the universe. And could there not be some self whose volitions had the appearance— which, though only an appearance, would be a *phenomenon bene fundatum*—of influencing the rest of the universe so profoundly that he would properly be called a god? There might be such a being, but there seems no evidence which should make his existence probable. And it must be noticed that, if our theory is true, the force of the argument from design would be greatly weakened, if not entirely destroyed, since it can be shown that a certain amount of order, and, as we shall see later, a certain direction towards the good, follows from the intrinsic nature of existence, and so does not suggest a conscious designer as its only possible cause.

It is clear that, if this is the real nature of what exists, it appears to be something very different from what it is. (1) It appears to include matter and sense-data, while really it includes nothing but spirit. (2) I appear to perceive myself, parts of myself, sense-data, and nothing else. But in reality I do not perceive sense-data, and I do perceive other selves and their parts. (3) I appear to have judgments, assumptions, and images, when in reality the whole content of myself consists in presentations. (4) Many of my volitions and emotions appear to be judgments, assumptions, or images, while in reality they are all perceptions. (5) All that I perceive appears to be in time, while in reality nothing is in time. Can we explain how reality should appear to be so different from what it really is?

This will involve our accepting the possibility of erroneous perception. Even if part of our cognition consisted of judgments, some of the errors in appearance mentioned above must be put down to perception. And, if our theory is true, all our cognition is really perception, and so all error must fall in perception. But is it not an essential and self-evident characteristic of perception that there is no possibility that it should be erroneous? And, if we remove this characteristic from anything, do not we thereby declare that it is not perception?

But when we look more closely we see that our certainty as to the correctness of perception is only that what I perceive exists, and exists as I perceive it, *at the time at which I perceive it,* and there is no certainty about any other time. Now we have seen that time is unreal. The condition "at the time at which I perceive it" must be translated into something else before it gives us the truth. And if that translation should allow for erroneous perception, we shall have achieved our end. It is clear, therefore, that the explanation of all error must be closely associated with the appearance of time.

It is only possible for me here to state what my theory is, omitting both the arguments which seem to me to render it impossible to accept various alternative theories, and also the exposition of the way in which I think that this theory does explain satisfactorily in detail the difference of the appearance from the reality.

The content of all selves, as we have seen, forms a system of perceptions which is determined by determining correspondence, and is in two dimensions—one dimension being the series of primary parts, secondary parts of the first grade, secondary parts of the second grade, and so on infinitely, while the other dimension is the series of parts in each grade. I believe that each of these parts is divided in another dimension into a series of other parts. The parts in this dimension are not determined by determining correspondence, and so must be simple parts, though, so far as I can see, there is nothing to determine whether their number is finite or infinite. (The series, as we shall see, is bounded at both ends, but might contain an infinite number of parts if there were no next terms.)

I hold that in any perception, G!H, all these parts are states of misperception by G of H, while G!H, of which they are parts, is a correct perception by G of H. (By a correct perception I mean one which, while not necessarily perceiving H as having all the qualities which it does have, perceives it as having some of the qualities which it does have, and does not perceive it as having any qualities which it does not have.)

Each of these states in the misperception series of G!H will be a misperception of H as a whole. H, like G, will have such a series within him and will be perceived by G as having it. But part of the erroneous element of G's perception of H will be to regard this C series as a B series, and consequently H will be misperceived by G as existing in time. (G, of course, can also perceive himself, in his perception G!G, and so misperceive himself as existing in time.)

Any perception in G will perceive at present whatever in H is at the same stage in the series as itself. It will perceive as future or as past whatever is at a different stage in the series. The only perceptions which are apparent perceptions—that is, which appear to be, as they are, perceptions—are *some* of those which are at the same stage in the series as their percepta. All others appear, not as perceptions, but as judgments, assumptions, or images. But even perceptions which are at the same stage of the series as their percepta, appear in some cases, not as perceptions, but as judgments, assumptions, or images.

What is the relation which connects the terms of the series—the relation which, when misperceived as temporal, appears as the relation of earlier and later? In view of the fact that the terms of the series are all states of misperception, while the whole of which they are parts is a state of correct perception, I believe that it can be shown that the terms of the series, though each a part of the whole, do not form a set of parts of the whole, and that no two of them can be mutually outside each other. The only alternative is that, of any two terms in the series, one must include the other.

We have thus an Inclusion Series, whose terms are related by the relation "included in," and the last term of which will be G!H itself, which includes all the others. All the terms of this series, with the exception of G!H itself, which is correct, form a Misperception

Series. And when the series is itself misperceived as being in time, the whole Inclusion Series acts as a C series—i.e., the series which is misperceived as a B series. The last member, however, G!H, can never appear as present. For it could only appear as present to a term which was at the same stage in a series as itself, i.e., was a final term in a series. And as the final terms are not misperceptions, they could not perceive anything as being in time.

It follows from the fact that the inclusion series appears as the time series, that the time series is limited at both ends, and that a finite number of durations which are next terms to each other will exhaust it, in the sense that from any point of it we shall reach either end of the series in a finite time.

When we consider what is meant by the time series in different selves having a common C series, it follows that (in either direction) the final terms of the time series of all selves will appear, *sub specie temporis,* to be simultaneous.

We have seen that the relations "inclusion of" and "included in" appear, *sub specie temporis,* as "earlier than" and "later than." But which of them appears as which? It appears clear that, in the time series, the relation "earlier than" is more fundamental than the relation "later than," since it arranges the terms in the order of actual change. And when we look into the exact nature of the inclusion series, there is good reason, I think, to regard the relation "included in" as more fundamental to it than the relation "inclusive of." And from these two results, I think that it is reasonable to conclude that it is the relation "included in" which appears as the relation "earlier than."

Then, in the inclusion series of H, it is H itself (which includes all the other terms, and is included in none of them), which, when the series appears as a temporal series, will appear as the latest term. (As this term contains all the content which is to be found in any part of the series, it may be called the whole of the series.) From the standpoint of any other term it will appear as future—never as past or present. From its own standpoint, however, it will not appear as present, but as timelessly eternal. For this case is not in the misperception series, and so cannot misperceive itself as in time.

It follows that the whole is, not really future, since nothing is really temporal, but as really future as my breakfast tomorrow is future.

We return to the question of immortality. After a finite time (speaking *sub specie temporis*), each self reaches the term of the whole, beyond which there is no other. But that term is the end of the time series. When this term is looked at from the standpoint of any earlier term, *sub specie temporis,* it will be perceived as unending (which it is, since there is nothing beyond it in that direction), and as being in time. And since we shall reach a state which *sub specie temporis* is an unending time, it will follow that, *sub specie temporis,* we are immortal. We are not really immortal, in the sense in which I have taken the word, but this is not because our lives really end (which they do not), but because their unendingness is not an unending duration in time. Thus the view, which has been maintained by some Christians, that heaven is both timeless and future, is not necessarily contradictory.

On the other hand, while, *sub specie temporis,* our lives never end, they do begin. For in this direction the birth of the series is a zero of content, which is not a term of the series of inclusive contents. And therefore the whole series will, in this direction, be limited by something outside itself, and so will appear as beginning in time.

How long, for each of us, the part of the series before, or after, the present life, is in comparison with that life, we cannot tell. But there seem empirical reasons for supposing that it is very great—that is that, *sub specie temporis,* a great length of time has passed from the beginning of time to the birth of my present body, and a great length will pass from the death of my present body till the attainment of the final term. There seem reasons to suppose that both these periods are divided up into a plurality of lives, separated from one another, as the present life of each of us is separated from all that goes before and all that goes after.

What can we say of the value in the universe, if our theory of the nature of the universe is true? People do not agree as to what qualities of the existent give it value. But I think that there would be general agreement that they would not include anything not included in the following list: knowledge, virtue, the possession of certain emotions, happiness, extent and intensity of consciousness, and harmony.

We decided of the final states of the inclusion series—those states which were the wholes of the determining correspondence parts, as distinguished from their parts in the discussion of inclusion—that in them the whole content of each self would consist in perceiving selves and their parts, and perceiving them correctly, that all their perceptions would be states of acquiescence in what was perceived, that each self would love all the other selves he perceived, and that this would determine his emotions toward himself, towards the selves perceived by the selves whom he perceived, and to the parts of all selves. Now if this state of things is judged by any or all of the criteria of goodness enumerated in the last paragraph, it will be very good. It will not possess complete good, which is impossible, since there is always a degree of good greater than any given degree of good, but it will possess very much greater good than we ever now experience, and the good will be unmixed with evil.

In all the other stages of the inclusion series, which are states of misperception, and whose nature will therefore be different, there is no guarantee that the states will be very good, or unmixed with evil. And since our present life is within those stages, we know empirically that they are partly good and partly bad.

Can we estimate all the values in the universe, including both the final and the pre-final stages? The pre-final stages appear, *sub specie temporis,* as finite in time, the final stage as infinite in time. The value of any stage varies, *caeteris paribus,* according to its duration in time. But, as the final stage does not appear to itself as in time at all, we cannot infer directly that the value of the final stage is infinitely greater than that of all the rest. I think, however, that good reasons can be given for holding that the limitation or non-limitation of value depends on boundedness or unboundedness, and not on whether this appears *sub specie temporis* or not. In that case the final stage will have infinitely more value than the aggregate of all the others. And as the final stage is unmixed good, and the others are mixed good and evil, the universe as a whole and every self in the universe, is infinitely more good than bad, although the evil—what there is of it—is just as real as the good.

There is, then, a state of very good and unmixed good, which, *sub specie temporis,* must be regarded as lying in the future, and as being reached in a finite time, while it is itself endless. But the time required to reach it may have any finite length, however great, and we do not know how much evil may await us during that period. What we do know, if our conclusions are correct, is that all the evil of the future and the past are surpassed infinitely in value by the good which lies at the end of time.

2.

The Unreality of Time

. . . PAST, PRESENT, AND FUTURE are incompatible determinations. Every event must be one or the other, but no event can be more than one. If I say that any event is past, that implies that it is neither present nor future, and so with the others. And this exclusiveness is essential to change, and therefore to time. For the only change we can get is from future to present, and from present to past.

The characteristics, therefore, are incompatible. But every event has them all. If *M* is past, it has been present and future. If it is future, it will be present and past. If it is present, it has been future and will be past. Thus all the three characteristics belong to each event. How is this consistent with their being incompatible?

It may seem that this can easily be explained. Indeed, it has been impossible to state the difficulty without almost giving the explanation, since our language has verb-forms for the past, present, and future, but no form that is common to all three. It is never true, the answer will run, that *M* *is* present, past, and future. It *is* present, *will be* past, and *has been* future. Or it *is* past, and *has been* future and present, or again *is* future, and *will be* present and past. The characteristics are only incompatible when they are simultaneous, and there is no contradiction to this in the fact that each term has all of them successively.

But what is meant by "has been" and "will be"? And what is meant by "is," when, as here, it is used with a temporal meaning, and not simply for predication? When we say that *X* has been *Y*, we are asserting *X* to be *Y* at a moment of past time. When we say that *X* will be *Y*, we are asserting *X* to be *Y* at a moment of future time. When we say that *X* is *Y* (in the temporal sense of "is"), we are asserting *X* to be *Y* at a moment of present time.

Thus our first statement about *M*—that it is present, will be past, and has been future—means that *M* is present at a moment of

This selection is from McTaggart's *The Nature of Existence*, Vol. II, Part I, edited after McTaggart's death by C. D. Broad. It was published in 1927 by Cambridge University Press, with whose kind permission it is reprinted.

present time, past at some moment of future time, and future at some moment of past time. But every moment, like every event, is both past, present, and future. And so a similar difficulty arises. If *M* is present, there is no moment of past time at which it is past. But the moments of future time, in which it is past, are equally moments of past time, in which it cannot be past. Again, that *M* is future and will be present and past means that *M* is future at a moment of present time, and present and past at different moments of future time. In that case it cannot be present or past at any moments of past time. But all the moments of future time, in which *M* will be present or past, are equally moments of past time. . . .

BENEDETTO CROCE

(1866-1952)

According to Croce mind or spirit is the whole of reality, but there is
no reason to suppose that it manifests itself in other than finite minds.
Mind is what it does. Hence Croce's form of idealism identifies reality
with history or process. His influence has been greatest in the field of
aesthetics, in which his idealism is shown by his view of natural beauty
as being really a human product in that it is all read into nature by
the person who sees it. The person who sees beauty is, in this context,
an artist, though natural beauty is thought by Croce inferior to art.
He recognises four and only four aspects or activities of mind—theoretical-individual, theoretical-universal, practical-individual, and practical-
universal. He brings everything under these classes. Hence the aesthetic
activity is classified as theoretical-individual, and most of the third
passage selected is concerned with distinguishing it from other aspects
—theoretical-universal (conceptual knowledge), practical-individual (utilitarian and hedonistic), and practical-universal (moral). Ugliness, error
and immorality consist in the intrusion of one activity into the field of
another; hence the great importance for him of these distinctions. Croce,
like Kant, repudiates "metaphysics," but he does not mean by this that
we cannot know reality, only that we must not assert the existence of
anything beyond finite minds and their experiences (transcendent metaphysics). The reduction of reality to these which he effects is in an
important sense itself a metaphysics.

1.

My Philosophy

I HAVE ALWAYS DECLINED the request to expound my philosophy
shortly in a popular way, partly because philosophy, like any other
work of man, can only be really understood by those who are of
the trade, and partly because this possessive "my" has a bad sound.

This is the first essay from Croce's book of the same name translated by E. F.
Carritt. It was published in London in 1949 by George Allen and Unwin Ltd. and
is here reprinted with the kind permission of the publishers.

Any craftsman who takes up the job which a fellow-worker or prede-
cessor has dropped, and carries it on towards perfection does not call
it "his" but "our" work. But I have now reached the age when, as
Giovanni Prati wrote, there arises in the heart "the sadness of the
days that are no more." It was his fortune to know sadness but not,
as we do, to despair in the encircling gloom of slaughter and destruction of all that we held dear or sacred. I have reached the age when
a man's life seems a past that he can survey at a single glance, and
when he himself takes his place in "history," or to put it more plainly,
he looks at himself as if he were dead. That is why I am now willing to comply briefly, as far as is modest and reasonable, with the
request.

Consistently with my simile of a craft as always a matter of
collaboration, we must get rid of the pretense or illusion that a
philosopher's work or "system" is a self-completed revelation of the
so-called "mystery of reality." A definitive pronouncement of total
truth would mean the burial of thought and all its doubts, and, with
them, of man himself, who would not know what to do with his
thought if he did not exercise it in order to live a human life. Man
thinks and will always think and always doubt, though he could not
think if he did not already live in the truth, in the light of God. In
his continual progress man stumbles from time to time upon obstacles
which have a common nature; he meets with clouds and darkness
and perplexity which he must clear away if he is to advance in
thought and in its corresponding action. A man is a philosopher in
the strict or eminent sense if he removes one more of these stumbling-
blocks, great or small, if he dispels one of these clouds, or lightens
one darkness, so that by the result of his work the activities of civilization and morality, slowly perhaps but certainly, enjoy increase.

Hence we see the folly of supposing that philosophies are like
either clever, "brainy" inventions or dreams, which may be believed
and arouse fanatical enthusiasm, but fade away, one after the other,
as each philosopher contradicts and supersedes the last. Such transitoriness is only found in the frivolous ignorance of vulgar and careless readers; the fact is quite different. The truths definitely attained
by philosophers are not mutually destructive but are accumulated
and integrated, and govern the life and thought even of the plain
man who may be quite unaware of it. When, pray, was destroyed the
truth which Socrates gave to men by emphasizing, as against the
rhetorical and dilettante skepticism of the sophist, the force of logical

conception, inference and definition? When was destroyed the truth
of Descartes which, by reminding man that he was thinking, gave
him the only proof of his own reality? When the truth of Vico, who
related thought with action and asserted that men can know their
history because they themselves made it? And when that of Kant,
who forever destroyed sensationalism and abstract intellectualism
by his discovery of the synthesis *a priori* and by his new idea of
judgment, which showed that categories would be empty without intuitions, and intuitions without categories blind? And who has ever
destroyed or eradicated the truth of Hegel, that the principle of
contradiction "A is A, and not-A is not-A" must be profoundly
modified, since reality is not static but living, not fixed but changing, and therefore demands the new principle that "A is both A and
not-A," so that rationalist logic gives place to the dialectic?

Some part of my philosophical work is conditioned by the demand so powerfully and persuasively expressed by Hegel. For while
I have not found it possible to substitute for the history that has
taken place, from which I must start, another history that has not
taken place, as he requires, yet my work, like that of every thinker,
great or little, could only be done in connection and correlation with
what preceded it. Hegel was the last great speculative genius who
has appeared in the history of philosophy, a genius of the class of
Plato and Aristotle, of Descartes, Vico and Kant. After him there
have only been minor talents, not to speak of mere followers who
do not count. But about Hegel I felt with distress, what I saw clearly,
that—quoting Catullus when in love with Lesbia—I could live neither
with him nor without out. Certainly I could not do without him,
though I was well aware of the bitter revolt against his philosophy
during the nineteenth century, which accused him of system-monger-
ing, of violence to the facts, of sophistic trickery and in general of
visionary raving, or, worse, of charlatanism. For all that, nobody
was able to refute effectively his criticism of the traditional logic,
and all attempts to do so by Trendelenburg and others remained
unconvincing and petty, the controversy ending with the proclama-
tion of a victory which was purely imaginary. What is more, the
substantial truth of his dialectic had been absorbed into the blood
of a whole generation, in whose minds the principle of historical
thinking, which he had put forward, flourished. Even the natural
sciences adopted a historical method of their own in the theory of
evolution, of which the new positivism claimed to be the philosophy.

Political thought also abandoned the eighteenth century faith in intellectualism, rationalism, enlightenment and jacobin radicalism, so that the new revolutionary movement, which was adumbrated as socialism or communism, aspired to scientific status by adopting and adapting to its own ends the historical method of Hegel; and in its theoretical expression in Russia today it still wears the Hegelian garment.

On the other hand the orthodox Hegelians, some of whom in Italy were worthy of all honor, treated the works of Hegel as gospel, and made of his philosophy a religion complete with exegesis, dogma and ancillary superstitions, so that his school became a congregation of the faithful. It was no longer possible to expect from them the necessary criticism and correction of the master's formulas, or even any incentive to such criticism, since Hegelianism, as they represented it, now crystallized into a hard and fast dogma, had lost the stimulus of the genuine Hegel, who had been his own constant critic and, to the day of his death, a prey to internal conflicts. Against this Hegel of theirs I rebelled; I rebelled because of my love for history which I saw either neglected by them or treated as *a priori* dialectic, not as the dialectic which ought to arise from the recorded facts and a sympathetic interpretation of the documents; I rebelled because of my love of poetry also, which I saw reduced, in the style of Baumgarten, to a confused perception and an immature philosophy which fused concepts and conceptual contrasts into imagery. Finally, I rebelled because I found it impossible to find any meaning for the dialectical transitions, asserted by this Hegel, from the "Idea" to Nature and Nature to Spirit or for the return from Spirit to a restoration of the "Idea"; in fact I found meaningless almost all the triads which at every step he constructed and overcame by sophistic solutions which gave his system a specious plausibility and coherence.

And yet one had to settle one's account with Hegel or not advance at all; nor did I find in myself the sublime courage of Campanella, in whose mouth the poem of Allessandro Poerio puts the proud defiance of Aristotle: "Nor, seated on the throne of centuries, could I tremble to challenge the Stagirite—You are my opponent!" Consequently, my opposition was cautious and even timid, accompanied by an uneasy feeling that there might be in Hegel some great truth hidden beneath his artificial formulas. I thought one could not have finished with the truth or with the formulas by contemptuously throwing all away in a bundle, without first finding out what the sticks in the bundle were and why they had been fastened together. At last, when my time had come, I saw before me the real logic of the philosophy Hegel had created, the Dialectic, taking shape out of the tangle. At the same time all the shackles fell away which had hampered and constricted this great thinker, and which owed their strength to the theological, academic and political traditions of his time and country and to his own ambition to herald a new and final philosophy that should say the last word on universal history. So soon as I had thus understood the all-too-human failings of his divine genius I was emboldened patiently to disentangle the knot which bound Hegel the philosopher to Hegel the man of human passions and designs, not yet or no longer a philosopher; which bound the discoverer of the dialectic to the builder of a closed system, the bold and deep thinker to the credulous weaver of dialectical triads. This conclusion took shape in my well known book: *What is Living and what is Dead in Hegel's Philosophy.*[1]

It is not worth while enumerating the criticisms which were at once made on this book by the surviving Hegelians or by their dwindling disciples and imitators. I was accused of deficiency in speculative method because I distinguished within a philosophic system what was living and what was dead, what was true and what false, whereas, as they said, echoing the words of Hegel like parrots, a system is the realization of a given principle, which may and should be criticized as a single whole on some different and better principle, but must not be divided up and criticized in its separate parts. But the very thing I was deliberately denying was the indivisible unity of philosophic systems. Apart from prejudice, I clearly saw behind the apparent unity a series or complex of particular problems, some successfully solved and others not, systematized up to a point, but only in provisional systems, which always must be and always are open to reconsideration in the light of later experience and later inevitable problems arising by historical necessity. I could not see in each system the realization of a new and limited principle exhausting itself therein, since in my view the one and only principle of philosophy is the eternal and universal nature of thought itself. So, too, I could not accept their demands that the categories or forms of spiritual activity should be deduced or developed one from another in an orderly progression by demonstrating their logical self-contradictions.

1. Bari, 1907. English translation: London, 1915.

Such a wearisome "ballet of bloodless categories,"[2] finding a final rest in one supreme ultimate category is precisely the "panlogism" of pure rationalism which weakened Hegel's vitality and effectiveness and against which I rebelled. For my part, I closed my account with Hegel, profiting, without scruple, by his great discoveries as the wherewithal to treat by different methods and different ideas those problems on which he had forced arbitrary and fanciful solutions.

Thus in aesthetics and the philosophy of language, in moral philosophy and the philosophies of economics and law, as well as elsewhere, I proposed and defended conclusions quite different from Hegel's. In logic also I saw clearly that the relations of the natural and historical sciences to philosophy compelled me to throw overboard the two imaginary sciences which he invented and elaborated, the *Philosophy of Nature* and the *Philosophy of History,* and to reinterpret his *Phenomenology of Spirit,* reshaping it as a *"Phenomenology of Error"* (and also of the search for truth). His treatment of the philosophy of history gave a new dignity to the subject, but I had to deny his historical order of categories in the development, while preserving his identification of philosophy with its history. And so it was with all his works. The main point is that the more I reflected on his dialectic, of which I recognized the substantial truth, the more I saw that it had been itself vitiated by theological and academic salvage from the traditional metaphysic, and by the habits of abstract logic, which accounted for his arbitrary and cursory treatment of particular problems, in spite of the flashes of genius, which his mind struck in every direction, and of his experience and penetration in human affairs. He had a manly, severe and at the same time wide view of morality; yet, constrained by his triadic scheme and his own German temperament, with too little political sense and too much reverence for authority, he subordinated it to the state and particularly to the Prussian state, which, to his mind, had achieved the perfect constitution. He had, what is rare among philosophers, a knowledge and a love for poetry, music and the arts of form; yet he corrupted their innocent nature, rationalizing them by introducing conceptual, cultural and social values instead of the purely esthetic. He had emphasized at least as strongly as any other thinker of his time the difference and the contrast between

---

2. The phrase is from F. H. Bradley: *Principles of Logic.* The Italian is *susseguirsi e inseguirsi di contradizione logiche* (translator's note).

the method of the understanding in sciences and that of the reason in philosophy; yet he fused the two in a single process where one was propaedeutic and the other completion. He had a conspicuously realistic temper, yet often forgot the clear evidence of fact; his philosophy was emphatically one of immanence, yet opened the door to transcendence. The systematic machinery which he had set in motion caught him and dragged him in its wheels, crushing the seeds of all his best thoughts.

How did he understand the kind of opposition which provides the "moments" or stages for his dialectic? What is the origin of the "contradiction" which for Hegel was not an insuperable exclusion, like that of good and evil for Parsees and Manicheans, but always leads to a reconciliation? As I investigated the origin of the contraries and analyzed the thought that lay behind them, I could not resist the conclusion that their opposition arises only within the nature of their own substratum; it is kindled precisely by the evolution from one form of that substrate to another, from one spiritual activity to another, the two being only distinguishable within a unity. Hegel, on the other hand, used the formula of mere contrariety, to which he obstinately adhered and which he carried so far as to make it generative of all reality. In this way he falsified the dialectical complex of spirit, one in its various activities, since he denied the reality of them all, interpreting them slightly as so many unsuccessful attempts at the truth of philosophy, which would be attained only in the mystic realization of the Idea. This was an initial error which had the gravest consequences, since as I have said, it infects and vitiates his whole system. And in spite of all, this force of contrariety, which had been miraculously dreamed of by the ancient Heraclitus, Heraclitus the Obscure, and which now was called up and reenlisted and marshalled by Hegel as a necessary instrument for the advance of modern thought, remains, with all his imperfections and eccentricities of expression, his immortal title to be called the regenerator of philosophy.

And so, since modern thought cannot do without this force of contrariety nor the synthesis which at once retains and overcomes the opposing elements, it is to be found throughout in the new philosophic home which I have made for myself and arranged and fitted up, a home new in its foundations and plans and passages and in the use of its rooms, since all are pretty different from those which Hegel had bequeathed. The relation which I there establish between mind or spirit and nature is no longer a dualistic one where the two terms are related by the mediation of God or the Idea, but a unity in which spirit, for its own purposes, fashions the idea of nature or the external world; and thus any intrusion of transcendence is absolutely excluded. The threefold classification, which goes back to the Stoics and was used for centuries by the Schoolmen, and which Hegel found surviving in the philosophy of Wolff, distinguished a "rational" philosophy, a "real" philosophy and a "metaphysic" which united them, corresponding severally to the "philosophy of spirit," the "philosophy of nature," and "metaphysical logic." My affirmation of the absolutely spiritual nature of reality annuls this distinction and leaves only the philosophy of spirit, which resolves the other two into itself. Hegel's categories or forms of the spirit were purely logical and therefore logically inadequate. The last of them, that was to comprise all the rest, cannot be defended in its unrelatedness to the others which it had superseded and resolved into itself. All of them, the last included, have now given place to the eternal alternation of the eternal values or categories or activities of spirit; each of them in its operation presupposes the others, since all are necessary to the whole, and no one can claim a primacy that belongs only to the whole cycle or to the spirit itself. Many criticisms and censures and even rather flat satires have been made on my "four" categories, as if truth, beauty, morality or goodness and utility were private inventions of mine rather than spiritual activities and ideals to which men constantly give these names—names that are not without meaning. And I have been insistently urged to unify these categories in the Hegelian way, that is to say, to annihilate them or give them up, which I steadily refused to do. In this philosophy of mine, then, poetry is poetry and not philosophy; action and morality are what they are, not poetry or philosophy; and philosophy is itself, neither poetry nor action nor morality, yet it concerns itself with all these as they concern themselves with it. Even morality, which from a certain point of view might be called the unifying capacity of the spirit, can only realize this capacity by interacting with the others at their own level, moderating and governing them indeed, but as a *primus inter pares,* respecting their autonomy, and not as a tyrant. Nor does historical knowledge any longer, as used to be thought, stand opposed and inferior to philosophy, since history is philosophy in the concrete. If we may elaborate and amend the Kantian definition of judgment, history is the only judgment properly so called, and includes in itself philosophy, which is only living philosophy in history and as history. That is why, since I had to find a name for my edifice, to the term "idealism," which has become vague and equivocal, I preferred "absolute history."

I must protest against the identification of this philosophy, some of whose features I have indicated, with Hegelianism, and against its baptism as "Italian neo-Hegelianism." I protest for the simple reason that we cannot believe in "schools" of philosophy, in revivals, returns, renewals or patchwork of any sort. We must hold fast to the truth that thinking, if it is really thinking, is always the thinking of the mind or, better, of the historical moment, in which it is done; that it is always original and not reducible or derivative; that only on these conditions can it be universal or necessary; and that to treat thought in any other way is to misunderstand its vertical character and to materialize it unphilosophically as an event conditioned and determined by the past. I hope it is not necessary to state that in these remarks I am not indulging the *laudum immensa cupido* which sometimes exhibits itself as the gross personal vanity of refusing to acknowledge the influence of a master. What can be more delightful or more restful than a loyal confidence in the person and the teaching of a master? Can anyone have failed to experience this delightful security, especially in his youth, or to long that it might last for ever, as one longs always for some faithful heart, the one heart faithful above all others, on which to rest one's own, in perfect confidence? I too have experienced this happiness; I remember with what longing and excitement I awaited, with what a thrill of joy I found the men or the books that could clear my confusion and dispel my doubts; by them I judged myself, with them I identified myself, in them I lost myself; they were my masters. But if an unchanging and untroubled bond is the rare gift that fortune gives to her favorites in love and in pure friendship, we must not expect it in our relations with the masters of our intellectual life, just because they help us to think for ourselves and to deal for ourselves with the new situations in which we are or shall be placed. So sometimes, though they may not know it or wish to know it, they make us different from themselves and even enemies or opponents. This is what has happened to me with the philosophy of Hegel. I salute him and shall always honor him as a master among the greatest I have had. But I should have been an unworthy disciple if I had failed, whenever I thought necessary and in whatever extent and degree, to develop or correct or harmonize or replace his doctrines and even to rebuild the whole structure. I had to criticize his idea of a final system from the idea, which I wish had been his, of a provisional dynamic system constantly developing and of provisional and dynamic systematization.

As to the future fate of this philosophy of "mine" (as I may call it for clearness in this last statement), like all others it will be superseded (as I have often superseded it in my lifetime and shall so long as I live and think) by the *unda quae supervenit undam,* by the growth and widening of the human spirit. And yet the truths which I have been able to discover and to establish remain and will remain. Great men or little men, we can neither hope nor look for more than that.

Sorrento, 4th January, 1945

2.
The Philosophy of the Spirit

WITH THE PHILOSOPHY of the Practical terminates the exposition that we had proposed to give of the Philosophy of the Spirit; and the exposition of the whole of Philosophy also terminates, because the Spirit is the whole of Reality.

Here at the end, this proposition has no need of such proof or verification as is customary in calculation. Because the proof of Philosophy is intrinsic to it and consists of the reciprocal confronting of the development of thought and its demands, between the System and Logic. And Logic, as we know, if it be in a certain sense the whole of Philosophy (philosophy in brief or in idea or in potentiality), is also a part among the parts of the philosophical system; so that the confrontation of the System and of Logic, of thought in act and thought in idea, between thought and the thought of thought, has been continuously present and active in the course of the exposition, and the coincidence of the two processes and their confluence into one has been clearly demonstrated.

Logic affirms the thinkability of the real and the inconceivability of any limit that could be put to thought, of every excogitation of the unknowable. And Philosophy, examining every part of the real, has not found any place in which to lodge the unknowable in thought. Logic posits as the ideal of the concept, that it should be universal and not general, concrete and not abstract; that it should be pure of intuitions such as those of mathematics and differ from them in being necessary and not conventional; fruitful in intuitions like those of the empirical sciences, but differing from them by its infinite fecundity which dominates every possible manifestation of the real. And the system has effectively shown that this desideratum of Logic is not a chimaera and that the Spirit is indeed that concept which corresponds to the ideal of the concept: there is nothing that is not a manifestation of the Spirit (an effectual manifestation, not con-

This selection is the concluding chapter of Croce's *Philosophy of the Practical*, translated by Douglas Ainslie and published by Macmillan and Co., London, in 1913. It is here reprinted with the kind permission of Mrs. Gladys C. Quinton.

ventional or metaphorical). Logic, rejecting all dualism and pluralism, wills that the philosophical concept shall be a unique concept
or of the One, and does not suffer heterogeneous concepts at its
side. And the system has confirmed that the concept of the Spirit
alone fulfills the logical condition of the concept; and that the concept of Nature, far from being a concept of something real, is the
hypostasis of a manner of elaborating reality; not philosophical but
practical; thus the concept itself of Nature, in so far as it is effectual,
is nothing but the product of a function of the Spirit.

On the other hand, the Logic of the idea of the concept deduces
that it must be synthesis of itself and of its opposite. For its opposite,
far from being heterogeneous and different, is flesh of the flesh and
blood of the blood of the concept itself, as negation is of affirmation.
And the system has led us before the Spirit or Reality as development, which is the true reality of the real and synthesis of opposites.
Logic deduces that the concept is synthesis of itself and of the
distinct from itself, of the universal and of the individual, and that
therefore Philosophy must flow in to History, and mediate its comprehension. And the system shows the capacity of its principles for
interpreting the complex reality of History, and above all the history
of philosophy itself, by solving its problems. Logic does not admit
other distinctions of the concept than those that are the outcome of
its own nature, such as the relations of subject-object and of indi-
vidual-universal; and the system has confirmed these distinctions,
duplicating itself as Philosophy of knowledge and Philosophy of
action, of theory and of practice; subdividing itself as to the first,
into Aesthetic and Logic; as to the second, into Economic and
Ethic. And since the demand of the concept has been entirely satisfied when these divisions have been exhausted, we have not found
the possibility of new subdivisions, for example into various esthetic
or into various ethical categories among the particular subforms of
the Spirit.

Some are seized as with a sense of dissatisfaction and delusion
when they arrive at the end of the philosophical system and at the
result that there is no reality save the Spirit and no other Philosophy
save the Philosophy of the Spirit; and they do not wish to resign
themselves to accepting that and nothing else as Reality, although
obliged to do so by logical necessity. A world beyond which there
is no other seems to them poor indeed; an immanent Spirit, tram-
melled and far inferior by comparison with a transcendental Spirit,

an omnipotent God outside the World; a Reality penetrable by
thought, less poetical than one surrounded with mystery; the vague
and indeterminate, more beautiful than the precise and determined.
But we know that they are involved in a psychological illusion, similar to his who should dream of an art so sublime that every work
of art really existing would by comparison appear contemptible; and
the dreamer of this turbid dream, should not succeed in achieving
a single verse. Impotent are those poets most refined; impotent those
insatiable philosophers.

But precisely because we know the genesis of their psychological
illusion, we know that there is in it (and there could not fail to be)
an element of truth. The infinite, inexhaustible by the thought of
the individual, is Reality itself, which ever creates new forms; Life
is the true mystery, not because impenetrable by thought, but because
thought penetrates it to the infinite with power equal to its own.
And since every moment, however beautiful, would become ugly,
were we to dwell in it, so would life become ugly, were it ever to
linger in one of its contingent forms. And because Philosophy, not
less than Art, is conditioned by Life, so no particular philosophical
system can ever contain in itself all the philosophable; no philosophical system is *definite,* because Life itself is never *definite.* A
philosophical system solves a group of problems historically given
and prepares the conditions for the posing of other problems, that
is, of new systems. Thus it has always been and thus it will always be.

In such a sense, Truth is always surrounded with mystery, an
ascending to ever greater heights, which are without a summit, as
Life is without a summit. At the end of one of his researches every
philosopher just perceives the uncertain outlines of another, which
he himself, or he who comes after him, will achieve. And with this
modesty, which is of the nature of things themselves, not my personal
sentiment; with this modesty, which is also confidence that I have
not thought in vain, I bring my work to a conclusion, offering it to
the well disposed as an *instrument of labor.*

3.
What Is Art?

. . . THE QUESTION as to what is art—I will say at once in the simplest manner, that art is *vision* or *intuition*. The artist produces an image or a phantasm; and he who enjoys art turns his gaze upon the point which the artist has indicated, looks through the chink which he has opened, and reproduces that image in himself. "Intuition," "vision," "contemplation," "imagination," "fancy," "figurations," "representations," and so on, are words continually recurring, like synonyms, when discoursing upon art, and they all lead to the same conceptual sphere, which indicates general agreement.

But this reply of mine, that art is intuition, obtains its force and meaning from all that it implicitly denies and distinguishes from art. What negations are implicit in it? I shall indicate the principal, or at least those that are the most important for us at this present moment of our culture.

It denies, above all, that art is a *physical fact*: for example, certain determined colors, or relations of colors; certain definite sounds, or relations of sounds; certain phenomena of heat or of electricity—in short, whatsoever be designated as "physical." The inclination towards this error of physicizing art is already present in ordinary thought, and as children who touch the soap-bubble and would wish to touch the rainbow, so the human spirit, admiring beautiful things, hastens spontaneously to trace out the reason for them in external nature, and proves that it must think, or believes that it should think, certain colors beautiful and certain other colors ugly, certain forms beautiful and certain other forms ugly. But this attempt has been carried out intentionally and with method on several occasions in the history of thought: from the "canons" which the Greek theoreticians and artists fixed for the beauty of bodies, through the speculations as to the geometrical and numerical relations of figures and sounds, down to the researches of the aestheti-

This selection is from *The Essence of Aesthetic*, translated by D. Ainslie and published by William Heineman, London in 1913. It is here reprinted with the kind permission of Mrs. Gladys C. Quinton.

[243]

cians of the nineteenth century (Fechner, for example), and to the "communications" presented in our day by the inexpert, at philosophical, psychological and natural science congresses, concerning the relations of physical phenomena with art. And if it be asked why art cannot be a physical fact, we must reply, in the first place, that physical facts *do not possess reality,* and that art, to which so many devote their whole lives and which fills all with a divine joy, is *supremely real;* thus it cannot be a physical fact, which is something unreal. This sounds at first paradoxical, for nothing seems more solid and secure to the ordinary man than the physical world; but we, in the seat of truth, must not abstain from the good reason and substitute for it one less good, solely because the first may have the appearance of a lie; and besides, in order to surpass what of strange and difficult may be contained in that truth, to become at home with it, we may take into consideration the fact that the demonstration of the unreality of the physical world has not only been proved in an indisputable manner and is admitted by all philosophers (who are not crass materialists and are not involved in the strident contradictions of materialism), but is professed by these same physicists in the spontaneous philosophy which they mingle with their physics, when they conceive physical phenomena as products of principles that are beyond experience, of atoms or of ether, or as the manifestation of an Unknowable; besides, the matter itself of the materialists is a supermaterial principle. Thus physical facts reveal themselves, by their internal logic and by common consent, not as reality, but as *a construction of our intellect for the purposes of science.* Consequently, the question whether art be a physical fact must rationally assume this different signification: that is to say, *whether it be possible to construct art physically.* And this is certainly possible, for we indeed carry it out always, when, turning from the sense of a poem and ceasing to enjoy it, we set ourselves, for example, to count the words of which the poem is composed and to divide them into syllables and letters; or, disregarding the aesthetic effect of a statue, we weigh and measure it: a most useful performance for the packers of statues, as is the other for typographers who have to "compose" pages of poetry; but most useless for the contemplator and student of art, to whom it is neither useful nor licit to allow himself to be "distracted" from his proper object. Thus art is not a physical fact in this second sense either; which amounts to saying that when we propose to ourselves to penetrate its nature and mode of action, to construct it physically is of no avail.

Another negation is implied in the definition of art as intuition: if it be intuition, and intuition is equivalent to *theory* in the original sense of contemplation, art cannot be a utilitarian act; and since a utilitarian act aims always at obtaining a pleasure and therefore at keeping off a pain, art, considered in its own nature, has nothing to do with the *useful* and with *pleasure* and *pain,* as such. It will be admitted, indeed, without much difficulty, that a pleasure as a pleasure, any sort of pleasure, is not of itself artistic; the pleasure of a drink of water that slakes thirst, or a walk in the open air that stretches our limbs and makes our blood circulate more lightly, or the obtaining of a longed-for post that settles us in practical life, and so on, is not artistic. Finally, the difference between pleasure and art leaps to the eyes in the relations that are developed between ourselves and works of art, because the figure represented may be dear to us and represent the most delightful memories, and at the same time the picture may be ugly; or, on the other hand, the picture may be beautiful and the figure represented hateful to our hearts, or the picture itself, which we approve as beautiful, may also cause us rage and envy, because it is the work of our enemy or rival, for whom it will procure advantage and on whom it will confer new strength: our practical interests, with their relative pleasures and pains, mingle and sometimes become confused with art and disturb, but are never *identified* with, our aesthetic interest. At the most it will be affirmed, with a view to maintaining more effectively the defition of art as pleasurable, that it is not pleasurable in general, but a *particular* form of the pleasurable. But such a restriction is no longer a defense, it is indeed an abandonment of that thesis; for given that art is a particular form of pleasure, its distinctive character would be supplied, not by the pleasurable, but by what distinguishes that pleasurable from other pleasurables, and it would be desirable to turn the attention to that distinctive element—more than pleasurable or different from pleasurable. Nevertheless, the doctrine that defines art as the pleasurable has a special denomination (hedonistic aesthetic), and a long and complicated development in the history of aesthetic doctrines: it showed itself in the Graeco-Roman world, prevailed in the eighteenth century, reflowered in the second half of the nineteenth, and still enjoys much favor, being especially well received by beginners in esthetic, who are, above all, struck by the fact that art causes pleasure. The life of this doctrine has consisted of proposing in turn one or another class of pleasures, or several classes together (the pleasure of the superior senses, the pleasure of play, of consciousness of our own strength, of criticism, etc., etc.), or of adding to it elements differing from the pleasurable, the useful, for example (when understood as distinct from the pleasurable), the satisfaction of cognoscitive and moral wants, and the like. And its progress has been caused by just this restlessness, and by its allowing foreign elements to ferment in its bosom, which it introduces through the necessity of somehow bringing itself into agreement with the reality of art, thus attaining to its dissolution as hedonistic doctrine and to the promotion of a new doctrine, or at least to drawing attention to its necessity. And since every error has its element of truth (and that of the physical doctrine has been seen to be the possibility of the physical "construction" of art as of any other fact), the hedonistic doctrine has its eternal element of truth in the placing in relief the hedonistic accompaniment, or pleasure, common to the aesthetic activity as to every form of spiritual activity, which it has not at all been intended to deny in absolutely denying the identification of art with the pleasurable, and in distinguishing it from the pleasurable by defining it as intuition.

A third negation, effected by means of the theory of art as intuition, is that of art as a *moral act;* that is to say, that form of practical act which, although necessarily uniting with the useful and with pleasure and pain, is not immediately utilitarian and hedonistic, and moves in a superior spiritual sphere. But the intuition, in so far as it is a theoretic act, is opposed to the practical of any sort. And in truth, art, as has been remarked from the earliest times, does not arise as an act of the will; good will, which constitutes the honest man, does not constitute the artist. And since it is not the result of an act of will, so it escapes all moral discrimination, not because a privilege of exemption is accorded to it, but simply because moral discrimination cannot be applied to art. An artistic image portrays an act morally praiseworthy or blameworthy; but this image, as image, is neither morally praiseworthy nor blameworthy. Not only is there no penal code that can condemn an image to prison or to death, but no moral judgment, uttered by a rational person, can make of it its object: we might just as well judge the square moral or the triangle moral as the Francesca of Dante or the Cordelia of

Shakespeare moral, for these have a purely artistic function, they are like musical notes in the souls of Dante and of Shakespeare. Further, the moralistic theory of art is also represented in the history of aesthetic doctrines, though much discredited in the common opinion of our times, not only on account of its intrinsic demerit, but also, in some measure, owing to the moral demerit of certain tendencies of our times, which render possible that refutation of it on psychological grounds, which should be made—and which we here make—solely for logical reasons. The end attributed to art, of directing the good and inspiring horror of evil, of correcting and ameliorating customs, is a derivation of the moralistic doctrine; and so is the demand addressed to artists to collaborate in the education of the lower classes, in the strengthening of the national or bellicose spirit of a people, in the diffusion of the ideals of a modest and laborious life; and so on. These are all things that art cannot do, any more than geometry, which, however, does not lose anything of its importance on account of its inability to do this; and one does not see why art should do so either. . . . And the moralistic doctrine of art was and is and will be perpetually beneficial by its very contradictions; it was and will be an effort, however unhappy, to separate art from the merely pleasing, with which it is sometimes confused, and to assign to it a more worthy post: and it also has its true side, because, if art be beyond morality, the artist is neither this side of it nor that, but under its empire, in so far as he is a man who cannot withdraw himself from the duties of man, and must look upon art itself—art, which is not and never will be moral—as a mission to be exercised, a priestly office.

Again, (and this is the last and perhaps more important of all the general negations that it suits me to recall in relation to this matter), with the definition of art as intuition, we deny that it has the character of *conceptual knowledge*. Conceptual knowledge, in its true form, which is the philosophical, is always realistic, aiming at establishing reality against unreality, or at reducing unreality by including it in reality as a subordinate moment of reality itself. But intuition means, precisely, indistinction of reality and unreality, the image with its value as mere image, the pure ideality of the image; and opposing the intuitive or sensible knowledge to the conceptual or intelligible, the aesthetic to the noetic, it aims at claiming the autonomy of this more simple and elementary form of knowledge, which has been compared to the dream (the dream, and not the sleep)

of the theoretic life, in respect to which philosophy would be the
waking. And indeed, whoever, when examining a work of art, should
ask whether what the artist has expressed be metaphysically and
historically true or false, asks a question that is without meaning
and commits an error analogous to his who should bring the airy
images of the fancy before the tribunal of morality: without meaning, because the discrimination of true and false always concerns
an affirmation of reality, or a judgment, but it cannot fall under the
head of an image or of a pure subject, which is not the subject of a
judgment, since it is without qualification or predicate. It is useless
to object that the individuality of the image cannot subsist without
reference to the universal, of which that image is the individuation,
because we do not here deny that the universal, as the spirit of God,
is everywhere and animates all things with itself, but we deny that
the universal is rendered logically explicit and is thought in the
intuition. Useless also is the appeal to the principle of the unity of
the spirit, which is not broken, but on the contrary strengthened by
the clear distinction of fancy from thought, because from the distinction comes opposition, and from opposition concrete unity.

Ideality (as has also been called this character that distinguishes
the intuition from the concept, art from philosophy and from history,
from the affirmation of the universal and from the perception or
narration of what has happened) is the intimate virtue of art: no
sooner are reflection and judgment developed from that ideality,
than art is dissipated and dies: it dies in the artist, who becomes a
critic; it dies in the contemplator, who changes from an entranced
enjoyer of art to a mediative observer of life.

But the distinction of art from philosophy (taken widely as including all thinking of the real) brings with it other distinctions,
among which that of art from *myth* occupies the foremost place.
For myth, to him who believes in it, presents itself as the revelation and knowledge of reality as opposed to unreality,—a reality
that drives away other beliefs as illusory or false. It can become art
only for him who no longer believes in it and avails himself of
mythology as a metaphor, of the austere world of the gods as a
beautiful world, of God as of an image of sublimity. Considered,
then, in its genuine reality, in the soul of the believer and not of
the unbeliever, it is religion and not a simple phantasm; and religion
is philosophy, philosophy in process of becoming, philosophy more
or less imperfect, but philosophy, as philosophy, is religion, more or

less purified and elaborated, in continuous process of elaboration and purification, but religion or thought of the Absolute or Eternal. Art lacks the thought that is necessary ere it can become myth and religion, and the faith that is born of thought; the artist neither believes nor disbelieves in his image: he produces it.

. . . But before having recourse to mystery (a refuge to which there is always time to fly), we must inquire whether the two elements have been correctly distinguished, and if an intuition without expression be conceivable. Maybe the thing is as little existing and as inconceivable as a soul without a body, which has certainly been as much talked of in philosophies as in religions, but to have talked about it is not the same thing as to have experienced and conceived it. In reality, we know nothing but expressed intuitions: a thought is not thought for us, unless it be possible to formulate it in words; a musical image exists for us, only when it becomes concrete in sounds; a pictorial image, only when it is colored. We do not say that the words must necessarily be declaimed in a loud voice, the music performed, or the picture painted upon wood or canvas; but it is certain that when a thought is really thought, when it has attained to the maturity of thought, the words run through our whole organism, soliciting the muscles of our mouth, and rising internally in our ears; when music is truly music, it trills in the throat and shivers in the fingers that touch ideal notes; when a pictorial image is pictorially real, we are impregnated with lymphs that are colors, and maybe, if coloring matters were not at our disposition, we might spontaneously color surrounding objects by a sort of irradiation, as is said of certain hysterics and of certain saints, who caused stigmata to appear upon their hands and feet by means of an act of imagination! Thought, musical fancy, pictorial image, did not indeed exist without expression, they did not exist at all, previous to the formation of this expressive state of the spirit. To believe in their pre-existence is simplicity, if it be simple to have a faith in those impotent poets, painters, or musicians, who always have their heads full of poetic, pictorial, and musical creations, and only fail to translate them into external form, either because, as they say, they are impatient of expression, or because technique is not sufficiently advanced to afford sufficient means for their expression: many centuries ago, it offered sufficient means to Homer, Pheidias, and Apelles, but it does not suffice for these, who, if we are to believe them, carry in their mighty heads an art greater than those others!

Sometimes, too, this ingenuous faith is due to keeping a bad account with ourselves and having imagined and consequently expressed some few images, we fancy we already possess in ourselves all the other images that go to form part of the work, which we do not yet possess, as well as the vital connection between them, which is not yet formed and therefore not expressed.

Art, understood as intuition, according to the concept I have exposed, having denied the existence of a physical world outside of it, which it looks upon simply as a construction of our intellect, does not know what to do with a parallelism of the thinking substance and of substance extended in space, and has no need to promote impossible marriages, because its thinking substance—or, rather, its intuitive act—is perfect in itself, and is that same fact which the intellect afterwards constructs as extended. And just as an image without expression is inconceivable, so an image which shall be also expression is conceivable, and indeed logically necessary; that is, provided that it be really an image. If we take from a poem its meter, its rhythm, and its words, poetical thought does not, as some opine, remain behind: there remains nothing. Poetry is born as those words, that rhythm, and that meter. Nor could expression be compared with the epidermis of organisms, unless it be said (and perhaps this may not be false even in physiology) that all the organism in every cell and in every cell's cell is also epidermis.

I should, however, be wanting in my methodological convictions and in my intention of doing justice to errors (and I have already done justice to the distinction of form and content by demonstrating the truth at which they aimed and failed to grasp), were I not to indicate what truth may also be active at the base of this attempted distinction of the indistinguishable, intuition and expression. Imagination and technique are reasonably distinguished, though not as elements of art; and they are related and united between themselves, though not in the field of art, but in the wider field of the spirit in its totality. Technical or practical problems to be solved, difficulties to be vanquished, are truly present to the artist, and there is truly something which, without being really physical, and being, like everything real, a spiritual act, can be metaphoricized as physical in respect to the intuition. What is this something? The artist, whom we have left vibrating with expressed images which break forth by infinite channels from his whole being, is a whole man, and therefore also a practical man, and as such takes measures against losing the result of his spiritual labor, and in favor of rendering possible or easy, for himself and for others, the *reproduction* of his images; hence he engages in practical acts, which assist that work of reproduction. These practical acts are guided, as are all practical acts, by knowledge, and for this reason are called technical; and since they are practical, they are distinguished from contemplation, which is theoretical, and seem to be external to it, and are therefore called physical: and they assume this name the more easily in so far as they are fixed and made abstract by the intellect. Thus writing and phonography are connected with words and music, with painting canvas and wood and walls covered with colors, stone cut and incised, iron and bronze and other metals, melted and molded to certain shapes, with sculpture and architecture. So distinct among themselves are the two forms of activity that it is possible to be a great artist with a bad technique, a poet who corrects the proofs of his verses badly, an architect who makes use of unsuitable material or does not attend to statics, a painter who uses colors that deteriorate rapidly: examples of these weaknesses are so frequent that it is not worth while citing any of them. But what is impossible is to be a great poet who writes verses badly, a great painter who does not give tone to his colors, a great architect who does not harmonize his lines, a great composer who does not harmonize his notes; and, in short, a great artist who cannot express himself. It has been said of Raphael that he would have been a great painter even if he had not possessed hands; but certainly not that he would have been a great painter if the sense of design and color had been wanting to him.

And (be it noted in passing, for I must condense as I proceed) this apparent transformation of the intuitions into physical things—altogether analogous with the apparent transformation of wants and economic labor into things and into merchandise—also explains how people have come to talk not only of "artistic things" and of "beautiful things," but also of "a beauty of nature." It is evident that, besides the instruments that are made for the reproduction of images, objects already existing can be met with, whether produced by man or not, which perform such a service—that is to say, are more or less adapted to fixing the memory of our intuitions; and these things take the name of "natural beauties," and exercise their fascination only when we know how to understand them with the same soul with which the artist or artists have taken and appropriated them, giving value to them and indicating the "point of view" from which we must look at them, thus connecting them with their own intuitions. But the always imperfect adaptability, the fugitive nature, the mutability of "natural beauties" also justify the inferior place accorded to them, compared with beauties produced by art. Let us leave it to rhetoricians or the intoxicated to affirm that a beautiful tree, a beautiful river, a sublime mountain, or even a beautiful horse or a beautiful human figure, are superior to the chisel-stroke of Michelangelo or the verse of Dante; but let us say, with greater propriety, that "nature" is stupid compared with art, and that she is "mute," if man does not make her speak.

BRAND BLANSHARD

(1892-—)

These selections are from the leading American idealist of the present day. The first opens with a summary of an epistemological argument akin to that of Royce and continues with a development of the conception of coherence. Of special importance is its statement of the argument that, if coherence is the test, it must also be the nature of truth. Blanshard also argues here that, if coherence is the test of truth, reality must be a coherent system. This conclusion is developed systematically and cogently in the second selection, in which Blanshard discusses the doctrine of internal relations. His main argument is derived from the nature of causation.

1.

The Nature of Truth

1. IT HAS BEEN CONTENDED in the last chapter that coherence is in the end our sole criterion of truth. We have now to face the question whether it also gives us the nature of truth. We should be clear at the beginning that these are different questions, and that one may reject coherence as the definition of truth while accepting it as the test. It is conceivable that one thing should be an accurate index of another and still be extremely different from it. There have been philosophers who held that pleasure was an accurate gauge of the amount of good in experience, but that to confuse good with pleasure was a gross blunder. There have been a great many philosophers who held that for every change in consciousness there was a change in the nervous system and that the two corresponded so closely that if we knew the laws connecting them we could infallibly predict one from the other; yet it takes all the hardihood of a behaviourist to

This selection is from Chapter XXVI of Blanshard's book *The Nature of Thought*, Vol. II, first published in 1939. All selections from this work are reprinted with kind permission of the author and George Allen & Unwin, Ltd.

say that the two are the same. Similarly it has been held that though coherence supplies an infallible measure of truth, it would be a very grave mistake to identify it with truth.

2. The view that truth *is* coherence rests on a theory of the relation of thought to reality, and since this is the central problem of the theory of knowledge, to begin one's discussion by assuming the answer to it or by trying to make one out of whole cloth would be somewhat ridiculous. But as this was our main problem in the long discussions of Book II, we may be pardoned here for brevity. First we shall state in *résumé* the relation of thought to reality that we were there driven to accept, and sketch the theory of truth implicit in it. We shall then take up one by one the objections to this theory and ask if they can pass muster.

To think is to seek understanding. And to seek understanding is an activity of mind that is marked off from all other activities by a highly distinctive aim. This aim, as we saw in our chapter on the general nature of understanding, is to achieve systematic vision, so to apprehend what is now unknown to us as to relate it, and relate it necessarily, to what we know already. We think to solve problems; and our method of solving problems is to build a bridge of intelligible relation from the continent of our knowledge to the island we wish to include in it. Sometimes this bridge is causal, as when we try to explain a disease; sometimes teleological, as when we try to fathom the move of an opponent over the chess board; sometimes geometrical, as in Euclid. But it is always systematic; thought in its very nature is the attempt to bring something unknown or imperfectly known into a sub-system of knowledge, and thus also into that larger system that forms the world of accepted beliefs. That is what explanation is. *Why* is it that thought desires this ordered vision? Why should such a vision give satisfaction when it comes: To these questions there is no answer, and if there were, it would be an answer only because it had succeeded in supplying the characteristic satisfaction to this unique desire.

But may it not be that what satisfies thought fails to conform to the real world? Where is the guarantee that when I have brought my ideas into the form my ideal requires, they should be *true?* Here we come round again to the tortured problem of Book II. In our long struggle with the relation of thought to reality we saw that if thought and things are conceived as related only externally, then knowledge is luck; there is no necessity whatever that what satisfies intelligence should coincide with what really is. It may do so, or it may not; on the principle that there are many misses to one bull's-eye, it more probably does not. But if we get rid of the misleading analogies through which this relation has been conceived, of copy and original, stimulus and organism, lantern and screen, and go to thought itself with the question what reference to an object means, we get a different and more hopeful answer. To think of a thing is to get that thing itself in some degree within the mind. To think of a color or an emotion is to have that within us which if it *were developed and completed,* would identify itself with the object. In short, if we accept its own report, thought is related to reality as the partial to the perfect fulfilment of a purpose. The more adequate its grasp the more nearly does it approximate, the more fully does it realize in itself, the nature and relations of its objects.

3. Thought thus appears to have two ends, one immanent, one transcendent. On the one hand it seeks fulfilment in a special kind of satisfaction, the satisfaction of systematic vision. On the other hand it seeks fulfilment in its object. Now it was the chief contention of our second book that these ends are one. Indeed unless they are accepted as one, we could see no alternative to scepticism. If the pursuit of thought's own ideal were merely an elaborate self-indulgence that brought us no nearer to reality, or if the apprehension of reality did not lie in the line of thought's interest, or still more if both of these held at once, the hope of knowledge would be vain. Of course it may really be vain. If anyone cares to doubt whether the framework of human logic has any bearing on the nature of things, he may be silenced perhaps, but he cannot be conclusively answered. One may point out to him that the doubt itself is framed in accordance with that logic, but he can reply that thus we are taking advantage of his logico-centric predicament; further, that any argument we can offer accords equally well with his hypothesis and with ours, with the view that we are merely flies caught in a logical net and the view that knowledge reveals reality. And what accords equally well with both hypotheses does not support either to the exclusion of the other. But while such doubt is beyond reach by argument, neither is there anything in its favor. It is a mere suspicion which is, and by its nature must remain, without any positive ground; and as such it can hardly be discussed. Such suspicions aside, we can throw into the scale for our theory the impressive fact of the advance of knowledge. It has been the steadfast assumption of science

whenever it came to an unsolved problem that there was a key to
it to be found, that if things happened thus rather than otherwise
they did so for a cause or reason, and that if this were not forth-
coming it was never because it was lacking, but always because of a
passing blindness in ourselves. Reflection has assumed that pursuit
of its own immanent end is not only satisfying but revealing, that
so far as the immanent end is achieved we are making progress toward the transcendent end as well. Indeed, that these ends coincide
is the assumption of every act of thinking whatever. To think is to
raise a question; to raise a question is to seek an explanation; to
seek an explanation is to assume that one may be had; so to assume
is to take for granted that nature in that region is intelligible. Certainly the story of advancing knowledge unwinds as if self-realization
in thought meant also a coming nearer to reality.

4. That these processes are really one is the metaphysical base
on which our belief in coherence is founded. If one admits that the
pursuit of a coherent system has actually carried us to what everyone
would agree to call knowledge, why not take this ideal as a guide
that will conduct us farther? What better key can one ask to the
structure of the real? Our own conviction is that we should take
this immanent end of thought in all seriousness as the clue to the
nature of things. We admit that it may prove deceptive, that somewhere thought may end its pilgrimage in frustration and futility before some blank wall of the unintelligible. There are even those who
evince their superior insight by taking this as a foregone conclusion
and regarding the faith that the real is rational as the wishful thinking of the "tender-minded." Their attitude appears to us a compound
made up of one part timidity, in the form of a refusal to hope lest
they be disillusioned; one part muddled persuasion that to be sceptical is to be sophisticated; one part honest dullness in failing to
estimate rightly the weight of the combined postulate and success
of knowledge; one part genuine insight into the possibility of surds
in nature. But whatever its motives, it is a view that goes less well
with the evidence than the opposite and brighter view. That view is
that reality is a system, completely ordered and fully intelligible, with
which thought in its advance is more and more identifying itself.
We may look at the growth of knowledge, individual or social, either
as an attempt by our own minds to return to union with things as
they are in their ordered wholeness, or the affirmation through our
minds of the ordered whole itself. And if we take this view, our

notion of truth is marked out for us. Truth is the approximation of thought to reality. It is thought on its way home. Its measure is the distance thought has travelled, under guidance of its inner compass, toward that intelligible system which unites its ultimate object with its ultimate end. Hence at any given time the degree of truth in our experience as a whole is the degree of system it has achieved. The degree of truth of a particular proposition is to be judged in the first instance by its coherence with experience as a whole, ultimately by its coherence with that further whole, all-comprehensive and fully articulated, in which thought can come to rest.

5. But it is time we defined more explicitly what coherence means. To be sure, no fully satisfactory definition can be given; and as Dr. Ewing says, "it is wrong to tie down the advocates of the coherence theory to a precise definition. What they are doing is to describe an ideal that has never yet been completely clarified but is none the less immanent in all our thinking."[1] Certainly this ideal goes far beyond mere consistency. Fully coherent knowledge would be knowledge in which every judgment entailed, and was entailed by, the rest of the system. Probably we never find in fact a system where there is so much of interdependence. What it means may be clearer if we take a number of familiar systems and arrange them in a series tending to such coherence as a limit. At the bottom would be a junk-heap, where we could know every item but one and still be without any clue as to what that remaining item was. Above this would come a stone-pile, for here you could at least infer that what you would find next would be a stone. A machine would be higher again, since from the remaining parts one could deduce not only the general character of a missing part, but also its special form and function. This is a high degree of coherence, but it is very far short of the highest. You could remove the engine from a motorcar while leaving the other parts intact, and replace it with any one of thousands of other engines, but the thought of such an interchange among human heads or hearts shows at once that the interdependence in a machine is far below that of the body. Do we find then in organic bodies the highest conceivable coherence? Clearly not. Though a human hand, as Aristotle said, would hardly be a hand when detached from the body, still it would be something definite enough; and we can conceive systems, in which even this something would be gone. Abstract a number from the number series, and it would

---

1. *Idealism*, p. 231.

be a mere unrecognizable x; similarly, the very thought of a straight line involves the thought of the Euclidean space in which it falls. It is perhaps in such systems as Euclidean geometry that we get the most perfect examples of coherence that have been constructed. If any proposition were lacking, it could be supplied from the rest; if any were altered, the repercussions would be felt through the length and breadth of the system. Yet even such a system as this falls short of ideal system. Its postulates are unproved; they are independent of each other, in the sense that none of them could be derived from any other or even from all the others together; its clear necessity is bought by an abstractness so extreme as to have left out nearly everything that belongs to the character of actual things. A completely satisfactory system would have none of these defects. No proposition would be arbitrary, every proposition would be entailed by the others jointly and even singly,[2] no proposition would stand outside the system. The integration would be so complete that no part could be seen for what it was without seeing its relation to the whole, and the whole itself could be understood only through the contribution of every part.

6. It may be granted at once that in common life we are satisfied with far less than this. We accept the demonstrations of the geometer as complete, and do not think of reproaching him because he begins with postulates and leaves us at the end with a system that is a skeleton at the best. In physics, in biology, above all in the social sciences, we are satisfied with less still. We test judgments by the amount of coherence which in that particular subject-matter it seems reasonable to expect. We apply, perhaps unconsciously, the advice of Aristotle, and refrain from asking demonstration in the physical sciences, while in mathematics we refuse to accept less. And such facts may be thought to show that we make no actual use of the ideal standard just described. But however much this standard may be relaxed within the limits of a particular science, its influence is evident in the grading of the sciences generally. It is precisely in those sciences that approach most nearly to system as here defined

<hr>

2. Coherence can be defined without this point, which, as Dr. Ewing remarks (*Idealism*, 231), makes the case harder to establish. In no mathematical system, for example, would anyone dream of trying to deduce all the other propositions from any proposition taken singly. But when we are describing an ideal, such a fact is not decisive, and I follow Joachim in holding that in a perfectly coherent system every proposition would entail all others, if only for the reason that its meaning could never be fully understood without apprehension of the system in its entirety.

that we achieve the greatest certainty, and precisely in those that are most remote from such system that our doubt is greatest whether we have achieved scientific truth at all. Our immediate exactions shift with the subject-matter; our ultimate standard is unvarying.

7. Now if we accept coherence as the test of truth, does that commit us to any conclusions about the *nature* of truth or reality? I think it does, though more clearly about reality than about truth. It is past belief that the fidelity of our thought to reality should be rightly measured by coherence if reality itself were not coherent. To say that the nature of things may be *in*coherent, but we shall approach the truth about it precisely so far as our thoughts become coherent, sounds very much like nonsense. And providing we retained coherence as the test, it would still be nonsense even if truth were conceived as correspondence. On this supposition we should have truth when, our thought having achieved coherence, the correspondence was complete between that thought and its object. But complete correspondence between a coherent thought and an incoherent object seems meaningless. It is hard to see, then, how anyone could consistently take coherence as the test of truth unless he took it also as a character of reality.

8. Does acceptance of coherence as a test commit us not only to a view about the structure of reality but also to a view about the nature of truth? This is a more difficult question. As we saw at the beginning of the chapter, there have been some highly reputable philosophers who have held that the answer to "What is the test of truth?" is "Coherence," while the answer to "What is the nature or meaning of truth?" is "Correspondence." These questions are plainly distinct. Nor does there seem to be any direct path from the acceptance of coherence as the test of truth to its acceptance as the nature of truth. Nevertheless there is an indirect path. If we accept coherence as our test, we must use it everywhere. We must therefore use it to test the suggestion that truth *is* other than coherence. But if we do, we shall find that we must reject the suggestion as leading to *in*coherence. Coherence is a pertinacious concept and, like the well-known camel, if one lets it get its nose under the edge of the tent, it will shortly walk off with the whole.

Suppose that, accepting coherence as the test, one rejects it as the nature of truth in favour of some alternative; and let us assume, for example, that this alternative is correspondence. This, we have said, is incoherent; why? Because if one holds that truth is correspondence, one cannot intelligibly hold either that it is tested by coherence or that there is any dependable test at all. Consider the first point. Suppose that we construe experience into the most coherent picture possible, remembering that among the elements included will be such secondary qualities as colors, odors, and sounds. Would the mere fact that such elements as these are coherently arranged prove that anything precisely corresponding to them exists "out there"? I cannot see that it would, even if we knew that the two arrangements had closely corresponding patterns. If on one side you have a series of elements a,b,c . . . , and on the other a series of elements a, β, γ . . . , arranged in patterns that correspond, you have no proof as yet that the *natures* of these elements correspond. It is therefore impossible to argue from a high degree of coherence within experience to its correspondence in the same degree with anything outside. And this difficulty is typical. If you place the nature of truth in one sort of character and its test in something quite different, you are pretty certain, sooner or later, to find the two falling apart. In the end, the only test of truth that is not misleading is the special nature or character that is itself constitutive of truth.

Feeling that this is so, the adherents of correspondence sometimes insist that correspondence shall be its own test. But then the second difficulty arises. If truth does consist in correspondence, no test can be sufficient. For in order to know that experience corresponds to fact, we must be able to get at that fact, unadulterated with idea, and compare the two sides with each other. And we have seen in the last chapter that such fact is not accessible. When we try to lay hold of it, what we find in our hands is a judgment which is obviously not itself the indubitable fact we are seeking, and which must be checked by some fact beyond it. To this process there is no end. And even if we did get at the fact directly, rather than through the veil of our ideas, that would be no less fatal to correspondence. This direct seizure of fact presumably gives us truth, but since that truth no longer consists in correspondence of idea with fact, the main theory has been abandoned. In short, if we can know fact only through the medium of our own ideas, the original forever eludes us; if we can get at the facts directly, we have knowledge whose truth is not correspondence. The theory is forced to choose between scepticism and self-contradiction.

Thus the attempt to combine coherence as the test of truth with correspondence as the nature of truth will not pass muster by its own test. The result is *in*coherence. We believe that an application of the test to other theories of truth would lead to a like result. The argument is: assume coherence as the test, and you will be driven by the incoherence of your alternatives to the conclusion that it is also the nature of truth. . . .

2.
Concrete Necessity and Internal Relations

Is THERE any positive reason for believing that the nature of things is intelligible? We have seen that the world could be accounted intelligible only if it were a system, all-inclusive and perfectly integrated, and that such integration would be achieved only if the parts were internally related. By an internal relation between two parts we mean a relation such that neither could be different without entailing a difference in the other. We have agreed that first appearances impose an all but overwhelming veto upon belief in such interdependence; and if it were not for the pressure of the implicit ideal of thought, making itself insistently felt in the scientific search for connection behind apparent irrelevance, and surging up continually in the long line of speculative thinkers who have held to the unity of things, the belief would probably have been discarded long ago as fanaticism or perversity. This verdict *may* be the right one. We have said repeatedly that *proof* of the rationality of things was not logically possible, since it would assume validity for a supposedly independent world of the very canons whose applicability was at issue. . . .

(1) Consider, first, an argument of Hegel's, which derives perhaps from Plato. It is an argument designed to show that the internal relation of each to each is a condition implicit in the very being of anything at all. For if a thing is to be at all, says Hegel, it must be this *rather than that,* and the "rather than that" belongs as truly to its essence as the "this." . . .

. . . Putting it generally, everything is related to everything else by the relation of difference at least. If it were not so related, it would clearly not be the thing it is, since then it would not differ from that which is admittedly other than itself. But a relation that could not be theoretically changed without changing the thing itself is precisely what we mean by an internal relation. Whence it follows that everything is related internally to everything else. . . .

This selection is from Chapter XXXII of *The Nature of Thought.*

(2) Consideration shows that what holds in this respect of the relation of difference holds of other relations also. The nature of any term, unless the term is itself a relation, consists of attributes or properties (in the non-technical sense); by the nature of an apple we mean its roundness, its redness, its juiciness, and so on. Thus a change in any of the properties would be a change in the apple's nature. Now is a relation a property? No. Nevertheless it seems clear that whenever a term does have a relation of any kind to anything else, it also has a property in virtue of that relation—what Dr. Moore calls a "relational property"—and that this property belongs to its nature as truly as does any other. "If A is father of B, then what you assert of A when you say that he is so is a *relational property*—namely the property of being father of B; and it is quite clear that this property is not itself a *relation,* in the same fundamental sense in which the relation of fatherhood is so. . . ."[1] A relation, then, though not a property, gives rise to a property. And these properties are part of the nature of that which has them; the properties of being "above the beasts of the field," "a little lower than the angels," and "the father of B," belong to A as part of his nature. Now could the relations be different without the properties also being different? Obviously not. Could they be different without a difference in the nature of their terms? Obviously not, again; for the properties *are* part of the nature of the terms. Thus it holds of all relations that if they were different, their terms would also be different. But this means that all relations are internal. . . .

(4) The argument just offered, however, has been applied only to the unique, and we shall at once be reminded that even if it holds of the unique, it may not hold of universals. And the case for internal relations must, if complete, apply to both. For the doctrine means that terms *as such or generally,* and not merely concrete existing things, are what they are in virtue of their relations. Now is there any reason to think that an abstract character or attribute is so connected with others, and ultimately with all others, that none of its relations to these could be different without involving a difference in itself? This is harder to believe. There are probably many persons who would admit that in order to say fully what this unique thing is, one must exhaust its relations to other things, but would draw back from the same suggestion as applied to a universal. Thus

---

1. G. E. Moore, *Philosophical Studies*, p. 281; his italics.

red-headedness may appear in a great variety of persons who have different temperaments, antecedents, and states of health. It therefore bears relations to all these characters, as it does indeed to countless others. Can one seriously say that red-headedness would not be red-headedness *unless* it were thus related? If this were true, we should have to hold that no one could know what red-headedness was without knowing all its relations to the mental and bodily traits of the people who had it. And is not that preposterous? For surely we do *not* know all these relations while we *do* know perfectly well what red-headedness is. That is, we actually possess knowledge which, on the theory, would be impossible. Hence the theory must be wrong.

But, for all its plausibility, this argument does not prove what it seeks to prove. What it proves is that we can have *some* knowledge of red-headedness without knowing all the relations of red-headedness. What it ought to prove is that we can know red-headedness *fully and as it really is* without such knowledge. And between these two there is an enormous difference. We admit that if the theory of internal relations asked us to deny the first, it would be asking something absurd. For it is obvious that we do attach some meaning to red-headedness even though we do not know all its relations. But what defender of internal relations has ever denied this? To deny it would be to take the self-destructive position that every bit of knowledge that we possess is equally and utterly illusion, since nothing ever comes before us whose relations we know exhaustively. And why anyone who holds, as do believers in internal relations, that all knowledge is a matter of degree, should be supposed to accept also this nihilism in knowledge is very far from apparent. Indeed it is the essence of the doctrine of degrees to hold that we can have some knowledge without an exhaustive grasp of relations. Between us and our critics, then, there is important common ground. It is agreed that when we use the term "red-headedness" we do use it with a meaning, we do have some knowledge of the attribute it names, even though we do not know all the relations of that attribute.

But is this equivalent to saying that the red-headedness now explicitly presented in thought is all there is to that attribute as it exists in the nature of things? That is what is implied in the criticism just offered us; for unless this criticism means that we can know the real nature of an attribute without knowing its relations, it is saying nothing from which we should differ. But to assume that

what is now presented in idea does give the whole nature of what
is referred to is not only to beg the question; it is to adopt a position
that we have already examined and found false. An idea always
points beyond itself; it always means more than it is; it always refers
to more than it includes within the circle of its explicit content.
Indeed that is what makes it an idea. This difference we have carefully studied under the head of immanent and transcendent meaning.
That there is such a difference is undeniable; it is the difference exemplified (though of course not perfectly, since transcendent meaning can never be captured wholly) by the interval between what
presents itself to the schoolboy when he thinks of Napoleon's loss
of Waterloo and what presents itself to the historian; both refer to
the same thing, but by general admission the historian's explicit
grasp is nearer to the fact than the schoolboy's. *What makes the
second grasp better than the first?* We have seen that it is the fuller
grasp of context, that is, of the antecedents, methods and bearings
of the engagement. The schoolboy must lay hold of these things
if he is to see the defeat as it really was, and as he apprehends the
context more fully his thought at once remolds itself internally and
approximates to the fact without. Similarly of the more trivial thought
we have taken in illustration. For purposes of everyday intercourse
on the level of common sense, the ordinary notion of it suffices.
Does our notion at this level therefore exhaust the nature of the
object? There is no more reason for thinking so than that our ideas
of anything else on this level are truly adequate to their objects.
Little, perhaps, as would be the point of reflecting on it ordinarily,
it still remains the fact that red-headedness is an integral part of
an organism, and indeed is so bound up, for example, with the
structure of hair-fibres, and this in turn with all manner of constitutional factors determining racial and individual differences that
our common notion of it supplies scarcely more than a sign-post to
its real or ultimate nature, i.e., to what it is as embedded in its own
context. As we grasp these further relations, our explicit thought
of the attribute is modified while our reference remains the same;
we see that we are advancing toward the character as it really is.
Our contention, in sum, is this: (1) in such a series of ideas, our
reference is the same throughout; (2) our comprehension of what
we refer to changes throughout; (3) the changes in comprehension
arise from the grasping of our original content in a fuller context of
relevant relations; (4) our comprehension at the end of the series

is a closer approach to the real character than our comprehension at the beginning; (5) further advance must be assumed to lie along the same line; (6) no limit can be set beforehand to the context that complete comprehension would demand. Do these propositions seem rash and irresponsible? To us they seem scarcely more than a report of what can be verified as fact in any process of improving knowledge.

They provide our comment on a suggestion made by some contemporary writers as to the limits of the internal relations theory. The theory, according to these writers, "cannot be applied to relation between abstract universals, e.g., the relation of equality between the pure number 4 and 2 + 2, because we cannot speak of the possibility of an abstract universal being different from what it is, but only to relations between concrete terms."[2] If an abstract universal means an *abstracted* universal, i.e., a universal considered by itself and apart from its context in nature, then it will not depend on its relations because we have expressly defined it as the sort of thing that does not. But the practice of using universals *as if* they were thus independent proves nothing as to whether they *are* so; and our argument is of course to the effect that they are *not* so as they exist in nature. In a sense, then, we hold, with these writers, that the doctrine of internal relations applies only to concrete terms. It applies only to things, attributes and relations taken *in situ,* though this does not necessarily mean that the *whole* of their concrete context must be exhausted before the internality is apparent. The doctrine does not apply to objects taken in that abstraction which would plainly beg the question, but in their real or natural habitat. . . .

(5) Further evidence for internal relations is to be found in the nature of causality. There are two propositions about causality which, if made out, would establish that everything in the universe is related internally to everything else. These propositions are, (i) that all things are *causally* related, directly or indirectly; (ii) that being causally related involves being *logically* related. We believe that there are sound reasons for accepting both propositions; and since the conclusion they carry with them is so important for our position, we must examine them, particularly the second, in some detail.

(i) First, is everything related causally to everything else? If anyone denies this, it is pretty certain to be on one or other of two grounds, either (a) that some events are not caused at all, or (b) that if all

---

2. Ewing, *Idealism,* pp. 130-31, where the same view is attributed to Dr. Moore.

events are caused, at least they are not each of them related causally to all of the others. . . .

. . . Our first proposition about causality was that every existent is causally related to every other. If the causal relation is really universal, which we saw no compelling reason to deny, and "causal relation" is interpreted to include indirect causal relation, this proposition has an excellent claim to be believed.

(ii) What about the other proposition? That proposition was that causality involves an element of necessity in the logical sense. This is far less likely to be accepted without protest than the first. Time was when it was accepted as evident by thinkers of the first rank, but this confidence was destroyed by Hume, and the prevailing tendency at present is to follow writers like Mach, Pearson and Russell in holding that there is nothing in causal law but regular antecedence and consequence. According to this view, all we are justified in meaning when we say that *a* causes *b* is that neither is ever found without the other. But it has become reasonably clear that this notion will not serve. There can be no doubt that we *mean* more than this by causality, and it can be established pretty certainly that there *is* more in it. We have not the space either for a complete discussion of the regularity theory or for an analysis of causality into its factors; but our purpose will be served if we show that among these factors logical necessity is one.

(a) That necessity does thus enter into causality is easier to see in some cases than in others, so we shall take at once the case in which its presence seems to us clearest. Consider any instance of reasoning, for example our old case of the abbé and the squire. "Ladies," says the abbé, "do you know that my first penitent was a murderer?" "Ladies," says the squire, entering shortly afterward, "do you know that I was the abbé's first penitent?" A conclusion was of course produced in the ladies' minds, and our question is as to the nature of the causation that produced it. It would be agreed between holders of the regularity theory and ourselves that the ladies' entertainment of the premises had something causally to do with the emergence in their minds of the conclusion. The question is whether, when we say that the one contributed causally to the other, our only proper meaning is that whenever the first appears the second does, or whether we must say also this, that the special logical relation in which the content of the premises stands to the content of the con-

clusion had something to do with the appearance of that conclusion.
To us it seems plain that it had. According to the regularity theory
our only ground for expecting the judgment that arose rather than
some other quite different one, e.g., that Florida raises grapefruit,
is that thoughts of the first kind have regularly been followed by
thoughts of the second; the question *why* what followed did follow
is one on which we are, and must remain, in total darkness; the
connection between the events is no more intelligible than the connection of lightning and thunder for a savage. We must confess to
feeling that there is something perverse in talk of this kind. If the
ladies were asked how they came to have the belief with which they
ended, they would say that it was because this belief was obviously
implied by what they were thinking the moment before; and we are
convinced that this answer, which is the natural one, is also sub-
stantially the right one. Not that no other causes contributed to the
result; we are not suggesting, of course, that causality *reduces* to logical necessity. What we hold is that when one passes in reasoning
from ground to consequent the fact that the ground entails the
consequent is one of the conditions determining the appearance of
this consequent rather than something else in the thinker's mind. . . .

. . . (b) But inference is of course only one of many mental
processes. Can the influence of necessity which is displayed in it so
plainly be traced in others also? We think it can. Not that its presence in those other processes is equally plain; nor would it be fair
to expect this, since inference is concerned with necessity in a
special manner. But we must remember what we have found earlier,
that necessity, whatever our first impressions, is a matter of more
and less, and that between a complete demonstration and a mere
accidental conjunction it may be present in very many degrees. A
process of rigorous inference approximates to the first of these extremes; association by mere contiguity approximates to the second;
and between them are numerous processes in which there is more
contingency than in inference, but more necessity than in association.
Consider some examples. A painter is painting a landscape that is
half completed, and he finds himself moved to put a tree in the
foreground. Is such a development normally quite unintelligible?
Certainly most painters would not say so. Is it then an example of
pure necessity? No again; it clearly falls somewhere between. Or let
us say that a man is intensely afraid of dogs. With the help of psycho-
analysis he discovers that at an early age he was badly injured by

the attack of a dog; it may come to him as a quasi-intuitive insight that it was this that caused his fear; and let us suppose that in this belief he is right. Can one say in such a case that it remains absolutely unintelligible to him how the fear arose? We do not think so. Again, "why are modest men grateful? Because they think lightly of their own deserts. This implies a syllogism in Barbara. All who think lightly of their own deserts are grateful, and modest men think lightly of their own deserts."[3] Does the major premise here, "All who think lightly of their own deserts are grateful," express a causal or a logical connection? We suggest that it expresses both. If a man whom we know to think little of himself proves grateful for another's esteem, is that, apart from inductions made on such people in the past, as startling a development, as unpredictable and unintelligible, as if he had begun talking in a Sumerian tongue or had run murderously amuck? Surely that is an odd view. We are not contending that between thinking lightly of oneself and being grateful there is the same simple abstract connection that one finds in geometry; it is true that one cannot isolate in human nature the precise reciprocating conditions of gratitude, or formulate one's law in anything better than a statement of tendency; but that, after all, is not utter darkness; we do have *some* insight into why the man of low self-esteem should be grateful for the esteem of others. And so of numberless other processes of the mind.

Dr. Ewing puts the case well:

It seems to me that we can see and to some extent really understand why an insult should tend to give rise to anger, why love should lead to grief if the object of one's love die or prove thoroughly unworthy, why a success should give pleasure, why the anticipation of physical pain should arouse fear. It does seem more reasonable on *other than inductive* grounds to suppose that if A loves B that will tend to make him sorry when B dies than to suppose that it will make him intensely glad. . . . At any rate anybody who denies altogether the insight for which I am contending will have to hold that it is just as reasonable to think of love as causing intense joy at the death of the person loved, except that this does not happen in fact.

Indeed, Ewing would go farther. He would hold that

if the regularity view were the whole truth, all practical life would become sheer nonsense. For all practical life presupposes that we can "do things" and are moved by motives and desires. . . . To say that such

---
3. Joseph, *Logic*, p. 306.
4. *Idealism*, pp. 176-78.

and such an action is due, e.g., to desire for power as a motive is more than to say that such actions generally are preceded by desire for power. . . . It is to say that in this particular case it does not merely follow on but is determined by the desire in question. And this view accepts causation in the sense not of regular sequence, but of genuine intrinsic connection. . . .[5]

. . . (c) There is thus good reason to think that not only in inference but also in many other mental processes the causal relation involves necessity. But what of causation in physical nature? This is the field in which most cases of causation are considered to fall, yet current philosophies of science are disposed to agree that no relation whatever is discoverable between physical cause and effect but one of regular conjunction. Certain it is that between the blow of a hammer and the sinking of a nail, or between the motion of one billiardball and that of a second, no one has shown the same transparent relation that appears in a course of inference and may be recognized under veils of varying depth in other processes of the mind. The challenge laid down by Hume to show *why* any particular physical event was followed by any other has not been met. Nor do we propose to add one more to the list of futile attempts to meet it. But we should be clear as to what is implied in the failure to meet it. Does such failure in particular cases show that causality generally is nothing but regular sequence? Very far from it. Indeed I think it can be shown that regular sequence is not enough, that there must be some intrinsic connection between cause and effect, and that this intrinsic connection probably is, or includes, one of logical necessity. We must dwell on this a little, since it is important for our position that it should be seen.

In order to overthrow the regular-sequence theory, nothing more, strictly speaking, need be shown than what has been contended for already. It will hardly be denied that mental processes supply genuine cases of causality, and any case at all in which the relation involves necessity is enough to invalidate an account which asserts that it never does. But we are dealing now with causality in physical nature. It seems to me that even there the theory has been disposed of by certain criticisms that have recently been made of it. . . .

. . . But further, even those who accept the regularity view are compelled, sometimes in the statement of this view itself, to assume that it is false. When they say that events have causes in the sense

---

5. *Ibid.*, pp. 161-62.

of regular and special antecedents, they intend this to apply to the future as well as to the past. But they have not experienced the future, and hence they must be using an *argument*: *Because b* has followed *a* in the past, it will continue to do so. Now unless *a* is connected with *b* by something more than mere conjunction, there is no ground for this argument whatever. What, apart from such connection, could be our reason for saying that uniform sequence in the past would carry with it uniform sequence in the future? We may say of course that when we have argued from such uniformities in the past to their continuance in the future, we have found our expectations verified, but plainly this will not do, for the uniform sequence of verification upon expectation is only another sequence, on a par with the original ones, and is entitled to no special privileges when the quesion is as to our right to argue from *any* past sequence to others. Again, if we make it a matter of probability, and say that a conjunction frequently recurrent is more likely to be maintained than broken, this either repeats the old assumption whose basis is in question, that the past is a guide to the future, or else is clearly false, since if *a* and *b* are really unconnected, there is no more reason to expect them to continue together than there is to expect an unloaded penny to go on giving heads because it has just done so ten times running. When this old puzzle about induction is raised, the answer usually given is that we "postulate" the uniformity of nature, viz., that the same cause is always followed by the same effect. But what is the status of this postulate? Is it merely an arbitrary assumption? Clearly not; in some sense it arises out of experience. Is it then a conclusion derived from experience? No, for, as has been pointed out times without number, the argument would be circular; unless we assumed "same cause, same effect," we could not argue that the same cause as in the past would be followed by the same effect. But then the question arises, what part *does* this assumption play in the argument? And the answer is that it is the *principle* of the inference, just as the principle of syllogism is the canon involved in any syllogistic reasoning. Now can the principle of an argument or inference be totally without necessity? We can only say that, if so, the "inference" to which it applies is no inference at all, and quite without cogency. We are not maintaining, of course, that the principle of uniformity has the clear and definite necessity of geometric demonstration, nor is that to be expected while the terms that pass muster as causes and effects remain so

loose and vague. We do maintain, however, that the passage from
past to future sequences is clearly an argument, that the principle
of the argument, as of inferences generally, must be more than a
chance conjunction of symbols or characters, and hence that the
linkage between cause and effect in virtue of which we predict their
future sequence is always implicitly taken as intrinsic.[6]

Indeed, whatever the difficulties of finding the true connection
between cause and effect, the difficulties of holding that they are
not connected at all except by *de facto* conjunction is far greater.
We have no room here to develop these in full, but by way of round-
ing out our brief case against this theory, we may set down the
following paradoxes. (1) If causality *means* regularity of sequence,
every unique event must be regarded as uncaused. An unexampled
biological sport could not even be set down as miracle since miracles
are supposed to be caused; it would have to be an explosion of
chance.[7] (2) No human action would ever spring from a self or
from a motive; there is no intrinsic connection between volition and
behaviour, character and conduct, motive and performance. Strictly
speaking, no one murders anyone, though in some cases homicide
has unhappily and quite inexplicably associated itself with certain
elements of a person's constitution. This association is the more un-
fortunate because, though wholly irrational, it is also permanent.
Such a view conflicts at a thousand points with our everyday judgments about practical action and moral accountability; and though
all these judgments may be mistaken, the fact that the sequence
view would *require* that they be mistaken is enough to impose on
it a heavy burden of proof.[8] (3) Note that we used the word "require." It was natural to use it, and those who hold the regularity
view do frequently use it. Yet, as we have seen, if they hold any
belief that is said to be required by their theory, its being required
can have nothing to do with their holding it. (4) Nor is their explanation of how we came to suppose that causality involved more

6. *Cf.* Mill's definition of cause as *unconditional* antecedent. On the argument
involved in induction, see Ewing, *Idealism,* pp. 151ff.; for the difficulties of the regular-
sequence view, see Ewing, *ibid.,* and Ducasse, *Causation and Types of Necessity,*
Chaps. I, II, V.
7. The converse criticism is also sometimes urged, that there are regular sequences where there is no causal or other intrinsic connection; day follows night,
ruminants are cloven-footed, white tom-cats that have blue eyes are deaf. The
argument is unconvincing. For there is usually, if not always, the suspicion that if
the terms are not themselves connected intrinsically, they are both so connected
with a third term.
8. See Ewing, *op. cit.,* p. 162.

than association at all convincing. The usual explanation is Hume's, that the regular repetition of *a* and *b* together produced a habit of conjoining them in thought. But apart from the difficulty that a habit or even a thought of uniform conjunction is clearly different from the thought of necessity, what is meant here by "produced"? When one says that regular repetition produces a habit, does one mean only that there is a regular repetition of regular-repetition's-being-followed-by-a-habit? It does not seem likely. (5) Hume's confident denial that we could perceive anything more than sequence in the connection of particular events becomes more doubtful the more one thinks about it. Mr. Montague has pointed out that though the way the body acts upon the mind remains in darkness, still, when we resolve to attend to something more closely and "in consequence" succeed in doing so, we have a sense of "enforcement" that does not leave us wholly blank as to the mode of connection; and Mr. Whitehead has urged that in particular cases of perception we are immediately aware of being causally acted upon by some external agency. (6) The position would guarantee a scepticism that may be unavoidable, but is not to be accepted till necessary. It says that between the percept and its cause there is no intrinsic connection. Now since we have no access to nature except through impressions that are presumably produced in us causally, we must depend for knowledge of nature on an argument from the character of the impressions to the character of their source. Such argument would be rendered impossible by the sort of causation before us. (7) Stout and Ewing have held, rightly I think, that the memory of our own experiences would be rendered impossible by it. When I recall a particular event that happened yesterday, one of the factors that led to the recall was the occurrence of the past event itself. And when we say that this event "conditioned" this recall, we do not mean that all similar events are followed by such recalls, for we plainly have in mind one particular event happening at a point in past time. (8) Finally, to say that causality involves nothing but regular sequence brings one into sharp conflict with both common sense and science. The plain man has undoubtedly got it fixed in his head that when he drives a nail with a blow of his hammer, there is an inner connection between these events which is not to be found between either of them and, say, a storm in the Antilles. If it is objected that his views are worthless, it may be pointed out that science from its birth has suffered from the same obsession. To be sure, in some manuals like Mill's and Pearson's the uniformity view is insisted on, and Mr. Russell has even suggested that the name and notion of causality should be dropped by science.[9] But we do not believe that scientific thought, even in physics, on which he too exclusively relies,[10] really has succeeded, or will succeed, in dispensing with it. The reason is that behind the scientist's desire to unbare the causes of things is his desire to understand, and his intuition that in mastering the cause of something he *has* to some extent understood it. We do not believe that the *only* reason why the scientific mind has rejected astrology is that the correlation between positions of the stars and the ups and downs of human fortune has been imperfectly made out. We do not believe that when the connection was revealed between tuberculosis and bacilli, physicians would have admitted that it gave no further understanding of the disease, but only a new fact, concomitant though wholly external. It is notorious that the physical scientist finds his ideal in mathematics; and if he continues to refine and purify his statements of abstract connection, it is surely because in doing so he feels himself approaching not only the precision but also the necessity of mathematical relations. Of course his conviction may have been a delusion from the beginning. But whoever says so assumes the burden of proof.[11]

For all these reasons we believe that the view which would deny to causality any intrinsic connection and reduce it to conjunction may be dismissed. *Some* intrinsic connection there must be. But of what sort? Does the insight that between cause and effect there is an intrinsic connection suffice to show that this is also a *necessary* connection? We believe that it does.

Consider the meaning of "same cause, same effect," which we have seen to be the principle of all inductive causal argument. Why do we accept it? We have seen that if it is taken as expressive of conjunction only, no evidence for it and no argument under it are possible; and we have suggested that if it is accepted nevertheless, that is because we have an insight that is felt as justifying it. The

9. *Mysticism and Logic,* p. 180.
10. Cf. Stebbing, *Modern Introduction to Logic,* p. 289.
11. We may repeat Bosanquet's question: "Is there any man of science who in his daily work, and apart from philosophic controversy, will accept a bare given conjunction as conceivably ultimate truth?" (*Distinction between Mind and Its Objects,* pp. 59-60); and Ewing: "Thinkers and scientists looked for causes because they wished to explain events, and if they had seriously held from the beginning the views of causation which most realist philosophers hold to-day, half the inspiration of the scientific search for causes would have been missing and induction would never have been trusted at all."—*Op. cit.,* p. 176.

nature of this insight will become clearer if we try for a moment to conceive the connection to be otherwise. Conceive a state of affairs in which there is causation but no uniformity; everything now has a cause, but the causes vary; everything produces effects, but the effects vary; the blow of the hammer sinks the nail today, but to-morrow under precisely the same conditions it fails to do so, and produces instead the *Melody in F* or a case of measles in Nov-gorod. We can talk thus, since we have just done it, but can we think thus? We cannot. For as Mr. Joseph says, "to say that any-thing may produce anything is to empty the word "produce" of all its meaning."[12] Why? Because it implies that when *a* produces *x,* the *nature* of *a* had nothing to do with the result; that result could equally have appeared if nothing resembling *a* had been on the scene. But if *a,* in virtue of its nature, exercised no constraining influence at all, why say *it* produced something? *It* is a thing of special character; this character makes it what it is; and we should be talking idly if we said that *it* produced something when this character was in no way engaged.

> To assert a causal connexion between *a* and *x* implies that *a* acts as it does because it is what it is. . . . For the causal relation which connects *a* with *x* connects a cause of the *nature a* with an effect of the *nature x.* The connexion is between them *as a* and *x,* and therefore must hold between any *a* and any *x.* . . .[13]

Now we suggest that when *a* is said to produce *x* in virtue of its nature as *a,* the connection referred to is not only an intrinsic rela-tion but a necessary relation. There are two considerations that make us think so. (1) Reflection seems to show that necessity is part of our *meaning* when we call such relations intrinsic. If we lay down a yellow card, then to the right of that an orange card, and to the right of that a red one, they have spatial relations to each other, but those relations are not *prima facie* intrinsic, for so far as we can see there is nothing about a card of one color *as such* to demand particular space relations to cards of other colors. Now consider the relations, not of the cards, but of the colours themselves. Regarded merely as color, orange comes between red and yellow. And that relation is intrinsic in the present sense, since it is obviously determined by the natures of the three colors. But note that it is also necessary; we see that, yellow, orange and red being what they are, orange must

---

12. *Logic,* p. 407.
13. Joseph, *ibid.,* pp. 408-9.

come between the other two, and could not possibly fall elsewhere. Is this not the case with all relations that turn on the content or character of the terms? It seems to us that it is. Not that the necessity is seen with equal purity or clearness in all such cases, but that whenever we see that a relation depends on *a*'s being what it is, we see *that* the relation is necessary whether we can isolate the nexus or not. Whether the tendency to gratitude, for example, follows from the nature of modesty we may not be quite sure, but *if* we are, we are sure that modesty *must* carry with it this tendency. Indeed to say that something follows from the nature of *a*, but not necessarily, seems meaningless.

But is this necessity in the logical sense, or have we smuggled into the term some meaning that is allied, perhaps, but distinct? That the necessity is genuinely logical will be clearer from our second point. (2) To say that *a* produces *x* in virtue of being *a* and yet that, given *a*, *x* might not follow, is inconsistent with the laws of identity and contradiction. Of course if *a* were a cluster of qualities abstracted from their relations, and its modes of causal behaviour were another set conjoined with the former externally, then one could deny the latter and retain the former with perfect consistency. But we have seen that when we say *a* causes *x*, we do *not* mean that sort of conjunction; we mean an intrinsic relation, i.e., a relation in which *a*'s behaviour is the outgrowth or expression of *a*'s nature. And to assert that *a*'s behaviour, so conceived, could be different while *a* was the same would be to assert that something both did and did not issue from the nature of *a*. And that is self-contradiction. The statement would also, though perhaps not so apparently, conflict with the law of identity. It implies that a thing may remain itself when you have stripped from it everything which it is *such* as to be and do. To strip it of these things would be to strip it, so to speak, of the suchness that makes it what it is, i.e., to say that it is other than it is.

We are now in a position to see the upshot of our long argument about causality. There were two propositions, we said, which if established would carry with them the conclusion that everything that exists is related internally to everything else, i.e., is so related that without this relation it would not be what it is. These propositions were that everything is *causally* connected with everything else, directly or indirectly, and that being causally connected involved being connected by a relation of logical *necessity*. The first proposition, while perhaps undemonstrable, we found probable enough to commend itself to most philosophers and scientists, and the arguments against it were unconvincing. The second proposition has given us far more trouble. Does causality involve intelligible necessity? We have seen that in some cases it does unquestionably, for it does in every case of genuine inference. But can we say the same of causality generally? We saw that the principle could be extended to a great many other mental processes, though the presence of necessity was here less clearly discernible. But what about the enormous range of causal processes in physical nature? Was any hint or trace of really intelligible connection to be found among them? Many writers on scientific method have denied this and have sought to commit science to the view that there is nothing in causality but regularity of sequence or functional dependence. This view we have found so full of para-doxical consequences as to be incredible. Its rejection left us with the result that between cause and effect there is some sort of intrinsic connection, a result confirmed by considering that ordinary inductive procedure involves an argument which without this would be invalid. But is this intrinsic connection necessary? Yes, for when anything is said to have a consequent or a consequence in virtue of its special nature, necessity is part of our meaning, and what follows cannot be denied except on pain of self-contradiction. Note that in this we have made no such unredeemable claim as that we can see *why* a particular hammerstroke should drive a particular nail. Despite all the changes in physics since the turn of the century, we are very far from the sort of insight into physical things that would enable us to isolate the nerve of a given physical interaction. But unless there is such a nerve, the principle is illusory on which all practice is conducted and all causal argument is based.

Now if all this is true, it is hard to see how the conclusion is to be resisted that the universe of existing things is a system in which all things are related internally. Let *a* and *x* be *any* two things in the universe. They are then related to each other causally. But if causally, then also intrinsically, and if intrinsically then also neces-sarily, in the sense that they causally act as they do in virtue of their nature or character, and that to deny such activity would entail denying them to be what they are. And to have this sort of relation to all other things is precisely what we mean by being related to them internally.

From this there is another important conclusion that in turn will follow: the immanent end of thought is no will-o'-the-wisp;

it is relevant to the experienced nature of things; to the best of our
knowledge the immanent and transcendent ends coincide. The aim
of thought from its very beginning, we saw, was at understanding.
To understand anything meant to apprehend it in a system that
rendered it necessary. The ideal of complete understanding would
be achieved only when this system that rendered it necessary was
not a system that itself was fragmentary and therefore contingent,
but one that was all-inclusive and so organized internally that every
part was linked to every other by intelligible necessity. But was this
more than an ideal? Was there any reason to suppose that by its
attainment thought would be nearer to its second end, the apprehension of things as they are? Such an ideal, as we have said, appears
ludicrously remote from the world of actual experience, where we
are met at every turn by seeming contingency and unintelligibility.
At least it is thus remote at the first glance, and perhaps also at the
second and third. But we have seen that in the very nature of terms
in relation, and in the nature of causality, there is ground for believing that such contingency is apparent only. In what we take as
the real world we can see the outlines of a necessary structure that
is the counterpart of thought's ideal. There is nothing to stay our
conclusion that with approximation to its immanent end, the
achievement of systematic necessity, thought is also approximating
its transcendent end, the apprehension of the real.

With this result we have reached the natural end of our inquiry.
We have sketched the ideal of thought, and shown, so far as we
could, that it is applicable to the real. If any reader is disposed to
complain that the idea of a completely coherent system is still
obscure, we may point out that in our present position there are
two kinds of obscurity. One is the kind that comes of relaxing logical
tension in the face of ultimate difficulty, of letting all holds go,
surrendering to "wishful thinking," and plunging blindly into the
mist. As one nears so high a conclusion, and one so much to be
desired, as the intelligibility of the world, the temptation to relapse
into a milky mysticism is strong. If there has been any compromise
with this sort of thing, we are culpable; we hope there has not. On
the other hand, there is a kind of vagueness whose condemnation,
on such an issue, would be far less reasonable. If thought is what
we hold it is, namely the pursuit of an end whose character can be
realized only as the pursuit advances, a full and clear account of
that end must in the nature of the case be impossible at any point

along the journey. An account that was really adequate would not now be intelligible; an account that was quite simple, neat and plain could only be suspicious. The tale we have told of the concrete universal, and concrete necessity, and a system of parts such that none can be known without the others, cannot be rendered entirely clear from the level of a logic of mosaics. And of this particular kind of obscurity we trust we have been adequately guilty.

Critics of Idealism

INTRODUCTORY NOTE

Two of these selections date from the period between 1900 and 1914, when the most famous and historically important objections to idealism were produced. In more recent years idealist arguments have been almost always ignored but very rarely refuted. Since a book of selections on Realism will also be published in this series, it could hardly be part of my function to represent the positive case on this side in full. I have confined myself to giving passages which point out clear fallacies that no doubt helped to influence philosophers in the direction of idealism and which were considered to have been the main basis of the case for idealism by many of their opponents.

Moore's argument has since been repudiated by its author, but I myself do not entirely agree with him in repudiating it. I would insist, however, that a man can be an idealist in spite of it, since one may see a synthetic *a priori* connection between the object and the experience[1] of sensing, and since it in any case does not affect all the epistemological and metaphysical arguments for idealism.

A similar criticism of idealism is found in the selection by Bertrand Russell.

The brief selection from Cook Wilson's *Statement and Inference* gives one of the most celebrated criticisms of Bradley's theory of relations.

Ernest Nagel's "Sovereign Reason" is a sustained attack from an empiricist point of view on Blanshard's defense of the doctrine of internal relations.

---

1. I much prefer the word "experience" here to the word "act."

JAMES COOK WILSON

(1849-1915)

Relation and Quality

. . . THERE IS a serious confusion in the chapter entitled "Relation and Quality" in Mr. F. H. Bradley's *Appearance and Reality*. Throughout this chapter there is not one single illustration, though it is of the last importance that there should be. The writer indeed takes the fallacy so seriously as to regard it as evidence of the necessarily illusive character of our experience. It is in fact a mistake of his own of a very inexcusable character which he thus naïvely thrusts upon the "appearance" of the object and treats as evidence of the unsoundness of phenomena. The fallacy is a supposed infinite regress which results from relating the relation of two terms to the terms of the relation themselves. The puzzle may be put briefly thus: let A and B be the terms of a relation, r the relation between A and B. A and r are different and, being different, stand in a relation, say r_1, to one another. Similarly let r_2 be the relation between B and r. Thus we have two new relations, r_1 and r_2, and r has itself become one of the terms of a relation. Now r_1 being different from A and r we similarly get two new relations, and the process is infinite, producing an infinite series with terms all different from one another.

The presupposition of this fallacy is that if two somethings are different from one another they must stand to one another in a relation which is different from either, not identical with nor included in the separate nature of either. In other words, r is not identical with A or B nor a part of what is already understood in A or B. So far from being always true, this presupposition can be shown to be never true where A and B are in fact properly described as related.

Take first the case in which, A and B being different from each

---

This selection is from Volume II of Cook Wilson's posthumously published book, *Statement and Inference*. It is here reprinted with the kind permission of the Clarendon Press, Oxford.

other, there really is a relation *r* between them different from either.
For instance, let *r* be equality in "A equals B." We have to ask
whether there is indeed a relation between A and *r* and what it is;
for the fallacy clearly lies in the first step, and it is presumed by the
writer that we do not go beyond the original A and B and *r* by any
new process of apprehension.

Now, if there really be such a thing as r_1, it is necessary that
it should be new and that the statement "A stands in the relation
r_1 to *r*" should be new and not a part of the original statement which
gave *r* as the relation between A and B. The question, then, what
r_1 is or what is the relation of A to *r* must be real and intelligible.
We shall find that there is, in fact, no new statement and that the
question is an unreal one, because the idea of a relation cannot be
applied, as is proposed, to a relation and a term of that relation
itself.

The ordinary statement of a relation does not contain the word
relation itself. A is B's father. So we say ordinarily A is equal to
B (where the relation between A and B is one of equality of magnitude), not A stands to B in a relation of equality. The latter
form, however, gives a convenient general formula. A stands to B
in a relation R, and if we define the kind of relation, *r*, this is the
particular of which R is the universal. Our question, then, is what
r_1 is which is the presumed relation of A to *r,* where *r* is the relation
of equality. Results can be obtained only by considering particular
instances, not by a symbolic method. Two replies, differing in completeness, are open to us. We may say that the relation of equality
to A is that it is the relation of A to B, or more accurately the kind
of relation which A has to B. Here equality is not the equality of
A to B, viz., *r,* but R the universal, that is, equality in general. The
answer, then, is simply a statement of what kind (viz., R) the relation *r* is. Thus we have not gone outside the nature of *r* itself nor
reached a new relation r_1. If, then, we are to give the full answer
and to use all the information which the question supplies, we may
reply; the relation of A to B is not R but the particular instance *r,*
which is the equality of A to B. If, then, with this in view we go
on to ask what is the relation to A of *r,* we can only reply that the
relation to A of A's equality to B (*r*) is that it is A's equality to B.
Here, instead of giving the genus R for our answer, we have *r,* the
being of R itself, yet we have not got beyond the original relation

r, nor in any sense beyond the original statement that A stands to B in a relation *r.*

The question, then, what the relation of A is to A's standing in the relation *r* to B is obviously unreal, for it contains everything necessary to its own answer; it puts as a question what is no question to the person asking it. There is a contradiction in the very asking, a contradiction between form and the matter to which it is applied. This is enough to show that to suppose a relation (r_1) of A to *r* is absurd; or (since the very question what that relation may be involves an absurdity) it must be an absurdity to suppose such a relation.

If now we try to avoid this by saying that r_1 is the difference between A and *r,* we can get the solution simply by asking what the difference is between A and *r.* To this question the only possible answer is that A is A and not the relation of A to B, and that the relation of A to B is the relation of A to B and not A. Thus the so-called difference is a way of restating the same facts as before and therefore a mere verbal difference. Moreover, it would be easy to show the futility of inquiring what the difference is between A and the last difference, as well as to show that the only possible answer gives nothing not already contained in A and *r.* The puzzle here is equally foolish with that puzzle which produces an infinite series by taking the difference between A and B as something different from each of them and then taking the difference between that difference and either A or B, and so on.

The formula, then, which the apparent puzzle presupposes being false in this particular case, we may next consider cases where it is equally false for other things than a relation and one of its terms. Here again we must proceed by particular concrete instances, not by a symbolic method. Consider, for example, the surface of a volume and the volume. These are clearly distinguishable, but what is the definition of a surface? It is the boundary of a volume. What, then, is the relation of the surface to the volume? We can only reply that it is that the surface is its boundary. If the word relation applies at all, clearly this must be the accurate account of the relation. Hence in the case of the two terms A, the surface, and B, the solid, the relation *r* (if there is any relation at all of A to B), instead of being, as the presupposition of the fallacy demands, neither identical with A nor included in what is understood in A, is either identical

with A, inasmuch as the description of *r* (being a boundary of the
solid) and the definition of A's being (being a boundary of the
solid) are the same, or at least something always included necessarily in what is already understood by A. This must always be the
case when A has no being except as an element in the being of B.
The same may easily be seen to be true of the so-called relation of
a subject to its attributes, the relation, for instance, between a body
and its weight or its motion. Thus, besides the particular case where
one something is a relation and the other a term of the relation,
there are other cases where the general formula is not true. There
may be two somethings different from one another, not being a
relation and one of its terms, which yet do not stand in a relation
different from either. . . .

G. E. MOORE

(1873-—)

The Refutation of Idealism

MODERN IDEALISM, if it asserts any general conclusion about the universe at all, asserts that it is *spiritual*. There are two points about this assertion to which I wish to call attention. These points are that, whatever be its exact meaning, it is certainly meant to assert (1) that the universe is very different indeed from what it seems, and (2) that it has quite a large number of properties which it does not seem to have. Chairs and tables and mountains *seem* to be very different from us but, when the whole universe is declared to be spiritual, it is certainly meant to assert that they are far more like us than we think. The Idealist means to assert that they are *in some sense* neither lifeless nor unconscious, as they certainly mean to be; and I do not think his language is so grossly deceptive, but that we may assume him to believe that they really are very different indeed from what they seem. And secondly when he declares that they are *spiritual*, he means to include in that term quite a large number of properties. When the whole universe is declared to be spiritual, it is meant not only that it is in some sense *conscious,* but that it has what we recognize in ourselves as the *higher* forms of consciousness. That it is intelligent; that it is purposeful; that it is not mechanical; all these different things are commonly asserted of it. In general, it may be said, this phrase "reality is spiritual" excites and expresses the belief that the *whole* universe possesses *all the qualities* the possession of which is held to make us so superior to things which seem to be inanimate: at least, if it does not possess exactly those which we possess, it possesses not one only, but several others, which, by the same ethical standard, would be judged equal to or better than our own. When we say it is *spiritual* we mean to say that it has quite a number of excellent qualities, different from any which we

This article was first published in *Mind*, 1903. It is here reprinted with the kind permission of the author and the editor of *Mind*.

commonly attribute either to stars or planets or to cups and saucers.

Now why I mention these two points is that when engaged in the intricacies of philosophic discussion, we are apt to overlook the vastness of the difference between this idealistic view and the ordinary view of the world, and to overlook the number of *different* propositions which the Idealist must prove. It is, I think, owing to the vastness of this difference and owing to the number of different excellences which Idealists attribute to the universe, that it seems such an interesting and important question whether Idealism be true or not. But, when we begin to argue about it, I think we are apt to forget what a vast number of arguments this interesting question must involve: we are apt to assume, that if one or two points be made on either side, the whole case is won. I say this lest it should be thought that any of the arguments which will be advanced in this paper would be sufficient to disprove, or any refutation of them sufficient to prove, the truly interesting and important proposition that reality is spiritual. For my own part I wish it to be clearly understood that I do not suppose that anything I shall say has the smallest tendency to prove that reality is not spiritual: I do not believe it possible to refute a single one of the many important propositions contained in the assertion that it is so. Reality may be spiritual, for all I know, and I devoutly hope it is. But I take "Idealism" to be a wide term and to include not only this interesting conclusion but a number of arguments which are supposed to be, if not sufficient, at least *necessary,* to prove it. Indeed I take it that modern Idealists are chiefly distinguished by certain arguments which they have in common. That reality is spiritual has, I believe, been the tenet of many theologians; and yet, for believing that alone, they should hardly be called Idealists. There are besides, I believe, many persons, not improperly called Idealists, who hold certain characteristic propositions, without venturing to think them quite sufficient to prove so grand a conclusion. It is, therefore, only with Idealistic *arguments* that I am concerned; and if any Idealist holds that *no* argument is necessary to prove that reality is spiritual, I shall certainly not have refuted him. I shall, however, attack at least one argument, which, to the best of my belief, is considered necessary to their position by *all* Idealists. And I wish to point out a certain advantage which this procedure gives me—an advantage which justifies the assertion that, if my arguments are sound, they will have refuted Idealism. If I can refute a single proposition which is a necessary and essential step in all Idealistic arguments, then, no matter how good the rest of these arguments may be, I shall have proved that Idealists have *no reason whatever* for their conclusion.

Suppose we have a chain of argument which takes the form: Since A is B, and B is C, and C is D, it follows A is D. In such an argument, thought "B is C" and "C is D" may both be perfectly true, yet if "A is B" be false, we have no more reason for asserting A is D than if all three were false. It does not, indeed, follow that A is D is false, nor does it follow that no other arguments would prove it to be true. But it does follow that, so far as this argument goes, it is the barest supposition, without the least bit of evidence. I propose to attack a proposition which seems to me to stand in this relation to the conclusion "Reality is spiritual"; I do not deny that there may be reasons for thinking that it is: but I do propose to show that one reason upon which, to the best of my judgment, all other arguments ever used by Idealists depend is *false*. These arguments may, for all I shall say, be eminently ingenious and true; they are very many and various, and different Idealists use the most different arguments to prove the same most important conclusions. Some of these *may* be sufficient to prove that B is C and C is D; but if, as I shall try to show, their "A and B" is false the conclusion A is D remains a pleasant supposition. I do not deny that to suggest pleasant and plausible suppositions may be the proper function of philosophy: but I am assuming that the name Idealism can only be properly applied where there is a certain amount of argument, intended to be cogent.

The subject of this paper is, therefore, quite uninteresting. Even if I prove my point, I shall have proved nothing about the Universe in general. Upon the important question whether Reality is or is not spiritual my argument will not have the remotest bearing. I shall only attempt to arrive at the truth about a matter, which is in itself quite trivial and insignificant, and from which, so far as I can see and certainly so far as I shall say, no conclusions can be drawn about any of the subjects about which we most want to know. The only importance I can claim for the subject I shall investigate is that it seems to me to be a matter upon which not Idealists only, but all philosophers and psychologists also, have been in error, and from their erroneous view of which they have inferred (validly or invalidly) their most striking and interesting conclusions.

And that it has even this importance I cannot hope to prove. If it
has this importance, it will indeed follow that all the most striking
results of philosophy—Sensationalism, Agnosticism, and Idealism
alike—have, for all that has hitherto been urged in their favor, no
more foundation than the supposition that a chimera lives in the
moon. It will follow that, unless new reasons never urged hitherto
can be found, all the most important philosophic doctrines have as
little claim to assent as the most superstitious beliefs of the lowest
savages. Upon the question what we have *reason* to believe in the
most interesting matters, I do therefore think that my results will
have an important bearing; but I cannot too clearly insist that upon
the question whether these beliefs are true they will have none
whatever.

The trivial proposition which I propose to dispute is this: that
esse is *percipi*. This is a very ambiguous proposition, but, in some
sense or other, it has been very widely held. That it is, in some
sense, essential to Idealism, I must for the present merely assume.
What I propose to show is that, in all the senses ever given to it, it
is false.

But, first of all, it may be useful to point out briefly in what
relation I conceive it to stand to Idealistic arguments. That wherever you can truly predicate *esse* you can truly predicate *percipi*,
in some sense or other, is, I take it, a necessary step in all arguments, properly to be called Idealistic, and, what is more, in all
arguments hitherto offered for the Idealistic conclusion. If *esse* is
percipi, this is at once equivalent to saying that whatever is, is
experienced; and this, again, is equivalent, in a sense, to saying that
whatever is, is something mental. But this is not the sense in which
the Idealist *conclusion* must maintain that Reality is *mental*. The
Idealist *conclusion* is that *esse* is *percipere;* and hence, whether *esse*
be *percipi* or not, a further and different discussion is needed to
show whether or not it is also *percipere*. And again, even if *esse* be
percipere, we need a vast quantity of further argument to show that
what has *esse* has also those higher mental qualities which are
denoted by spiritual. But, on the other hand, I believe that every
argument ever used to show that reality is spiritual has inferred this
(validly or invalidly) from *"esse* is *percipere"* as one of its premises; and that this again has never been pretended to be proved
except by use of the premise that *esse* is *percipi*. The type of argument used for the latter purpose is familiar enough. It is said that

since whatever is, is experienced, and since some things are which are not experienced by the individual, these must at least form part of some experience. Or again that, since an object necessarily implies a subject, and since the whole world must be an object, we must conceive it to belong to some subject or subjects, in the same sense in which whatever is the object of our experience belongs to us. Or again, that, since thought enters into the essence of all reality, we must conceive behind it, in it, or as its essence, a spirit akin to ours, who think: that "spirit greets spirit" in its object. Into the validity of these inferences I do not propose to enter: they obviously require a great deal of discussion. I only desire to point out that, however correct they may be, yet if *esse* is not *percipi,* they leave us as far from a proof that reality is spiritual, as if they were all false too.

But now: Is *esse percipi?* There are three very ambiguous terms in this proposition, and I must begin by distinguishing the different things that may be meant by some of them.

And first with regard to *percipi.* This term need not trouble us long at present. It was, perhaps, originally used to mean "sensation" only; but I am not going to be so unfair to modern Idealists—the only Idealists to whom the term should now be applied without qualification—as to hold that, if they say *esse* is *percipi,* they mean by *percipi* sensation only. On the contrary, I quite agree with them that, if *esse* be *percipi* at all, *percipi* must be understood to include not sensation only, but that other type of mental fact, which is called "thought"; and, whether *esse* be *percipi* or not, I consider it to be the main service of the philosophic school, to which modern Idealists belong, that they have insisted on distinguishing "sensation" and "thought" and on emphasizing the importance of the latter. Against Sensationalism and Empiricism they have maintained the true view. But the distinction between sensation and thought need not detain us here. For, in whatever respects they differ, they have at least this in common, that they are both forms of consciousness or, to use a term that seems to be more in fashion just now, they are both ways of experiencing. Accordingly, whatever *esse* is *percipi* may mean, it does *at least* assert that whatever is, is *experienced.* And since what I wish to maintain is, that even this is untrue, the question whether it be experienced by way of sensation or thought or both is for my purpose quite irrelevant. If it be not experienced at all, it cannot be either an object of thought or an object of sense. It is only if being involves "experience" that the question, whether it involves sensation or thought or both, becomes important. I beg, therefore, that *percipi* may be understood, in what follows, to refer merely to what is *common* to sensation and thought. A very recent article states the meaning of *esse* is *percipi* with all desirable clearness in so far as *percipi* is concerned. "I will undertake to show," says Mr. Taylor, "that what makes [any piece of fact] real can be nothing but its presence as an inseparable aspect of *a sentient experience.*" I am glad to think that Mr. Taylor has been in time to supply me with so definite a statement that this is the ultimate premise of Idealism. My paper will at least refute Mr. Taylor's Idealism, if it refutes anything at all: for I *shall* undertake to show that what makes a thing real cannot possibly be its presence as an inseparable aspect of a sentient experience.

But Mr. Taylor's statement though clear, I think, with regard to the meaning of *percipi* is highly ambiguous in other respects. I will leave it for the present to consider the next ambiguity in the statement: *Esse* is *percipi*. What does the copula mean? What can be meant by saying that *Esse* is *percipi?* There are just three meanings, one or other of which such a statement must have, if it is to be true; and of these there is only one which it can have, if it is to be important. (1) the statement may be meant to assert that the word "esse" is used to signify nothing either more or less than the word "percipi"; that the two words are precise synonyms: that they are merely different names for one and the same thing: that what is meant by *esse* is absolutely identical with what is meant by *percipi*. I think I need not prove that the principle *esse* is *percipi* is *not* thus intended merely to define a word; nor yet that, if it were, it would be an extremely bad definition. But if it does *not* mean this, only two alternatives remain. The second is (2) that what is meant by *esse,* though not absolutely identical with what is meant by *percipi,* yet *includes* the latter as *part* of its meaning. If this were the meaning of *esse* is *percipi,* then to say that a thing was real would not be the same thing as to say that it was experienced. That it was *real* would mean that it was experienced and *something else besides*: "being experienced" would be *analytically essential* to reality, but would not be the whole meaning of the term. From the fact that a thing was real we should be able to infer, by the law of contradiction, that it was experienced; since the latter would be *part* of what is meant by the former. But, on the other hand, from the fact a thing was experienced we should *not* be able to infer that it was real; since it would not follow from the fact that it had one of the attributes essential to reality, that it *also* had the other or others. Now, if we understand *esse* is *percipi* in this second sense, we must distinguish *three* different things which it asserts. First of all, it gives a definition of the word "reality," asserting that word stands for a complex whole, of which what is meant by *percipi* forms a part. And secondly, it asserts that "being experienced" forms a part of a certain whole. Both these propositions may be true, and at all events I do not wish to dispute them. I do not, indeed, think that the word "reality" is commonly used to include *percipi*: but I do not wish to argue about the meaning of words. And that many things which are experienced are also something else—that to be experienced forms part of certain wholes, is, of course, indisputable. But what I wish to point out is, that neither of these propositions is of any importance, unless we add to them a *third*. That "real" is a convenient name for a union of attributes which *sometimes* occurs, it could not be worth any one's while to assert: no inferences of any importance could be drawn from such an assertion. Our principle could only mean that when a thing happens to have *percipi* as well as the other qualities included under *esse*, it has *percipi*: and we should never be able to *infer* that it was experienced, except from a proposition which already asserted that it was both experienced and something else. Accordingly, if the assertion that *percipi* forms part of the whole meant by reality is to have any importance, it must mean that the whole is organic, at least in this sense, that the other constituent or constituents of it *cannot* occur without *percipi*, even if *percipi* can occur without them. Let us call these other constituents *x*. The proposition that *esse* includes *percipi*, and that therefore from *esse percipi* can be inferred, can only be important if it is meant to assert that *percipi* can be inferred from *x*. The only importance of the question whether the whole *esse* includes the part *percipi* rests therefore on the question whether the part *x* is necessarily connected with the part *percipi*. And this is (3) the third possible meaning of the assertion *esse* is *percipi*: and, as we now see, the only important one. *Esse* is *percipi* asserts that wherever you have *x* you also have *percipi* that whatever has the property *x* also has the property that it is *experienced*. And this being so, it will be convenient if, for the future, I may be allowed to use the term "*esse*" to denote *x alone*. I do not wish thereby to beg the

question whether what we commonly mean by the word "real" does
or does not include *percipi* as well as *x*. I am quite content that my
definition of *esse* to denote *x*, should be regarded merely as an
arbitrary verbal definition. Whether it is so or not, the only question
of interest is whether from *x percipi* can be inferred, and I should
prefer to be able to express this in the form: can *percipi* be inferred
from *esse?* Only let it be understood that when I say *esse,* that term
will not for the future *include percipi:* it denotes only that *x,* which
Idealists, perhaps rightly, include *along with percipi* under *their*
term *esse.* That there is such an *x* they must admit on pain of
making the proposition an *absolute* tautology; and that from this
x percipi can be inferred they must admit, on pain of making it a
perfectly barren analytic proposition. Whether *x* alone should or
should not be called *esse* is not worth a dispute: what is worth
dispute is whether *percipi* is necessarily connected with *x.*

We have therefore discovered the ambiguity of the copula in
esse is *percipi,* so far as to see that this principle asserts two distinct
terms to be so related, that whatever has the *one,* which I call *esse,*
has *also* the property that it is experienced. It asserts a necessary
connection between *esse* on the one hand and *percipi* on the other;
these two words denoting each a distinct term, and *esse* denoting
a term in which that denoted by *percipi* is not included. We have,
then in *esse* is *percipi,* a *necessary synthetic* proposition which I
have undertaken to refute. And I may say at once that, understood
as such, it cannot be refuted. If the Idealist chooses to assert that
it is merely a self-evident truth, I have only to say that it does not
appear to me to be so. But I believe that no Idealist ever has maintained it to be so. Although this—that two distinct terms are necessarily related—is the only sense which *esse* is *percipi* can have
if it is to be true and important, it *can* have another sense, if it is to
be an important falsehood. I believe that Idealists all hold this
important falsehood. They do not perceive that *Esse* is *percipi* must,
if true, be *merely* a self-evident synthetic truth: they either identify
with it or give as a reason for it another proposition which must
be false because it is self-contradictory. Unless they did so, they
would have to admit that it was a perfectly unfounded assumption;
and if they recognized that it was *unfounded,* I do not think they
would maintain its truth to be evident. *Esse* is *percipi,* in the sense
I have found for it, *may* indeed be true; I cannot refute it: but if

this sense were clearly apprehended, no one, I think, would *believe* that it was true.

Idealists, we have seen, must assert that whatever is experienced, is *necessarily* so. And this doctrine they commonly express by saying that "the object of experience is inconceivable apart from the subject." I have hitherto been concerned with pointing out what meaning this assertion must have, if it is to be an important truth. I now propose to show that it may have an important meaning, which must be false, because it is self-contradictory.

It is a well known fact in the history of philosophy that *necessary* truths in general, but especially those of which it is said that the opposite is inconceivable, have been commonly supposed to be *analytic,* in the sense that the proposition denying them was self-contradictory. It was in this way, commonly supposed, before Kant, that many truths could be proved by the law of contradiction alone. This is, therefore, a mistake which it is plainly easy for the best philosophers to make. Even since Kant many have continued to assert it; but I am aware that among those Idealists, who most properly deserve the name, it has become more fashionable to assert that truths are *both* analytic and synthetic. Now with many of their reasons for asserting this I am not concerned: it is possible that in some connections the assertion may bear a useful and true sense. But if we understand "analytic" in the sense just defined, namely, what is proved by the law of contradiction *alone,* it is plain that, if "synthetic" means what is *not* proved by this alone, no truth can be both analytic and synthetic. Now it seems to me that those who do maintain truths to be both, do nevertheless maintain that they are so in this as well as in other senses. It is, indeed, extremely unlikely that so essential a part of the historical meaning of "analytic" and "synthetic" should have been entirely discarded, especially since we find no express recognition that it is discarded. In that case it is fair to suppose that modern Idealists have been influenced by the view that certain truths can be proved by the law of contradiction alone. I admit they also expressly declare that they can *not*: but this is by no means sufficient to prove that they do not also think they are; since it is very easy to hold two mutually contradictory opinions. What I suggest then is that Idealists hold the particular doctrine in question, concerning the relation of subject and object in experience, because they think it is an analytic truth in this restricted sense that it is proved by the law of contradiction alone.

I am suggesting that the Idealist maintains that object and subject are necessarily connected, mainly because he fails to see that they are *distinct,* that they are *two,* at all. When he thinks of "yellow" and when he thinks of the "sensation of yellow," he fails to see that there is anything whatever in the latter which is not in the former. This being so, to deny that yellow can ever *be* apart from the sensation of yellow is merely to deny that yellow can ever be other than it is; since yellow and the sensation of yellow are absolutely identical. To assert that yellow is necessarily an object of experience is to assert that yellow is necessarily yellow—a purely identical proposition, and therefore proved by the law of contradiction alone. Of course, the proposition also implies that experience is, after all, something distinct from yellow—else there would be no reason for insisting that yellow is a sensation: and that the argument thus both affirms and denies that yellow and sensation of yellow are distinct, is what sufficiently refutes it. But this contradiction can easily be overlooked, because though we are convinced, in other connections, that "experience" does mean something and something most important, yet we are never distinctly aware *what* it means, and thus in every particular case we do not notice its presence. The facts present themselves as a kind of antinomy: (1) Experience *is* something unique and different from anything else; (2) Experience of green is entirely indistinguishable from green; two propositions which cannot both be true. Idealists, holding both, can only take refuge in arguing from the one in some connections and from the other in others.

But I am well aware that there are many Idealists who would repel it as an utterly unfounded charge that they fail to distinguish between a sensation or an idea and what I will call its object. And there are, I admit, many who not only imply, as we all do, that green is distinct from the sensation of green, but expressly insist upon the distinction as an important part of their system. They would perhaps only assert that the two form an inseparable unity. But I wish to point out that many, who use this phrase, and who do not admit the distinction, are not thereby absolved from the charge that they deny it. For there is a certain doctrine, very prevalent among philosophers nowadays, which by a very simple reduction may be seen to assert that two distinct things both are and are not distinct. A distinction is asserted; but it is *also* asserted that the things distinguished form an "organic unity." But, forming such a unity, it is held, each would not be what it is *apart from its relation to the other*. Hence to consider either by itself is to make an *illegitimate abstraction*. The recognition that there are "organic unities" and "illegitimate abstractions" in this sense is regarded as one of the chief conquests of modern philosophy. But what is the sense attached to these terms? An abstraction is illegitimate, when and only when we attempt to assert of *a part*—of something abstracted —that which is true only of the *whole* to which it belongs: and it may perhaps be useful to point out that this should not be done. But the application actually made of this principle, and what perhaps would be expressly acknowledged as its meaning, is something much the reverse of useful. The principle is used to assert that certain abstractions are *in all cases* illegitimate; that whenever you try to assert *anything whatever* of that which is *part* of an organic whole, what you assert can only be true of the whole. And this principle, so far from being a useful truth, is necessarily false. For if the whole can, nay *must,* be substituted for the part in all propositions and for all purposes, this can only be because the whole is absolutely identical with the part. When, therefore, we are told that green and the sensation of green are certainly distinct but yet are not separable, or that it is an illegitimate abstraction to consider the one apart from the other, what these provisos are used to assert is, that though the two things are distinct yet you not only can but must treat them as if they were not. Many philosophers, therefore, when they admit a distinction, yet (following the lead of Hegel) boldly assert their right, in a slightly more obscure form of words, *also* to deny it. The principle of organic unities, like that of combined analysis and synthesis, is mainly used to defend the practice of holding *both* of two contradictory propositions, wherever this may seem convenient. In this, as in other matters, Hegel's main service to philosophy has consisted in giving a name to and erecting into a principle, a type of fallacy to which experience had shown philosophers, along with the rest of mankind, to be addicted. No wonder that he has followers and admirers.

I have shown then, so far, that when the Idealist asserts the important principle *"Esse* is *percipi"* he must, if it is to be true, mean by this that: Whatever is experienced also *must* be experienced. And I have also shown that he *may* identify with, or give as a reason for, this proposition, one which must be false, because it is self-contradictory. But at this point I propose to make a complete break in my argument. *"Esse* is *percipi,"* we have seen, asserts of two terms, as distinct from one another as "green" and "sweet," that whatever has the one also has the other: it asserts that "being" and "being experienced" are necessarily connected: that whatever *is* is *also* experienced. And this, I admit, cannot be directly refuted. But I believe it to be false; and I have asserted that anybody who saw that *"esse"* and *"percipi" were* as distinct as "green" and "sweet" would be no more ready to believe that whatever *is* is *also* experienced, than to believe that whatever is green is also sweet. I have asserted that no one would believe that *"esse* is *percipi"* if they saw how different *esse* is from *percipi*: but *this* I shall not try to prove. I have asserted that all who do believe that *"esse* is *percipi"* identify with it or take as a reason for it a self-contradictory proposition: but this I shall not try to prove. I shall only try to show that certain propositions which I assert to be believed, are false. That they are believed, and that without this belief *"esse* is *percipi"* would not be believed either, I must leave without a proof.

I pass, then, from the uninteresting question "Is *esse percipi?"* to the still more uninteresting and apparently irrelevant question "What is a sensation or idea?"

We all know that the sensation of blue differs from that of green. But it is plain that if both are *sensations* they also have some point in common. What is that they have in common? And how is this common element related to the points in which they differ?

I call the common element "consciousness" without yet attempting to say what the thing I so call *is*. We have then in every sensation two distinct terms, (1) "consciousness," in respect of which all sensations are alike; and (2) something else, in respect of which one sensation differs from another. It will be convenient if I may be allowed to call this second term the "object" of a sensation: this also without yet attempting to say what I mean by the word.

We have then in every sensation two distinct elements, one which I call consciousness, and another which I call the object of consciousness. This must be so if the sensation of blue and the sensation of green, though different in one respect, are alike in another: blue is one object of sensation and green is another, and consciousness, which both sensations have in common, is different from either.

But, further, sometimes the sensation of blue exists in my mind and sometimes it does not; and knowing, as we now do, that the sensation of blue includes two different elements, namely consciousness and blue, the question arises whether, when the sensation of blue exists, it is the consciousness which exists, or the blue which exists, or both. And one point at least is plain: namely that these three alternatives are all different from one another. So that, if any one tells us that to say "Blue exists" is the *same* thing as to say that "Both blue and consciousness exist," he makes a mistake and a self-contradictory mistake.

But another point is also plain, namely, that when the sensation exists, the consciousness, at least, certainly does exist; for when I say that the sensations of blue and of green both exist, I certainly mean that what is common to both and in virtue of which both are called sensations, exists in each case. The only alternative left, then, is that *either* both exist or the consciousness exists alone. If, therefore, any one tells us that the existence of blue is the same thing as the existence of the sensation of blue he makes a mistake and a self-contradictory mistake, for he asserts *either* that blue is the same thing as blue together with consciousness *or* that it is the same thing as consciousness alone.

Accordingly to identify either "blue" or any other of what I have called *"objects"* of sensation, with the corresponding sensation is, in every case, a self-contradictory error. It is to identify a part either with the whole of which it is a part or else with the other part of the same whole. If we are told that the assertion "Blue exists" is *meaningless* unless we mean by it that "The sensation of blue exists," we are told what is certainly false and self-contradictory. If we are told that the existence of blue is inconceivable apart from the existence of the sensation, the speaker *probably* means to convey to us, by this ambiguous expression, what is a self-contradictory error. For we can and must conceive the existence of blue as something quite distinct from the existence of the sensation. We can and must conceive that blue might exist and yet the sensation of blue not exist. For my own part I not only conceive this, but conceive it to be true. Either therefore this terrific assertion of inconceivability means what is false and self-contradictory or else it means only that *as a matter of fact* blue never can exist unless the sensation of it exists also.

And at this point I need not conceal my opinion that no philosopher has ever yet succeeded in avoiding this self-contradictory error: that the most striking results both of Idealism and of Agnosticism are only obtained by identifying blue with the sensation of blue: that *esse* is held to be *percipi,* solely because *what is experienced* is held to be identical with *the experience of it.* That Berkeley and Mill committed this error will, perhaps be granted: that modern Idealists make it will, I hope, appear more probable later. But that my opinion is plausible, I will now offer two pieces of evidence. The first is that language offers us no means of referring to such objects as "blue" and "green" and "sweet," except by calling them sensations: it is an obvious violation of language to call them "things" or "objects" or "terms." And similarly we have no natural means of referring to such objects as "causality" or "likeness" or "identity," except by calling them "ideas" or "notions" or "conceptions." But it is hardly likely that if philosophers had clearly distinguished in the past between a sensation or idea and what I have called its object, there should have been no separate name for the latter. They have always used the same name for these two different "things" (if I may call them so): and hence there is some probability that they have supposed these "things" *not* to be two and different, but one and the same. And, secondly, there is a very good reason why they should have supposed so, in the fact that when we refer to introspection and try to discover what the sensation of blue is, it is very easy to suppose that we have before us only a single term. The term "blue" is easy enough to distinguish, but the other element which I have called "consciousness"—that which sensation of blue has in common with sensation of green—is extremely difficult to fix. That many people fail to distinguish it at all is sufficiently shown by the fact that there are materialists. And, in general, that which makes the sensation of blue a mental fact seems to escape us: it seems, if I may use a metaphor, to be transparent—we look through it and see nothing but the blue; we may be convinced that there *is some-thing* but *what* it is no philosopher, I think, has yet clearly recognized.

But this was a digression. The point I had established so far was that in every sensation or idea we must distinguish two elements, (1) the "object," or that in which one differs from another; and (2) "consciousness," or that which all have in common—that which makes them sensations or mental facts. This being so, it followed that when a sensation or idea exists, we have to choose between the alternatives that either object alone, or consciousness alone, or both, exist; and I showed that of these alternatives one, namely that the object only exists, is excluded by the fact that what we mean to assert is certainly the existence of a mental fact. There remains the question: Do both exist? Or does the consciousness alone? And to this question one answer has hitherto been given universally: That both exist.

This answer follows from the analysis hitherto accepted of the relation of what I have called "object" to "consciousness" in any sensation or idea. It is held that what I call the object is merely the "content" of a sensation or idea. It is held that in each case we can distinguish two elements and two only, (1) the fact that there is feeling or experience, and (2) *what* is felt or experienced; the sensation or idea, it is said, forms a whole, in which we must distinguish two "inseparable aspects," "content" and "existence." I shall try to show that this analysis is false; and for that purpose I must ask what may seem an extraordinary question: namely what is meant by saying that one thing is "content" of another? It is not usual to ask this question; the term is used as if everybody must understand it. But since I am going to maintain that "blue" is *not* the content of the sensation of blue, and what is more important, that, even if it were this analysis would leave out the most important element in the sensation of blue, it is necessary that I should try to explain precisely what it is that I shall deny.

What then is meant by saying that one thing is the "content" of another? First of all I wish to point out that "blue" is rightly and properly said to be part of the content of a blue flower. If, therefore, we also assert that it is part of the content of the sensation of blue, we assert that it has to the other parts (if any) of this whole the same relation which it has to the other parts of a blue flower and we assert only this: we cannot mean to assert, that it has to the sensation of blue any relation which it does not have to the blue flower. And we have seen that the sensation of blue contains at least one other element beside blue—namely, what I call "consciousness," which makes it a sensation. So far then as we assert that blue is the content of the sensation we assert that it has to this "consciousness" the same relation which it has to the other parts of a blue flower: we do assert this and we assert no more than this. Into the question what exactly the relation is between blue and a blue flower in virtue of which we call the former part of its "content" I do not propose to enter. It is sufficient for my purpose to point out

that it is the general relation most commonly meant when we talk
of a thing and its qualities; and that this relation is such that to say
the thing exists implies that the qualities also exist. The *content* of
the thing is *what* we assert to exist, when we assert *that* the thing
exists.

When, therefore, blue is said to be part of the content of the
"sensation of blue," the latter is treated as if it were a whole constituted in exactly the same way as any other "thing." The "sensation of blue," on this view, differs from a blue bead or a blue beard,
in exactly the same way in which the two latter differ from one
another: the blue bead differs from the blue beard, in that while
the former contains glass, the latter contains hair; and the "sensation
of blue" differs from both in that, instead of glass or hair, it contains consciousness. The relation of the blue to the consciousness is
conceived to be exactly the same as that of the blue to the glass or
hair: it is in all three cases the *quality* of a *thing*.

But I said just now that the sensation of blue was analyzed into
"content" and "existence," and that blue was said to be *the* content
of the idea of blue. There is an ambiguity in this and a possible
error, which I must note in passing. The term "content" may be used
in two senses. If we use "content" as equivalent to what Mr. Bradley calls the *"what"*—if we mean by it the *whole* of what is said
to exist, when the thing is said to exist, then blue is certainly not
the content of the sensation of blue: part of the *content* of the sensation is, in this sense of the term, that other element which I have
called consciousness. The analysis of this sensation into the "content" "blue," on the one hand, and mere existence on the other, is
therefore certainly false; in it we have again the self-contradictory
identification of "Blue exists" with "The sensation of blue exists."
But there is another sense in which "blue" might properly be said
to be *the* content of the sensation—namely, the sense in which "content," like εἶδος, is opposed to "substance" or "matter." For the
element "consciousness," being common to all sensations, may be
and certainly is regarded as in some sense their "substance," and by
the "content" of each is only meant that in respect of which one
differs from another. In this sense then "blue" might be said to be
the content of the sensation; but, in that case, the analysis into "content" and "existence" is, at least, misleading, since under "existence"
must be included *"what* exists" in the sensation other than blue.

We have it, then, as a universally received opinion that blue is

related to the sensation or idea of blue, as its *content,* and that this
view, if it is to be true, must mean that blue is part of *what* is said to
exist when we say that the sensation exists. To say that the sensation
exists is to say both that blue exists and that "consciousness," whether
we call it the substance of which blue is *the* content or call it another
part of the content, exists too. Any sensation or idea is a *"thing,"* and
what I have called its object is the quality of this thing. Such a "thing"
is what we think of when we think of a *mental image.* A mental image
is conceived as if it were related to that of which it is the image (if
there be any such thing) in exactly the same way as the image in a
looking-glass is related to that of which it is the reflection; in both
cases there is identity of content, and the image in the looking-glass
differs from that in the mind solely in respect of the fact that in the
one case the other constituent of the image is "glass" and in the other
case it is consciousness. If the image is of blue it is not conceived
that this "content" has any relation to the consciousness but what it
has to the glass: it is conceived *merely* to be its *content.* And owing
to the fact that sensations and ideas are all considered to be *wholes*
of this description—things in the mind—the question: What do we
know? is considered to be identical with the question: What reason
have we for supposing that there are things outside the mind *corresponding* to these that are inside it?

What I wish to point out is (1) that we have no reason for
supposing that there are such things as mental images at all—for
supposing that blue *is* part of the content of the sensation of blue,
and (2) that even if there are mental images, no mental image and
no sensation or idea is *merely* a thing of this kind: that "blue," even
if it is part of the content of the image or sensation or idea of blue,
is always *also* related to it in quite another way, and that this other
relation, omitted in the traditional analysis, is the *only* one which
makes the sensation of blue a mental fact at all.

The true analysis of a sensation or idea is as follows. The element
that is common to them all, and which I have called "consciousness,"
really *is* consciousness. A sensation is, in reality, a case of "knowing"
or "being aware of" or "experiencing" something. When we know
that the sensation of blue exists, the fact we know is that there exists
an awareness of blue. And this awareness is not merely, as we have
hitherto seen it must be, itself something distinct and unique, utterly
different from blue: it also has a perfectly distinct and unique relation
to blue, a relation which is *not* that of thing or substance to content,

nor of one part of content to another part of content. This relation
is just that which we mean in every case by "knowing." To have in
your mind "knowledge" of blue, is *not* to have in your mind a "thing"
or "image" of which blue is the content. To be aware of the sensation of blue is not to be aware of a mental image—of a "thing," of
which "blue" and some other element are constituent parts in the
same sense in which blue and glass are constituents of a blue bead.
It is to be aware of awareness of blue; awareness being used, in both
cases, in exactly the same sense. This element, we have seen, is
certainly neglected by the "content" theory: that theory entirely fails
to express the fact that there is, in the sensation of blue, this unique
relation between blue and the other constituent. And what I contend
is that this omission is *not* mere negligence of expression, but is due
to the fact that though philosophers have recognized that *something*
distinct is meant by consciousness, they have never yet had a clear
conception of what that *something* is. They have not been able to
hold *it* and *blue* before their minds and to compare them, in the same
way in which they can compare *blue* and *green*. And this for the
reason I gave above: namely that the moment we try to fix our
attention upon consciousness and to see *what*, distinctly, it is, it
seems to vanish: it seems as if we had before us a mere emptiness.
When we try to introspect the sensation of blue, all we can see is
the blue: the other element is as if it were diaphanous. Yet it *can*
be distinguished if we look attentively enough, and if we know that
there is something to look for. My main object in this paragraph has
been to try to make the reader *see* it; but I fear I shall have succeeded
very ill.

It being the case, then, that the sensation of blue includes in its
analysis, beside blue, *both* a unique element "awareness" *and* a
unique relation of this element to blue, I can make plain what I
meant by asserting, as two distinct propositions, (1) that blue is
probably not part of the content of the sensation at all, and (2)
that, even it were, the sensation would nevertheless not be the sensation *of* blue, if blue had only this relation to it. The first hypothesis
may now be expressed by saying that, if it were true, then, when the
sensation of blue exists, there exists a *blue awareness*: offense may
be taken at the expression, but yet it expresses just what should be
and is meant by saying that blue is, in this case, a *content* of consciousness or experience. Whether or not, when I have the sensation
of blue, my consciousness or awareness is thus blue, my introspection

does not enable me to decide with certainty: I only see no reason for thinking that it is. But whether it is or not, the point is unimportant, for introspection *does* enable me to decide that something else is also true: namely that I am aware *of* blue, and by this I mean, that my awareness has to blue a quite different and distinct relation. It is possible, I admit, that my awareness is blue *as well* as being *of* blue: but what I am quite sure of is that it is *of* blue; that it has to blue the simple and unique relation the existence of which alone justifies us in distinguishing knowledge of a thing from the thing known, indeed in distinguishing mind from matter. And this result I may express by saying that what is called the *content* of a sensation is in very truth what I originally called it—the sensation's *object*.

But if all this be true, what follows?

Idealists admit that some things really exist of which they are not aware: there are some things, they hold, which are not inseparable aspects of *their* experience, even if they be inseparable aspects of some experience. They further hold that some of the things of which they are sometimes aware do really exist, even when they are not aware of them: they hold for instance that they are sometimes aware of other minds, which continue to exist even when they are not aware of them. They are, therefore, sometimes aware of something which is *not* an inseparable aspect of their own experience. They do *know* *some* things which are *not* a mere part or content of their experience. And what my analysis of sensation has been designed to show is, that whenever I have a mere sensation or idea, the fact is that I am then aware of something which is equally and in the same sense *not* an inseparable aspect of my experience. The awareness which I have maintained to be included in sensation is the very same unique fact which constitutes every kind of knowledge: *"blue"* is as much an object, and as little a mere content, of my experience, when I experience it, as the most exalted and independent real thing of which I am ever aware. There is, therefore, no question of how we are to "get outside the circle of our own ideas and sensations." Merely to have a sensation is already to *be* outside that circle. It is to know something which is as truly and really *not* a part of *my* experience, as anything which I can ever know.

Now I think I am not mistaken in asserting that the reason why Idealists suppose that everything which *is* must be an inseparable aspect of some experience, is that they suppose some things, at least, to be inseparable aspects of *their* experience. And there is

certainly nothing which they are so firmly convinced to be an inseparable aspect of their experience as what they call the *content*
of their ideas and sensations. If therefore, *this* turns out in every
case, whether it be also the content or not, to be at least *not* an
inseparable aspect of the experience of it, it will be readily admitted
that nothing else which *we* experience ever is such an inseparable
aspect. But if we never experience anything but what is *not* an
inseparable aspect of *that* experience, how can we infer that anything whatever, let alone *everything,* is an inseparable aspect of
any experience? How utterly unfounded is the assumption that *"esse*
is *percipi"* appears in the clearest light.

But further I think it may be seen that if the object of an
Idealist's sensation were, as he supposes, *not* the object but merely
the content of that sensation, if, that is to say, it really were an
inseparable aspect of his experience, each Idealist could never be
aware either of himself or of any other real thing. For the relation
of a sensation to its object is certainly the same as that of any other
instance of experience to its object; and this, I think, is generally
admitted even by Idealists: they state as readily that *what* is judged
or thought or perceived is the *content* of that judgment or thought
or perception, as that blue is the content of the sensation of blue.
But, if so, then when any Idealist thinks he is *aware* of himself or
of any one else, this cannot really be the case. The fact is, on his
own theory, that himself and that other person are in reality mere
contents of an awareness, which is aware *of* nothing whatever. All
that can be said is that there is an awareness in him, *with* a certain
content: it can never be true that there is in him a consciousness *of*
anything. And similarly he is never aware either of the fact that
he exists or that reality is spiritual. The real fact, which he describes
in those terms, is that his existence and the spirituality of reality
are *contents* of an awareness, which is aware of nothing—certainly
not, then, of its own content.

And further if everything, of which he thinks he is aware, is in
reality merely a content of his own experience he has certainly no
reason for holding that anything does exist except himself: it will,
of course, be possible that other persons do exist; solipsism will not
be necessarily true; but he cannot possibly infer from anything he
holds that it is not true. That he himself exists will of course follow
from *his* premise that many things are contents of *his* experience.
But since everything, of which he thinks himself aware, is in reality

merely an inseparable aspect of that awareness; this premise allows no inference that any of these contents, far less any other consciousness, exists at all except as an inseparable aspect of his awareness, that is, as part of himself.

Such, and not those which he takes to follow from it, are the consequences which *do* follow from the Idealist's supposition that the object of an experience is in reality merely a content or inseparable aspect of that experience. If, on the other hand, we clearly recognize the nature of that peculiar relation which I have called "awareness of anything"; if we see that *this* is involved equally in the analysis of *every* experience—from the merest sensation to the most developed perception or reflection, and that *this* is in fact the only essential element in an experience—the only thing that is both common and peculiar to all experiences—the only thing which gives us reason to call any fact mental; if, further, we recognize that this awareness is and must be in all cases of such a nature that its object, when we are aware of it, is precisely what it would be, if we were not aware: then it becomes plain that the existence of a table in space is related to my experience of *it* in precisely the same way as the existence of my own experience is related to my experience of *that*. Of both we are merely aware: if we are aware that the one exists, we are aware in precisely the same sense that the other exists; and if it is true that my experience can exist, even when I do not happen to be aware of its existence, we have exactly the same reason for supposing that the table can do so also. When, therefore, Berkeley supposed that the only thing of which I am directly aware is my own sensations and ideas, he supposed what was false; and when Kant supposed that the objectivity of things in space *consisted* in the fact that they were "Vorstellungen" having to one another different relations from those which the same "Vorstellungen" have to one another in subjective experience, he supposed what was equally false. I am as directly aware of the existence of material things in space as of my own sensations; and *what* I am aware of with regard to each is exactly the same—namely that in one case the material thing, and in the other case my sensation does really exist. The question requiring to be asked about material things is thus not: What reason have we for supposing that anything exists *corresponding* to our sensations? but: What reason have we for supposing that material things do *not* exist, since *their* existence has precisely the same evidence as that of our sensations? That either exist *may* be false; but if it is a reason for doubting the existence of matter, that it is an inseparable aspect of our experience, the same reasoning will prove conclusively that our experience does not exist either, since that must also be an inseparable aspect of our experience of *it*. The only *reasonable* alternative to the admission that matter exists *as well as* spirit, is absolute Scepticism— that, as likely as not *nothing* exists at all. All other suppositions— the Agnostic's, that something, at all events, does exist, as much as the Idealist's, that spirit does—are, if we have no reason for believing in matter, as baseless as the grossest superstitions.

BERTRAND RUSSELL

(1872-—)

The Fallacies of Idealism

. . . THE GROUNDS on which idealism is advocated are generally grounds derived from the theory of knowledge, that is to say, from a discussion of the conditions which things must satisfy in order that we may be able to know them. The first serious attempts to establish idealism on such grounds was that of Bishop Berkeley. He proved first, by arguments which were largely valid, that our sense-data cannot be supposed to have an existence independent of us, but must be, in part at least, "in" the mind, in the sense that their existence would not continue if there were no seeing or hearing or touching or smelling or tasting. So far, his contention was almost certainly valid, even if some of his arguments were not so. But he went on to argue that sense-data were the only things of whose existence our perceptions could assure us, and that to be known is to be "in" a mind, and therefore to be mental. Hence he concluded that nothing can ever be known except what is in some mind, and that whatever is known without being in my mind must be in some other mind.

In order to understand his argument, it is necessary to understand his use of the word "idea." He gives the name "idea" to anything which is *immediately* known, as, for example, sense-data are known. Thus a particular color which we see is an idea; so is a voice which we hear, and so on. But the term is not wholly confined to sense-data. There will also be things remembered or imagined, for with such things also we have immediate acquaintance at the moment of remembering or imagining. All such immediate data he calls "ideas."

He then proceeds to consider common objects, such as a tree, for instance. He shows that all we know immediately when we "per-

This selection is taken from Chapter IV of *The Problems of Philosophy*, which was first published in 1912. It is reprinted with the kind permission of the author and the Oxford University Press.

ceive" the tree consists of ideas in his sense of the word, and he argues that there is not the slightest ground for supposing that there is anything real about the tree except what is perceived. Its being, he says, consists in being perceived: in the Latin of the schoolmen its *"esse"* is *"percipi."* He fully admits that the tree must continue to exist even when we shut our eyes or when no human being is near it. But this continued existence, he says, is due to the fact that God continues to perceive it; the "real" tree, which corresponds to what we called the physical object, consists of ideas in the mind of God, ideas more or less like those we have when we see the tree, but differing in the fact that they are permanent in God's mind so long as the tree continues to exist. All our perceptions, according to him, consist in a partial participation in God's perceptions, and it is because of this participation that different people see more or less the same tree. Thus apart from minds and their ideas there is nothing in the world, nor is it possible that anything else should ever be known, since whatever is known is necessarily an idea.

There are in this argument a good many fallacies which have been important in the history of philosophy, and which it will be as well to bring to light. In the first place, there is a confusion engendered by the use of the word "idea." We think of an idea as essentially something *in* somebody's mind, and thus when we are told that a tree consists entirely of ideas, it is natural to suppose that, if so, the tree must be entirely in minds. But the notion of being "in" the mind is ambiguous. We speak of bearing a person in mind, not meaning that the person is in our minds, but that a thought of him is in our minds. When a man says that some business he had to arrange went clean out of his mind, he does not mean to imply that the business itself was ever in his mind, but only that a thought of the business was formerly in his mind, but afterwards ceased to be in his mind. And so when Berkeley says that the tree must be in our minds if we can know it, all that he really has a right to say is that a thought of the tree must be in our minds. To argue that the tree itself must be in our minds is like arguing that a person whom we bear in mind is himself in our minds. This confusion may seem too gross to have been really commited by any competent philosopher, but various attendant circumstances rendered it possible. In order to see how it was possible, we must go more deeply into the question as to the nature of ideas.

Before taking up the general question of the nature of ideas, we must disentangle two entirely separate questions which arise concerning sense-data and physical objects. We saw that, for various reasons of detail, Berkeley was right in treating the sense-data which constitute our perception of the tree as more or less subjective, in the sense that they depend upon us as much as upon the tree, and would not exist if the tree were not being perceived. But this is an entirely different point from the one by which Berkeley seeks to prove that whatever can be immediately known *must* be in a mind. For this purpose arguments of detail as to the dependence of sense-data upon us are useless. It is necessary to prove, generally, that by being known, things are shown to be mental. This is what Berkeley believes himself to have done. It is this question, and not our previous question as to the difference between sense-data and the physical object, that must now concern us.

Taking the word "idea" in Berkeley's sense, there are two quite distinct things to be considered whenever an idea is before the mind. There is on the one hand the thing of which we are aware—say the color of my table—and on the other hand the actual awareness itself, the mental act of apprehending the thing. The mental act is undoubtedly mental, but is there any reason to suppose that the thing apprehended is in any sense mental? Our previous arguments concerning the color did not prove it to be mental; they only proved that its existence depends upon the relation of our sense organs to the physical object—in our case, the table. That is to say, they proved that a certain color will exist, in a certain light, if a normal eye is placed at a certain point relatively to the table. They did not prove that the color is in the mind of the percipient.

Berkeley's view, that obviously the color *must* be in the mind, seems to depend for its plausibility upon confusing the thing apprehended with the act of apprehension. Either of these might be called an "idea"; probably either would have been called an idea by Berkeley. The act is undoubtedly in the mind; hence, when we are thinking of the act, we readily assent to the view that ideas must be in the mind. Then, forgetting that this was only true when ideas were taken as acts of apprehension, we transfer the proposition that "ideas are in the mind" to ideas in the other sense, i.e., to the things apprehended by our acts of apprehension. Thus, by an unconscious equivocation, we arrive at the conclusion that whatever

we can apprehend must be in our minds. This seems to be the true
analysis of Berkeley's argument, and the ultimate fallacy upon which
it rests.

This question of the distinction between act and object in our
apprehending of things is vitally important, since our whole power
of acquiring knowledge is bound up with it. The faculty of being
acquainted with things other than itself is the main characteristic
of a mind. Acquaintance with objects essentially consists in a relation between the mind and something other than the mind; it is
this that constitutes the mind's power of knowing things. If we say
that the things known must be in the mind, we are either unduly
limiting the mind's power of knowing, or we are uttering a mere
tautology. We are uttering a mere tautology if we mean by "*in* the
mind" the same as by "*before* the mind," i.e., if we mean merely
being apprehended by the mind. But if we mean this, we shall have
to admit that what, *in this sense,* is in the mind, may nevertheless
be not mental. Thus when we realize the nature of knowledge,
Berkeley's argument is seen to be wrong in substance as well as in
form, and his grounds for supposing that "ideas"—i.e., the objects
apprehended—must be mental, are found to have no validity whatever. Hence his grounds in favor of idealism may be dismissed.
It remains to see whether there are any other grounds.

It is often said, as though it were a self-evident truism, that we
cannot know that anything exists which we do not know. It is inferred that whatever can in any way be relevant to our experience
must be at least capable of being known by us; whence it follows
that if matter were essentially something with which we could not
become acquainted, matter would be something which we could
not know to exist, and which could have for us no importance
whatever. It is generally also implied, for reasons which remain
obscure, that what can have no importance for us cannot be real,
and that therefore matter, if it is not composed of minds or of mental
ideas, is impossible and a mere chimaera.

To go into this argument fully at our present stage would be
impossible, since it raises points requiring a considerable preliminary discussion; but certain reasons for rejecting the argument may
be noticed at once. To begin at the end: there is no reason why
what cannot have any *practical* importance for us should not be
real. It is true that, if *theoretical* importance is included, everything
real is of *some* importance to us, since, as persons desirous of know-

ing the truth about the universe, we have some interest in everything that the universe contains. But if this sort of interest is included, it is not the case that matter has no importance for us, provided it exists, even if we cannot know that it exists. We can, obviously, suspect that it may exist, and wonder whether it does; hence it is connected with our desire for knowledge, and has the importance of either satisfying or thwarting this desire.

Again, it is by no means a truism, and is in fact false, that we cannot know that anything exists which we do not know. The word "know" is here used in two different senses. (1) In its first use it is applicable to the sort of knowledge which is opposed to error, the sense in which what we know is *true,* the sense which applies to our beliefs and convictions, i.e., to what are called *judgments*. In this sense of the word we know *that* something is the case. This sort of knowledge may be described as knowledge of *truths*. (2) In the second use of the word "know" above, the word applies to our knowledge of *things,* which we may call *acquaintance*. This is the sense in which we know sense-data. (The distinction involved is roughly that between *savoir* and *connaitre* in French, or between *wissen* and *kennen* in German.)

Thus the statement which seemed like a truism becomes, when re-stated, the following: "We can never truly judge that something with which we are not acquainted exists." This is by no means a truism, but on the contrary a palpable falsehood. I have not the honor to be acquainted with the Emperor of China, but I truly judge that he exists. It may be said, of course, that I judge this because of other people's acquaintance with him. This, however, would be an irrelevant retort, since, if the principle were true, I could not know that any one else is acquainted with him. But further: there is no reason why I should not know of the existence of something with which *nobody* is acqainted. This point is important, and demands elucidation.

If I am acquainted with a thing which exists, my acquaintance gives me the knowledge that it exists. But it is not true that, conversely, whenever I can know that a thing of a certain sort exists, I or some one else must be acquainted with the thing. What happens, in cases where I have true judgment without acquaintance, is that the thing is known to me by *description,* and that, in virtue of some general principle, the existence of a thing answering to this description can be inferred from the existence of something with which I am acquainted. In order to understand this point fully, it will be well first to deal with the difference between knowledge by acquaintance and knowledge by description, and then to consider what knowledge of general principles, if any, has the same kind of certainty as our knowledge of the existence of our own experiences. These subjects will be dealt with in the following chapters.

ERNEST NAGEL

(1903-—)

*"It is a habit of mankind to entrust to careless hope
what they long for, and to use sovereign reason to
thrust aside what they do not fancy."*—THUCYDIDES.

Sovereign Reason

1.

THE INJUNCTION to take Reason as one's guide has fallen repeatedly on men's ears at least since classical antiquity; and the place
of Reason in nature and society has been an oft-recurring theme in
the history of thought. Philosophers have been perennially occupied with analyzing Reason's anatomy and function; poets and
moralists have celebrated its worth and dignity; and even those
engrossed in the conquest and cynical use of power have not sel-
dom made formal obeisance to its authority. If men have so often
been found wanting in adapting their conduct and beliefs to the
precepts of Reason, it has surely not been for lack of frequent
verbal encouragement to do so.

Men's failure to live reasonably is in large measure a consequence
of the fact that though man is by nature a rational animal, the
proficient exercise of rational powers is not a natural blessing but
a difficult achievement. For the full realization of those powers is
the end-product of an arduous personal discipline, to which only
a few of mankind have been able to subject themselves; and the
exercise of those powers is also contingent upon favorable material
and social circumstances, not easily called into existence, and not
generally available in human epochs when a rigid tradition or
brutal compulsion is the primary determinant of personal and
social action. However, mankind's alleged failure to take Reason

---

This essay was first published in 1947 in *Freedom and Experience*, a collection
edited by Sidney Hook and Milton R. Konvitz. It is reprinted with the kind permission of the author and the Cornell University Press.

for its guide cannot always be explained in such terms. For the allegation is often the consequence of the fact that human beliefs and actions are being judged on the basis of conflicting conceptions as to what it is *to be rational*. Though the name of Reason is frequently invoked to sanction or to condemn various practices and beliefs, Reason's ostensible spokesmen do not always speak with a single voice. In short, men have been confronted with incompatible ideals of Reason, not all of which can be congruent with human powers and nature's organization. Whatever else one may learn from the study of philosophy and its history, one cannot easily escape the fact that the canons which mankind has employed in evaluating the reasonableness of conduct and belief have varied with local tradition and historical circumstance.

Systems of philosophy can indeed be profitably studied as explicit and refined formulations of standards of rationality, proposed as ideals against which conduct and claims to genuine knowledge are to be measured. These standards, whatever may be the evidence on which their proponents formally accept them, have in general not been the exclusive creations of those who thus explicitly propose them: they have frequently been the symptoms and intellectual expressions of pervasive tensions and needs operating in various forms in the inclusive social matrix within which philosophical systems come to birth or find wide acceptance. It is thus undoubtedly illuminating to examine philosophical doctrines in terms of their origins and causes and to determine to what extent the perspectives from which philosophers view the world are formed by current customs, current beliefs, and current moral and intellectual problems.

However, philosophical ideas are not simply otiose by-products of cultural processes, exercising no reciprocal influence upon their matrix cultures. On the contrary, the standards of rationality explicitly or implicity contained in philosophic systems have repeatedly served as guides in resolving practical and intellectual issues and in directing theoretical inquiry. The general acceptance of a system of philosophy thus frequently leads to consequences of far-reaching importance to both society and science. Accordingly, the analysis of the canons of rationality involved in philosophic doctrines, with a view to evaluating their adequacy and authority, as distinct from investigating their causes and their matter-of-fact consequences, is a contribution, however indirect, to serious social criticism.

It is with such an examination of the canons of rationality implicit in one historically influential system of philosophy—that of philosophical idealism—that the present paper is concerned. Few would care to deny that the domination which this system of ideas once exercised over thinking minds in this country is now a thing of the past. Nevertheless, the conception of Reason proposed by it is still worth serious attention. It is a conception which satisfies the deep-seated need of sensitive minds for an ideal that is inclusive and worthy of human devotion. It is a view of the goal of thought and of the power of reason that appears to many as the sole alternative to accepting dogmatic preference and brute power as ultimate standards. And it is an interpretation of the office of Reason which still controls the minds of many men eminent in science and art, and which in various guises guides much recent discussion in social and moral philosophy. One is therefore not engaging in a gratuitous intellectual exercise in attempting a fresh evaluation of this ideal of Reason. Is it an ideal firmly rooted in the character of the world and implicit in the actual operations of human reflection? Or is it a conception of the goal of thought that is fundamentally irrelevant to the procedures and conclusions of controlled inquiry, inherently incapable of even partial attainment, the vain pursuit of which leads only to an enervating scepticism and an eventual despair?

This ideal of Reason has been argued in recent years with great vigor and unusual clarity by Professor Brand Blanshard. His presentation of the case for it has in addition the merit of recognizing many of the deficiencies and obscurities of earlier formulations of the doctrine and of exhibiting considerable familiarity with relevant developments in modern logic and science. The task of evaluating the standard of rationality proposed by philosophic idealism has thus become a relatively easy one, for it is now possible to concentrate on Mr. Blanshard's presentation of the evidence for this ideal, in the confident belief that no presentation of the case for it more cogent than his could be made. Accordingly, the present paper will be devoted exclusively to appraising some of the considerations advanced by Mr. Blanshard in favor of this ideal. It will be impossible, naturally, to deal with all the issues he raises in all their dimensions, and in particular it will be necessary to pass by in silence his own criticisms of alternative standards of rationality that have been proposed by contemporary pluralistic naturalists. But while much in his argument must be neglected, it is hoped that what will be discussed is at any rate near the center of his vision.

What, then, is the proper goal of Reason, as Mr. Blanshard envisages it, and what are the arguments upon which he rests his case? The very end and goal of Reason, he declares,

is to understand, and to understand is always to follow an objective pattern or order. What kind of order is this? If it is to satisfy reason, it must be an intelligible order, and what is that? It is an order that never meets our question Why? with a final rebuff, one in which there is always an answer to be found, whether in fact, we find it or not. And what sort of answer would satisfy that question? Only an answer in terms of necessity, and ultimately of logical necessity, since of any answer that falls short of this the question Why? can be raised again. When we reach an answer that is necessary, we see that to repeat the question is idle. Of any statement of merely causal necessity, such as the law of gravitation, or Ohm's law, or Boyle's law, we can intelligibly ask why things should behave in this manner. But when we see that things equal to the same thing are equal to each other, we cannot sensibly ask why, because we are at the end of the line to which such questioning can take us. We have already reached the logically necessary.[1]

And as he explains more fully elsewhere,

Fully coherent knowledge would be knowledge in which every judgment entailed, and was entailed by, the rest of the system. Probably we never find in fact a system where there is so much of interdependence. . . . It is in such systems, perhaps, as Euclidean geometry that we get the most perfect examples of coherence that have been constructed. If any proposition were lacking, it could be supplied from the rest; if any were altered, the repercussions would be felt through the length and breadth of the system. Yet even such a system as this falls short of ideal system. Its postulates are unproved; they are independent of each other, in the sense that none of them could be derived from any other or even from all the others together; its clear necessity is brought by an abstractness so extreme as to have left out nearly everything that belongs to the character of actual things. A completely satisfactory system would have none of these defects. No proposition would be arbitrary, every proposition would be entailed by the others jointly and even singly, no proposition would stand outside the system. . . .[2]

---

1. "Current Strictures on Reason," *Philosophical Review*, LIV (July, 1945), pp. 360-361.
2. *The Nature of Thought* (New York, 1940), II, pp. 264-266.

But this ideal of knowledge is a valid ideal, and something other than the expression of undisciplined self-indulgence, Mr. Blanshard believes, only if the world which thought seeks to apprehend is one "in which intelligence finds an answering intelligibility,"[3] only if reality likewise is an "all-inclusive and perfectly integrated system"[4] whose parts logically imply each other. It is upon this view of reality that he ultimately rests his case for the ideal of reason he professes, and it is to a defense of this theory of reality that he devotes his best efforts.

At this point, however, a reader not antecedently committed to Mr. Blanshard's canons of intelligibility might enter a protest. Why should the goal of human reason, such a reader might ask, be dictated by this alleged character of reality, even if this all-inclusive reality does have the character Mr. Blanshard believes it to have? What logical compulsion is there that even if the world does possess such a perfectly integrated logical structure, human thought should seek to encompass it? Are not the actual tasks of human reason set by *specific* problems, involving only a sector of what exists, whose successful resolution does not, in point of fact, require a consideration of the rest of nature? And should not, therefore, the ideals of human reason, and the principles of criticism that men ought to employ in evaluating proposed solutions to their problems, be established by considering the ways in which specific problems do become resolved, rather than by trying to ground those ideals and principles in the character of an all-inclusive reality that is only vaguely present to men's vision?

Mr. Blanshard is not entirely unmindful of such objections; nor does he conceal from himself that the ideal of knowledge he portrays is in conflict with the general positivistic tenor of modern science as well as with many current naturalistic interpretations of the function of thought. Nevertheless, he attempts to show that the ideal he invokes for human reason is implicit in the tasks human reason normally undertakes. He rejects the view, common since Hume, that all propositions about matters of fact are contingent; for he maintains and tries to prove that "in the end" no propositions are devoid of logical necessity, and that only on the supposition that no proposition is "altogether contingent"[5] can responsible

---

3. "Current Strictures on Reason," p. 361.
4. *The Nature of Thought*, II, p. 475.
5. "Current Strictures on Reason," p. 368.

inquiry be distinguished from arbitrary postulation. Objections of the type briefly cited above do not therefore lead Mr. Blanshard to doubt his fundamental commitments, and a critic who wishes to come to grips with him must consider the positive arguments he employs to support his thesis. The foundation upon which Mr. Blanshard builds his case is the doctrine of internal relations, and it is with an examination of his arguments for this doctrine that the remainder of this paper will be concerned.

2.

The issue raised by the doctrine of internal relations is "whether a term could be what it is apart from the relations it bears to others." Mr. Blanshard explains this issue more fully as follows:

A relation is internal to a term when in its absence the term would be different; it is external when its addition or withdrawal would make *no* difference to the term. . . . Those who accept the theory of internal relations . . . hold that everything, if we knew enough, would turn out to be internally related to everything else. . . .[6]

But this formulation, he believes, is not free from ambiguity, and he therefore amplifies it into the following statment:

. . . Everything is so integral a part of a context that it can neither be nor be truly conceived apart from that context. Put more formally, the theory is this: (1) that every term, i.e., every possible object of thought, is what it is in virtue of relations to what is other than itself; (2) that its nature is affected thus not by some of its relations only, but in differing degrees by all of them, no matter how external they may seem; (3) that in consequence of (2) and of the further obvious fact that everything is related in *some* way to everything else, no knowledge will reveal completely the nature of any term until it has exhausted that term's relations to everything else.[7]

Mr. Blanshard's statement of the doctrine of internal relations has undoubted advantages of greater clarity over other formulations. Nevertheless, one crucial point in it seems to me essentially obscure, and something must be said about it before I turn to his detailed defense of his thesis. For in the statement of his doctrine as well as in the ensuing discussion of it Mr. Blanshard uses the phrase "the nature of a term," though I have been unable to discover in his writings any explicit explanation of what he means by

6. *The Nature of Thought*, II, p. 451.
7. *Ibid.*, p. 452.

it; yet everything depends upon the sense that is to be assigned to it. What ought we to understand by the expression?

At least three uses of the word "nature" can be distinguished when the word occurs in such contexts as "the nature of x."

(1) In the first place, it frequently occurs in questions and answers such as the following: "What is the nature of a circle?"— "The nature of a circle is to be a closed plane curve, all of whose points are equidistant from a fixed point"; "What is the nature of electricity?"—"The nature of electricity is to be a mode of physical behavior specified by Maxwell's equations"; "What is the nature of man?" "The nature of man is to be a rational animal." It is clear that in this usage, the terms whose natures are being discussed are *kinds, characters,* or *universals,* are capable of repeated exemplification in concrete individuals and processes but are not themselves concrete individuals or processes. Successful inquiries into natures, in this sense of the word, terminate in what has traditionally been called *definition,* though the outcome of such research might more appropriately be designated as *theory.* The intellectual service that is rendered when the natures of universals are satisfactorily formulated is that other generic characters associated with the former can be exhibited as logical implicates of those universals.[8] I shall call this use of the word "nature" its *primary* use.

An allied sense of the word "nature" is illustrated by such statements as "The nature of gold is to be malleable" and "It is the nature of cats to catch mice." Here again natures are predicated of universals or characters, not of individuals. However, what is said in such statements to be the nature of a kind is not a definition or complete theory of the kind but is regarded as merely a logical implicate of some assumed complete theory. Thus, the dispositional predicate "being malleable" is generally not taken to constitute the definition of gold, though it is commonly supposed to follow logically from such a definition.

(2) A second important sense of the word "nature" is illustrated by such statements as: "It is the nature of this particular figure to have an angle-sum equal to two right-angles," "To be

---

8. Although I am employing realistic language throughout this paper, and am thus assuming that there are such things as universals, this is done primarily for the sake of expediting the present discussion. Whether, and in what sense, one *must* make this assumption is another question, whose resolution does not, I think, affect the argument in this paper.

rust-resisting is the nature of this knife," or "The nature of Socrates is to be mortal." In these contexts natures are being predicated of concrete things or individuals, rather than of universals or characters as in the previous examples. However, statements like the present ones must frequently be understood as elliptic formulations, in which something is predicated to *be* the nature, or to be *of* the nature, of an individual, only in the sense that the individual has the character designated as its nature as a consequence of his displaying some *other* character. Thus, the mortality which is asserted to be of the nature of Socrates belongs to him *insofar* as Socrates is human; for if Socrates is a man, and assuming an appropriate formulation of the nature of the generic character *man* (in the primary sense of the word "nature"), it follows that Socrates is mortal. In this usage of the word "nature," therefore, to be snub-nosed is not part of the nature of Socrates, since though he is a man, it does not follow from his being one that he is snub-nosed. In this usage, also, though to be mortal is if the nature of Socrates insofar as he is human, mortality need not be part of his nature insofar as he may exhibit some other generic character, for example having a physical body of a determinate shape. Accordingly, when, in the present sense of the word "nature," an individual is said to have a specified nature, what is being asserted is a connection between characters or universals. Since, however, an individual possesses an indefinite number of characters, not all of which logically entail one another, whether a given trait the individual exhibits does or does not belong to his nature is relative to what other character is selected for describing the individual.

(3) I come finally to a third and most puzzling use of the word "nature," according to which individuals are said to have intrinsic natures, where the predication of such natures is supposed to be made without ellipsis. Thus, it is frequently said that the nature of a given individual (e.g., Socrates) is to be a man, or that the nature of the moon is to be a satellite, not insofar as those individuals exhibit some further character, but absolutely and without qualification. What are we to understand by the word "nature" when it is used in this manner?

There is one interpretation that seems obvious, though it may not carry us far. On this interpretation the character attributed to an individual as its nature is one which permits the systematic organization and logical derivation of a large number of other traits the individual exhibits. For example, in asserting that the nature of Socrates is to be a man, what we are asserting on the proposed interpretation is that many other characters possessed by Socrates, such as the ability to see and hear, to experience joy and sorrow, to resent injury, to remember and reflect, are logical consequences of his being a man. However, this interpretation of the word "nature" does not require us to say that *every* trait an individual thing possesses is a consequence of its nature. Thus, even if on some theory of man it would follow from the fact that Socrates is a man that he must be capable of sexual passion, it would not follow from his *nature alone* that he must be fond of music, or that he must be a lover of Alcibiades. In brief, on this interpretation of the term, in predicating a character of an individual as its nature we bring into systematic order only a *selected* group of traits and actions it exhibits.

It is at this point that our difficulties begin, for there apparently are some people, among whom Mr. Blanshard is perhaps to be included, who conceive the nature of an individual as something which logically determines all the thing's attributes and relational properties and not merely *some* of them. But such a use of the word "nature" seems to me to lead to fatal consequences.

In the first place, it is quite clear that just what characters are included in an individual, and just where the boundaries of an individual are drawn, depend on decisions as to the use of language. These decisions, though motivated by considerations of practical utility, are *logically arbitrary*. Thus, the expression "the sun" is generally understood to cover an object confined to a certain apparent volume possessing a certain shape, and exhibiting certain radiant properties; it is usually not employed so as to cover the innumerable spatial relations that object has to other things, nor the energies that had been radiated from the object but are now millions of miles away from it. Nevertheless, the phrase "the sun" *could* be used so that the individual thing to which it refers will include not only the items just mentioned but also all the physical events that stand to the thing (as initially specified) in relations of causal antecedents and consequences, and even all the images and ideas which men have had or ever will have of it. Accordingly, just what qualities and relations are to be included as parts or elements of an individual thing is not a question to be settled by empirical investigation of facts, but a question which calls for a practical delimitation.

However, if the word "individual" is so used that an individual will include *all possible* attributes, relations, and relational properties it may possess, two consequences immediately follow: there will be only one individual, which will coincude with the conjectural "totality" of all things, events, and relations; and secondly, every statement containing the name of an individual will express an analytical proposition. Both consequences are practically undesirable, for reasons too obvious to need mention. But these consequences can be avoided only by restricting the use of the word "individual," as is normally done, so that individuals will include only a proper subset of their possible attributes and relational properties, however vaguely this subset might be delimited and however inexhaustible its membership may be.

But if this is so, and if, as is generally admitted, in the normal use of the word "individual" individuals are not logically definable (because they are taken to include an inexhaustible set of *logically independent* characters), what are we to understand by assertions concerning the nature of an individual thing, in the absolute, unqualified sense of the word "nature"? We must remind ourselves that, in this absolute sense, the nature of an individual is supposed to determine *logically all* the thing's traits and behaviors, its enduring as well as its passing qualities. On the other hand, it is demonstrable that if the nature of a thing is something that is capable of formulation and definition, the nature of a thing cannot by itself determine *all* of its characteristics. For example, if to be a metal is taken to be the nature of a concrete thing, this nature *may* entail the fact that the thing is malleable; but this nature will not, by itself, determine the specific degree of malleability exhibited by the thing, nor will it determine the specific shapes the thing may assume at various times. Such further statements about the thing are derivable from a statement about its nature only if the latter is supplemented by other, logically independent statements, which are instantial in form and specify the contingent initial and boundary conditions under which the thing happens to exist. Accordingly, on the supposition that the natures of things are statable and definable, the nature of a thing cannot determine *every* character the thing may possess.

As far as I can see, however, this conclusion can be avoided in only one way—by equating the nature of a thing with the thing itself. But such an attempted escape from difficulties leads to consequences no less disastrous. In the first place, the nature of a thing, like the thing itself, would be something that is in principle indefinable and could not therefore be made the basis for bringing into systematic order any of the characters which the thing displays. In the second place, every statement which mentions the nature of an individual would express no more than a trivial analytical proposition. And in the third place, since discursive thought would be inherently inadequate to the task of discovering the natures of things, the goal of understanding the natures of things could not be a pertinent ideal for human reason.

Should these difficulties be brushed aside with the comment that they arise only for finite minds and not for an "infinite intelligence," the appropriate rejoinder is close at hand. Why *should* finite minds adopt an ideal of reason that is suitable for an intelligence totally different from theirs? Moreover, would not even an all-encompassing mind fail to achieve the "fully coherent knowledge" that Mr. Blanshard envisages as the ultimate aim of thought? For the characters things possess fall into a large number of subclasses which are demonstrably independent of each other *logically*. If, therefore, an infinite mind did ever come to know the nature of a thing, it would know it only as a miscellaneous collection of attributes and relational properties, some of which do logically entail others, and some of which are logically independent of others. Accordingly, even such a mind would be compelled to recognize an ineradicable contingency in the very heart of the nature of things.

I have spent much time on matters that are preliminary to a discussion of Mr. Blanshard's arguments for the doctrine of internal relations. I hope the time has not been misspent. Mr. Blanshard nowhere states explicitly what he understands by the phrase "the nature of a term"; but his rejection of the false or abstract universal in favor of the true or concrete universal suggests that for him the nature of a thing simply *is* the total set of characters included in the thing. Indeed, he does say that

the nature of any term, unless the term is itself a relation, consists of attributes or properties (in the non-technical sense); by the nature of an

apple we mean its roundness, its redness, its juiciness, and so on. Thus
a change in any of the properties would be a change in the apple's
nature.[9]

And such a statement does provide some ground for the suspicion
that this is the way he is using the expression "the nature of a
thing." But in any event, I shall try to show that only on such
an interpretation of this expression do his arguments for the doctrine of internal relations fail to illustrate the fallacy of *non sequitur*.

3.

I shall examine Mr. Blanshard's arguments for the doctrine of
internal relations under three divisions into which they can be
conveniently placed: arguments concerned with the relations of
concrete things to one another; those dealing with the relations
of universals; and finally those addressed to the nature of causal
relations.

Although Mr. Blanshard offers several grounds for his theory
under the first head, they seem to me to be homogeneous in type,
and I shall therefore comment on only one, in the belief that it is
representative of the others. According to this argument, "everything is related to everything else by the relation of difference at
least," so that if A and B are two concrete (and therefore distinct)
individuals, A must be related to B by the relation of *difference*.
However, were this relation altered, A would no longer be the
thing it is, since it would then not differ from that which, by
hypothesis, is distinct from itself. But "a relation that could not
be theoretically changed without changing the thing itself is precisely what we mean by an internal relation."[10] Hence the relation of difference is internal to A; indeed, everything is therefore
internally related in this manner to everything else. And by a
strictly parallel argument Mr. Blanshard also tries to show that
"what holds in this respect of the relation of difference holds of
other relations as well."[11]

I fear, however, that though this argument has the impressive
quality of great simplicity, its only merit is that it establishes a
truism. To show that this is so, I shall restate it in terms of a
special example. Suppose A and B are two individual plane figures,

9. *The Nature of Thought*, II, p. 478.
10. *Ibid.*, pp. 476-477.
11. *Ibid.*, p. 478.

A having the shape of a circle, *B* that of a triangle. *A* and *B* are surely different, both numerically and with respect to the shapes they possess. Mr. Blanshard's claim is that the relation of being different from *B* is internal to *A*, because if *A* did not stand in this relation to *B*, *A* would be different from what it in fact is. Does the argument establish what Mr. Blanshard believes it does?

(a) Notice, in the first place, that if the nature of a thing is distinguished from the thing, the admitted facts of the example do not yield the conclusion that the relation of difference is internal to the individual *A*. Undoubtedly, given that *B* is triangular in shape, *A* could not be circular unless *A* differed in shape from *B*. But to say that *A* would fail to have the shape it does in fact have, did it not differ in shape from *B*, is *prima facie* not equivalent to saying that *A*'s *nature* would be affected were *A* not different in shape from *B*. However, on Mr. Blanshard's explicit formulation of the doctrine of internal relations, it is this *latter* claim that must be made good if the relation of *difference* is to be established as internal to *A*. But Mr. Blanshard offers no reasons why his readers should accept this claim, unless indeed he assumes, contrary to the hypothesis, that *A* and *A*'s nature are one and the same. If, however, he does assume this, the relation of difference is internal to *A*, but only because of some initial (though perhaps not explicit) practical decision as to what attributes and relational properties are to be included in the individual *A*. Accordingly, Mr. Blanshard has supplied adequate grounds for the statement that difference is a relation internal to *A* if, and only if, this statement is construed as a glaring tautology.

(b) Let us consider the matter in another light. Suppose that the individual figure *B* were to be destroyed so that *A*, though retaining its circular shape, would no longer be different from *B*—for the simple reason that there no longer would be the figure *B* from which it could differ. It seems, therefore, that *A* remains the thing it is in spite of the fact that one of its relations is altered.

I do not know what Mr. Blanshard would say to this objection to his argument, but his reply might conceivably take the following form: To be sure, he might say, the shape of *A* need not be affected by the destruction of the individual *B*, but its *nature* would be. For the nature of *A* is something such that the fact that *A* stands in some relation *R* to a thing follows logically from that nature. But since, on the hypothesis under discussion, *A* ceases to have a relation to a thing that it did have, A's nature must be acknowledged to have undergone alteration, on pain of logical contradiction.

If this is Mr. Blanshard's reply, he requires us to consider again the cryptic notion of the nature of an individual thing. Now it is certainly the case that the proposition, A is different in shape from B, follows logically from the two propositions that A is circular in shape and B is triangular, where A and B are two plane figures. But it is well to note that the conclusion of this inference is entailed by propositions about the *shapes* of the two individuals. If, then, the relational property of being different from B is alleged to be internal to A, it is internal to it only relative to the contingent facts that A is circular and B is triangular. Accordingly, to assert that A is necessarily related to B by the relation of difference, is simply an *elliptic* formulation of the fact that the *characters* A and B possess logically exclude one another. On the other hand, neither the proposition that A is circular in shape nor the proposition that B is triangular in shape is logically necessary; and we cannot therefore conclude that the relational property of being different from B is internal to A without further qualification. On the contrary, though the relation of difference may be internal to A relative to A's possessing one character, it will not in general be internal to A relative to A's possessing some other character. For example, if A and B are figures constructed out of white chalk, the relational property of being different from B is not internal to A relative to its being white in color.

Mr. Blanshard's hypothetical reply to the objection does not therefore dispose of it, unless indeed he construes the nature of a thing to be identical with the total set of attributes and relational properties the thing possesses. In that case, however, he has been arguing strenuously for a truism that no one would care to dispute.

(c) It is pertinent to note, moreover, that even if one were to grant Mr. Blanshard's claim that all the characters a thing possesses are internal to it, his major task would still be ahead of him. For he would still have to show that the necessary relations in which individuals stand to one another satisfy his requirements for a perfectly coherent rational system. In particular, there would remain the task of showing that the complex of characters which constitute an individual thing's nature do indeed form such a system—so that if P and Q are any two characters that are elements in a thing's nature, P and Q mutually entail one another. On the face of it, this seems like a hopeless undertaking, if modern mathematics and natural science do not deceive us in asserting that there are many characters which are logically independent of one another. And unless Mr. Blanshard can find an answer to what appear to be cogent demonstrations of such independence, he must surrender his conception of what is the ultimate ideal of reason.

4.

This last observation leads directly to the second division of Mr. Blanshard's arguments, which attempts to show that every universal is internally related to every other.

One approaches the discussion of this part of Mr. Blanshard's thesis in the cheerful hope that the obscurities surrounding the claim that concrete things are internally related to one another will no longer plague us. For there is a fairly clear sense in which relations between universals may be said to be internal to their natures. Thus, the relational property of having an area greater than that of any other closed plane figure with the same perimeter may be said to be internal to a Euclidean circle, because this property is logically entailed by the nature of Euclidean circles. On the other hand, the character of having radii of four feet is not internal to Euclidean circles, because neither this character nor any of its contraries are logically implied by that universal. In this sense of the word "internal" it would appear therefore that some universals are internally related while others are not, so that in consequence the doctrine of internal relations ought to be judged as false.

However, Mr. Blanshard does not permit us to decide the merits of the doctrine so quickly. For he makes plain that he is affirming the validity of the doctrine for what he designates as "concrete universals," not for the "false" or "abstract" universals of which examples have just been given. To be sure, this qualification carries with it at least the tacit acknowledgment that the doctrine is false when abstract universals are taken to fall within its scope, and so much at any rate may perhaps be regarded as settled. And since, as I believe, it is with the interrelations of abstract universals that discursive thought (in the sciences and elsewhere) is primarily concerned, an ideal of reason that is based on the pre-

sumed truth of the doctrine that concrete universals are internally
related does not appear to be obviously relevant to the normal
operations of reflective inquiry. But I must also confess that I am
quite unclear as to what one is to understand by the phrase "concrete universals," if the expression does not signify *concrete individuals* in all their manifold relations and dependencies; and if
this is at least approximately the meaning of the phrase, all the
obscurities which attend the doctrine of internal relations when
applied to individuals make their unwelcome reappearance when
the doctrine is applied to concrete universals.

However this may be, Mr. Blanshard defends his claim that all
universals are internally related, chiefly by trying to dispose of a
number of standard objections to this thesis. His replies to these
objections bring to a focus several crucial questions, and I shall
therefore examine two series of representative comments he makes
that bear upon them.

(1) A typical criticism of the doctrine, formulated by Mr.
Blanshard runs as follows: "Certain abstractions in the field of
quantity, for example the number three, remain the same and un-
affected through every possible embodiment, and in every possible context."[12] But since the embodiment of such universals does
not necessarily involve the embodiment of other abstract characters, the former are not internally related to the latter. Hence
not all universals are internally related.

Mr. Blanshard counters this criticism with a threefold rejoinder.

(a) His first comment is that the alleged independence of the
number three from context is not an independence in all respects,
"for it is so intimately bound up with the other members of the
number series that if its relations to any one of them were altered, if three were no longer greater than two, for example, or
less than four, it would simply vanish."[13] I am afraid, however,
that Mr. Blanshard is here scoring only against mythical opponents and against those who confuse the contradictory of a proposition with its contrary. His present remark carries no weight
against those of his critics who, in denying that *all* relations of
the number three are internal to its nature, no *not* deny that *some*
of its relations are internal.

(b) The second part of Mr. Blanshard's rejoinder asserts that

___
12. *Ibid.*, p. 471.
13. *Ibid.*, p. 472.

"identity in difference" creeps into even purely arithmetical analysis. According to him, the equation "3 = 2 + 1" asserts that "in
some respect or other the two sides are the same." But if the two
sides are "merely and abstractly the same, i.e., the same with no
difference at all," a distinction is asserted without difference; and
if they are "merely different," the equation asserts what is not,
for the equation "expressly declares that they are *not* different
wholly."[14]

I have not been able to discover what direct bearing these remarks have on the question whether all the relations of the number
three are internal to it. The remarks do reveal, however, a common
mistake in analysis, the mistake of confusing a sign with what the
sign expresses. The essential point to note is that the *equation*
"3 = 2 + 1" is a complex linguistic sign, whose two members
are different *symbolic expressions*. What the equation asserts (assuming that it is not being used to state the nominal definition of
the *numeral* "3"), is that the number referred to by its left-hand
member is identically the same as the number *described* by the
right-hand member, where the descriptive phrase describes the
number in terms of a certain operation upon two other numbers.
The identity in difference which Mr. Blanshard finds in the equation thus reduces itself to the following: the same *number* is denoted by two different *expressions*. But surely this fact cannot be
used to cast doubt on the claims of Mr. Blanshard's critics that a
universal may appear in two different contexts without undergoing
any alteration in its nature.

(c) The remaining part of Mr. Blanshard's rejoinder asserts
that the alleged indifference of abstracted quantities to concrete
contexts is simply the consequence of a definition and cannot
therefore be taken as decisive evidence against his view. He thus
declares that

when it is asked whether . . . purely numerical differences, or the assem-
blies of them of which the several numbers are composed, depend on
the special differences of the terms, the answer presumably is No. But
does this prove that there are purely numerical differences in nature?
It is hard to see that it does. All that it shows is that if one *defines* one's
units as independent of special differences, then they will be independent
of special differences. It does not show that one's definition corresponds
to anything in reality.[15]

---

14. *Ibid.*, p. 472.
15. *Ibid.*, p. 473.

This curious comment seems to me a child of desperation. Mr. Blanshard is apparently not denying that the number three is a universal. But if the number is a universal, and if its presumed *logical independence* from various other universals with which it may sometimes be conjoined is simply the consequence of its definition, just how, one would like to know, is the number to be conceived so that this logical independence is irrelevant for understanding the true nature of three? Moreover, what good reasons are there for doubting that the number three as defined corresponds, or may correspond, to something in reality? When we discover that two sets of elements in nature (say, the individuals gathered to play Beethoven's Opus 70, No. 1, and the principal planets whose orbits are interior to the orbit of Mars) can be matched in a one-to-one fashion, do we not discover a genuine fact in the real—a fact which is expressed by saying that the two sets possess the common cardinal number three? The obvious truth seems to be that the cardinal numbers, like other universals, are properties of groups of elements that are *invariants* under certain transformations and conditions; and although they are properties which can be defined, the fact *that* they are invariants is not simply a matter of definition. Nor does the assumption that cardinal numbers are invariants entail the conclusion that "there are purely numerical differences in nature." On the contrary, they could not very well be invariants unless the groups of things which they characterize were distinguishable in various respects. Accordingly, to say that the cardinals are invariants is simply another way of saying that they are not internally related to every other character with which they may jointly occur.

(2) Mr. Blanshard's rejoinder to one criticism of the theory of internal relations thus seems to me to be somewhat less than conclusive. I now turn to his comments upon a second objection, which maintains that we *can* have adequate knowledge of a universal (say redheadedness) without knowing all its relations to every other universal that might be exemplified by the individuals possessing the first—for example, without knowing all the relations of redheadedness to the mental and bodily traits of redheaded people. The crux of Mr. Blanshard's reply to this is that while we can, and do, have some knowledge of redheadedness without knowing all its relations, we cannot know "red-headedness *fully and as it really is* without such knowledge."[16]

---
16. *Ibid.*, p. 488.

This reply is certainly conclusive if the phrase "to have full knowledge" simply *means* to know *all* the relations of a character; and perhaps at bottom Mr. Blanshard does rest his case on what is essentially a stipulation as to his use of language. Nevertheless, there are some indications that he is aiming at a less arbitrary disposition of a serious criticism of his views. For he declares that the "red-headedness now explicitly presented to thought" is not "all there is to that attribute as its exists in the nature of things," since an idea "always points beyond itself; it always means more than it is; it always refers to more than it includes within the circle of its explicit content."[17] He continues:

Red-headedness is an integral part of an organism, and indeed is so bound up, for example, with the structure of hair-fibres, and this in turn with all manner of constitutional factors determining racial and individual differences that our common notion of it supplies scarcely more than a sign-post to its real or ultimate nature, i.e., to what it is as embedded in its own context.[18]

But do these explanations remove the force of the criticism? I think not, and for the following reasons:

(a) In the first place, the point of the criticism (namely, that one could have adequate knowledge of redheadedness without knowing all its relations) does not reside in the claim that the redheadedness explicitly presented to thought is "all there is" to this character; at any rate, there are many who raise that objection to Mr. Blanshard's thesis and at the same time deny such a claim. The point of the criticism is that the adequacy of one's knowledge of redheadedness is to be measured in terms of its relevance to the specific problems which may generate inquiry into that character. There are, however, *many distinct* problems which may generate such inquiry, and not just one all-encompassing difficulty; and there is no good reason to suppose that what may be an adequate resolution of one problem is either adequate or relevant to every other. The problem a redheaded woman faces who wishes to adorn herself attractively is not the problem which may agitate the physiologist or geneticist, and neither of these problems coincides with the question that a student of the physics of color may put to himself. Why should one imagine that these various problems are simply limited aspects of one inclusive

17. *Ibid.,* p. 489.
18. *Ibid.,* p. 490.

problem, or that the several answers to them are necessarily relevant to one another? And why should one suppose, *in advance of specific inquiry,* that in the attempt to answer any one question about redheadedness one is inevitably and necessarily led to the consideration of *every* relation in which that character stands to others?

(b) I come to my second reason. A customary way of distinguishing between universals and concrete individuals is to say that the former, unlike the latter, are capable of repeated exemplification and are often definable. But according to Mr. Blanshard, redheadedness is no more repeatable and definable than are the individuals who may happen to illustrate it. For if I read him aright, the redheadedness embodied in Frederick Barbarossa is regarded by him to have a "real or ultimate nature" which is different from the nature of redheadedness embodied in one of Barbarossa's ancestors. And if this is so, in what sense is the redheadedness Mr. Blanshard is discussing a universal, and in what way are his remarks relevant to the criticism he is nominally discussing?

(c) I have one final point in this connection. Mr. Blanshard is presumably considering the question whether all of the relations which redheadedness may have to other characters are internal to redheadedness. His aim must therefore be to determine whether, if an individual A is redheaded, it *logically follows* that A possesses every one of the traits it does in fact possess—for example, that A is blue-eyed, brachycephalic, right-handed, and so on. But what he is actually discussing is the question whether these other traits are *causally related* to A's hair being reddish in color. Now while it may indeed be the case that the occurrence of redheadedness has causal conditions and consequences, it is a complete *non sequitur* to conclude from this fact that the characters causally connected with redheadedness are *internally* related to it—it is a conclusion which is warranted only if it can be shown, what thus far Mr. Blanshard has not shown, that logical entailment is an essential ingredient in all causal relations.

I must therefore conclude that Mr. Blanshard does not establish his claim that the relations of universals are all internal, whether the universals are taken to be concrete or abstract. In particular, he presents no plausible reasons for doubting that the demonstrations contained in the modern literature of logic and mathematics concerning the logical independence of various universals do prove what they say they do. The challenge that these demonstrations offer to the doctrine of internal relations is certainly not a negligible one; and one of the strange anomalies of his defense of the doctrine is that he addresses himself to it only incidentally.

5.

I have now examined two of Mr. Blanshard's three classes of arguments for the doctrine of internal relations. There remains for consideration his third group, which attempts to find support for the doctrine in the alleged nature of causal relations. Two important claims are made by him in this connection. The first is that "all things are *causally* related, directly or indirectly"; and the second is that "being causally related involves being *logically* related."[19] I shall, however, not stop to examine the evidence Mr. Blanshard offers for the first claim, chiefly because if, as I hope to show, his grounds for the second are insufficient to establish it, his first claim even if sound would not by itself suffice to prove the doctrine of internal relations. Certainly many thinkers have held that all things are causally related but have rejected the doctrine without demonstrated inconsistency.

Three lines of evidence are presented by Mr. Blanshard to show that causal connections involve logical necessity.

(1) In the first he maintains that whenever we engage in deductive inference, "the fact that the ground entails the consequent is one of the conditions determining the appearance of this consequent rather than something else in the thinker's mind."[20] Accordingly, the answer to the question "Why does the conclusion of an argument appear in the mind of a reasoner?" is that the *thought* of the premise, which constitutes the cause (or part of the cause) for the occurrence of the *thought* of the conclusion, *logically necessitates* this latter thought. There is therefore an element of logical necessity relating the cause and the effect.

Mr. Blanshard appears to take much stock in this argument, for he has used it on more than one occasion to win assent for his views. Nevertheless, I find it singularly unimpressive.

(a) It is not an unfamiliar fact that at least in some cases when a man thinks of a premise he subsequently thinks of a proposi-

19. *Ibid.*, p. 492.
20. *Ibid.*, p. 496.

tion which, though he believes it to be the logical consequence of the premise, is in fact not a valid consequence at all. If we admit that in such cases the thought of the premise is a cause (or part of the cause) of the thought of the conclusion, we must also admit that thoughts may be causally related, though the propositions to which these thoughts are addressed do not stand to each other in the relation of logical entailment. There is therefore some ground for believing that the presence of the implicative relation between propositions is not a *sine qua non* for the alleged causal connection between *thoughts* about those propositions.

It is also well known that men often entertain propositions with a view to deducing conclusions from them but nevertheless fail to do so, even though various conclusions may in fact be entailed by the premises. Evidently the presence of the implicative relation between propositions, therefore, is not a *sufficient* condition for the causal determination of a thought about a conclusion by a thought about the premises.

It sometimes happens, moreover, that each of two men will think of a premise and also come to think of a conclusion implied by it, where one of the thinkers perceives the logical connection between the propositions while the other, luckily hitting upon the conclusion, does not obtain it by following the chain of logical implication. Such a situation is almost ideal for the application of the familiar canons of induction; and if we rely on the Method of Difference, we must conclude that though the thought of one proposition may be the cause (or part of the cause) of the thought of a second implied by the first, the relation of implication is not an element in the causal transaction. Contrary to Mr. Blanshard's contention, his argument thus supplies no credible reasons for supposing that causal connections involve logical necessity.

(b) There is, however, an even more serious flaw in his argument. What is it, we must ask, which is properly characterized as "necessary" when what is called a "necessary inference" is drawn? When, for example, we draw the conclusion that Smith is younger than Brown from the premise that Brown is older than Smith, is it the *inference* which is necessary, or is it the *proposition* that if Brown is older than Smith then Smith is younger than Brown? The answer is clearly in favor of the second alternative. For it is of the *proposition,* not of the inference that it is correct to say: it is necessary because it is *impossible* for its antecedent to be true and its consequent false;

it is not at all impossible for an *inference* to occur whose antecedent is true and its consequent false. In characterizing an inference as necessary we are thus using an elliptic form of speech, and the phrase "necessary inference" must be construed as signifying the fact that the consequent of a necessary conditional proposition is being deduced from its antecedent.

Accordingly, to argue that the causal relation between the thought of a premise and the thought of the conclusion (when the premise entails the conclusion) involves logical necessity is to confuse the thought of a necessary relation with the necessity of a thought; it is to confound the nontemporal logical relation of entailment or implication with the temporal process of inference that recognizes or discovers such implicative relations.

Mr. Blanshard is not unaware of this apparently fatal objection to his argument. But his reply to it is regrettably not to the point and succeeds only in raising irrelevant issues. His rejoinder considers the objection as if the latter rested on the assumption that causal connections hold between "mere event[s], endowed with no sort of character";[21] and in opposition to this assumption he maintains, quite rightly, that the "contents or characters of events" enter into causal processes. He therefore concludes that the logical relations between these characters also enter into these processes and declares: "In explicit inference we have a process in which we can directly see not only *that* one event succeeds another, but in large measure *why* it succeeds."[22]

But just what is the pertinence of these remarks to the matter at stake? For suppose we admit that the thoughts which are said to be causally related in inference are not naked events, stripped of all characters. It does not follow from this admission alone that the *logical relations* between the *objects* of those thoughts enter into the causal processes involving those *thoughts;* and it certainly does not follow from that admission that it is the *thoughts as existents,* rather than the *propositions* to which those thoughts may be addressed, which logically imply one another. Mr. Blanshard cannot be acquitted of the charge that he is confusing implication with inference.

Moreover, is it the case that we do directly see, as Mr. Blanshard maintains, *why* in an explicit inference one event follows an-

21. *Ibid.*, p. 497.
22. *Ibid.*, p. 498.

other? Do we see *why,* when we think of Brown as older than Smith, we subsequently think that Smith is younger than Brown? It has already been noted that though the first proposition entails the second, the *thought* of the first is not invariably followed by the *thought* of the second; and it is not unreasonable to suppose therefore that the causal sequence of such thoughts involves the operation of a complicated physiological and psychological mechanism, whose detailed structure and conditions of effective performance are still only partly understood. Accordingly, there seems to be some basis for the suspicion that when Mr. Blanshard believes he sees *why* one event in inference is followed by another, and not merely *that* there is such a succession, he is being deceived by the happy working of his own body into identifying his *apprehension* of necessary relations with an alleged necessity of his apprehending those relations.

(c) There is one other aspect of Mr. Blanshard's discussion that requires brief comment. For he believes that serious consequences for morals and the life of reason follow from the denial that logical necessity is involved in causal relations; and he declares that "unless necessity does play a part in the movement of inference, no argument will establish anything,"[23] since on the hypothesis that no such necessity exists the distinction between being "moved by reasons" and being moved by causes is simply an illusion.

Now, no doubt, all who love the life of the intellect and hate brutal unreason will recoil in horror from any philosophy which would deny this distinction. But can one retain it only on Mr. Blanshard's terms and only within the framework of his philosophy? Surely not. Why is it impossible to be moved by reasons if the *temporal passage* from premise to conclusion in a valid inference does not involve a relation of logical necessity? A man who first notes a premise *A,* and then perceives that *A logically implies B,* is moved by reasons when he accepts *B* on the evidence of the premise—even if the causal sequence, the thought of *A,* the perception of the connection between *A* and *B,* the assertion of *B,* is a logically contingent one. Such a thinker might not assert *B* did he not *perceive* the connection between *A* and *B;* and his *perception* of this connection is doubtless one of the factors which causally determine his thought and acceptance of *B.* But is there

23. *Ibid.*

any reason for maintaining that if the connection between this factor and the effect attributed to it is a logically contingent one, its manifest operation is illusory?

(2) So much for Mr. Blanshard's first argument for the presence of logical necessity in causal relations. He next comes to alleged cases of such necessity in mental activities other than inference. And he offers as an example of such necessity the proposition that all who think lightly of their own deserts are grateful, in which, according to himself, both a causal and a logical connection is asserted between low self-esteem and gratefulness for the esteem of others.[24]

As far as I can make out, Mr. Blanshard rests his case that this is so on the alleged fact that though "one cannot isolate in human nature the precise reciprocating conditions of gratitude, or formulate one's law in anything better than a statement of tendency," nevertheless "we do have *some* insight into why the man of low self-esteem should be grateful for the esteem of others."[25] He therefore cites with approval Ewing's assertion:

It seems to me that we can see and to some extent really understand why an insult should tend to give rise to anger, why love should lead to grief if the object of one's love die or prove thoroughly unworthy, why a success should give pleasure, why the anticipation of physical pain should arouse fear. It does seem more reasonable *on other than inductive* grounds to suppose that if *A* loves *B* that will tend to make him sorry when *B* dies than to suppose that it will make him intensely glad.

I will not venture to challenge Mr. Blanshard's contention that in such matters as he mentions he *does* possess an "insight" into the presence of a necessary logical bond, especially since he specifies no general rules that might serve to define the character of that necessity. If he does have the insight, he must be congratulated on possessing what is surely a rare power. However, Mr. Blanshard himself admits that the alleged law connecting low self-esteem and gratitude states only a "tendency," not an invariable connection, to which therefore exceptions may (and presumably do) occur. And I confess that the sense in which a law expressing only such a tendency *also* expresses a logical necessity is to me entirely obscure.

Moreover, it is surely no news that many men with a low self-

---

24. *Ibid.*, p. 500.
25. *Ibid.*

esteem exhibit an attitude quite the reverse of gratitude for the esteem of others. Spinoza had suggested as much, and in the light of contemporary psychological investigations the absence of feelings of gratitude in such cases appears eminently plausible. The chief point to note, however, is that whether a certain type of human response to an indicated situation appears "reasonable" and "logically necessary" or not, is a function of what theory of human nature is explicitly or implicity assumed. But one must not overlook the crucial fact that though many propositions about human action may be necessary consequences from the main principles of the theory, neither those principles nor those propositions are' logically necessary truths. For example, Mr. Ewing's example of love for a person leading to grief if that person dies is a theorem in Spinoza's *Ethics;* but its "necessity" is relative to the postulates of this system, postulates which, if they are true, are clearly only contingently true.

Apropos of the suggestion that certain general propositions about human actions are "reasonable" inherently and "on other than inductive grounds," I must add the obvious but unfortunately still needed reminder that the pages of the history of thought are strewn with exploded claims concerning the "necessary" character of various "truths" alleged to be revealed to immediate vision. The tendency to see something final and necessary in what subsequently turns out to be transitory and contingent has been no minor hindrance to the development of knowledge, especially in the social and moral disciplines. To be sure, Mr. Blanshard's claim to have discovered such logically necessary propositions about human actions may meet a better fate than have similar claims by countless other men. It is nevertheless curious that such a claim should come from one who, in terms of his professed philosophy, might be expected to deny that necessity and self-evidence characterize propositions isolated from their relations to some system in which they are elements.

(3) I turn finally to Mr. Blanshard's discussion of the question whether logical necessity is present even in the causal processes found in physical nature, which clearly constitutes what is perhaps the most crucial part of the defense of his general thesis. However, his discussion is predicated on the assumption that only two views as to the nature of causal connections are possible, one represented by what is known as the regularity view, the other by the con-

ception which he himself favors. He therefore devotes his best
efforts to a criticism of the regularity view, in the apparent belief
that if he can exhibit its inadequacy he will thereby have established the validity of his own conception. Unfortunately for the
argument, the two alternative analyses Mr. Blanshard considers
do not exhaust the possibilities; in fact, a number of contemporary writers (for example, Cohen, Dewey, Parker, and at one time
Broad), have offered accounts of causality which are incompatible
both with the regularity and the entailment views. Accordingly,
even if Mr. Blanshard's reasons for rejecting the regularity view
were entirely cogent, he would still not have produced compelling
evidence for adopting his own analysis of causality.

In what follows I shall therefore not consider his criticisms of
the regularity view, and shall restrict myself to examining the
few grounds he presents for the entailment view. These grounds
are, I think, just two in number.

(a) Mr. Blanshard requires of any analysis of causality that it
be compatible with the fact that successful predictions concerning
the future can often be made on the basis of past observations on
the sequences of events. And he maintains that when we predict
that *b* will follow *a* in the future as it has followed in the past,
there must be a logical bond between *a* and *b* which warrants the
prediction. "Unless *a* is connected with *b* by something more than
mere conjunction," he declares, "there is no ground . . . whatever"
for the argument from past to future.[26]

It will be admitted, I think, that if all causes *entail* their effects,
and if we knew not only this but *also* that a specific phenomenon
a which is suspected of being the cause of *b* entails the latter, then
a prediction concerning the future occurrence of *b* on the strength
of observing *a* would be fully warranted. However, if we knew
only that the entailment view is true but did *not* know that *a*
logically implies *b* (though events of the type *a* may have been observed in the past to be followed by the events of type *b*), we would
certainly not possess what Mr. Blanshard would regard as rationally
satisfactory grounds for predicting the future occurrence of *b*
as an effect of *a*. Evidently, therefore, the acceptance of the entailment view of causality is not sufficient for justifying any particular prediction.

But though some defenders of the entailment view claim to have

26. *Ibid.*, p. 507.

an "insight" into the logical structures of specific causal processes in physical nature, Mr. Blanshard makes no such pretensions; he modestly limits his own claims to matters pertaining to mental actions. And there is little doubt that most men who venture to predict physical occurrences also lack such insight. What then can the entailment view of causality, assuming that it is the correct view, offer to Mr. Blanshard and the rest of mankind in the way of a "rational justification" of predictive inferences? Must not he, like everybody else, fall back upon the evidence provided by past conjunctions of characteristics to support the hypothesis that they may be causally related? Is he any better off in this respect than are those who subscribe to the regularity view of causality? Must we not conclude that the entailment view contributes *nothing* toward advancing the aims of specfic inquiries into the causal dependencies of physical nature, that it provides no rational foundation for the successful predications that are often made, and that therefore Mr. Blanshard's present line of reasoning supplies no support for the entailment view?

(b) Mr. Blanshard's remaining argument for the entailment view rests upon a consideration of general statements *about* causality (such as the maxim "Same cause, same effect"), rather than upon a study of specific causal propositions (such as that the earth's rotation is the cause of day and night). He maintains that we can safely assert such general propositions about causality because we possess an "insight" that justifies our doing so. This insight consists in recognizing that "when *a* is said to produce *x* in virtue of its nature as *a,* the connection referred to is not only an intrinsic relation but a necessary relation."[27] And as he goes on to explain, "To say that *a* produces *x* in virtue of being *a* and yet that, given *a, x* might not follow, is inconsistent with the laws of identity and contradiction." For *a* is not a mere "cluster of qualities abstracted from their relations"; on the contrary,

a's behavior is the outgrowth or expression of *a*'s nature. And to assert that *a*'s behavior, so conceived, could be different while *a* was the same would be to assert that something both did and did not issue from the nature of *a*. And that is self-contradiction. The statement would also . . . conflict with the law of identity. It implies that a thing may remain itself when you have stripped from it everything which it is *such as* to be and do. To strip it of these things would be to strip it, so to speak,

---

27. *Ibid.*, p. 512.

of the suchness that makes it what it is, i.e., to say that it is other than
it is.[28]

Old acquaintances thus greet us once more, the puzzle as to
what is to be included in a thing and the obscure notion of a
thing's nature. Let us make one final effort to penetrate into these
mysteries, by applying Mr. Blanshard's present argument to the
proposition that Brutus caused the death of Caesar. On that argument, Brutus' action was the outgrowth of Brutus' special nature,
and to suppose that Brutus had not acted as he in fact did would
be to strip him of the "suchness" that made him what he was. The
argument thus requires us to say that the compound proposition,
Brutus did cause the death of Caesar but it is nevertheless logically possible for Brutus not to have done so, is logically impossible. More briefly and generally, Mr. Blanshard's position as
revealed by the present argument reduces to this: every true proposition which imputes a causal action to Brutus is logically necessary.

This is certainly an amazing conclusion. But is it true? It can be
shown to be true if, and only if, the *individual* Brutus is conceived
as including every possible attribute that may be truly predicated
of him, while at the same time the *nature* of Brutus is equated with
the total set of characters Brutus is thus made to include. In short,
it can be shown to be true only by a violent redefinition of the
expressions "individual" and "the nature of an individual." But as
I have tried to show earlier, by this device Mr. Blanshard's entire
thesis is reduced to a trivial tautology.

I therefore conclude that Mr. Blanshard's heroic efforts in be-
half of the doctrine of internal relations have failed of their intended objective. He has not succeeded in showing that contingency is not an irreducible feature of the world, and in urging upon
men an ideal of reason which ignores this character of things he
must be judged as an advocate of a false and irrelevant ideal. The
vision he has called up of the scope and office of human reason is
not without grandeur and inspiring power, and its insistence on
system and rational order reveals its sources in human aspirations.
But like all visions which feed on uncontrolled and exaggerated
hopes and fancies, it is a vision that cannot permanently serve to
guide the energies of sober men.

---

28. *Ibid.*, pp. 513-514.

BIBLIOGRAPHY

Compiled by James Bayley and Herbert Heidelberger

The following abbreviations are used in this list:
Arist. Soc. for *Proceedings of the Aristotelian Society*
Educ. Rev. for *Educational Review*
Harvard Theol. Rev. for *Harvard Theological Review*
Int. J. of Ethics for *International Journal of Ethics*
J. Philo. for *Journal of Philosophy*
J. Philo., Psych. and Sc. Meth. for *Journal of Philosophy, Psychology & Scientific Method*
Philos. Rev. for *Philosophical Review*
All references to *Mind*, unless otherwise indicated, are to the new series.

Berkeley, George

COLLECTED WORKS

Fraser, A. Campbell, Ed., *The Works of George Berkeley,* 4 vols., Oxford: The Clarendon Press, 1871

Jessop, T. E., and Luce, A. A., Eds., *The Works of George Berkeley, Bishop of Cloyne,* London: Nelson & Co., publication in progress

SELECTED WORKS

Berkeley, George, *New Theory of Vision and Other Selected Philosophical Writings,* London: Dent, New York: Dutton, 1910 (Everyman's Library Edition), with Introduction by A. D. Lindsay

Berkeley, George, *Three Dialogues between Hylas and Philonous,* Chicago: Open Court, 1925

Calkins, M. W., Ed., *Essays, Principles and Dialogues,* New York: Scribners, 1929

Johnston, G. A., Ed., *Commonplace Book,* London: Faber & Co., 1930

COMMENTARIES

Broad, C. D., "Berkeley's Argument About Material Substance," London: H. Milford, 1942; also in *Proceedings of the British Academy,* Volume 28

Fraser, A. Campbell, *Berkeley,* Philadelphia: J. B. Lippincott, 1899

Hicks, G. Dawes, *Berkeley,* London: Benn, 1932

Hone, J. M., Rossi, M. M., *Bishop Berkeley His Life, Writings, and Philosophy,* New York: Macmillan, 1931

Huxley, T. H., *Hume, with Helps to the Study of Berkeley,* New York: Appleton & Co., 1896

Jessop. T. E., *et al., Homage to George Berkeley,* Hodges Figges for Trinity College, Dublin, 1953
        Contributors: Jessop, T. E.; Luce, A. A.; Leroy, A. L.; Dobree, B.; Johnston, J.; Witrow, G. J.; Ramsey, I. T.; Popkin, R. H.

Johnston, G. A., *The Development of Berkeley's Philosophy*, New York: Macmillan, 1923
Luce, A. A., *Berkeley and Malebranche*, London: Oxford Univ. Press, 1934
Luce, A. A., *The Life of George Berkeley Bishop of Cloyne*, London: Nelson, 1949
Warnock, G. J., *Berkeley*, Hammondsworth and Baltimore: Penguin, 1953
Wild, J., *George Berkeley*, Cambridge: Harvard Univ. Press., 1936
Wisdom, J. O., *The Unconscious Origin of Berkeley's Philosophy*, London: Hogarth, 1953
Johnston, G. A., "The Influence of Mathematical Conceptions on Berkeley's Philosophy," *Mind* 25, 1916
Laird, J., "Berkeley's Realism," *Mind* 25, 1916

Kant, Immanuel

COLLECTED WORKS

Sämtliche Werke, Berlin: Preussische Akadamie der Wissenschaften, 1802-1910, 22 volumes
Several other editions

SELECTED WORKS IN ENGLISH

Critique of Judgement, Tr. Meredith, J. C., Oxford: The Clarendon Press, 1952
Critique of Practical Reason, and Other Writings in Moral Philosophy, Tr. Beck, L. W., Chicago: Univ. of Chicago Press, 1949
Critique of Pure Reason, Tr. Kemp Smith, N., London: Macmillan, 1929
The Moral Law on the Groundwork of the Metaphysic of Morals, Tr. Paton, H. J., London: Hutchinson's Univ. Libr., New York: Barnes & Noble, 1950
Prolegomena to Any Future Metaphysics, Tr. Carus, P., Chicago: Open Court, 1902
Religion Within the Limits of Reason Alone, Tr. Greene, T. M., and Hudson, H. H., Chicago: Open Court, 1934
Selections, Ed. Greene, T. M., New York: Scribner's, 1929

COMMENTARIES
Books
Caird, E., *A Critical Account of the Philosophy of Kant*, London and New York: Macmillan, 1877
Cassirer, Ernst, *Kants Leben und Lehre*, Berlin: B. Cassirer, 1918
Cassirer, Ernst, *Rousseau, Kant, Goethe*, Princeton: Princeton Univ. Press, 1945
Cassirer, H. W., *A Commentary on Kant's Critique of Judgement*, London: Methuen, 1938
Cassirer, H. W., *Kant's First Critique*, London: Allen and Unwin, 1954
Ewing, A. C., *A Short Commentary on Kant's Critique of Pure Reason*, Chicago: Univ. of Chicago Press, 1950
Kemp Smith, N., *A Commentary to Kant's Critique of Pure Reason*, London: Macmillan, 1923
Körner, S., *Kant*, Hammondsworth and Baltimore: Pelican, 1955
Lindsay, A. D., *Kant*, London: Benn, 1934
Paton, H. J., *Kant's Metaphysic of Experience*, 2 vols., New York: Macmillan, 1936
Paulsen, Friedrich, *Immanuel Kant, His Life and Doctrine*, Tr. Creighton, T. E., and Lefevre, A., New York: Scribner's, 1902

Prichard, H. A., *Kant's Theory of Knowledge,* Oxford: Clarendon, 1909
Ross, W. D., *Kant's Ethical Theory,* Oxford: Clarendon, 1954
Vaihinger, H., *Die Transcendentale Deduktion der Kategorien,* Halle: Nie-meyer, 1902
Weldon, T. D., *Introduction to Kant's Critique of Pure Reason,* Oxford: Clarendon, 1945
Whitney, G. T., and Bowers, D. F. (Eds.), *The Heritage of Kant,* Princeton: Princeton Univ. Press, 1939

Articles

Bowman, A. A., "Kant's Phenomenalism in its Relation to Subsequent Meta-physics," *Mind* 25, 1916
Bowman, A. A., "Kant's View of Metaphysics," *Mind* 25, 1916
Hicks, G. Dawes, "Recent Criticism of Kant's Theory of Knowledge," *Mind* 22, 1913
Hyslop, J. H., "Kant's Doctrine of Time and Space," *Mind* 7, 1898
Moore, G. E., "Kant's Idealism," *Arist. Soc.* 4, 1904
Munitz, M. K., "Kantian Dialectic and Modern Scientific Cosmology," *J. Philo.* 47, 1950
Stirling, J. H., "The Question of Idealism in Kant," *Arist. Soc.* 8, 1908
Walsh, C. M., "Kant's Transcendental Idealism and Empirical Realism," *Mind* 12 and 13, 1903, 1904

Hegel, Georg Wilhelm Friedrich

COMPLETE WORKS

Georg Wilhelm Friedrich Hegel's Werke, Berlin: Duncker and Humboldt, 1840-54, 19 vols.
Several other editions, the most recent one: Berlin: F. Meiner, 1920-55

ENGLISH TRANSLATIONS

The Philosophy of Hegel, Ed. Friedrich, C. J., New York: Modern Library, 1953
Hegel, Selections, Ed. J. Lowenberg, New York: Scribners, 1929
Lectures on the History of Philosophy, Tr. Haldane, E. S., London: Kegan Paul, Trench, Trübner & Co., 1892
Lectures on the Philosophy of Religion, together with a work on the proof of the existence of God, Tr. Speirs, E. B., and Sanderson, J. B., London: Kegan Paul, Trench, Trübner & Co., 1895
The Phenomenology of Mind, Tr. Baillie, J. B., 2 vols., New York: Macmillan, 1931
The Philosophy of Art, Tr. Bryant, W. M., New York: Appleton & Co., 1879
The Philosophy of Fine Art, Tr. Bosanquet, B., London: Kegan Paul, Trench, Trübner & Co., 1886
The Philosophy of History, Tr. Sibree, J., New York: Colonial Press, 1899
The Philosophy of Mind, Tr. Wallace, W., Oxford, 1894
The Philosophy of Right, Tr. Knox, T. M., Oxford: Clarendon, 1942

COMMENTARIES
Books

Caird, E., *Hegel,* Philadelphia: Lippincott & Co., 1891
Croce, B., *What Is Living and What Is Dead in the Philosophy of Hegel,* Tr. Ainslie, D., London: Macmillan, 1915

Foster, Michael B., *The Political Philosophies of Plato and Hegel,* Oxford: Clarendon, 1935
Marcuse, Herbert, *Reason and Revolution: Hegel and the Rise of Social Theory,* New York: Humanities Press, 1954
McTaggart, J. M. E., *Studies in Hegelian Cosmology,* Cambridge, 1918
McTaggart, J. M. E., *Studies in Hegelian Dialectic,* Cambridge, 1922
McTaggart, J. M. E., *A Commentary on Hegel's Logic,* Cambridge, 1910
Maier, J., *On Hegel's Critique of Kant,* New York: Columbia Univ. Press, 1939
Mure, G. R. G., *An Introduction to Hegel,* Oxford: Clarendon, 1940
Mure, G. R. G., *A Study of Hegel's Logic,* Oxford, 1950
Stace, W. T., *The Philosophy of Hegel,* New York: Dover, 1955
Stirling, J. H., *The Secret of Hegel,* London: Longmans, Roberts and Green, 1865, 2 vols.

Articles

Alexander, S., "Hegel: His Conception of Nature," *Mind,* Old Series, 11, 1886
Bosanquet, B., "Hegel's Theory of the Political Organism," *Mind* 7, 1898
Calkins, M. W., "The Order of the Hegelian Categories in the Hegelian Argument," *Mind* 12, 1903
Findlay, J. N., "Some Merits of Hegelianism," *Arist. Soc.* 56, 1956
Mackenzie, J. S., "The Hegelian Point of View," *Mind* 11, 1902
McTaggart, J. M. E., "The Changes of Method in Hegel's Dialectic," *Mind* 1, 1892
McTaggart, J. M. E., "Hegel's Treatment of the Categories of the Idea," *Mind* 9, 1900
McTaggart, J. M. E., "Hegel's Treatment of the Categories of the Objective Notion," *Mind* 8, 1899
McTaggart, J. M. E., "Hegel's Treatment of the Categories of Quality," *Mind* 11, 1902
McTaggart, J. M. E., "Hegel's Treatment of the Categories of Quantity," *Mind* 13, 1904
McTaggart, J. M. E., "Hegel's Treatment of the Categories of the Subjective Notion," *Mind* 6, 1897
McTaggart, J. M. E., "Time and the Hegelian Dialectic," *Mind* 3, 1894
Ritchie, D. G., "Hegelianism and Its Critics," *Mind* 3, 1894
Rogers, A. K., "The Absolute of Hegelianism," *Mind* 9, 1900
Seth, A., "Hegelianism and Its Critics," *Mind* 3, 1894

Schopenhauer, Arthur

COMPLETE WORKS
Sämtliche Werke, Wiesbaden: Brockhaus, 1946-50, other editions

MAJOR WORKS TRANSLATED
The World as Will and Idea, Tr. Haldane, R. B., and Kemp, J., 8th ed., London: Trübner, 1886, 3 vols.
The Works of Schopenhauer, Ed. Edman, I., New York: Modern Library, 1928
Schopenhauer (Selections), Ed. Parker, D., New York: Scribners, 1928
The Basis of Morality, London: Sonnenschien, 1903
Selected Essays, London: Bell, 1926
Studies in Pessimism, London: Allen & Unwin, 1937
The Wisdom of Life, Tr. Saunders, B., and Box, B., London: Dunne, 1901

COMMENTARIES

Bullock, A., *The Supreme Human Tragedy*, London: Daniel, 1920
Caldwell, W., *Schopenhauer's System in Its Philosophical Significance*, Edinburgh: Blackwood, 1896
Fischer, Kuno, *Geschichte der Neuern Philosophie*, Bd. 8, Mannheim: Bassermann and Mathy, 1893
Hasse, H., *Schopenhauer*, Munich: Reinhardt, 1926
Hedge, F. H., *Atheism in Philosophy, and Other Essays*, Boston: Roberts, 1884
Hubbard, E., *Schopenhauer*, E. Aurora, New York: Roycrofter's, 1904
Kelly, M., *Kant's Ethics and Schopenhauer's Criticism*, London: Sonnenschein, 1910
Kelly, M., *Kant's Philosophy as Rectified by Schopenhauer*, London: Sonnenschein, 1909
Knox, I., *The Aesthetic Theories of Kant, Hegel, and Schopenhauer*, New York: Columbia Univ. Press, 1936
Mann, Thomas, *Schopenhauer*, Stockholm: Bermann-Fischer, 1938
Mann, Thomas, *The Living Thoughts of Schopenhauer*, New York: Longmans Green & Co., 1939
McGill, V. J., *Schopenhauer*, New York: Brentano, 1931
Nietzsche, F., "Thoughts out of Season" (in his *Complete Works*, Vols. IV & V, Ed. Levy, O), New York: Macmillan, 1910-1927
Saltus, Edgar E., *The Anatomy of Negation*, Chicago: Belford, Clarke & Co., 1889
Tsanoff, R., *Schopenhauer's Criticism of Kant's Theory of Experience*, New York: Longmans, Green & Co., 1911
Zimmern, H., *Arthur Schopenhauer*, rev. ed., London: Allen & Unwin, 1932

Fichte, Johann Gottlieb

COLLECTED WORKS

Fichte's Werke, Berlin: Veit, 1865-66, other editions
Appelation gegan die Anklage des Atheismus, Jena: C. E. Gabler, 1799
Atheismus-Streit, Ed. Lindau, H., Munich: Georg Müller, 1912

ENGLISH TRANSLATIONS OF HIS WORKS

Addresses to the German Nation, Tr. Gray, L. H., New York: 1913-14
The Science of Knowledge, Tr. Kroeger, A. E., London: Trübner, 1889
The Science of Rights, Tr. Kroeger, A. E., Philadelphia: Lippincott, 1869
The Vocation of Man, Tr. Smith, W., Chicago: Open Court, 1910

COMMENTARIES

Adamson, R., *Fichte*, Edinburgh: Blackwood, 1881
Ellis, R. S., *A Criticism of Fichte's "Science of Knowledge,"* Chicago: Griggs, 1884
Everett, C. C., *Fichte's "Science of Knowledge,"* Chicago: Griggs, 1884
Leighton, J. A., *Typical Modern Conceptions of God*, New York: Longmans, Green, 1901
Smith, W., *Memoir of J. G. Fichte*, Boston: Munroe, 1846
Talbot, E. B., *The Fundamental Principle of Fichte's Philosophy*, New York: Macmillan, 1901
Thompson, A. B., *The Unity of Fichte's Doctrine of Knowledge*, Boston: Ginn, 1895

Wundt, M., *Fichte, Forschungen,* Stuttgart: Frommann, 1929
Wundt, M., *Johann Gottlieb Fichte,* Stuttgart: Frommann, 1927
Moore, G. E., Review of "The Science of Ethics as based on The Science of Knowledge," *Int. J. of Ethics* 9, 1898

Schelling, Friedrich von

COLLECTED WORKS

F. W. J. von Schelling's Sämtliche Werke, Stuttgart: Cotta, 1856-61, other editions

ENGLISH TRANSLATIONS

The Ages of the World, Tr. Balmon, F. W., New York: Columbia, 1942
Of Human Freedom, Tr. Gutman, J., Chicago: Open Court, 1936

COMMENTARIES

Hartmann, E. von, *Schelling's Positive Philosophie Als Einheit von Hegel und Schopenhauer,* Berlin: 1869
Tillich, P., *Mystik und Schuldbewusstsin in Schelling's Philosophischer Entwicklung,* Guterslott: Betelsmann, 1912

Lotze, R. H.

MAJOR WORKS IN GERMAN

Geschichte der Deutschen Philosophie seit Kant, Leipzig: Herzel, 1883
Grundzüge der Aesthetik, Leipzig: Herzel, 1884
Grundzüge der Logik und Encyclopadie der Philosophie, Leipzig: Herzel, 1884
Grundzüge der Metaphysik, Leipzig: Herzel, 1883
Grundzüge der Religionsphilosophie, Leipzig: Herzel, 1894

ENGLISH TRANSLATIONS

Logic, Tr. Bosanquet, B., Oxford: Clarendon, 1884
Microcosmus, Tr. Hamilton, E. Jones, C., and Welford, E. E., New York: Scribner, 1887
Outlines of Aesthetics, Tr. Ladd, G. T., Boston: Ginn, 1886
Outlines of Metaphysic, Tr. Ladd, G. T., Boston: Ginn, 1884
Outlines of the Philosophy of Religion, Tr. Ladd, G. T., Boston: Ginn, 1885

COMMENTARIES

Hartmann, E. von, *Lotze's Philosophie,* Leipzig: Friedrich, 1888
Moore, V. F., *The Ethical Aspect of Lotze's Metaphysics,* New York: Macmillan, 1901
Thomas, E. E., *Lotze's Theory of Reality,* London: Longmans, Green, 1901
Wentscher, M., *Fechner und Lotze,* Munich: Reinhardt, 1925
Eastwood, A., "Lotze's Antithesis between Thought and Things," *Mind* 3, 1894
Thomas, E. E., "Lotze's Relation to Idealism," *Mind* 24, 1915

British Idealists

Bosanquet, Bernard

The Civilization of Christendom, New York: Macmillan, 1899
The Distinction between Mind and Its Objects, Manchester: Manchester Univ., 1913
Essentials of Logic, New York: Macmillan, 1895
A History of Aesthetics, London: Allen & Unwin, 1934
Implication and Linear Inference, London: Macmillan, 1920
Knowledge and Reality, London: Sonnenschein, 1892
Logic, or the Morphology of Knowledge, 3 vols., London: Oxford Univ., 2nd ed., 1911
The Meeting of Extremes in Contemporary Philosophy, London: Macmillan, 1924
The Philosophical Theory of the State, 3rd ed., London: Macmillan, 1920
The Principle of Individuality and Value, London: Macmillan, 1927
Science and Philosophy, New York: Macmillan, 1927
Three Chapters on the Nature of Mind, London: Macmillan, 1923
Three Lectures on Aesthetics, London: Macmillan, 1915
The Value and Destiny of the Individual, London: Macmillan, 1923
"Life and Philosophy," in *Contemporary British Philosophy,* First Series, Ed. Muirhead, J. H., London: Allen & Unwin, New York: Macmillan, 1924

Bradley, Francis Herbert

Appearance and Reality, Oxford: Clarendon, 1930, 2nd ed.
Collected Essays, Oxford: Clarendon, 1935, 2 vols.
Essays on Truth and Reality, Oxford: Clarendon, 1914
Ethical Studies, Oxford: Clarendon, 1927
The Principles of Logic, London: Oxford Univ. Press, 1922, 2 vols.

Green, Thomas Hill

Works of T. H. Green, Ed. Nettleship, R. L., London: Longmans, Green, 1885, 3 vols.
Lectures on the Principle of Political Obligation, London: Longmans, Green, 1924
Prolegomena to Ethics, Oxford: Clarendon, 1906

Haldane, R. B.

Essays in Philosophical Criticism, London: Longmans, 1883
The Pathway to Reality, London: John Murray, 1903, 2 vols.
The Reign of Relativity, London: John Murray, 1921
The Philosophy of Humanism, London: John Murray, 1922
"The Function of Metaphysics in Scientific Method," in *Contemporary British Philosophy,* First Series, Ed. Muirhead, J. H.

[354] *Bibliography*

Hoernle, R. F. A.

Idealism as a Philosophy, New York: Harcourt, Brace, 1927
Studies in Contemporary Metaphysics, New York: Harcourt, Brace, 1920
Matter, Life, Mind and God, London: Methuen, 1926, 2nd ed.
"On the Way to a Synoptic Philosophy," in *Contemporary British Philosophy*, Second Series, Ed. Muirhead, J. H., London: Allen and Unwin, New York: Macmillan, 1925

Inge, W. R.

Christian Ethics and Modern Problems, New York: Putnam, 1930
Christian Mysticism, London: Methuen, 1925
Personal Idealism and Mysticism, London: Longmans, Green, 1907
"Philosophy and Religion," in *Contemporary British Philosophy*, First Series Ed., Muirhead, J. H.

Joachim, H. M.

Logical Studies, Oxford: Clarendon, 1948
The Nature of Truth, London: Oxford Univ. Press, 1906

McTaggart, J. M. Ellis

The Nature of Existence, Cambridge: Cambridge Univ. Press, 1921 and 1927, 2 vols., Vol. II ed. by C. D. Broad
Philosophical Studies, Ed. Keeling, S. V., New York: Longmans, Green, 1936
Some Dogmas of Religion, London: E. Arnold, 1906
"An Ontological Idealism," in *Contemporary British Philosophy*, First Series Ed., Muirhead, J. H.

Rashdall, Hastings

Is Conscience an Emotion?, New York: Houghton Mifflin, 1914
Ideas and Ideals, Oxford: Blackwell, 1928
Philosophy and Religion, London: Duckworth, 1911
The Theory of Good and Evil, Oxford: Clarendon, 1910, 2 vols.

Sorley, W. R.

Moral Values and the Idea of God, Cambridge: Cambridge Univ. Press, 1930
"Value and Reality," in *Contemporary British Philosophy*, Second Series, Ed., Muirhead, J. H.

Taylor, A. E.

The Christian Hope of Immortality, New York: Macmlilan, 1917
Does God Exist?, London: Macmillan, 1947

Elements of Metaphysics, New York: Macmillan, 1907
The Faith of a Moralist: Gifford Lectures 1926, London: Macmillan, 1930, 2 vols.
Philosophical Studies, London: Macmillan, 1936

Commentaries on British Idealism

Books
Broad, C. D., *Examination of McTaggart's Philosophy,* Cambridge: Cambridge Univ. Press, 1933-38, 3 vols.
Ewing, A. C., *Idealisms, A Critical Survey,* London: Methuen, 1936
Lofthouse, W. F., *F. H. Bradley,* London: Epworth, 1949
Muirhead, J. H., *The Platonic Tradition in Anglo-Saxon Philosophy;* studies in the history of idealism in England and America, London: Allen & Unwin, 1931
Muirhead, J. H., *Bernard Bosanquet and His Friends;* letters illustrating the sources and development of his philosophical opinions, London: Allen & Unwin, 1935

Articles
Balfour, A. J., "A Criticism of Current Idealistic Theories," *J. Philo.* 2, 1905
Blanshard, B., "Francis Herbert Bradley," *J. Philo.* 22, 1925
Bosanquet, B., "Contradiction and Reality," *Mind* 15, 1906
Bosanquet, B., "F. H. Bradley on Fact and Inference," *Arist. Soc.* 10, 1910
Bosanquet, B., "Hedonism among the Idealists," *Mind* 12, 1903
Bosanquet, B., "Idealism and the Reality of Time," *Mind* 23, 1914
Bosanquet, B., "Moore's 'Principia Ethica'," *Mind* 13, 1904
Bradley, A. C. *et al.,* "Bernard Bosanquet, 1838-1923," *Proceedings of the British Academy* 10, 1923
Bradley, F. H., "Consciousness and Experience," *Mind* 2, 1893
Bradley, F. H., "A Defense of Phenomenalism in Psychology," *Mind* 9, 1900
Bradley, F. H., "On Floating Ideas and the Imaginary," *Mind* 15, 1906
Bradley, F. H., "Our Knowledge of Immediate Experience," *Mind* 18, 1909
Bradley, F. H., "Reality and Thought," *Mind* 2 (old series), 1877
Bradley, F. H., "On Some Aspects of Truth," *Mind* 20, 1911
Bradley, F. H., "On Truth and Copying," *Mind* 16, 1907
Broad, C. D., "Mr. Bradley on Truth and Reality," *Mind* 23, 1914
Carr, H. W., "Impressions and Ideas—The Problem of Idealism," *Arist. Soc.* 8, 1908
Castaner, C., "The Ideal and the Real," *Arist. Soc.* 30, 1930
Cooke, H. P., "On Certain Idealistic Arguments," *Mind* 27, 1918
Cuning, A., "Lotze, Bradley and Bosanquet," *Mind* 26, 1915
Eastwood, A., "Mr. Balfour's Refutation of Idealism," *Mind* 3, 1894
Eliot, T. S., "F. H. Bradley," in his *Essays Ancient and Modern,* London: Faber & Faber, 1936; also in *Selected Essays,* New York: Harcourt, Brace, 1950
Galloway, G., "Idealism and the External World," *Mind* 29, 1920
Hicks, G. Dawes, "Are the Materials of Sense Affections of the Mind?," *Arist. Soc.* 17, 1917
Hicks, G. Dawes, "The Belief in External Realities," *Arist. Soc.* 1, 1901
Hoernle, R. F. A., "On Bosanquet's Idealism," *Philos. Rev.* 32, 1923
Hoernle, R. F. A., "Image, Idea and Meaning," *Mind* 16, 1907

Hoernle, R. F. A., "Pragmatism vs. Absolutism," *Mind* 14, 1905
Hoernle, R. F. A., "Professor Baillie's Idealistic Construction of Experience," *Mind* 16, 1907
Jones, H., "Idealism and Epistemology," *Mind* 2, 1893
Joseph, H. W. B., "The Psychological Explanation of the Development of the Perception of External Objects," *Mind* 19, 1910
Knox, H. V., "Mr. Bradley's Absolute Criterion," *Mind* 14, 1905
Ladd, G. T., "A Defence of Idealism," *Mind* 23, 1914
Laird, J., "The Nature of Ideas," *Arist. Soc.* 25, 1925
Lamont, F. C., "Bosanquet's 'The Distinction between Mind and It's Objects'," *J. Philo.* 12, 1915
Mackenzie, J. S., "Mr. Bradley's View of the Self," *Mind* 3, 1894
Mackenzie, J. S., "The Infinite and the Perfect," *Mind* 13, 1904
Mackenzie, J. S., "The New Realism and the Old Idealism," *Mind* 15, 1906
McTaggart, J. E. M., "The Meaning of Causality," *Mind* 24, 1915
McTaggart, J. E. M., "The Relation of Time and Eternity," *Mind* 18, 1909
Moore, G. E., "Are the Materials of Sense Affections of the Mind?" *Arist. Soc.* 17, 1917
Moore, G. E., "The Refutation of Idealism," *Mind* 12, 1903
Moore, G. E., Review of Bosanquet's "Implication and Linear Inference," *Mind* 29, 1920
Rashdall, H., "Professor Watson on Personal Idealism," *Mind* 18, 1909
Reyburn, H. A., "The Ego-Centric Predicament," *Mind* 25, 1916
Reyburn, H. A., "Idealism and the Reality of Time," *Mind* 22, 1913
Rogers, A. K., "The Absolute as Unknowable (A Criticism of Bradley's 'Appearance and Reality')," *Mind* 12, 1903
Schiller, F. C. S., "The New Developments of Mr. Bradley's Philosophy," *Mind* 24, 1915
Schiller, F. C. S., "Is Neo-Idealism Reduceable to Solipsism?," *Arist. Soc. Supp.* Vol. 3
Schiller, F. C. S., "The Present Phase of 'Idealist' Philosophy," *Mind* 19, 1910
Schiller, F. C. S., "Reality and Idealism," *Philos. Rev.* 1 and 2, 1892, 1893
Schiller, F. C. S., "Solipsism," *Mind* 18, 1909
Sidgwick, H., "Mr. Bradley and the Sceptics," *Mind* 3, 1894
Sidgwick, H., "The Philosophy of T. H. Green," *Mind* 10, 1901
Strange, E. H., "Mr. Bradley's Doctrine of Knowledge," *Mind* 20, 1911
Strong, C. A., "Has Mr. Moore Refuted Idealism?," *Mind* 14, 1905
Taylor, A. E., *et al.*, "F. H. Bradley," *Mind* 34, 1925
Taylor, A. E., "Francis Herbert Bradley, 1896-1924," *Proceedings of the British Academy* 11, 1925
Turner, J. E., "Mr. Alexander on Mind and its Objects," *Mind* 24, 1915
Turner, J. E., "Dr. Bosanquet's Theory of Mental States, Judgment and Reality," *Mind* 27, 1918
Ward, J., Review of Bradley's *Appearance and Reality*, *Mind* 3, 1894
Watson, J., "Mr. Rashdall's Defence of Personal Idealism," *Mind* 18, 1909
Wollheim, R. A., "F. H. Bradley," in Ayer, A. J., *et al.*, *The Revolution in Philosophy*, London: Macmillan, 1956

Indian Idealists

Rhadhakrishnan, Sarvapalli

The Hindu View of Life, New York: Macmillan, 1927
An Idealist View of Life, New York: Macmillan, 1932
Indian Philosophy, New York: Macmillan, 1932
The Philosophy of the Upanisads, New York: Macmillan, 1924

Commentaries on Indian Idealism

Belvalkar, S. K., *History of Indian Philosophy,* Poona: Bilvakunja, 1933
Deussen, Paul, *Outlines of Indian Philosophy,* Berlin: K. Curtius, 1907
Muirhead, J. H., and Rhadhakrishnan, E. (Eds.), *Contemporary Indian Philosophy,* London: Allen & Unwin, 1936
Schilpp, P. A., Ed., *The Philosophy of Sarvapalli Rhadhakrishnan,* Tudor, N. Y.: Library of Living Philosophers Series, 1952

Italian Idealists

Croce, Benedetto

Aesthetic as Science of Expression and General Linguistic, Tr. Ainslie, D., London: Macmillan, 1922
The Conduct of Life, Tr. Livingstone, G., New York: Harcourt, Brace, 1924
History as the Story of Liberty, Tr. Sprigge, S., London: Allen & Unwin, 1941
History, Its Theory and Practice, Tr. Ainslie, D., New York: Harcourt, Brace, 1921
Historical Materialism and the Economics of Karl Marx, Tr. Meredith, C. M., with an introd. by A. D. Lindsay, New York: Macmillan, 1914
Logic, Tr. Meyer, B. E., London: Macmillan, 1913
Logic as the Science of the Pure Concept, Tr. Ainslie, D., London: Macmillan, 1917
My Philosophy and Other Essays, Tr. Carritt, E. T., London: Allen & Unwin, 1949
Philosophy of the Practical, Tr. Ainslie, D., London: Macmillan, 1913
Politics and Morals, London: Allen and Unwin, 1946, New York: Philosophical Library, 1945

Gentile, Giovanni

The Theory of Mind as Pure Act, Tr. Carr, H. W., London: Macmillan, 1922

Commentaries on Italian Idealism

Books

Carr, H. W., *The Philosophy of Benedetto Croce; the Problem of Art and History,* London: Macmillan, 1917

Holmes, R. W., *The Idealism of Giovanni Gentile*, New York: Macmillan, 1937

Articles

Bosanquet, B., "The Philosophy of Benedetto Croce," *Quarterly Review* 231, London and New York, 1919
Carr, H. Wildon, " 'Time' and 'History' in Contemporary Philosophy," *British Acad. Proceedings*, London 1918
Collingwood, R. G., "Croce's Philosophy of History," *Hibbert Journal* 19, London 1921
Crespi, A., "Idealism and Religion in Contemporary Italian Philosophy," *Mind* 24, 1915
Harford, G., "Croce's Philosophical System," *Church Quarterly Review* 89, London 1920
Pellizi, C., "The Problems of Religion for Modern Italian Idealists," *Arist. Soc.* 24, 1924

American Idealists

Adams, G. P.

Idealism and the Modern Age, New Haven: Yale Univ. Press, 1919
"Naturalism or Idealism," in *Contemporary American Philosophy*, Vol. 1, Eds., Adams, G. P., and Montague, W. P., London: Allen & Unwin, New York: Macmillan, 1930

Blanshard, Brand

The Impasse in Ethics and a Way Out, Berkeley: Univ. of California, 1955
The Nature of Thought, London: Allen & Unwin, 1939, 2 vols.
On Philosophical Style, Manchester: Manchester Univ. Press, 1954

Bowne, B. P.

Kant and Spencer, Boston: Houghton, Mifflin, 1912
Metaphysics, New York: American Book Co., 1882
Personalism, Boston: Houghton, Mifflin, 1908
Philosophy of Theism, New York: Harper, 1892
Principles of Ethics, New York: Harper, 1892
Theory of Thought and Knowledge, New York: Harper, 1897

Brightman, E. S.

Immortality in Post-Kantian Idealism, Cambridge: Harvard Univ. Press, 1925
An Introduction to Philosophy, New York: Holt, 1925
A Philosophy of Ideals, New York: Holt, 1928
A Philosophy of Religion, New York: Prentice-Hall, 1940
The Problem of God, New York: Abingdon, 1930
Religious Values, New York: Abingdon, 1925
The Spiritual Life, New York: Abingdon, 1942

Calkins, M. W.

The Persistent Problems of Philosophy, New York: Macmillan, 1907
"The Philosophical Credo of an Absolutistic Personalist," in *Contemporary American Philosophy,* vol. I, Eds., Adams, G. P., and Montague, W. P.

Creighton, J. E.

Studies in Speculative Idealism, Smart, H. R., Ed., New York: Macmillan, 1925

Cunningham, G. Watts

Five Lectures on the Problem of Mind, Austin: Univ. of Texas Press, 1925
The Idealistic Argument in Recent British and American Philosophy, New York: Century, 1933
Thought and Reality in Hegel's System, New York: Longmans, Green, 1910
Problems of Philosophy, New York: Holt, 1935 (rev. ed.)

Harris, W. Torrey

Hegel's Logic: A Book on the Genesis of the Categories of the Mind, Chicago: Griggs, 1890
Introduction to the Study of Philosophy, New York: Appleton, 1890

Hocking, W. E.

The Meaning of God in Human Experience, New Haven: Yale Univ. Press, 1912
The Self, its Body and Freedom, New Haven: Yale Univ. Press, 1928
Human Nature and its Remaking, New Haven: Yale Univ. Press, 1929
Living Religions and a World Faith, New York: Macmillan, 1940
Man and the State, New Haven: Yale Univ. Press, 1926
Science and the Idea of God, Chapel Hill: Univ. of N. Carolina Press, 1944
Types of Philosophy, New York: Scribner, 1929
"Some Second Principles," in *Contemporary American Philosophy,* vol. I Eds. Adams, G. P., and Montague, W. P.

Howison, G. H.

The Limits of Evolution, and other Essays, New York: Macmillan, 1904
Philosophy and Science, Berkeley: Univ. of California Press, 1902

Royce, Josiah, et al.

The Conception of God, New York: Macmillan, 1897

Royce, Josiah

The Conception of Immortality, New York: Houghton, Mifflin, 1900
Lectures on Modern Idealism, New Haven: Yale Univ. Press, 1923

Logical Essays, Ed., Robinson, D. S., Dubuque, Iowa: Brown Press, 1951
The Philosophy of Loyalty, New York: Macmillan, 1908
The Problem of Christianity, New York: Macmillan, 1913
The Religious Aspect of Philosophy, Boston: Houghton, Mifflin, 1885
The Spirit of Modern Philosophy, New York: Houghton, Mifflin, 1892
Studies of Good and Evil, New York: Appleton, 1898
The World and the Individual, New York: Macmillan, 1900-1901, 2 vols.

Urban, W. M.

Beyond Realism and Idealism, London: Allen & Unwin, 1949
Humanity and Deity, London: Allen & Unwin, 1951
The Intelligible World, New York: Macmillan, 1929
Language and Reality, London: Allen & Unwin, 1951
Valuation; Its Nature and Laws, New York: Macmillan, 1909
"Metaphysics and Value," in *Contemporary American Philosophy,* vol. II, Eds.,
    Adams, G. P., and Montague, W. P.

Commentaries on American Idealism

Books

Barrett, C., Ed., *Contemporary Idealism in America,* New York: Macmillan, 1932
Brightman, E. S., Ed., "Personalism and the Influence of Bowne," *Proceedings of the Sixth International Congress of Philosophy,* New York: Longmans, Green, 1927
Buckham, J. W., and Stratton, J. M., Eds., *George Holmes Howison: Philosopher and Teacher,* selections with a biographical sketch, Berkeley: Univ. of California Press, 1934
Cotton, J. H., *Royce on the Human Self,* Cambridge: Harvard Univ. Press, 1954
Harmon, F. A., *The Social Philosophy of the St. Louis Hegelians,* New York: Columbia University Press, 1943
Knudson, A. C., *The Philosophy of Personalism,* New York: Abingdon, 1927
Leidecker, K. F., *Josiah Royce and Indian Thought,* New York: Kailas Press, 1931
Leidecker, A. F., *Yankee Teacher: The Life of William Torrey Harris,* New York: Philosophical Library, 1946
Marcel, G., *Royce's Metaphysics,* New York: Henry Regnery, 1956
McConnell, F. J., *Borden Parker Bowne,* New York: Abingdon, 1929
Perry, C. M., *The St. Louis Movement in Philosophy,* Norman, Okla.: Univ. of Oklahoma Press, 1930
Riley, I. W., *American Thought,* New York: Holt, 1923
Rogers, A. K., *English and American Philosophy Since 1800,* New York: Macmillan, 1922
Santayana, G., *Character and Opinion in the United States,* New York: Scribners, 1920
Schaub, E. L., Ed., *William Torrey Harris,* Chicago: Open Court, 1936
Schneider, H. W., *A History of American Philosophy,* New York: Columbia Univ. Press, 1946
Smith, J. E., *Royce's Social Infinite,* New York: Liberal Arts Press, 1950
Townsend, H. G., *Philosophical Ideas in the United States,* New York: American Book Co., 1934

Werkmeister, W. H., *A History of Philosophical Ideas in America,* New York: The Ronald Press, 1949

Articles

Ames, C. H., "William Torrey Harris," *J. Philo., Psych. & Sc. Meth.* 6, 1909
Bakewell, C. M., "Idealism and Realism," *Philos. Rev.* 22, 1914
Bakewell, C. M., "The Issue between Idealism and Immediate Empiricism," *J. Philo.* 2, 1905
Bakewell, C. M., "Royce as an Interpreter of American Ideals," *Int. J. of Ethics* 27, 1917
Barrow, G. A., "A Via Media between Realism and Idealism," *J. Philo.* 17, 1920
Benett, C. A., "Josiah Royce," *Philos. Rev.* 25, 1916
Blanshard, B., "Current Strictures on Reason," *Philos. Rev.* 54, 1945
Blanshard, B., "The Nature of Mind," *J. Philo.* 38, 1941
Bode, B. H., "Objective Idealism and its Critics," *Philos. Rev.* 19, 1910
Brightman, E. S., "The Definition of Idealism," *J. Philo.* 30, 1953
Brightman, E. S., "Modern Idealism," *J. Philo.* 17, 1920
Brosnahan, T., "Dr. Harris and the Agnostic School-House," New York: *The Messenger,* 1904
Buckham, J. W., "The Contributions of Professor Howison to Christian Thought," *Harvard Theol. Rev.* 9, 1916
Buckham, J. W., "The Contributions of Professor Royce to Christian Thought," *Harvard Theol. Rev.* 8, 1915
Calkins, M. W., "The Foundation in Royce's Philosophy for Christian Theism," *Philo. Rev.* 25, 1916
Calkins, M. W., "The Idealist to the Realist," *J. Philo.* 8, 1911
Calkins, M. W., "Idealist to Realist Once More," *J. Philo.* 11, 1914
Calkins, M. W., "The New Rationalism and Objective Idealism," *Philos. Rev.* 28, 1919
Calkins, M. W., "The Personalistic Conception of Nature," *Philos. Rev.* 28, 1919
Colain, S. S., "Is Subjective Idealism a Necessary Point of View for Psychology?," *J. Philo.* 2, 1905
Creighton, J. E., "Two Types of Idealism," *Philos, Rev.* 26, 27, 1915 1916
Dewey, J., "Experience and Objective Idealism," *Philos. Rev.* 15, 1906
Drake, D., "Where Do Perceived Objects Exist?," *Mind* 24, 1915
Greenwood, J. M., "William Torrey Harris—Educator, Philosopher and Scholar," *Educ. Rev.* 39, 1910
Howison, J. H., "Josiah Royce," *Philos. Rev.* 25, 1916
Kitchel, A. T., "Idealism on an Azalea Bush; or Practice and the Egocentric Predicament," *J. Philo.* 15, 1918
Loewenberg, J., "The Apotheosis of Mind in Modern Idealism," *Philos. Rev.* 31, 1922
McGilvary, E. B., "The Chicago 'Idea' and Idealism," *J. Philo.* 5, 1908
Mead, G. H., "The Philosophy of Royce, James and Dewey in their American Setting," *Int. J. of Ethics* 40, 1930
Montague, W. P., "Professor Royce's Refutation of Realism," *Philos. Rev.* 11, 1902
Moore, J. S., "Idealism, Irrationalism and Absolute," *J. Philo.* 7, 1910
Morris, F. E., "An Approach to Idealism," *Philos. Rev.* 31, 1922
Perry, R. B., "The Cardinal Principle of Idealism," *Mind* 19, 1910

Perry, R. B., "The Egocentric Predicament," *J. Philo., Psych. and Sc. Meth.* 7, 1910

Perry, R. B., "Mind Within and Mind Without," *J. Philo.* 6, 1909

Rogers, A. K., "G. E. Moore's Refutation of Idealism," *Philos. Rev.* 28, 1919

Rogers, A. K., "Professor Royce and Monism," *Philos. Rev.* 12, 1903

Russell, J. E., "Idealism and Revised Empiricism," *Philos. Rev.* 15, 1906

Sabine, G. H., "Idealism: The Social Origin of the Absolute," *J. Philo.* 12, 1915

Sabine, G. H., "The Philosophy of James Edwin Creighton," *Philos. Rev.* 34, 1925

Scott, W., "Idealism as Tautology or Paradox," *Philos. Rev.* 22, 1913

Sheldon, W. H., "The Consistency of Idealism with Realism," *Philos. Rev.* 21, 1912

Sheldon, W. H., "The Task of Present-Day Metaphysics," *American Philosophy Today and Tomorrow,* Kallen, H. M., and Hook, S., Eds., New York: Furman, 1935

Sorley, W. R., "Josiah Royce, 1855-1916," *British Academy Proceedings,* 1916

Strong, C. A., "Idealism and Realism," *J. Philo.* 1, 1904

Thilly, F., "The Philosophy of James Edwin Creighton," *Philos. Rev.* 34, 1925

Turner, J. E., "Miss Calkins on Idealism and Realism," *J. Philo.* 11, 1914

Urban, W. M., "Two Types of Idealism," *Philos. Rev.* 63, 1954

Watson, J., "The Critical Philosophy and Idealism," *Philos. Rev.* 1, 1892

INDEX

Index [365]

design argument for, 222
existence unnecessary, 215 (intro.)
Hegel on, 99
idealist argument for, 203-06
Kant on, 17, 81-84
and *percipi,* 312
and sorrow, 198-200
Goethe, 101
good, as the real, 152
Green, 7, 155

hedonism, 159
hedonistic, aesthetics, 245
Hegel
  Bosanquet on, 156-59, *passim*
  Caird on, 85-91
  Croce on, 232ff
  ed. discussion of, 19-21
  and internal relations, 262
  Moore on, 299
  and the romantic movement, 102
  Royce on, 92ff
  and the state, 184
Hegelianism, Croce on, 233ff
Heraclitus, 236
history, philosophy of, 235ff
Holy Spirit, 94
Hook, S., 317n.
Hume
  and Kant, 14
  Kant on, 82-83, 126, 267, 270

idea
  Berkelian, 311ff
  and object, 189ff
  reference of, 265
  and sensation, 140
  world as, 111ff
ideas, objects of knowledge, 29
Idealism
  absolute, 210
  contradictory of, 3
  critical, 52
  difficulty in defining, 3
  and ethics, 25, 129-30
  Green's definition of, 126
  and experience, 8
  hard to refute, 11
  influence of today, 4
  Kant's definition of, 47
  mental, 204-06
  objective, 85 (intro.)
  ontological, 215ff

personal, 210
and phenomenalism, 5
pluralistic, 207 (intro.)
and politics, 153 (intro.)
as process, 230
Schopenhauer's definition of, 111-12
subjective, 85 (intro.)
transcendental, 14, 52
types of, 24-25
ideals, root principles of life, 213
identity-in-difference
  Bosanquet on, 180
  Bradley on, 145
  Nagel on, 88, 328ff,
identity, law of, 86
illegitimate abstractions, 299
imagination, Kant on, 57
immortality
  Howison on, 211ff
  McTaggart, 225-227
imperatives, 80
implication, Bosanquet on, 173ff
individual
  and community, 181
  and the universal, 241
individuality, 144-52
induction, problem of, 271
Infinite, as reality, 242
infinitude, of world, 74ff
infinity, problem of, 12
intelligence, 125-26
internal relations
  Blanshard on, 253ff
  Bosanquet on, 176ff
  Hegel on, 262
  Nagel on, 322ff
  ten views on distinguished, 21
  and universals, 263ff
introspection, and consciousness, 306
intuition
  in art, 243ff
  of being of external world, 7
  in Kant, 38

James, William, 98
Joachim, 258n.
Joseph, H. W. B., 269n.
judgments
  and art, 248
  and coherence theory, 257ff

Kant
  Bosanquet on, 158-59
  Croce on, 232